College Success Version 2.0

By

Bruce Beiderwell, Linda Tse, Thomas Lochhaas and
Nicholas deKanter

S-2451113-CO

flatworld
KNOWLEDGE

9 781453 373163

College Success Version 2.0

Bruce Beiderwell, Linda Tse, Thomas Lochhaas and Nicholas deKanter

Published by:

Flat World Knowledge, Inc.
1111 19th St NW, Suite 1180
Washington, DC 20036

Brief Contents

Contents

About the Authors

BRUCE BEIDERWELL

Bruce Beiderwell (PhD, UCLA) has served as director of the UCLA Writing Programs since 2001. He regularly teaches developmental writing classes that serve students who arrive at the university without the preparation or skills they will need to succeed. This teaching role links him to broad efforts from across the campus, particularly the library and the College Learning Center. In this respect, he works with colleagues in English as a Second Language, Library Science, Athletics, and Counseling. In addition, Bruce's role as a faculty mentor to student athletes in the University's "Community of Learners" program connects directly to his work identifying, placing, and instructing at-risk students. Bruce has also overseen and taught in UCLA's Transfer Intensive Program built upon the notion that the crucial part of a successful transfer is the ability to write. For his work with nontraditional students seeking admission (or readmission) to the university through UC extension courses he received a UCLA Teaching Award.

While Bruce has spent most of his professional life as a writing teacher and administrator, his PhD is in English literature, and his first publications focused on nineteenth-century fiction. His book, *Power and Punishment in Scott's Novels*, was nominated for a McVities Prize. Bruce was also guest editor of a special edition of *European Romantic Review* that was devoted to essays on Walter Scott. In addition, he is the coauthor of the widely used literature anthology *The Literary Experience* (coauthored with Jeff Wheeler and published by Wadsworth).

Bruce's teaching interests along with his concern for undergraduate education have moved him outside this fairly narrow scholarly world. He has taught a wide range of literature and composition courses in the past twenty years—everything from courses on Faulkner to business writing workshops. He has been involved in administrative work (e.g., student placement, curriculum development). And he has consulted in the development of teaching materials for use in business settings.

LINDA F. TSE

Linda F. Tse (MS, Minnesota State University, Mankato) has been an educator for over two decades, first as a high school English teacher in Hong Kong and currently at Minneapolis Community and Technical College (MCTC). Since 1997, Linda has been working as a counselor on college campuses, initially at four-year comprehensive universities before finding her passion working with the student body at MCTC, where 43 percent of the students are non-Caucasian and more than eighty different languages are spoken on campus. New immigrants for whom English is a second language, first-generation college students, nontraditional students, single parents, and students living below the poverty line make up the majority of the college's student population.

Born to refugee parents in Hong Kong, Linda came to the United States on a student visa with the help of a scholarship. Her personal struggle together with her professional training have enabled her to relate readily to underrepresented and underserved students who aspire to higher education in the face of adversity and disadvantage. In this regard, she provides academic, career, and personal counseling, while teaching classes in Career Development and Life Planning, and College Success Strategies. In addition to her academic responsibilities, Linda works professionally with dislocated workers and people with disabilities.

TOM LOCHHAAS

Tom Lochhaas is a teacher, a writer, an editor, and a consultant. He received his MFA in writing from the University of Arizona and is ABD in English from Washington University. He is a member of Phi Beta Kappa.

Tom has taught at the University of Arizona, Pima Community College, Otterbein College, Washington University, Saint Louis Community College, and the University of California at Los Angeles. His teaching focus has been on freshman courses with an emphasis on reading, writing, and study and communication skills. Tom's special interests are in working with unprepared students and recent immigrants.

As a college instructor, Tom has always focused on what students actually need—not necessarily what professors might think they need—to succeed in their studies, regardless of the particular topic. In an academic world where many students do not read their textbooks at all, or have difficulty understanding them when they do, it is critical to be realistic about how today's students learn and how best to reach them. "A weighty traditional tome might look like the best classic student success textbook to some instructors," Tom says, "but such a text fails if students can't or won't read it. Students quickly become frustrated by reading materials not useful to them as students or appropriate for their needs." His expertise in how to shape an effective textbook is part of what he brings to this authorship team.

As a professional college textbook editor and writer, Tom specializes in making textbooks accessible for students in many curriculum areas, including communications, software and technical manuals, and public health information. In his work with public organizations such as the American Red Cross and the National Safety Council, he has brought an expertise in language and reading level to ensure that a wide range of publications are appropriate for their intended audiences. He has written or ghostwritten several dozen textbooks and other books.

NICHOLAS B. DEKANTER

Nick deKanter (MA, Tufts University) is an educational advocate, consultant, and marketing professional. As founder and president of the Vision 21 Education Group, he is working to support schools seeking to transform into twenty-first-century learning environments that help students master core subjects, connect subjects to real-world needs, think critically, communicate clearly, and practice collaboration and innovation.

Acknowledgments

Flat World Knowledge would like to thank the following reviewers whose comprehensive feedback and suggestions for improving the material helped make this a better text:

- Henry F. Algera, Seattle Pacific University
- Lenore Arlee, University of Oklahoma, Norman Campus
- Katie Cerrone Arnold, The University of Akron, Summit College
- Steven R. Boyd, University of Texas at San Antonio
- Mark Brennaman, University of Central Oklahoma
- Kathryn Burk, Jackson Community College
- Christi Duque, Tarrant County College
- Debby Espinor, George Fox University
- Lameteria D. Hall, The Community College of Baltimore County
- Sheryl Hartman, Miami Dade College
- Ann Iseda, Jackson Community College Extension Centers
- Dan Issler, University of Pennsylvania
- Timothy J. Jones, University of Oklahoma
- Lucas Keefer, University of Kansas
- Sharon Kousaleos, Ohio University
- Carla Kulinsky, Salt Lake Community College
- Patricia McGee, University of Texas at San Antonio
- Ted Miller, Jackson Community College
- Penny Pasque, University of Oklahoma
- Said Sewell, The Fort Valley State University
- Melissa Thomas, University of Texas at San Antonio
- John Timmons, Winthrop University
- Patrick Raphael Toney, Bowie State University

Preface

Our goal in writing *College Success* is to help you succeed in college.

According to Department of Education data, 30% of college freshmen leave school in their first year, and as many as 50% never graduate. *College Success* is designed to help change that—and to help ensure that you yourself are among those who succeed.

College Success has a student-friendly format arranged to help you develop the essential skills and provide the information you need to succeed in college. This is not a textbook full of theory and extensive detail that merely *discusses* student success; rather, this is a how-to manual for succeeding in college. The book provides realistic, practical guidance ranging from study skills to personal health, from test taking to managing time and money. Furthermore, *College Success* is accessible—information is presented concisely and as simply as possible.

College Success has the following features to help you achieve your goals: Each chapter asks you to evaluate yourself because success starts with recognizing your strengths and weaknesses, your hopes and desires, and your own personal, individual realities. You'll develop your own goals based on these self-assessments, determining what success in college really means for you as an individual. Throughout the book, you will find numerous interactive activities created to help you improve your skills. To assist you with this, the material is presented in short sections of information that you can begin applying immediately in your own life—and get the most out of your college education.

Welcome aboard!

New in this Second Edition

College education continues to change and evolve, and the second edition of *College Success* has evolved similarly. In addition to thoroughly updated content in all chapters, chapters are more concise and revised to be as practical as possible for new college students facing time constraints.

New content has been added in many areas, including these:

- Taking online courses, blended or flipped courses; online instructor and student interaction
- Taking digital exam, computer-scored tests and essays
- Digital learning tools and apps in all areas: note taking, writing, health and fitness, time management, finances and budgeting, and more
- Financing of college, risks of student loans, career guidance
- Mindfulness and commitment

In addition to new content, new pedagogy and learning aids have been added throughout, including:

- Class discussion questions for all chapters
- Embedded and linked videos (e.g., memory tips, time management)
- Increased links for web resources on all topics
- File attachments for digital readers to print out exercises involving written responses

Thanks to the many instructors using the first edition who took the time to give us suggestions for the new edition and thus helped make *College Success* even more successful.

CHAPTER 1
You and Your College Experience

FIGURE 1.1

© *Thinkstock*

Where Are You Now?

Assess your present knowledge and attitudes.

	Yes	Unsure	No
1. I understand the benefits of a college education for my future life.			
2. My career interests are clear and I have already planned my college program to prepare me best for my future.			
3. I understand how my previous education has prepared me for college work.			
4. I have all the personal traits of a successful college student.			
5. I know how people learn and make an effort to maximize my learning at each step in this process.			
6. I know my personal learning style and use it to my advantage when learning new things.			
7. I know how to pay attention to gain the most from my classes.			
8. I know my college's policies for academic honesty and behavior on campus.			
9. I know where to find my college's resources that can help me succeed both academically and personally.			
10. I am confident I can earn the grades I need to succeed in my courses.			
11. I know the first year of college will be the most difficult, but I am fully prepared and take responsibility for my own success.			
12. I am taking steps every day to make sure I succeed in every aspect of college.			

Where Do You Want to Go?

Think about how you answered the questions above. Be honest with yourself. On a scale of 1 to 10, how would you rate your present skills for succeeding in college?

Not very strong					Very strong				
1	2	3	4	5	6	7	8	9	10

In the following list, circle the three most important areas in which you think you can improve:

- Having strong personal values for education
- Choosing a program or degree major
- Finding the best career for my interests and skills
- Being prepared for college-level work
- Developing a positive attitude for college
- Successfully using each step of the learning process
- Adapting and broadening my personal learning style
- Getting the most out of classes large and small
- Following all college policies
- Taking advantage of college resources
- Getting the best grades I can
- Successfully transitioning to college and completing my first year
- Doing everything I can every day to ensure I succeed in college

Are there other areas or skills that need more attention in order for you to succeed in college? Write down other things you feel you need to work on.

_____
_____
_____

How to Get There

Here's what we'll work on in this chapter:

- Viewing college in terms of your personal values
- Recognizing the importance of making a commitment to succeed in the first year of college
- Discovering the career and college major that best match your interests and skills
- Understanding the obstacles students like you may have to overcome when transitioning into college
- Figuring out how to learn best in each step of the learning process
- Using your personal learning style effectively while also including other forms of learning
- Staying motivated and succeeding in large lecture classes as well as small discussion classes
- Working with your academic advisor to select courses and plan your program
- Discovering the resources your college offers for succeeding not only in classes but also in your personal and social life
- Understanding why grades matter
- Understanding the financial costs and benefits of college
- Understanding why the first year of college is so critical and how to ensure you make it through
- Knowing what steps you can take starting today and every day to ensure your success in college

1.   WELCOME TO COLLEGE!

Congratulations on your decision to attend college! For the great majority of college students, it really was your *decision*—not just an automatic thing to do. If you happen to be one of the few who just sort of ended up in college for want of anything better to do, the benefits of college will soon become obvious. But you also need to understand the costs—and the risks.

The reason for this book, and for almost all college courses, is that college does require commitment and effort. Like everything else in life that leads to meaningful results, success in college is not automatic. But when you apply yourself to your studies using the skills you'll learn in this book, you'll find you can succeed.

1.1   The Value of College

When asked, most students say they're in college primarily for the job or career they expect to follow after college. And they are correct that a college degree pays off enormously in terms of future earnings, job security and stability, and job satisfaction. Every statistic shows that people with a college education will make much more in their lifetime (much, much more than the cost of college itself) and be much happier with the work they do.

But your future career is only a part of the big picture. A college education results in many other personal benefits, and these also should be part of your motivation for doing well and continuing with your college plans. Here are a few other benefits of a college education:

- You will have a fuller life and a better understanding of the world around you.
- You will gain decision-making and problem-solving skills.
- You will meet many interesting and diverse people and have a richer social life.
- You will gain self-confidence.
- You will gain learning skills that can continue for a lifetime.
- You will make wiser decisions about lifestyle issues and live healthier.
- You will make wiser economic decisions the rest of your life.

- You will be better equipped to deal with other people, organizations, governmental agencies, and all the hassles of daily life.
- You will feel more fully a part of your community, the larger culture, and history.

A college education leads to greater success in all those areas, even though most students are usually more concerned with making it through the next class or test than the rest of their lives. But sometimes it helps to recall what a truly great step forward you are taking!

A book like this one can help you stay motivated when things get tough, but it can't necessarily *give* you motivation to start with. You have to bring that to college yourself. What we can promise you is that if you are committed, you can learn the skills for succeeding in college.

Special skills are needed because college isn't the same as high school. Throughout this book, we'll look at the many ways college is different from high school. To name just a few, college is different in study skills needed, in personal skills related to being independent, in social skills for getting along with instructors and others on campus, in financial realities, in matters of personal health, and more.

Remember, you can learn whatever you need in order to succeed. That's what this book is all about. You'll learn how to get the most out of going to class. You'll learn how to study in ways that use your time efficiently and help you pass tests. You'll even learn how to remember what you read in your college textbooks. You'll learn how to manage your time more effectively than you might have in the past, so that studying is less a burden and becomes more a simple routine. You'll even learn how things like eating well and getting enough sleep and exercise make it easier to do well in your classes.

One warning: you might not at first see an immediate payoff for everything you read here. When it comes to certain things, such as tips for how to take good notes in class to help you study later for a test, you will get specific, practical advice you can put to use immediately to get a better grade. But not everything is as obvious or immediately beneficial. You'll need to think about some of the things you'll read about here. Some things will help you get to know yourself better and understand more clearly what you really want from your education and how to go about attaining them.

But we promise you this: if you care enough to want to succeed in college and care enough to read these chapters and try to use the information, suggestions, and tips presented here, you *will* succeed in college.

1.2 The Risk of Not Finishing College

To be fair, it is important to realize also that not everyone makes it through college—that there is in fact a rather high dropout rate rate at many colleges. Typically, students who do not succeed in college drop out within the first year. Sometimes it's due to an unsolvable financial problem or a personal or family crisis, but most of the time students drop out because they're having problems passing their courses. The two biggest causes of this problem are a lack of motivation and not having learned the skills needed to succeed in college. This book addresses those issues.

You may have read or heard stories in the media about college students with enormous student loans who feel they will never earn enough in their jobs to pay it all back. These stories can be very discouraging, but they also are often misleading. Most students who complete their degree do in fact earn more than they would have without a degree and do not find it that difficult to repay their student loans. On the other hand, students who drop out after amassing a large student debt do suffer in the future because they don't get a higher-paying job requiring a degree but still have large loan payments to make. This problem emphasizes the crucial need to be committed to your college education once you begin. Dropping out after taking student loans is about the worst thing you can do. But don't worry: if you choose to succeed, as we hope you will with the help of tips and information throughout this book, you can succeed in college and earn your degree and go on to a successful future. (The later chapter Taking Control of Your Finances will offer many ways to help you avoid a large student debt.)

2.   WHO ARE YOU, REALLY?

LEARNING OBJECTIVES

1. **List your most important personal values and relate them to a college education.**
2. **Think about what kind of career will best match your interests, skills, and personality.**
3. **Understand how college is different from high school in many ways.**
4. **Develop a positive attitude about yourself as a college student.**
5. **Accept responsibility for your college experience and your life.**

Succeeding in college is somewhat like succeeding in life. It's really much more about *you* than it is about *college*. The most important place to start is to consider why you're here, what matters to you, and what you expect to get out it. Even if you have already thought about these questions, it's good to reaffirm your commitment to your plan.

2.1   What's Your Plan?

Take a few minutes and write down short answers to the questions in Activity 1. Be honest with yourself, and write down what *you* really feel. You are not writing for an instructor here, and you are not being graded on your answers!

ACTIVITY 1: YOUR COLLEGE PLAN

How long do you think you will be in college?

_____

How many courses will you need to take per term to finish college in your planned time period?

_____

What do you anticipate will be the most difficult part of completing college?

_____

Are you confident you can overcome difficulties to complete college?

_____

Could you easily answer the questions in Activity 1? How confident are you about your plan?

These are important questions to think about for the simple reason that students who have a clear plan and who are prepared to overcome possible obstacles that may arise along the way are much more likely to succeed in college. In other words, *just thinking in a positive way about your future can help that future come true*!

2.2   What If You Have Doubts?

If you're feeling very positive about college and are committed to do what you need to do to succeed, great! But what if you have doubts? What if you're not even sure you should be in college and aren't feeling much motivated at all?

In that case, you may be at a crossroads. Despite all the benefits of a college education as described earlier, college may not be right for you or you for college. If you truly feel that way, you owe it to yourself to do a little hard thinking about why you're here. Think about possible results of not feeling very committed to being in college. If you do poorly because you just don't care much, you'll likely get poor grades that will follow you into the rest of your education. If you have a student loan, you could end up dropping out but still having the debt, the worst possible situation. Go talk to a college counselor or your instructor to work through your feelings. When you've resolved your doubts and feel committed to your education, you're ready to start the road to success.

2.3 What Matters to You?

values

An object or quality a person believes is desirable.

The word **values** refers to things that matter to a person. What makes you feel good? What would you be doing if you had all the time, money, and opportunities in the world? Questions like these help us define our own values. Every individual has his or her own values.

Thinking about your own values can help you know what you want from life and from college. Take a moment and consider the list of things in Activity 2 that are valued by some people. Rate how important each thing is to you.

ACTIVITY 2: YOUR VALUES

Following is a list of things that different people say they value. For each item on this list, indicate how important it is to you yourself by ranking it as very important (5), not important (0), or somewhere in between.

Value	Not important					Very important
Making a good income	0	1	2	3	4	5
Having good friends	0	1	2	3	4	5
Learning interesting new things	0	1	2	3	4	5
Having a nice car	0	1	2	3	4	5
Having intelligent conversations	0	1	2	3	4	5
Staying current with the news	0	1	2	3	4	5
Playing sports	0	1	2	3	4	5
Hanging out with friends	0	1	2	3	4	5
Playing computer or video games	0	1	2	3	4	5
Cooking	0	1	2	3	4	5
Online social networking	0	1	2	3	4	5
Sleeping	0	1	2	3	4	5
Reading a good book	0	1	2	3	4	5
Traveling to new places	0	1	2	3	4	5
Shopping	0	1	2	3	4	5
Being liked by others	0	1	2	3	4	5
Studying and reading textbooks	0	1	2	3	4	5
Having nice clothing	0	1	2	3	4	5
Watching television	0	1	2	3	4	5
Enjoying time alone	0	1	2	3	4	5
Getting out in nature	0	1	2	3	4	5
Working your job	0	1	2	3	4	5
Looking good, personal hygiene	0	1	2	3	4	5
Meeting new people	0	1	2	3	4	5
Going to movies or entertainments	0	1	2	3	4	5
Eating nice meals out	0	1	2	3	4	5
Exercising, being physically active	0	1	2	3	4	5
Being your own boss	0	1	2	3	4	5
Having a romantic relationship	0	1	2	3	4	5
Engaging in your hobbies	0	1	2	3	4	5
Setting your own schedule	0	1	2	3	4	5
Volunteering for a good cause	0	1	2	3	4	5
Cleaning house	0	1	2	3	4	5
Attending classes	0	1	2	3	4	5
Going to religious services	0	1	2	3	4	5
Talking on the telephone, texting, e-mail	0	1	2	3	4	5
Going to parties	0	1	2	3	4	5
Participating in clubs, organized activities	0	1	2	3	4	5
Other: _____	0	1	2	3	4	5
Other: _____	0	1	2	3	4	5

Look back at the values you rated highly (4 or 5) in Activity 2, which probably show how you enjoy spending your time. But now think about how each relates to managing your time (and money) effectively while in college. Most college students feel they don't have enough time for everything they like to do. Do some of the activities you value contribute to your college experience, or could they distract you from being a good student?

Students who enter college with their eyes open and who think about their own values and motivations will be more successful. We'll start right away in Chapter 2 by helping you stay motivated and manage your time well. The following chapters will then lead you through learning how to study well and everything else.

2.4   Thinking Ahead to a Major and Career

major

A subject or field of study chosen by a college student representing his or her principal interest.

liberal arts education

A college program that provides general knowledge about the humanities, arts, and natural and social sciences, rather than professional or technical subjects.

If you've just begun college, should you already know what career you seek in the future and what courses you should take or what you should **major** in? Good question!

Some students say they have known from a very early age what they want to do after college, choose the college that is best for that plan, never waiver from the plan and choose each course with the one goal in mind, and then enter their chosen career after college or graduate school. At the other extreme, some students have only a vague sense of direction before beginning college, take a wide variety of courses, select a major only when they reach the point that they must major in something (or perhaps change majors multiple times), and then after college choose to work in an entirely different field.

Some students choose to major in an academic subject simply because they enjoy that subject, never concerned with what kind of job they may get afterward. The traditional idea of the **liberal arts education** is that you can go to college not to prepare for a specific career but to become a well-educated person who is then in a better position to work in any number of careers.

You'll also hear debates about whether it's best to choose a major that lets you "follow your dream" or better to direct yourself specifically to a future career. None of these different approaches to choosing a major and a career is automatically better than others. As long as you work to succeed, you will receive the many benefits of college and are likely to end up in a fulfilling career.

So where are *you* in this great variety of attitudes about career and major choices?

You may have entered a very specific college program designed specifically for a certain career. This is often true with community college programs and other two-year settings. But if you are in the first year of a four-year college program, you probably don't need to decide yet. Chances are, as you take a variety of courses and meet people in different fields, you'll discover something about what you really enjoy doing and the career you may choose to pursue.

On the other hand, help is available for discovering your interests, strengths, and personality factors related to careers. You can learn a lot about your options and what you would be good at by visiting your college's advising or counseling department. Almost all colleges have tools to help you discover what careers you would most enjoy.

The Strong Interest Inventory is an assessment tool used by many colleges and universities. You answer a series of simple questions and get back information about your interests, strengths, and personality related to different types of careers. This tool can also suggest specific courses, jobs and internships, and extracurricular activities related to your interests. Ask your college's career counseling center about what tools they have, such as a personality inventory to help you find the best career for you.

The CareerLink Inventory (http://www.mpcfaculty.net/CL/climain.htm) is a free, simple online tool that can teach you a lot about yourself. Follow the steps in the "Outside the Book" section at the end of this chapter to maximize your results.

Although there's nothing wrong with starting out without an intended major or career path, take care not to accidentally take courses that end up not counting toward your degree. You could end up in college longer than needed or have to pay for additional courses. Be sure to read your college catalog carefully and to talk to your academic advisor.

FIGURE 1.2

Talk with your advisor or visit the career counseling center to learn more about what future careers you may be interested in.

© *Thinkstock*

2.5 Your Past Educational Experience

Because college is so different from high school, students need to understand how well their past educational experiences have prepared them for college. Entering college with your eyes wide open is important.

Regardless of whether you just graduated from high school or are returning to education after years of working, you are now experiencing something new. Many students have difficulty because of the differences like these between college and high school.

- Time management is more important in college because of varying class and work schedules and other time commitments.
- College instructors seldom seek you out to offer extra help if you're falling behind. You are on your own and expected to do the work and meet deadlines without someone looking over your shoulder.
- There may be no attendance policy in some classes. You are expected to be mature enough to come to class without fear of penalties.
- Many classes are large, making it easy to feel lost in a crowd.
- Many instructors, especially in large classes, teach by lecture—which can be difficult for those whose high school teachers interacted a great deal with students.
- College courses require more study time and require you to work on your own.
- Your social and personal life in college may be less supervised. Younger students may not cope well with suddenly having freedom to do what they want.
- You will meet more people from more diverse backgrounds in college.
- All of these differences, along with a change in living situation for many students, can lead to emotional changes—both positive and negative.

What does all this add up to? For some students, this freedom can lead in negative directions: sleeping late, skipping classes, missing deadlines, failing to study adequately for tests, and so on. Even students who work hard in their classes may also have difficulty transitioning to the higher academic standards of college. Suddenly, you're responsible for everything. That can be a challenge to get used to. All the chapters in this book will help you make this transition successfully.

2.6 Liking Yourself as a Student and Why That Matters

Of all the factors that affect how well one does in college, attitude is probably the most important. A positive attitude leads to motivation, and someone who is strongly motivated to succeed can overcome obstacles that may occur.

In Chapter 2, we'll discuss how you can keep a positive attitude about college and stay motivated in your studies. But your attitude toward yourself as a student matters just as much. Now that you are in college, you are a new person, not just the same person who happens now to be a college student. What do you think of this new person?

If you're feeling excited, enthusiastic, capable, and confident in your new life—great! Skip ahead to the next section. But if you're less sure how well you'll do in your new role, take comfort in knowing that you're not alone. A lot of new college students, once they begin experiencing the differences from high school, start having doubts. Some may start to feel "I'm not a good enough student" or "I can't keep up with all this." Some may become fearful or apathetic.

These feelings, while perfectly natural, can hinder one's motivation and ability to succeed. If you think you can't make it, that might become true. If you're sure you'll make it, you will.

Again, think honestly about this. If you have these thoughts sometimes, why is that? Are you just reacting to a low grade on your first test? Are you just feeling this way because you see other students who look like they know what they're doing and you're feeling out of place? Most likely, if you have doubts about being able to do well, this is just a reaction to college being more difficult than what you're used to. It's mostly a matter of having the right skills for succeeding in college. This book will help you learn them—everything from how to study effectively to how to do better on tests and even how to read your textbooks more effectively.

Why do some students have to work on their student skills after beginning college while others seem to waltz right in and do well from the start?

The answer sounds simple but is actually rather complex. In part, there are just many differences among people. There are differences among high schools, past teachers, peer groups, families, cultural backgrounds, and many other factors. As a result of many different things, some students just need a little more help to succeed in college. But no student is better or automatically more capable than another, and everyone can learn the skills to succeed.

2.7 Self-Management

ethical code

A system of principles for acceptable conduct.

To succeed in college, you need to take control of your life. Gone are the days when you could just cruise through school, or life, or let others motivate you or set your schedule for you. But this is an exciting opportunity. It's your first step in your new life and the key to your future. Here are a few thoughts to get you started in the right direction:

- **Accept responsibility for your life.** You are on equal footing with everyone else and have the same opportunities to succeed.
- **Decide what you want to do.** Don't let things just happen—*make* them happen by deciding that they should happen.
- **Realize you can change.** You can change your habits to become a better student. You can change your attitudes and become a more positive, motivated student.
- **Develop a personal ethical code.** Do what is right for you and for others. College rewards responsible, ethical behavior. Be proud of who you are and your good decisions.
- **Enjoy your life!** Going to college might seem overwhelming at times, but no one is asking you to give up your life to succeed in college. Enjoy meeting new people, learning new things, and experiencing the diversity of the college experience. Most college graduates look back on their college years as one of the best periods in their whole lives!

KEY TAKEAWAYS

- A college education provides many benefits as well as much better prospects for a career you will enjoy.
- Thinking about your personal values and how they relate to your education can help you stay motivated to succeed in college.
- Personality and skill inventories can help you discover the right career for your future and your college major.
- Because college is a new and different life experience for most students, taking responsibility for new freedoms and managing time well are critical.

CHECKPOINT EXERCISES

1. Which of the following are benefits of a college education?

    a. A better understanding of the world

    b. Developing problem-solving skills

    c. Meeting interesting people

    d. Making wiser financial decisions in the future

    e. All of the above

2. What do you value that will make your future life richer when you have a college education?

   _____

   _____

   What do you value that will you likely have less time or money to spend on while in college?

   _____

   _____

3. Students usually find their college life different from their previous life in high school or in the workforce. What are the biggest changes you are experiencing now or anticipate experiencing this term?

   _____

   _____

   _____

   _____

4. For each of the following statements, circle T for true or F for false:

T	F	Attitude is one of the most important factors affecting college success.
T	F	If you sit back, wait patiently, and stick it out long enough, success in college will inevitably come to you.
T	F	To do well in college, you basically have to give up everything else in life for a while.
T	F	Most college graduates later look back on their college years as one of the best times in their lives.

3. DIFFERENT WORLDS OF DIFFERENT STUDENTS

LEARNING OBJECTIVES

1. **Understand how you may be similar to, and different from, other traditional students or returning students.**
2. **Describe the characteristics of successful students.**

Not all college students are the same, and college is usually a different experience for different students. Students answer the following questions in a variety of different ways:

1. Are you attending college directly from high school or within a year of graduation?

2. Are you a full-time student?

3. Is English your first language?

4. Are you the first person in your family to attend college?

5. Have you spent most of your life in a country other than the United States?

6. Are you married or living with a partner? Do you have children?

7. Are you working full time now or have you in the past?

When thinking about different "types" of students, be careful to avoid stereotyping. While there are genuine differences among individual students, never assume an individual person has certain characteristics simply because he or she is a certain "type" of student. For example, if you answered yes to questions 1 through 3 and no to the other questions, you may be called a **"traditional" student**—young and attending college after high school. The word "traditional" is used simply because, in the past, this was often the largest group of college students—even though, at many colleges, these students are now the minority. On the other hand, if you are older and have worked for some years before going to college, or if you are an international student or are working and attending classes part time,

"traditional" student

A college student, typically age seventeen to nineteen, attending college directly or soon after completing high school.

you might be considered a "nontraditional" student. Again, this term comes from past statistics, even though very many colleges now have more "nontraditional" students than "traditional" students.

FIGURE 1.3

Colleges have students of all ages and with diverse backgrounds.

© Thinkstock

What should that mean to you? First, not everything discussed in this book will apply to you. If you're eighteen and living away from your family for the first time in a college dormitory, you will likely not face the same issues of finding time for studying as an older student working full time and having children at home. If you're thirty and returning to school after years of successfully managing a job, you may have to reestablish your study skills but will not face the same issues as a younger student who may be tempted by the sudden freedom of college and have difficulty setting boundaries.

Every student has certain advantages from their background experience. Every student may also face certain kinds of difficulties. Understanding how your own background may impact your own preparedness for college can help you make a good start in college.

3.1 "Traditional" Students

We put quotation marks around the word "traditional" because this group of college students is no longer the majority at many colleges, although the term is still sometimes used by educators. Coming directly or almost directly from high school, "traditional" students are used to attending classes, reading textbooks, and studying and thus may find the transition to college easier. Many are single and unattached and have fewer time commitments to others. Although many do work while in college, the work is typically part time or during the summer and often does not have a severe time impact on their studies. As first-year students, usually living on campus at a four-year college or university, they do not lose time to commuting, and typically their housing plan includes meals and otherwise simplifies their living arrangements. In all, many have few responsibilities other than their academic work.

On the other hand, "traditional" students living away from home for the first time may face more psychological and social issues than other student groups. They may be away from family and old friends, perhaps forced to cope with an incompatible roommate or living arrangements, and facing all sorts of new temptations. With this new freedom, many students develop habits such as a poor diet and little sleep, a lack of exercise, and sometimes substance abuse or other behaviors that disrupt their academic routine and study habits. Some students who do not adjust to the freedoms of college end up dropping out in their first year.

3.2 Returning Students

returning students

A college student, typically over age twenty, who has worked or engaged in other significant activities between high school and college.

Students returning to their education are often older, may have worked for a number of years, and may be used to living on their own and being financially and psychologically independent. They are often more mature and know what they want from college; they may be more goal driven. They are likely to be paying their own way through college and want to get their money's worth. They may be full-time students but frequently are still working and can take only a part-time course load. They often live off campus and may own a home and have a mortgage. They may have children. Because they have made a very deliberate decision to go to college, **returning students** are often serious students and are motivated to do the work. Having spent time in the work world, they may also have developed good problem-solving and decision-making skills as a result of their "real-world" experience.

extracurricular

Activities at college, usually organized and involving a group, outside academic activities related to one's courses.

On the other hand, returning students may have less time for studying because of work and family commitments. They may feel more stress because of the time and financial requirements of college. Spending less time on campus may contribute to not feeling completely at home in the academic world. They may not have time for many **extracurricular** and campus activities. Although they may be dedicated and hardworking students, they may also be less patient with learning "theory" in their courses and want all their coursework to relate directly to the real world.

Returning students may also be able to attend college intermittently—sometimes just one term at time, then back to work for a while, then back for another term, usually for financial reasons. Such students can experience frustration when it feels like it's taking forever to finish, and it can take a lot of will power to keep coming back. Staying motivated may be particularly important.

3.3 Transfer Students

A transfer student begins at one college but then switches to another college at some point—for any of many reasons. With the high costs of many four-year colleges, some students begin at a less expensive community college planning to transfer after a year or two to a four-year college. While this can help save in overall costs, they should look ahead to make sure all their college credits will transfer to the new college, since they certainly don't want to pay to take similar courses again. Other students transfer if they realize their first school does not offer the educational program they now want. It is especially important for students contemplating a transfer to talk with their academic advisor about their plans.

3.4   Other Student Groups

Other common differences also affect students' college experience. Students in the following groups may be either "traditional" students by age or returning students.

Commuter Students

Many working students commute to campus for classes. Many young people also continue to live at home after high school and come to campus only for classes. Commuter students often face the same issues of limited time as returning students. They may find it difficult to find time to talk with an instructor outside of class. At a four-year college they may feel less involved in college overall if they do not take part in any campus life. At many community colleges, however, all students are commuters.

First-Generation Students

The phrase "first-generation student" refers to students who are the first in their families to attend college. These students may be "traditional" students enrolled right after high school or may be returning students. Students whose parents did not attend college may be less familiar with some or all aspects of the college experience and may face a bigger transition into their new life.

Recent Immigrant and International Students

Many college students have recently **immigrated** to the United States or may be attending college here from their native country. Students coming from a different culture, and possibly speaking English as a second language, may have to make cultural accommodations. Language issues can be a serious obstacle for some, since so much of college education is based on reading and writing in English.

Immigrated

To move to a country of which one is not a native, usually for permanent residence.

Students with Disabilities

The Americans with Disabilities Act prohibits colleges and universities from discriminating on the basis of disabilities and ensures that both classes and extracurricular activities are accessible to students with disabilities. This includes both physical accessibility to campus buildings and housing and accessibility to services and aids necessary for effective communication. Students with disabilities have the right to request any accommodations needed to allow them to succeed in college. For more information or for answers to any specific questions, contact the Association on Higher Education And Disability (AHEAD) at http://www.ahead.org.

Students Who Are Working

The key issue for working students often is time—how to find enough time to study enough to do well. Since it is very difficult to maintain two full-time schedules—work and school—one or the other may suffer. For those working long hours, Chapter 2 presents many tips for managing your time when you have less of it; Chapter 11 also suggests ways to cut back on expenses while in college so that you don't have to work so many hours.

Students with a Family

Returning students often have families of their own. Having children of your own means you have different priorities from most some students, but a family shouldn't be viewed as an obstacle to college success. Time may be short, but you can learn to manage it carefully to avoid falling behind in your studies. Chapter 2 describes some creative ways students can involve their families in the experience to prevent student stresses from disrupting family happiness.

3.5 Profile of a Successful Student

While all types of students can succeed, it's important to develop a plan to make sure you have the knowledge and skills needed to succeed. Following are some of the characteristics of successful students you should strive for:

- Successful students have a good attitude and know how to stay motivated. You will learn about this in Chapter 2.
- Successful students have developed good time management strategies, such as scheduling study time and getting started early on assignments and projects. You will also learn about this in Chapter 2.
- Successful students develop their critical thinking skills and apply them in their studies. Chapter 3 gets you started in this direction.
- Successful students have effective strategies for taking good notes in class and using them. Chapter 4 guides you through this learning process.
- Successful students gain the most from their assigned readings for classes. Chapter 5 presents guidelines for effective reading and taking notes to help you understand and retain information.
- Successful students know how to prepare for and take tests successfully. Chapter 6 tells you what you need to know and presents tips for effective test taking.
- Successful students interact well with their instructors and fellow students in and outside of class. Chapter 7 helps you gain these skills.
- Successful students write well in their classes, an essential aspect of college education. Chapter 8 introduces key principles of effective college writing to get you started.
- Successful students have social relationships that contribute to, rather than detract from, their educational experiences. Chapter 9 will show you how to manage your social life.
- Successful students stay healthy with good habits that help them be better students and feel less stress. Chapter 10 can help you get started on good habits.
- Successful students control their finances. Because getting into debt is a common reason why students drop out of college, it's important to control expenditures and manage your finances well, as we'll see in Chapter 11.
- Successful students are able to transition well from the world of college into their future careers. You will learn these important principles in Chapter 12 to carry forward into your future.

KEY TAKEAWAYS

- College students vary widely in terms of age, work experience, cultural background, family, and other factors that may affect how they learn.
- Young students just out of high school face a transition involving new freedoms and new situations they may need to master in order to succeed academically.
- Returning students who work and may also have family responsibilities often have time issues and may feel out of place in the college environment.
- Other student groups include commuters, first-generation students, immigrant and international students, students with disabilities, and others, each of whom may need to face additional issues to be successful.
- Regardless of individual differences, all successful students share a number of traits, including a good attitude, effective time management strategies, good studying and test-taking skills, and more.

CHECKPOINT EXERCISES

1. Are you a "traditional" or "returning" student? List an important advantage you have as a result of being this sort of student:

   _____

2. Check off which traits in this list are true of successful students:

	They know how to stay motivated.
	They don't need to schedule study periods because they study at every available moment every day.
	They know better than to try to think on their own.
	They know how to speed-read so they don't have to underline or highlight in their textbooks.
	They avoid talking with their instructors, so they can remain anonymous.
	They develop their writing skills.
	They eat fast food so they have more time for studying.
	They have few friends, because social relationships distract one from academics.
	They use several credit cards so they don't have to worry about finances until after graduation.

4. HOW YOU LEARN

LEARNING OBJECTIVES

1. **Understand and make effective use of the four steps of the learning process.**
2. **Describe the different learning styles of different college students and recognize your own learning preferences.**
3. **Know how to benefit from your own learning style and how to develop new learning skills.**
4. **Take action to learn effectively when your learning style differs from your instructor's teaching style.**

One of the first steps for becoming a successful student is to understand how people learn. Certain characteristics of effective learning, including the four-step learning process, are true of all people. At the same time, people have different learning styles. Understanding how you learn is important for your college success.

4.1   The Learning Cycle: Four Steps to Learning

Adult learning in college is different from learning in primary and secondary school. In high school, teachers often take much of the responsibility for how students learn—encouraging learning with class discussions, repeating key material, creating study guides, and looking over students' shoulders to make sure no one falls behind. In college, most of the responsibility for learning falls on the student. You're free to fail—or succeed—as you choose. This also applies to how well you learn.

Learning an academic subject means really understanding it, being able to think about it in meaningful ways and to apply that understanding in new situations. This is very different from simply memorizing something and repeating it back on a test. Academic learning occurs most effectively in a cycle of four steps:

1. Preparing
2. Absorbing
3. Capturing
4. Reviewing

Think first about the different situations in which you learn. Obviously you learn during class, whether by listening to the instructor speak or in class discussions in which you participate. But you also learn while reading your textbooks and other materials outside of class. You learn when you talk with an instructor during office hours. You learn by talking with other students informally in study groups. You learn when you study your class notes before an exam. All of these different learning situations involve the same four-step process.

FIGURE 1.4 The Learning Cycle

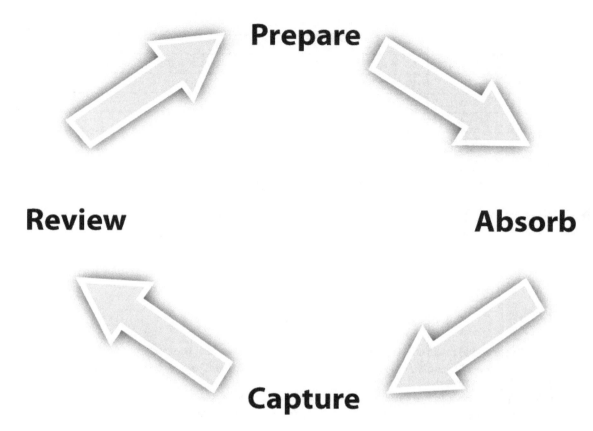

Prepare

One student rolls out of bed a few minutes before class and dashes across campus and grabs the last seat in the hall just as the instructor begins a lecture; it takes him a few minutes to find the right notebook in his backpack, and then he can't find a pencil. He's thinking about how he should've set his alarm a little earlier so he'd have had time to grab a cup of coffee, since he's having trouble waking up. Finally he settles in his seat and starts listening, but now he can't figure out what the instructor is talking about. He starts jotting down phrases in his notes anyway, thinking he'll figure it out later.

Another student looks over his notes from the previous class and glances back at passages he'd highlighted in the textbook reading. He arrives at class a few minutes early, sits up front where he can hear well, and has his notebook open and pencil out. While waiting for the instructor to arrive, he talks to another student about her ideas for the class paper due next week.

It's obvious which of these students will learn more during today's class lecture. One has prepared and the other has not, and there will be a huge difference in how well they understand today's topic. Preparing to learn is the first step for learning. The same is true when you sit down to read your textbook, to study for an exam, or to work on a class project. Partly you are putting yourself in the right mindset to learn. But when you review yesterday's notes to prepare for today's class, you are also solidifying yesterday's learning.

Absorb

"Absorbing" refers to taking in new ideas, information, or experience. This is what happens when a student listens to a class lecture or reads a textbook. In high school, this is sometimes the only learning step some students took. They listened to what the instructor said and "regurgitated" it back on the test. But this won't work in college because learning now requires *understanding* the topic, not just repeating facts or information. In coming chapters you'll get tips for improving in this step.

Capture

"Capturing" refers to taking notes. No matter how good your memory, you need to take good notes in college simply because there is so much to learn. Just hearing or reading something once is not enough. You have to go back over the material again, sometimes several times again, thinking about it and seeing how it all fits together.

The more effective your note-taking skills, the better your learning abilities. Take notes also when reading your textbooks. You'll learn methods for taking good notes in later chapters.

Review

The step of reviewing—your class notes, your readings and notes, and any other course materials possibly including recordings, online media, **podcasts**, and so on—is the next step for solidifying your learning. This is how you reach a real understanding of the topic. Reviewing is also a way to prepare for new information and ideas. That's why this is a learning cycle: the end of the process loops back to the beginning as you prepare for additional learning.

Reviewing is also the step in which you discover whether you really understand the material. If you do not understand something fully, you may need to reread a section of the book, talk it over with a friend in the class, or go see your instructor.

podcasts
An audio or video recording, such as of a class lecture, made available online; so named because podcasts were originally developed to be downloaded and played on iPods.

4.2 What's Your Learning Style?

Different people have different **learning styles**. Style refers to a person's specific learning preferences and actions. One student may learn more effectively from listening to the instructor. Another learns more effectively from reading the textbook, while another student benefits most from charts, graphs, and images the instructor presents during a lecture.

Learning style is important in college. Each different style, described later in more detail, has certain advantages and disadvantages compared with other styles. None is "right" or "wrong." You can learn to use your own style more effectively.

College instructors also have different **teaching styles**, which may or may not match up well with your learning style. Although you may personally learn best from a certain style of teaching, you cannot expect that your instructors will use exactly the style that is best for you. Therefore you need to know how to adapt to teaching styles used in college.

The different ways in which people learn have been given different names in different systems. Some describe the differences between how extroverts (outgoing, gregarious, social people) and introverts (quiet, private, contemplative people) learn. Some divide people into "thinkers" and "feelers." A popular theory of different learning styles is Howard Gardner's "multiple intelligences," based on eight different types of intelligence:

1. Verbal (prefers words)
2. Logical (prefers math and logical problem solving)
3. Visual (prefers images and spatial relationships)
4. **Kinesthetic** (prefers body movements and doing)
5. Rhythmic (prefers music, rhymes)
6. Interpersonal (prefers group work)
7. Intrapersonal (prefers introspection and independence)
8. Naturalist (prefers nature, natural categories)

The multiple intelligences approach recognizes that different people have different ways, or combinations of ways, of relating to the world.

Another approach to learning styles is called the VARK approach, which focuses on learning through different senses (**V**isual, **A**ural, **R**eading/Writing, and **K**inesthetic):

- Visual learners prefer images, charts, and the like.
- Aural learners learn better by listening.
- Reading/writing learners learn better through written language.
- Kinesthetic learners learn through doing, practicing, and acting.

You can learn more about your VARK learning style and take a self-assessment at http://www.businessballs.com/freepdfmaterials/vak_learning_styles_questionnaire.pdf. You can also take a quick learning style inventory that provides some good study tips at http://www.educationplanner.org/students/self-assessments/learning-styles.shtml.

learning styles
A person's preferred approach to or way of learning most effectively.

teaching styles
The preferred methods or techniques an instructor uses to teach students, often based on personal preferences, individual skills, and the norms of the academic discipline.

Kinesthetic
Referring to the sensation of body movement or position.

Still more systems have been used by educators to describe the various ways how people learn. All of these systems can help you learn how **you as an individual person and college student learn best.** You can use the assessment in the "Outside the Book" section at the end of this chapter to learn more about your style.

Just knowing your preferred style, however, doesn't automatically tell you how to do your best in college. For example, even if you are a kinesthetic learner, you'll likely still have reading assignments (verbal learning) as well as lecture classes (listening). All students need to adapt to other ways of learning.

The following sections look at the key ways in which learning occurs in college classes and offer some suggestions about how to adapt your strengths for success.

Reading

Reading skills are very important in college. Most classes involve reading assignments. Although some instructors cover some of the textbook's content in lectures or class discussions, students cannot skip the reading assignments and expect to do well.

If your personal learning style is verbal and independent—that is, if you learn well by sitting alone and reading—then you will likely not have difficulty with your college reading. Here are some tips to maximize your learning:

- Underline and highlight key ideas when reading.
- Take good notes on your reading, using your own words.
- Write descriptions that summarize information presented in nonverbal modes, such as through charts and graphs.
- Do all optional and supplemental readings.
- Take good notes in class, as you may remember more from your written words than from the instructor's spoken words.
- If a class involves significant nonreading learning, such as learning hands-on physical processes, study with other students who are kinesthetic or "doing" learners.

If you have a different learning style, then you may need to give more attention to your reading skills. Always allow plenty of time for reading assignments—rushing makes it harder to understand what you are reading. Do your reading at times of the day when you are most alert. Find a quiet, comfortable place conducive to reading.

Try also to maximize your learning through your personal style. If you learn better by listening, for example, sit up front in lecture classes where you can see and hear the instructor better. Ask if you can record an instructor's lectures and then listen again at a convenient time, such as when commuting to class or work. If you are more of a visual learner, sit in class where you can see **PowerPoint** slides and other visual presentations most clearly. Use a visual approach in your class notes, as described in Chapter 4. See whether video podcasts are available for reviewing lectures. Try to relate all of these visual images to the textbook's content when you're reading an assignment. In addition, pay special attention to illustrations and diagrams in the book. If you are more of an interpersonal learner, form a study group with other students and talk with others about the course topics. Take advantage of your instructors' office hours to help clarify your understanding after reading assignments.

Listening

Listening skills are as important in college as reading skills. College students are expected to listen to their instructors in class and remember and understand what is said. In discussion classes, listening is important also for participating well in discussions.

PowerPoint

The name of a specific software presentation program (within Microsoft Office) used in many educational and business settings to produce and deliver "slides" containing text and graphics to a group via a projected computer screen.

If your personal learning style favors listening, then you may already be good at understanding class lectures. Chapter 4 provides tips to help you pay close attention, take good notes, and recall what you have heard. Here are some more tips:

- Sit where you can best hear the instructor, away from other distractions.
- Study with other students and listen to what they say about course topics. Hearing them talk from their class notes may be more helpful than reviewing your own written notes.
- Record lectures and listen to them again later when reviewing material before a test.
- When studying, read your notes aloud. Review previous tests by reading the questions aloud and speaking your answers. If a section in your textbook seems confusing, read it aloud.
- Talk with your instructor if you feel you are not understanding course readings.
- Use rhymes or **acronyms** to recall verbal information. For more information, see Chapter 4.
- Explore supplemental learning aids, such as audio and video podcasts and YouTube videos (even from other colleges and universities) on the course's subject matter.

Seeing

A "seeing" learner learns more effectively through seeing than through reading or listening. Your instructor may do demonstrations, for example. If you are a visual learner, work on developing your reading and listening skills, too, because you will need to learn in these ways as well. Here are some tips to improve learning related to seeing:

- Pay special attention in class to visual presentations, such as charts, diagrams, and images.
- Take lecture notes using a visual approach. Do the same when taking notes on class readings. Use diagrams, different colors, lists, and sketches to help you remember. For more information, see Chapter 4.
- Use videos and other visual aids for reviewing lectures.
- Pay special attention to your textbooks' illustrations and diagrams.
- If your instructor or textbook uses few visuals to help you understand and recall information and ideas, try to imagine how you would present this information visually to others if you were giving a class presentation. In your notes, create sketches for a PowerPoint slideshow capturing the highlights of the material.
- Study with other students who may learn better by reading or listening, and watch how they explain the material.

Doing

People who learn best by doing are often attracted to careers with a strong physical or hands-on component, which can vary from athletics to engineering. But these students will need to use other learning skills as well. Here are some tips to help maximize your learning related to doing:

- Try to engage all your senses when learning. Even when reading about something, try to imagine what it would feel like if you touched it, how it might smell, how you could physically manipulate it, and so forth.
- Think about how you would teach the topic you are presently learning. What visuals could you make to demonstrate the idea or information? Imagine a class lecture as a train of boxcars and think about what things you would put in those cars to represent the lecture topics.
- When it becomes difficult to concentrate when reading while sitting in a quiet place, get up and move around while studying; make gestures as you read aloud.
- Use your hands to create a range of study aids rather than just taking notes: make charts, posters, flash cards, and so on.
- When taking notes, sketch familiar shapes around words and phrases to help you remember them. Try to associate abstract ideas with concrete examples.
- The act of writing—handwriting more than typing at a keyboard—may increase retention; write key things several times.
- Study with other students who may learn better by reading or listening.

FIGURE 1.5

Many college classes involve lectures.

© Thinkstock

FIGURE 1.6

Instructors often use visual aids to help explain concepts and ideas. This helps students with visual learning styles.

© Thinkstock

acronyms

A word formed from the initial letters of words in a phrase or series of words, such as "USA" for "United States of America."

Feeling

Feeling learners focus on the emotional side of information and learn through personal connections. They may feel that a college textbook or a class is "dry" or "boring" if it focuses exclusively on written information. In addition to improving their reading and listening skills, students with this style can enrich their learning by focusing on what they and others feel about the information and ideas being learned. Here are some tips to help maximize your learning related to feeling:

- Try to establish an emotional connection with the topic you are learning. In a history class, for example, imagine yourself as someone living in the period you are studying: what would you feel about the forces at work in your life? In a science class, think about what the implications of a particular scientific principle or discovery might mean for you as a person or how you yourself might have felt if you had been the scientist making that discovery.
- Talk with your instructor during office hours. Express your enthusiasm and share your feelings about the subject. Even instructors who may seem "dry" in a lecture class often share their feelings toward their subject in conversation.
- Do supplemental reading about the people involved in a subject you're studying. For example, reading a Wikipedia biographical sketch of a historical figure, scientist, or theorist may open your eyes to a side of the subject you hadn't seen before and increase your learning.
- Study with other students who may learn better by reading or listening. Talk with them in a personal way about what the material means to them. Try teaching them about the topic while explaining your feelings about it.
- Also try the strategies listed for the "doing" learning style.

Your Style, Your Instructor's Style

Many college classes tend to focus on certain learning styles. Instructors in large lecture classes, for example, generally emphasize listening carefully and reading well. But don't worry if these are not your particular strengths, for much of this book focuses on learning study skills related to these. Take responsibility for your own learning, since you can't expect the instructor to help you through the subject in your own personal way. For example, if you are a visual learner but your instructor simply stands at a podium and lectures, then provide your own visual stimulation by sketching concept maps in your notes or by visualizing how information being presented might look in a pie chart or graph. For more information, see Chapter 4.

As you move further into your college curriculum, you will likely have more small classes with class discussions, demonstrations, group presentations, and other learning activities. Once you are in classes closely related to a career path that interests you, you will find you are learning more with your personal style.

Much learning in college also comes from interactions with others, who often have different learning styles. Be open to interacting with other students and instructors who are different from you, and you will find yourself learning in ways that may be new to you.

Finally, if your instructor's teaching style seems to be keeping you from succeeding in a course, talk to your instructor privately during office hours. You can explain how you best learn and ask for suggestions about other resources that may help you.

KEY TAKEAWAYS

- People learn through a four-step process, and you can maximize your learning by paying attention to all steps.
- The first step of the learning cycle is to prepare in advance for classes, reading, tests, and other learning.
- The second step is to absorb information and ideas effectively during classes, reading, and other learning experiences.
- The third step, capturing, typically involves taking notes while learning to increase your understanding and retention.
- The fourth step is to review your notes, to help solidify the learning and to prepare for repeating the cycle in the next class or reading assignment.
- People have natural learning preferences, affecting how they learn best, such as learning by reading, by listening, by seeing, by doing, and by feeling.
- Students should learn how to use their own learning style to their best advantage while also becoming flexible and working to develop other learning styles.

CHECKPOINT EXERCISES

1. Number each the following actions to put them in the correct order of the four steps of the learning cycle:

   - ___ Review your class notes to make sure you understand.
   - ___ Listen carefully to what your instructor says.
   - ___ Get ready for today's class by looking over your notes on the reading you did for today.
   - ___ Take effective notes.

2. How would you describe your personal learning style?

   _____

   Name an activity from which you generally learn very well.

   _____

   Name a type of learning experience you may have difficulty with.

   _____

   For the activity above, list at least two strategies you can use to improve your learning effectiveness when in that situation next time.

   _____

   _____

3. If you experience a situation in which your personal learning style seems to clash hopelessly with an instructor's teaching style, what is your best course of action?

   a. Ask the instructor to teach in a different way.
   b. Drop the class.
   c. Adapt your style or study with other students.
   d. Complain to the dean.

5. WHAT IS COLLEGE, REALLY?

LEARNING OBJECTIVES

1. **Describe differences between large and small college classes and discuss the implications for learning.**
2. **Understand different kinds of courses within your own college program: core courses, electives, and major courses.**
3. **Describe the different skills needed for online courses.**
4. **Know how to learn your college's policies and understand their importance.**
5. **Know what resources your college has for students and how to access them.**

5.1 Big Classes, Small Classes

While most high school classes are fairly small, many college classes are large—up to several hundred students in a large lecture class. Other classes may be as small as high school classes. In large lecture classes you may feel totally anonymous or even invisible. This feeling can get some students in trouble. Here are some common mistaken assumptions and attitudes about large classes:

- The instructor won't notice me sitting there, so I can check e-mail or Facebook or even read for a different class.
- Since the instructor doesn't know me, I don't even need to go to class as long as I can borrow someone's notes to find out what happens.
- I hate listening to lectures, so I might as well think about something else because I'm not going to learn anything this way anyway.

These comments all share the same flawed attitude about college: it's up to the instructor to keep me interested and entertained, and it's actually the college's or instructor's fault that I'm stuck in this large class, so they're to blame if I get bored and do other things. But remember, *in college, you take responsibility for your own learning*. Sure, a student is free to try to sleep in a lecture class, or not attend the class at all—the same way a student is "free" to fail any class he or she chooses!

FIGURE 1.7

In a lecture class, avoid the temptation to cruise the Web or engage in other activities that will distract you from paying attention.

© *Thinkstock*

If you dislike large lecture classes but can't avoid them, the best solution is to learn how to learn in them. Later chapters will give you tips for improving this experience. Just remember that it's up to you to actively engage in your own learning—it's not the instructor's job to entertain you enough to "make" you learn.

There is one thing you need to know right away. Even in a lecture hall holding three hundred students, your instructors *do* know who you are. They may not know your name right away or even by the end of the term, but they see you sitting there, doing whatever you are doing, looking wherever you are looking—and you do make a impression on them. Instructors probably won't lower your grade on an exam because you slept once in class, but the impression you make can affect how far instructors go out of their way to offer a helping hand. Interacting with instructors is a crucial part of education—and a primary way students learn. Successful interaction begins with good communication and mutual respect. If you want your instructors to respect you, then you need to show respect for them and their classes as well.

5.2 Core Courses, Electives, Majors, and Credits

Every college has its own course requirements for different programs and degrees. This information is available online at the college's website or in a printed course catalog. While you should have an academic advisor to help you plot your path through college and take the best courses, you should also make sure yourself that you are registering for courses that fit well into your plan to graduate. In general there are three types of courses:

1. **Core courses,** sometimes called general education requirements, involve a range of courses from which you can choose to meet a general requirement. You may need to take one or more English classes and possibly math or science requirements. You will need a certain number of credits or course hours in certain types of core courses, but you can often choose among various specific courses for how you meet these requirements.

2. **Required courses in your major** are set by academic departments. Whether you choose to major in English, math, engineering, history, a health field, chemistry, business, or any other field, your department requires certain courses you must take and gives you options for a additional required credits. You may not need to declare a major for a while, but this is something you can start thinking about now.

3. **Electives** are courses you choose freely to complete the total number of college credits needed for your program or degree. How many electives you may take, how they count toward your total, and what kinds of courses are acceptable as electives all vary considerably among different schools and programs.

Most important is that you understand what courses you need and how each counts. Study the college catalog carefully and talk things over fully with your advisor. Don't just sign up for courses that sound interesting—you might end up taking courses that don't count toward your degree at all.

In addition, each term you may have to choose how many courses or hours to take. Colleges have rules about the maximum number of hours allowed per term, but this may be more than you want to manage—especially if you work or have other responsibilities. Still, taking a light course load can add up over time and result in an extra full year of college (or more)—at significant additional expense. At many colleges, the average full-time student takes five years to graduate, and that's a lot of extra money to have to spend! Part-time students often have to decide based on time issues. Since everyone's situation is unique, you should talk this issue over with your advisor each year or term.

5.3 Online Courses

online

Referring to a computer connected to other computers, typically through the Internet; online education, for example, may occur entirely through the computer.

Most colleges offer some online courses or regular courses with an **online** component. There are many different types, but in almost all online courses you work independently and communicate with the instructor (and sometimes other students) primarily through your computer. If you have never taken an online course, carefully the following issues to ensure you will succeed:

- You need to own or have frequent access to a recent model of computer with a high-speed Internet connection. Don't even think about taking a course on your cellphone or small tablet because the screen is too small for much of the experience.

- Without set hours, you need to stay motivated to schedule your time and participate regularly.

- Without an instructor or other students in the room, you need to be able to pay attention effectively and stay engaged. Learning on a computer is not as simple as passively watching television! Learn to interact fully with the online course and take notes.

- Without reminders in class and peer pressure from other students, you'll need to take responsibility to complete all assignments and papers on time.

- Since your instructor will evaluate you primarily through your writing and test scores, you need good writing and test-taking skills (discussed in later chapters). If you believe you need to work on these, put off taking an online course until you feel better prepared.

- You must take the initiative to ask questions if you don't understand something.

- You may need to be creative to find other ways to interact with other students in the course. You could form a study group and get together regularly in person with other students in the same course.

If you feel you are ready to take on these responsibilities and are attracted to the flexibility of an online course and the freedom to schedule your time in it, see what your college has available.

Note also that many "regular" college courses also have an online component in addition to classroom learning. In a "blended" course, for example, you might be asked to view video content or read special materials online before coming to class, or to work through exercises or other activities online after class. In a "flipped" class, the instructor may present the lecture or readings online in advance of classroom discussions—and you are expected to experience the online content first in order to participate in classroom activities. Any online component in any class will demand the same skills and responsibilities as a full online course.

FIGURE 1.8

Online courses are increasingly common at colleges and require independent learning.

© *Thinkstock*

5.4   Online Degree Programs

In the last decade many schools have developed complete online degree programs, and these have become more popular because they allow for more flexible schedules and may be less expensive than other traditional settings. This area of education is rapidly changing, however, with new programs in wide-ranging fields sprouting up all over. If you are considering doing your entire degree through an online program, make sure you spend some time thinking about it and researching the possibilities.

First, carefully consider whether online learning is best for you. Many younger students, especially, do better in classrooms with other students—while some older students who have developed self-discipline on the job may thrive in an online environment. Before plunging in, take an online course or two to experience how well you learn independently on your computer and how much you enjoy that approach.

In addition, fully research the different institutions offering online degree programs. Not all are fully accredited, and your degree may not be as fully valued by future employers. Be wary of "get your degree quick!" advertisements. Reputable online degree programs take as much time as classroom programs and are as rigorous in the learning process as traditional college programs. Be suspicious of any online school promising a shortcut or easy path, especially among for-profit schools.

5.5   Class Attendance and Promptness

In some classes at some colleges, attendance is required and absences can affect your course grade. But even when attendance is not required, missing classes will also hurt your grade. You're not learning if you're not there. Reading another student's notes is not the same.

Arriving in class on time is also important. Walking into a class that has already begun is rude to the instructor (remember the impression you're making) and to other students. A mature student respects the instructor and other students and in turn receives respect back.

5.6   College Policies

A college campus is almost like a small town—or country—unto itself. The campus likely has its own police force, its own government, its own stores, its own ID cards, its own parking rules, and so on. Colleges also have policies about acceptable behaviors. Students who do not understand the rules can find themselves in trouble.

academic honesty

Fundamental principle that a student does his or her own work and does not interfere with the honest work of others; violations of academic honesty include cheating, plagiarism, fabrication of false authorities, misrepresentation, inappropriate assistance from others, acting to prevent others from accomplishing their own work, and so on.

The most important policy is **academic honesty**. Cheating is taken very seriously. Some high school students may have only received a slap on the wrist if caught looking at another student's paper during a test or turning in a paper containing sentences or paragraphs found online or purchased from other sources. In many colleges, academic dishonesty like this results in automatic failure of the course—or even expulsion from college. The principle of academic honesty is simple: all students must do their own work. If you have any doubt of what this means for a paper you are writing, a project you are doing with other students, or anything else, check the college website for policy statements or talk with your instructor.

Colleges also have policies about alcohol and drug use, sexual harassment, hazing, hate crimes, and similar behaviors. Residence halls have policies about noise limits, visitors, hours, alterations of university property, and so on. The college registrar has policies about course add and drop dates, payment schedules and refunds, and the like. Such policies help ensure all students have the same right to a quality education—one not unfairly interrupted by the actions of others. You can find these policies on the college website or in the catalog.

5.7 College Resources

To succeed in college, you need to be fully informed and make smart decisions about the courses you register for, college policies, and additional resources. Always remember that your college *wants* you to succeed. That means that if you are having any difficulties or have questions you can't get answered, there are college resources available to help you. This is true of both academic and personal issues that could potentially disrupt your college experience. *Never* hesitate to go looking for help or information—but realize that usually **you have to take the first step**.

The college's website and catalog have already been mentioned as great sources of many kinds of information. Students are often surprised to see how much information is available online about college programs, offices, special assistance programs, and so on, as well as helpful information such as studying tips, personal health, financial help, and other resources. Explore your college's website and learn what is available—this could save you a lot of time in the future if you experience any difficulty.

In addition, many colleges have offices that can help in a variety of ways. Following are some of the resources your college may have:

- **Academic advising office.** This office helps you choose courses and plan your program or degree. You should have a personal meeting at least once every term.
- **Counseling office.** This office helps with personal problems, including health, stress management, interpersonal issues, and more.
- **Financial aid office.** If you are presently receiving financial aid or may qualify for assistance, you should know this office well.
- **Tutoring or skill centers.** The title of this resource varies among colleges, but most have special places where students can go for additional help for their courses. There may be a separate math center, writing center, or general study skills center.
- **Computer lab.** In the past before most students were skilled with computers, colleges built labs where students could use campus computers and receive training or help resolving technical problems. Many campuses still maintain computer centers to assist students with technical issues.
- **Student health clinic.** In addition to providing some basic medical care and making referrals, most college student health centers also help with issues such as diet and exercise counseling, birth control services, and preventive health care.
- **Career guidance or placement office.** This center can help you find a student job or internship, plan for your career after graduation, and receive career counseling.

- **Office for students with disabilities.** This office provides various services to help students with disabilities adapt within the college environment.
- **Housing office.** This office controls campus residential housing and also often helps students find off-campus housing.
- **Diversity office.** This office promotes cultural awareness on campus, runs special programs, and assists diverse students with adjusting to campus culture.
- **Office of student affairs or student organizations.** Participating in a group of like-minded students often supports academic success.
- **Athletic center.** Most colleges have exercise equipment, pools, courts and tracks, and other resources open to all students. Take advantage of this to improve or maintain your personal health, which promotes academic success.
- **Special offices for student populations.** These may include an office supporting students who speak English as a second language, adult students returning to college, international students, religious students, students with children (possibly a child-care center), veterans of the armed services, students preparing for certain types of careers, and so on.
- **Your instructors.** It never hurts to ask a friendly instructor if he or she knows of any additional college resources you haven't yet discovered. There may be a brand new program on campus, or a certain department may offer a service not widely promoted through the college website.

Everyone needs help at some time—you should never feel embarrassed or ashamed to seek help. Part of your tuition and fees are going to these offices, and you have every right to take advantage of them.

FIGURE 1.9

Your college has many resources and many professionals available to help you with any issue that may affect your success as a student.

© *Thinkstock*

KEY TAKEAWAYS

- Even in large classes, attendance is important; make a good impression and learn to stay attentive.
- Study the college catalog and talk with your advisor to ensure you understand the role of core classes, electives, and major courses in your program or degree requirements.
- Online courses are another option in many colleges but require preparedness and a heightened sense of responsibility.
- Know your college's policies for academic issues and campus behavior.
- Taking advantage of college resources for a wide range of academic and personal matters is essential for success in college.

CHECKPOINT EXERCISES

1. For each of the following statements, circle T for true or F for false:

T	F	If your instructor in a large lecture class is boring, there's nothing you can do except to try to stay awake and hope you never have him or her for another class.
T	F	In a large lecture hall, if you sit near the back and pretend to listen, you can send text messages or check Facebook without your instructor noticing.

2. List three things a student need to be good at to succeed in an online course.

   _____

   _____

   _____

3. Using your imagination, describe three different actions that would violate your college's academic honesty policy.

   _____

   _____

   _____

4. Where on campus would you first go for help choosing your courses for next term?

   _____

   For help with your math class?

   _____

   For a problem coping with a lot of stress?

   _____

   To learn about your options for student loans?

   _____

   To find a better apartment?

   _____

---

6. LET'S TALK ABOUT SUCCESS

LEARNING OBJECTIVES

1. **Understand that success in college means much more in the long term than simply passing or getting good grades.**
2. **Describe situations in which grades do matter—and why it's important to do as well as you can.**
3. **Describe why it is so important to succeed in your first year of college.**
4. **List steps you can begin taking immediately to ensure your success.**

Success in college is the theme of this book, and you'll be learning more about everything involved in success in the following chapters. Let's first define what success really means so that you can get started, right now, on the right foot.

Understand first that no book can "make" you be successful—it can only offer the tools for you to use if you want. What are you thinking now as you read these words? Are you reading this right now only because you *have* to, because it is assigned reading in a course you have to take—and your mind keeps drifting to other things because you're feeling bored? Or are you interested because you've decided you *want* to succeed in college?

We hope it's the latter, that you're feeling motivated—and excited, too—to do a great job in college. But even if you aren't presently concerned about these issues, we hope you'll keep reading and do some thinking about why you're in college and how to get motivated to do well.

6.1 "Success" and "Failure"

So what does "success" actually mean in college? Good grades? That's what many students would say—at least toward the beginning of their time in college.

When you ask people about their college experience a few years later, grades are seldom one of the first things mentioned. College graduates reflecting back typically emphasize the following:

- The complete college experience (often "the best years of my life")
- Exploring many different subjects and discovering one's own interests
- Meeting a lot of interesting people, learning about different ways to live
- Learning how to make decisions and solve problems—skills now used in one's career
- Gaining the skills needed to get the job—and life—one desires

When you are achieving what you want in life and when you are happy and challenged and feel you are living life to its fullest and contributing to the world, then you likely feel successful. When you reach this point, your grades in college are about the last thing you'll think of.

But that doesn't mean that grades don't matter—just that getting good grades is not the ultimate goal of college or the best way to define personal success while in college. Five or ten years from now, no one is going to care much about what grade you got in Freshman English or Biology 101. Success in college does include acceptable grades, of course, but in the end—in your long-range goals—grades are only one component of a larger picture.

6.2 How Much Do Grades Matter?

As you begin college, it's good to think about your attitude toward grades, since grades often motivate students to study and do well on assignments.

Valuing grades too highly, or not highly enough, can cause problems. A student who is determined to get only the highest grade can easily be frustrated by difficult college classes. Expectations that are too high may lead to disappointment, and possibly depression or anxiety, and may become counterproductive. At the other extreme, a student who is too relaxed about grades, who is content simply with passing courses, may not be motivated to study enough even to pass—and may be at risk for failing courses.

What is a good attitude to have toward grades? The answer depends in part on how grades do matter generally—and specifically in your own situation. Here are some ways grades clearly do matter:

- At most colleges, all students must maintain a minimum **grade point average (GPA)** to be allowed to keep taking courses and to graduate.
- Financial aid and scholarship recipients must maintain a minimum grade in all courses, or a minimum GPA overall, to continue receiving their financial award.
- In some programs, the grade in certain courses must be higher than simply passing to count toward the program or major.

After graduation, it may be enough for some careers just to have completed the program or degree. But in many situations, how well one did in college remains important. Employers often ask how well you did in college (new graduates at least—this becomes less important after you have more job experience). Students who are proud of their grades usually include their GPA on their résumé. Students with a low GPA may avoid including it on their résumé, but employers may ask on the company's application form or in an interview (and being caught in a lie can lead to being fired). An employer who asks for a college transcript will see all your grades, not just the overall GPA.

In addition to the importance for jobs, grades matter if you plan to continue to **graduate school**, **professional school**, or other educational programs—all of which require your transcript.

Certainly grades are not the only way people are judged, but along with all forms of experience (work, volunteer, internship, hobbies) and personal qualities and the recommendations of instructors and others, they are an important consideration. After all, an employer may think, if you goofed off so much in college that you got low grades, how can I expect you not to goof off on the job?

How to Calculate Your GPA

Because of various requirements for maintaining a GPA at a certain level, you may need to know how to calculate your GPA before grades come out at the end of the term. The math is not difficult, but you need to consider both the grade in every course and the number of credit hours for that course when calculating your overall GPA. Here is how to do the calculation using the traditional four-point scale. First, translate each letter grade to a numerical score:

A = 4

B = 3

grade point average (GPA)

A numerical score representing the average of a student's grades in all courses during a term and cumulatively through the student's duration at the particular high school or college.

graduate school

A division of a university with masters or doctorate degree programs, typically first requiring completion of a bachelor's degree.

professional school

An academic program to prepare for certain professions after completion of a bachelor's degree, such as medical school, law school, business school, and others.

C = 2

D = 1

Then multiply each grade's numerical score by the number of units or hours for that course:

B in Math 101 × 5 hours = 3 × 5 = 15

B in English 4 × 3 hours = 3 × 3 = 9

C in Humanities 1 × 5 hours = 2 × 5 = 10

A in College Success × 3 hours = 4 × 3 = 12

Then add together those numbers for each course:

15 + 9 + 10 + 12 = 46.

Then divide that total by the total number of credit hours:

46 / 16 = 2.87 = GPA of 2.87.

Consult your college's policies regarding the numeric weighting of + and − grades.

The best attitude to take toward grades in college is simply to do the best you can do. There's no need to kill yourself, but if you're not going to make an effort then there's not much reason to be there in the first place. Almost everything in this book—from time management to study skills to social skills and staying healthy—will contribute to your overall success and, yes, to getting better grades.

If you have special concerns about grades, such as feeling unprepared in a certain class and at risk of failing, talk with your academic advisor. If a class requires more preparation than you have from past courses and experience, you might be urged to drop that class and take another—or to seek extra help. Your advisor can help you work through any individual issues related to doing well and getting the best grade you can.

Can You Challenge a Grade?

Yes and no. College instructors are very careful about how they assign grades, based on clear-cut standards often stated in the course syllabus. The likelihood of an instructor changing your grade if you challenge it is very low. On the other hand, we're all human, and mistakes can happen, and if you truly feel a test or other score was miscalculated, you can ask your instructor to review the grade. Just be sure to be polite and respectful.

Most situations in which students want to challenge a grade, however, result from a misunderstanding about the grading scale or the instructor's standards. Students may simply feel they deserve a higher grade because they think they understand the material well or spent a lot of time studying for a test or doing an assignment. The grade, however, is based on your actual responses on a test, a paper, or another assignment. The instructor is grading not how many hours you spend or what he or she thinks is in your head, but what you actually wrote down.

If you are concerned that your grade does not accurately reflect your understanding or effort, you should still talk with your instructor—not to argue for a grade change but to gain a better understanding of the course's expectations so that you'll do better next time. Instructors respect students who want to improve. Visit the instructor during office hours or ask for an appointment and prepare questions ahead of time to help you better understand how to improve your performance and better understand the material.

Learning how to accept criticism is a challenge for some students. Your instructors hold you to high standards and expect you to have the maturity to understand that a lower grade is not a personal attack on you or a statement that you're not smart enough to do the work. Since none of us is perfect, we all can improve in almost everything we do—and the first step is accepting evaluation of our work. If you receive a grade lower than you think you have earned, take the responsibility to learn what you need to do to earn a higher grade next time.

6.3 What Else Matters?

So far we've talked mostly about grades, but that's not all that matters or the only measure of success. Sometimes a student will work hard to get good grades but do very little else, thinking the GPA and degree are all that matter. (High school sometimes gives people that impression.) But a future employer or graduate program is looking for other things too, possibly including the ability to act independently, to show initiative or leadership, to work well in a group, to find creative solutions, and many other qualities important for some careers. How can simple grades show these qualities? They can't—they may show only that you're smart or know how to study and take tests.

So don't obsess over grades or forget other aspects of life and the college experience. What you do in a job while a student, or your success as a volunteer or paid intern, or your leadership in group projects as noted by your instructor in a letter of recommendation—all these are also important for your future. We'll be talking more about these things in later chapters; for now, just try to avoid the trap of thinking of success only in terms of grades

6.4   Succeeding in Your First Year

The first year of college is almost every student's most crucial time. Statistics show a much higher dropout rate in the first year than thereafter. Why? Because for many students, adjusting to college is not easy. You may have to wrestle with managing your time, your freedom, and your other commitments to family, friends, and work. It's important to recognize that it may not be easy for you.

On the other hand, when you do succeed in your first year, the odds are very good that you can continue to succeed and complete your program or degree.

Are you ready? Remember that everything in this book will help you succeed in your first year. Motivation and a positive attitude are the keys to getting off to a running start. The next section lists some things you can do to start right now, today, to ensure your success.

6.5   Getting Started on the Right Foot Right Now

- Make an appointment to talk with your academic advisor if you have any doubt about the courses you have already enrolled in or about the direction you're taking. Start watching how you spend your time, and ensure you make enough time to keep up with your courses.

- Check for tutoring assistance if you feel you may need it, and make an appointment or schedule time to visit tutoring centers on your campus to see what help you can get if needed.

- Like yourself. You've come a long way to reach this point, you have succeeded in taking this first step toward meeting your college goal, and you are fully capable of succeeding the rest of the way. Don't start feeling down on yourself if you're struggling with any classes. Know you can meet the challenges ahead.

- Pay attention to your learning style and your instructors' teaching styles. Begin immediately applying the guidelines discussed earlier for situations in which you do not feel you are learning effectively.

- Plan ahead. Check your syllabus for each class and highlight the dates of major assignments and tests. Write on your calendar the important dates coming up. (We'll be talking more about time management soon.)

- Look around your classroom and plan to introduce yourself right away to one or two other students. Talking with other students is the first step in forming study groups that will help you succeed.

- Introduce yourself to your instructors, if you haven't already. In a large lecture, go up to the instructor after class and ask a question about the lecture or about an upcoming assignment.

FIGURE 1.10

Start getting to know other students right away by talking before or after class. This is often a good way to start a study group.

- Participate in your classes. If you're normally a quiet person who prefers to observe others rather than ask questions or join class discussions, you need to take the first step toward becoming a participating student—another characteristic of the successful student. Find something of particular interest to you and write down a question for the instructor. Then raise your hand at the right time and ask. You'll find it a lot easier than you may think!

- Vow to pay more attention to how you spend your money. Debt is a major reason why some students have to drop out. (We'll talk more about this in a later chapter.)

- Take good care of your body. Good health makes you a better student. Vow to avoid junk food, to get enough sleep, and to move around more. When you're done reading this chapter, take a walk!

© Thinkstock

Excellent! Start doing these few things, and already you'll be a step or two ahead—and on your way to a successful first year!

KEY TAKEAWAYS

- While success in college involves many benefits and experiences, grades are an important measure of success.
- Acceptable grades are important for continuing your college program and financial aid, for graduate school or other future educational opportunities, and for obtaining a good job in many careers.
- Succeeding is especially important in the first year of college to avoid the factors that lead to many students dropping out.
- You can launch yourself on a path of success immediately by taking the first steps: developing a positive attitude, taking advantage of your personal learning style, practicing time management, meeting your instructors and other students, participating actively in your classes, and taking control of your personal health and finances.

CHECKPOINT EXERCISES

1. In your college or your specific program, do you need to maintain a minimum GPA to continue in the program? (If you don't know, check your college catalog or website.) What is that minimum GPA?

   _____

   What was your cumulative GPA in high school?

   _____

   Because college classes are usually more difficult than high school classes, figure—purely as a starting point—that with the same effort, your college GPA could be a full point (or more) lower than your high school GPA. Does that give you any cause for concern? If so, what do you think you should work on most to ensure you succeed in college?

   _____

   _____

2. For each of the following statements, circle T for true or F for false:

T	F	See your academic advisor only when it's time to register for courses or when the college requires you to.
T	F	The best way to get help with a class is to pick whoever looks like the smartest student in class and offer to pay that person for tutoring.
T	F	A positive attitude about yourself as a college student helps you stay motivated in your classes.
T	F	Understanding your learning style makes it easier to understand how to apply your strengths when studying and to overcome learning obstacles by adapting in other ways.
T	F	Meeting other students in your classes is important early on because you can skip classes once you arrange to borrow other people's notes.
T	F	Participating in class is a key to being successful in that class.

7. CHAPTER ACTIVITIES

Chapter Takeaways

- The first year of college is the most critical. Make the commitment to overcome any obstacles to a successful transition and stay committed and motivated to succeed.
- Although college students differ in many ways, all successful students share certain common traits, including a positive attitude, effective critical thinking skills, good time management skills, effective study skills, interactions with instructors and other students, and good habits for personal health and financial stability.
- You can learn to maximize your learning by attending to each step of the learning process: preparing, absorbing, capturing, and reviewing.
- It is important to understand your personal learning style and use it well in classes, while also making the effort to learn in new ways and work with other students for a more effective overall learning experience.
- Working with your academic advisor and taking advantage of the many resources available at your college are key actions to ensure success.

- Understanding all aspects of college success leads to a richer college experience, supplementing the value of good grades.
- While it may take a few weeks to develop all the skills needed for success in college, there are many steps you can begin taking today to get moving in the right direction.

CHAPTER REVIEW

Check off every action on the following list that you plan to use in your first year of college to help you be as successful as you can be.

	Approach classes and homework exactly as I did in high school
	View college as a vital experience preparing me for the rest of my life
	Decide immediately what I want to major in and never change my mind as I move forward through my courses
	Manage my time well so that I have enough time to study and start on assignments well ahead of the due dates
	Attend classes when I think something important will be said and I can't find someone to borrow class notes from
	Adopt a positive attitude and work on staying motivated to succeed
	Give up everything else in life while in college
	Talk to my advisor so that I take only those classes where the teacher's style matches my own learning style
	Form study groups with other students different from me so I can take advantage of how they learn as well
	Be sure to tell all my instructors what I think they want to hear, not what I might really think
	Sit in the back row where I won't be noticed or get asked a question I might not be able to answer
	Make good friendships and interact with a wide range of people on campus
	Pay close attention in class so that I don't have to be concerned with reviewing the course material later
	Prepare for each class every day
	If I read too slowly, read only the chapter summaries and key points so I don't lose time reading whole textbook chapters
	Talk to other students to find out what classes and instructors are easiest to keep my GPA up
	Take as many online courses as I can so that I can sleep late and get help from friends doing online assignments
	To save time, go first to a friendly instructor to learn about any resources the college may have to help me
	Take it easy my first year in college, not worrying about grades, to avoid burnout
	Check out tutoring services only as a last resort at the end of the term if I'm in danger of failing
	Check the class syllabus for important assignments and exam dates and begin scheduling study periods well ahead of time
	Get to know my instructors and other students in the class right away

OUTSIDE THE BOOK

1. Go online to the free CareerLink Inventory Web site at http://www.mpcfaculty.net/CL/cl.htm and spend a few minutes taking this free assessment of your interests and personality. Completion leads to a statement of your Career Inventory Results, with different career clusters matched to your assessment.

   Click on the "cluster title" for several of your best-matched career areas to view specific career possibilities. Clicking on specific career titles will then provide a wealth of career information from the United States Department of Labor, Bureau of Labor Statistics, including data about the following:

   This information will get you started thinking about possible careers that may match your interests. For a more complete survey of your interests, personality, and strengths, visit your college's career counseling center.

   - The nature of the work
   - Education and training required
   - Employment possibilities and future job outlook
   - Earnings
   - Related occupations

2. Go to http://www.businessballs.com/howardgardnermultipleintelligences.htm#multiple% 20intelligences tests and scroll down to the link for "free Multiple Intelligences test (based on Howard Gardner's model)—in Microsoft Excel self-calculating format" and other versions. You need Microsoft Excel on your computer to take this free online assessment of your learning style.

   Clicking the link will download an Excel spreadsheet with 74 questions. Answer each as directed on the 1 to 4 scale. Your score totals are then shown for each of the "multiple intelligences" learning styles presented earlier in this chapter.

   What are your two strongest "intelligence types"?

   _____
   _____

   What are your two weakest "intelligence types"?

   _____
   _____

   Based on this evaluation, what aspects of college learning might you want to give more attention to? (Refer to Chapter 1, Section 4 for ideas to think about.)

   _____
   _____
   _____
   _____

3. Visit your college's website and spend at least thirty minutes exploring available resources. Usually there is a section called "Students" or "Present Students" or "Student Resources" or something similar—apart from all the other information for prospective future students, parents, faculty, courses, and so on. Jot down some of the topics here that you might want to consult again in the future if you were to experience a problem involving money, personal health, academic success, emotional health, social problems, discrimination, or other issues.

   _____
   _____
   _____
   _____
   _____
   _____
   _____
   _____
   _____

MAKE AN ACTION LIST

Attitude

My most negative attitude toward college is

_____

_____

Here's what I'll do to be more positive:

_____

_____

Values

My personal values most closely related to a college education are

_____

_____

I may have to put these values on hold while in college:

_____

_____

Transitioning to College

The most likely problems I'll have (as a traditional or returning student) transitioning to college are

_____

_____

Here's what I'll do to stay focused in my first year:

_____

_____

Learning Process

In the past, I have paid too little attention to these steps of the learning process:

_____

_____

Here's what I will begin doing now in my classes to fully use all steps of the process:

_____

_____

Learning Style

This is my preferred learning style:

_____

_____

I will begin working to strengthen my learning through these other styles:

_____

_____

Lecture Classes

When I'm bored in a large lecture hall, I frequently do this:

_____

_____

To pay closer attention, I will try the following:

_____

_____

College Resources

I have not paid much attention to these available resources on my campus:

_____

_____

In the coming weeks, I will check online or in person for information about these offices that may be able to help me succeed:

_____

_____

College Grades

My grades generally suffer when I

_____

_____

To ensure I do well in all my classes, I will now begin to focus on

_____

_____

Immediate Steps to Success

I have not used my time as well as I might because I've been doing the following:

_____

_____

I will immediately start taking these steps to ensure I succeed in my classes:

_____

_____

CLASS DISCUSSION QUESTIONS

1. What is your *primary* reason for going to college? (Let several students answer this aloud before any discussion.) Is there any one best answer? Why is it important to think about your own reasons? Discuss.
2. Why is it important to *review* something you've just learned (the fourth step in the learning process) even if you're sure you understand it well?
3. How difficult was it to read and understand this chapter? Are you convinced by reading things in a textbook? If not, what would make this information more meaningful to you? What does that say about your preferred learning style?

CHAPTER 2
Staying Motivated, Organized, and On Track

FIGURE 2.1

© *Thinkstock*

Where Are You Now?

Assess your present knowledge and attitudes.

	Yes	Unsure	No
1. I have clear, realistic, attainable goals for the short and long term, including for my educational success.			
2. I have good priorities that help ensure I always get the important things done, including my studies, while balancing my time among school, work, and social life.			
3. I have a positive attitude toward being successful in college.			
4. I know how to stay focused and motivated so I can reach my goals.			
5. When setbacks occur, I work to solve the problems effectively and then move on.			
6. I have a good space for studying and use my space to avoid distractions.			
7. I do not attempt to multitask when studying.			
8. I schedule my study periods at times when I am at my best.			
9. I use a planner to schedule study periods and other tasks in advance and to manage my time well.			
10. I am successful at not putting off my studying and other important activities or being distracted by other things.			

Where Do You Want to Go?

Think about how you answered the questions above. Be honest with yourself. On a scale of 1 to 10, how would you rate how well you stay focused on your goals and use your time?

Need to improve					Very successful				
1	2	3	4	5	6	7	8	9	10

In the following list, circle the three most important things you think you need to improve:

- Setting goals
- Staying focused on goals
- Keeping strong priorities
- Maintaining a positive attitude
- Staying motivated for academic work
- Solving and preventing problems
- Having an organized space for studying
- Avoiding the distractions of technology
- Preventing distractions caused by other people
- Managing time well when studying
- Overcoming a tendency to put things off
- Using a planner to schedule study periods
- Using a to-do list to ensure all tasks are done
- Finding enough time to do everything

Are there other areas in which you can improve your time management skills so that you can study effectively in the time you have, while still managing the rest of your life? Write down other things you feel you need to work on.

_____

_____

_____

_____

How to Get There

Here's what we'll work on in this chapter:

- Setting and focusing on goals that are specific, realistic, and attainable
- Setting priorities for managing your time
- Adapting a positive attitude to succeed and to overcome any fear of failure or negativity
- Developing and practicing strategies for staying focused
- Preventing or solving problems that might threaten your success in college
- Choosing a study space and using it to your advantage to avoid distractions
- Understanding why multitasking, such as using your computer or cell phone while studying, is inefficient and actually wastes time
- Using your "time personality" to perform at your best and to plan ahead
- Using a planner to schedule study periods, get started on projects well in advance, and manage your time well
- Developing and practicing strategies for preventing procrastination

1. GOALS AND TIME MANAGEMENT

Since you're reading this now, chances are very good you're in college now or about to start. That means you've already set at least one goal for yourself—to get a college education—and that you've been motivated to come this far. Feel good about that, because lots of people don't make it this far. You're off to a great first step!

But did you know that in many colleges in the United States, almost half of first-year students will not make it to graduation? This varies widely among different schools. Ask your instructor if he or she knows the graduation rate at your college, or research this online. Knowing this can be important, because peer pressure (whether to succeed or to be lax and possibly drop out later) can be an important factor in your success.

If you want to be among the students who do succeed, begin by accepting that college is not easy for most students. Still, the evidence shows that the huge majority of those who really want to finish college can do so successfully, if they stay motivated and learn how to succeed. That's what this book is all about—just know that it may take some effort.

The two most common reasons students drop out are financial difficulties and falling behind in studying. If money is an issue for you, there are many ways you can cut costs and make it easier to get through. Chapter 11 has lots of tips.

This chapter looks at the other big issue: succeeding in your courses. The first step is to be committed to your education. You've been motivated to start college—now you need to keep that motivation going through your classes. Attitude and time management are two important factors we'll discuss in this chapter.

In fact, time management skills can make the difference between those who graduate from college and those who drop out. Time management is actually about managing yourself: knowing what you want, deciding how to get what you want, and then efficiently and effectively getting it. That applies to fun things, too. Think of the goal of this chapter as managing your time not just for studying but also for still enjoying your life while in college!

2. SETTING AND REACHING GOALS

LEARNING OBJECTIVES

1. **Make short-, mid-, and long-term goals that are realistic and specific, and commit to them.**
2. **Set priorities for reaching your goals as a basis for time management.**
3. **Develop an attitude for success.**
4. **Learn to use strategies for staying focused and motivated.**
5. **Network with other students to help ensure academic success.**
6. **Solve problems and overcome setbacks that threaten your goals.**

goal

A result or achievement toward which one directs one's efforts.

priorities

Something that is more important than other things or given special attention.

Some people are goal oriented and seem to easily make decisions that lead to achieving their **goals**, while others seem just to "go with the flow" and accept what life gives them. While the latter may sound pleasantly relaxed, moving through life without goals may not lead anywhere at all. The fact that you're in college now shows you already have the major goal to complete your college program.

A goal is a result we intend to reach mostly through our own actions. Things we do may move us closer to or farther away from that result. Studying moves us closer to success in a difficult course, while sleeping through the final examination may completely prevent reaching that goal. Extreme cases are fairly obvious, yet still a lot of college students don't reach their goal of graduating. Students may not be committed to their goal, or they may have conflicting goals. One way to prevent problems is to think about *all* your goals and **priorities** and to learn ways to manage your time, your studies, and your social life to best reach your goals. Consider these four students:

To help his single mother, Juan went to work full time after high school, but now, a few years later, he's dissatisfied with the kinds of jobs he has been able to get and has begun taking computer programming courses in the evening. He's often tired after work, however, and his mother would like him to spend more time at home. Sometimes he cuts class to stay home and spend time with her.

In her senior year of college, Becky is elected president of her sorority and is excited about planning a community service project. She knows she should be spending more time on her senior thesis, but she thinks that in her sorority project she will make new contacts that will help her find a better job after graduation. Besides, the sorority project is a lot more fun, and she's enjoying the esteem of her position. Even if she doesn't do well on her thesis, she's sure she'll pass.

After an easy time in high school, James is surprised his college classes are so hard. He's got enough time to study for his courses, but he also has a lot of friends and fun things to do. Sometimes he's surprised to look up from his computer to see it's midnight already and he hasn't started reading that chapter yet. Where does the time go? When he's stressed, he can't study well, so he tells himself he'll get up early and read the chapter before class, and then he turns back to his computer to post to Facebook.

Sachito was successful in cutting back her hours at work to give her more time for her engineering classes, but it's hard to get much studying done at home. Her husband has been wonderful about taking care of their young daughter, but he can't do everything, and lately he's been hinting that she needs to help more. Sometimes when she has to study on the weekend, he goes out with his friends, and Sachito ends up spending the day with her daughter—and not getting much studying done.

What do these very different students have in common? Each has goals that conflict in one or more ways. Each needs to develop strategies to meet their other goals if they are to succeed in college. And all of them have time management issues to work through: three because they feel they don't have enough time to do everything they want or need to do and one because even though he has enough time, he needs to learn how to manage it better. For all four of them, motivation and attitude will be important as they develop strategies to achieve their goals.

It all begins with setting goals and thinking about your priorities.

When you think about your own goals, include more than just being a student. There are other things you like to do too. Your long-term goals likely include graduation and a career but may also involve social times with others, a romantic relationship, family, hobbies or other activities, where and how you live, and so on. As a student you might not pursue all your goals with the same fervor, but they remain goals and are still important in your life.

Goals also have different time frames. Short-term goals focus on today and the next few days and weeks. Mid-term goals involve plans for this school year and your total time in college. Long-term goals may begin with graduating college and what you want to happen then. Often your long-term goals (such as the career you want) guide your mid-term goals (getting the right education for that career), and your short-term goals (such as doing well on an exam) are steps for reaching the larger goal. Thinking about goals in this way helps you realize how even the little things you do everyday can keep you moving toward your most important long-term goals.

Write out your goals in Activity 1. You should literally *write* them down, because the act of finding the best words to describe your goals helps you think more clearly about them. Follow these guidelines:

- **Goals should be realistic.** It's good to dream and to challenge yourself, but your goals should relate to your personal strengths and abilities—and the amount of time and money you have.

- **Goals should be specific.** Don't write, "I will become a great musician"; instead, write, "I will finish my music degree and become employed in a symphony orchestra."

- **Goals should have a time frame.** You won't feel very motivated if your goal is vaguely "to finish college someday." If you're realistic and specific in your goals, you should also be able to project a time frame for reaching the goal.

- **You should really want to reach the goal.** People are willing to work hard to reach goals they really care about, but they're likely to give up when they encounter obstacles if they don't feel strongly about the goal. If you're doing something only because your parents or someone else wants you to, then it's not your own personal goal—and you may need to do some more thinking about your life.

ACTIVITY 1: PERSONAL GOALS

Write your goals in the following blanks. Be sure to consider all areas of your life—consider *everything import-ant* that you want to do between this moment and old age. (While you might aim for three to eight goals in each section, remember that everyone is unique, and you may be just as passionate about just one or two goals or more than eight.)

Short-term goals (today, this week, and this month):

_____
_____
_____
_____
_____
_____
_____
_____
_____
_____

Mid-term goals (this year and while in college):

_____
_____
_____
_____
_____
_____
_____
_____
_____
_____

Long-term goals (from college on):

_____
_____
_____
_____
_____
_____
_____
_____
_____
_____

2.1 Priorities

Thinking about your goals gets you started, but it's also important to think about priorities. We often use that word to refer to how important something is to us. We might think, *This* is a really important goal, and *that* is less important. Try this experiment: go back to the goals you wrote in Activity 1 and see if you can rank each goal as a 1 (top priority), 2 (middle priority), or 3 (low priority).

It sounds easy, but do you actually feel comfortable doing that? Maybe you gave a priority 1 to passing your courses and a priority 3 to playing your guitar. So what does that mean—that you never play guitar again while in college? Whenever you have an hour free between class and work, do you have to study because that's the higher priority? What about all your other goals—do you have to ig-nore *everything* that's not a priority 1? And what happens when you have to choose between two differ-ent number 1 priorities?

In reality, priorities don't work quite that way. It doesn't make a lot of sense to try to rank goals as *always* more or less important. The question of priority is really a question of what is more important *at a specific time*. It is important to do well in your classes, but it's also important to have a social life and enjoy time off from studying. You shouldn't have to choose between the two—except *at any given time.* Priorities always involve time: what is most important to do *right now* or *tomorrow.* As we'll see later, time management is mostly a way to juggle priorities so you can meet all your goals.

But time management works only when you're committed to your goals. Attitude and motivation are very important. If you haven't yet developed an attitude for success, all the time management skills in the world won't keep you focused and motivated to succeed.

2.2   An Attitude for Success

What's your attitude *right now*—what ran through your mind as you saw the "An Attitude for Success" heading above? Did you groan and think, "No, not the attitude thing again!" Or maybe you thought, "Great! Now I'll learn everything I need to get through college without a problem!" Those are two attitude extremes, one negative and skeptical, the other positive and hopeful. Most students are somewhere in between—but *everyone* has an attitude of one sort or another.

Everything people do and how they do it starts with attitude. One student gets up on time and prepares for the day, planning to study for a couple hours between classes, go jogging later, and see a friend at dinner. Another student oversleeps after partying too late last night, decides to skip his first class, somehow gets through later classes fueled by fast food and energy drinks while dreading tomorrow's exam, and then goes out with a friend in the evening instead of studying. Both students could have identical situations, classes, finances, and academic preparation. There may be just one big difference—but it's the one that matters.

Here's a picture of a positive attitude:

- Enthusiasm for and enjoyment of daily activities
- Acceptance of responsibility for one's actions and feeling good about success
- Generally upbeat mood and positive emotions, cheerfulness with others, and satisfaction with oneself
- Motivation to get the job done
- Flexibility to make changes when needed
- Ability to make a good use of available time

And here's a picture of a negative attitude:

- Frequent complaining
- Blaming others for anything that goes wrong
- Frequent negative emotions: anger, depression, resentment
- Lack of motivation for work or studies
- Hesitant to change or seek improvement
- Unproductive use of time, procrastination

We started this chapter talking about goals, because people's goals and priorities have a huge effect on their attitude. Someone who really wants to do well in college is better motivated and can develop a more positive attitude to succeed. But what if you feel doubtful or worried or even down on yourself even if you are committed to succeeding—what can you do then? Can people really change their attitude? Aren't people just "naturally" positive or negative or whatever?

The good news is there's no "attitude gene" that makes you one way or another. It's not as simple as taking a pill, but attitude can be changed. If you're committed to your goals, you can learn to adjust your attitude. Here are some things you can start doing.

Be More Upbeat with Yourself

We all have conversations with ourselves. I might do badly on a test and start thinking things like, "I'm just not smart enough" or "That teacher is so hard no one could pass that test." The problem when we talk to ourselves this way is that we're listening too—and we start believing what we're hearing. Think about what you've been saying to yourself since your first day at college. Have you been negative or making excuses, maybe because you're afraid of not succeeding? You *are* smart enough or you wouldn't be here. Even if you did poorly on a test, you can turn that around by taking responsibility. "OK, I goofed off too much when I should have been studying. I learned my lesson—now it's time to buckle down and study for the next test. I'm going to ace this one!" Hear yourself saying that enough and guess what—you soon find out you *can* succeed even in your hardest classes.

Choose Whom You Spend Time With

We all know negative and positive people. Sometimes it's fun to hang out with someone with a funny, sarcastic, negative person. If we've just failed a test, we might enjoy being with someone else who also blames the instructor or "the system" for things that go wrong—misery loves company. But being with negative people too often is one of the surest ways to stay negative yourself. You'll hear your self-talk making excuses and blaming others, and you'll hear other people saying it, too. After a while you're convinced it's true. You've developed a negative attitude that sets you up for failure.

College offers a great opportunity to make new friends. Friendships and other social relationships are especially important to students because of the stresses of college. Later chapters have some tips for making new friends and getting actively involved in campus life, if you're not already there. Do try to choose friends with a positive attitude. It's more fun to be with people who are upbeat and enjoying life, people whom you respect—and who, like you, are committed to their studies and are motivated. A positive attitude can really be contagious.

Overcome Resistance to Change

It's natural to shy away from change, but many kinds of change are good and should be welcomed. College is a big change from high school or working. Sure, you have to study more, and the classes are harder. You may be working more and have less time for fun things. But worrying about these changes only leads to a negative attitude. Look instead at the positive changes: the exciting and interesting people you're meeting, the education you're getting that will lead to a bright future, and the mental challenges and stimulation you're feeling every day.

The first step may be simply to see yourself succeeding in your new life. Visualize yourself as a student taking control, enjoying classes, studying effectively, getting good grades. It all begins with the right attitude.

Overcome Fears

College students are often afraid of failure—of not being able to make the grade. In life, everyone experiences some sort of failure at some time—and everyone has fears. The question is what you do about it.

Again, think about your goals. You've enrolled in college for good reasons, and you've already shown your commitment by coming this far. If you still have any fear of failure, turn it around and use it in a positive way. If you're afraid you may not do well on an upcoming exam, don't mope around—sit down and schedule times to start studying. It's mostly a matter of attitude adjustment.

2.3 Stay Focused and Motivated

Okay, now you've got a positive attitude. But you've got a lot of reading for classes to do tonight, a test tomorrow, and a paper due the next day. Maybe you're a little bored with one of your reading assignments. Maybe you'd rather play a computer game. Uh oh—now what? Attitude can change at almost any moment. One minute you're enthusiastically starting a class project, and then you get a text message or a friend drops by and suddenly all you want to do is close the books and relax a while, just hang out.

One of the characteristics of successful people is accepting that life is full of interruptions and change—and planning for it. Staying focused does not mean you become a boring person who does nothing but go to class and study all the time. You just need to make a plan.

Planning ahead is the single best way to stay focused and motivated to reach your goals. Don't wait until the night before an exam. If you know you have a major exam in five days, start by reviewing the material and deciding how many hours of study you need. Then schedule those hours spread out over the next few days—at times when you are most alert and least likely to be distracted. Allow time for other activities, too, to reward yourself for successful studying. Then when the exam comes, you're relaxed, you know the material, you're in a good mood and confident, and you do well.

Here are some other tips for staying focused and motivated:

- If you're not feeling motivated, think about the results of your goals, not just the goals themselves. If just thinking about finishing college doesn't sound all that exciting, then think instead about the great, high-paying career that comes afterward and the things you can do with that income.

- Say it aloud—to yourself or a friend with a positive attitude: "I'm going to study now for another hour before I take a break—and I'm getting an A on that test tomorrow!" Sometimes all it takes is saying it aloud.

- Remember your successes, even small successes. When you begin a project or start studying for a test, think about your past success on a different project or test. Remember how good it feels to succeed. Know you can succeed again.

- Focus on the here and now. For some people, looking ahead to goals, or to anything else, may lead to daydreaming that keeps them from focusing on what they need to do right now. Don't worry about what you're doing tomorrow or next week or month. If your mind keeps drifting off, you may need to reward or even trick yourself to focus on the here and now. For example, if you can't stop thinking about the snack you're going to have when you finish studying in a couple hours, change the plan. Tell yourself you'll take a break in twenty minutes if you really need it—but only if you really work well first.

- If you just can't focus in on what you should be doing because it seems too big and daunting, break the task into smaller, manageable pieces. Don't start out thinking "I need to study the next four hours," but think "I'll spend the next thirty minutes going through my class notes from the last three weeks and figure out what topics I need to spend more time on." It's a lot easier to stay focused when you're sitting down for thirty minutes at a time.

- Never, ever multitask while studying! You may think that you can monitor e-mail and send text messages while studying, but in reality, these other activities lower the quality of your studying.

- Imitate successful people. Does a friend always seem better able to stick with studying or work until they get it done? What are they doing that you're not? We all learn from observing others, and we can speed up that process by using the same strategies we see working with others. *Visualize yourself* studying in the same way and getting that same high grade on the test or paper.

- Separate yourself from unsuccessful people. This is the flip side of imitating successful people. If a roommate or a friend is always putting off things until the last minute or is distracted with other interests and activities, tell yourself how different you are. When you hear other students complaining about how hard a class is or bragging about not studying or attending class, visualize yourself as not being like them at all.

- Reward yourself when you complete a significant task—but only when you are done. Some people seem able to stay focused only when there's a reward waiting.

- Get the important things done first. We'll talk about managing your academic planner and to-do lists later in the chapter, but for now, to stay focused and motivated, concentrate on the things that matter most. Say you're about to sit down to read a chapter in a book you're not much enjoying, and you suddenly notice some clothing piled up on a chair. "I really should clean up this place," you think. "And I'd better get my laundry done before I run out of things to wear." Don't try to fool yourself into feeling you're accomplishing something by doing laundry rather than studying. Stay focused!

2.4 Be Mindful

Do you know the word *mindfulness?* The concept of mindfulness has become increasingly popular in many different fields, ranging from Eastern philosophy to modern psychology to business practices in Fortune 500 corporations. Mindfulness can be thought of a mental state in which you stop what you are doing and focus on what you are feeling and thinking in the present moment without making any judgments. You examine your thoughts and feelings in an accepting way, especially if they are negative. You observe what you are thinking and feeling but do not try to change your thoughts and feelings at this time. For some, mindfulness is a form of meditation that is calming and can lead to insights about oneself. The key thing is to *accept* what you are feeling and thinking in the moment.

Have you ever tried to force yourself *not* to think of a certain thing? "I will *not* think about that test I bet I failed this morning." Trying not to think about something is often the surest way to keep thinking about it! Instead, you might try to sit quietly for a few minutes and observe yourself in an accepting way. "Yes, I'm still thinking about that test. It's OK to feel that way. I shouldn't worry about feeling depressed about it." Then bring your thoughts back to the present moment. If they drift back to the test, don't fight them—but focus on the present, observing your thoughts, not dwelling on them. Concentrate on the present, the room you are in, how your body feels, the sound of your breathing. Be accepting, and do not judge yourself. Many people have found that this sort of mindfulness helps them accept who they are and allows for more calmly moving forward rather than being caught up in negative emotions. Your college may even have a program for learning mindfulness meditation.

2.5 Network for Success

Making friends with people who have a positive attitude not only helps you maintain a positive attitude yourself, but it gets you started networking with other students in ways that will help you succeed.

Did you study alone or with friends in high school? Because college classes are usually more challenging, many students discover they do better, and find it much more enjoyable, if they study with other students in the course. You might organize a study group or just get together with a friend to review material before a test. It's good to start thinking right away about networking with other students in your classes.

If you consider yourself an independent person and prefer studying and doing projects on your own rather than with others, think for a minute about what happens in most careers and what the business world is like. Most work today is done by teams or individuals collaborating. In very few jobs does a person working alone most of the time. The more you learn to study and work with other students now, the more skills you are mastering for a successful career.

Studying with other students has immediate benefits. You can quiz each other to make sure everyone understands the course material; if you're not clear about something, someone else can help teach it to you. You can read and respond to each other's writing and other work. You can divide up the work in group projects. And you might have more fun than if you were doing it on your own.

Studying together is also a great way to start networking—a topic we'll hear more about later on. Networking can have many benefits for your future and right now can help you be more successful in college.

Tips for Success: Staying Motivated

- Keep your eye on your long-term goals while working toward immediate goals.
- Keep your priorities straight—but also save some time for fun.
- Work on keeping your attitude positive.
- Keep the company of positive people; imitate successful people.
- Don't let past habits drag you down.
- Plan ahead to avoid last-minute pressures.
- Focus on your successes.
- Break large projects down into smaller tasks or stages.
- Reward yourself for completing significant tasks.
- Avoid multitasking.
- Network with other students; form a study group.

2.6 Problem Solving: When Setbacks Happen

Even when you have clear goals and are focused to achieve them, problems sometimes happen. Accept that they *will* happen, as they do for everyone. What is important is knowing how to cope when a problem occurs.

Here are a few examples of common problems in life:

- A financial crisis
- An illness or injury
- A crisis involving family members or loved ones
- Stress related to frequently feeling you don't have enough time
- Stress related to relationship problems

While some problems cannot be prevented, others can. You can take steps to stay healthy, as you'll learn in Chapter 10. You can take control of your finances and avoid most of the money problems college students have, as you'll learn in Chapter 11. You can learn how to get along better with your instructors, with other students, and in personal relationships. You can learn how to use your time effectively for studying. Most of the chapters in this book also provide study tips and guidelines to help you do well in your classes with effective reading, note-taking, test-taking, and writing skills for classes. *Preventing* the problems that typically keep college students from succeeding is much of what this book is all about.

But not all problems can be avoided. Illness or a financial problem can significantly set one back—especially when you're on a tight schedule and budget. What then?

First, work to resolve the immediate problem:

1. Stay motivated and focused. Don't let frustration, anxiety, or other negative emotions make the problem worse than it already is.

2. Analyze the problem to consider all possible solutions. An unexpected financial setback doesn't automatically mean you have to drop out of school. Alternatives such as student loans, less expensive living arrangements, or other possible solutions may be available. Failing a midterm exam doesn't automatically mean you're going to fail the course—not when you make the effort to determine what went wrong, work with your instructor and others on an improved study plan, and use better strategies to prepare for the next test.

3. Seek help when you need to. It's not a sign of weakness to see your academic advisor or a college counselor if you have a problem.

4. When you've developed a plan for resolving the problem, work to follow through. If it will take a while before the problem is completely solved, track your progress in smaller steps so that you can see you really are succeeding. Every day will move you one step closer to putting it behind you.

After you've solved a problem, be sure to avoid it again in the future:

1. Be honest with yourself: how did you contribute to the problem? Drinking heavily at a party the night before a big test rather obviously contributes to doing poorly on the exam. Frequent colds and other mild illnesses might keep another student from doing his best, but how much better would he feel if he ate well, got plenty of exercise, and slept enough every night? If you don't honestly explore all the factors that lead to the problem, it's more likely to happen again.

2. Take responsibility for your life and your role in what happens to you. Earlier we talked about people with negative attitudes, who are always blaming others, fate, or "the system" for their problems. It's no coincidence that they keep having problems. Unless you *want* to keep having problems, don't keep blaming others.

3. Taking responsibility doesn't mean being down on yourself. Failing at something doesn't mean *you* are a failure. Adjust your attitude so you're ready to get back on track and feel happy that you'll never make that mistake again!

4. Make a plan. You might still have a problem on that next big test if you don't have an effective study plan and stick to it. You may need to change your behavior in some way, such as learning time management strategies. (Read on!)

KEY TAKEAWAYS

- Goals should be realistic, specific, and time oriented, and you should be committed to them.
- Setting priorities helps keep you focused on your goals but doesn't mean you can't enjoy life too.
- Attitude is often the major reason students succeed or fail in college. Everyone can work on developing a more positive, motivating attitude.
- Planning, the essence of time management, is necessary to keep moving toward your goals.
- Networking with other students helps you stay motivated and can make studying more effective.
- Since problems and setbacks are inevitable, knowing how to solve (or prevent) problems is important for reaching goals.

CHECKPOINT EXERCISES

1. Which of the following goal statements is written in a way that shows the person has carefully considered what he or she wants to achieve?

    a. I will do better in my math course.

    b. I will earn at least a B on my next English paper.

    c. I will study more this term.

2. List ways in which a negative attitude can prevent students from being successful in college.

    _____
    _____
    _____
    _____

3. Think about your friends in college or other students you have observed in one of your classes. Choose one who usually seems positive and upbeat and one who sometimes or frequently shows a negative attitude about college. Visualize both their faces—side by side—as if you are talking to both of them. Now imagine yourself sitting down to study with one of them for a final exam. Describe how you imagine that study session going.

    _____
    _____
    _____

4. Look back at the four students described at the beginning of the chapter. Each of them is experiencing some sort of problem that could interrupt their progress toward their goals. Think about each student and write down a solution that you would try, if you were that person.

    For Juan:

    _____
    _____

    For Becky:

    _____
    _____

    For James:

    _____
    _____

    For Sachito:

    _____
    _____

5. List a few things you can do if you're having trouble getting motivated to sit down to study.

    _____
    _____
    _____
    _____

3. ORGANIZING YOUR SPACE

LEARNING OBJECTIVES

1. **Recognize the importance of organizing your space to your best advantage for studying.**
2. **Avoid distractions where you are studying.**
3. **Understand the myth of multitasking and avoid distractions from your personal technology.**

Now that you've worked up an attitude for success and are feeling motivated, it's time to organize both your space and your time.

Space is important for many reasons—some obvious, some less so. People's moods, attitudes, and levels of work productivity change in different spaces. Learning to use space to your own advantage helps get you off to a good start in your studies. Here are a few of the ways space matters:

- **Everyone needs his or her own space.** As simple as this is, everyone needs some physical area, regardless of size, that is really his or her own—even if it's only a small part of a shared space. Within your own space, you generally feel more in control.

- **Physical space reinforces habits.** For example, using your bed primarily for sleeping makes it easier to fall asleep there than elsewhere and also makes it *not* a good place to try to stay awake and alert for studying. Using a desk consistently for studying makes it easy to study once you sit there.

- **Different places create different moods.** While this may seem obvious, students don't always use places to their best advantage. One place may be bright and full of energy, with happy students passing through and enjoying themselves—a place that puts you in a good mood. But that may also make it more difficult to concentrate on studying. Yet the opposite—a totally quiet, austere place devoid of color and sound and pleasant decorations—can be just as unproductive if it makes your studying unpleasant. Everyone needs to discover what space works best for himself or herself—and then let that space reinforce good study habits.

3.1 Use Space to Your Advantage and to Avoid Distractions

Begin by analyzing your needs, preferences, and past problems with study places. Where do you usually study? What are the best things about that place for studying? What distractions are most likely to occur there?

The goal is to find, or create, the best place for studying, and then to use it regularly so that studying there becomes a good habit.

- **Choose a place you can associate with studying.** Don't choose a place already associated with other activities (eating, watching television, sleeping, etc.). Over time, the more often you study in this space, the stronger will be its association with studying, so that eventually you'll be completely focused as soon as you enter that place and begin.

- **Your study area should be available whenever you need it.** If you want to use your home, apartment, or dorm room but you never know if another person may be there and possibly distract you, then it's better to look for another place, such as a study lounge or an area in the library. Look for locations open in the hours when you may be studying. You may also need two study spaces—one in or near where you live, another on campus. Maybe you study best at home but have an hour free between two classes, and the library is too far away to use for only an hour? Look for a convenient empty classroom.

- **Your study space should meet your study needs.** An open desk or table surface usually works best for writing, and you'll tire quickly if you write notes sitting in an easy chair (which might also make you sleepy). You need good light for reading, to avoid tiring from eyestrain. If you use a laptop for writing notes or reading and researching, you need a power outlet so you don't have to stop when your battery runs out.

FIGURE 2.2

Choose a pleasant, quiet place for studying, such as the college library.

© Thinkstock

- **Your study space should meet your psychological needs.** Some students may need total silence with absolutely no visual distractions; they may find a perfect study carrel hidden away on the fifth floor in the library. Other students may be unable to concentrate for long without looking up from reading and momentarily letting their eyes move over a pleasant scene. Some students find it easier to stay motivated when surrounded by other students also studying; they may find an open space in the library or a study lounge with many tables spread out over an area. Experiment to find the setting that works best for you—and remember that the more often you use *this same space*, the more comfortable and effective your studying will become.

- **You may need the help of others to maintain your study space.** Students living at home, whether with a spouse and children or with their parents, often need the support of family members to maintain an effective study space. The kitchen table probably isn't best if others pass by frequently. Be creative, if necessary, and set up a card table in a quiet corner of your bedroom or elsewhere to avoid interruptions. Put a "do not disturb" sign on your door.

- **Keep your space organized and free of distractions.** You want to prevent sudden impulses to neaten up the area (when you should be studying), do laundry, wash dishes, and so on. Unplug a nearby telephone, turn off your cell phone, and use your computer only as needed for studying. If your e-mail or message program pops up a notice every time an e-mail or message arrives, turn off this notification or your Wi-Fi to prevent such intrusions.

- **Plan for breaks.** Everyone needs a break occasionally when studying. Think about the space you're in and how to use it when you need a break. If in your home, stop and do a few exercises to get your blood flowing. In the library, take a walk up a couple flights of stairs and around the stacks before returning to your study area.

- **Prepare for human interruptions.** Even if you hide in the library to study, a friend may happen by. At home with family members or in a dorm room or common space, the odds increase greatly. Be ready in case someone pops in and asks you to join them in some fun activity. Know what time you will finish your studying so that you can tell them what time you'll meet them later—or for tomorrow at a set time.

3.2   The Distractions of Technology

Multitasking

The performing of multiple tasks at the same time, often involving technology and communications. The term originates in computer science, referring to how a computer's CPU can be programmed to function. (Importantly, the human brain does not function the same as a computer!)

Multitasking is the term for being engaged in two or more different activities at the same time, often referring to activities using devices such as smartphones, computers, and so on. Some people claim to be able to do as many as four or five things simultaneously, such as writing an e-mail while responding to a text message and reading a tweet, all while watching a video on their computer monitor or talking on the phone—or studying. Many people who have grown up with computers consider this kind of multitasking a normal way to get things done. Even people in business sometimes speak of multitasking as an essential component of today's fast-paced world.

It is true that *some* things can be attended to while you're doing something else, such as checking e-mail while you watch television news—but *only when* none of those things demands your full attention. You can concentrate 80% on the e-mail, for example, while 20% of your attention is listening for something on the news that catches your attention. Then you turn to the television for a minute, watch that segment, and go back to the e-mail. But you're not actually watching the television *at the same time* you're composing the e-mail—you're rapidly going back and forth. In reality, the mind can focus only on one thing at any given moment. Even things that don't require much thinking are severely impacted by multitasking, such as driving while talking on a cell phone or texting. An astonishing number of people end up in the emergency room from just trying to walk down the sidewalk while texting, so common is it now to walk into a pole or parked car while multitasking!

You might be thinking, "So why should it matter if I write my paper first and then answer e-mails or do them back and forth at the same time?" **It actually takes you longer to do two or more things at the same time than if you do them separately**—at least with anything that you actually have to focus on, such as studying. That's true because each time you go back to studying after reading a text or tweet, it takes time for your mind to shift gears to get back to where you were. Every time your attention shifts, more downtime adds up—and pretty soon it's evident that multitasking is costing you a lot more time than you think. And that's assuming that your mind *does* fully shift back to where you were every time, without losing your train of thought or forgetting an important detail. It doesn't always.

The other problem with multitasking is the effect it can have on the person's attention span—and even on how the brain works. Scientists have shown that when people constantly shift their attention from one thing to another in short bursts, the brain forms patterns that make it more difficult to keep sustained attention on any one thing. So when you really do need to concentrate for a while on one thing, such as when studying for a big test, it becomes more difficult to do even if you're not multitasking at that time. It's as if your mind makes a habit of wandering from one thing to another and then can't stop.

So stay away from multitasking whenever you have something important to do, like studying. If it's already a habit for you, don't let it become worse. It's best to prevent the temptations altogether. Turn your computer off—or shut down e-mail and messaging programs if you need the computer for studying. Turn your phone off: even if you just tell yourself not to answer it but still glance at it each time to see who sent or left a message, you're still losing your studying momentum and have to start over again. For those who are really addicted to technology (you know who you are!), go to the library and don't take your laptop or phone.

In the later section in this chapter on scheduling your study periods, we recommend that you schedule breaks too, usually for a few minutes every hour. If you're really hooked on checking for messages, plan to do that at scheduled times.

What about listening to music while studying? Some don't consider that multitasking, and many students say they can listen to music without it affecting their studying. Studies are inconclusive about the positive or negative effects of music on people's ability to concentrate, because music affects people in different ways. There's a huge difference between listening to your favorite CD while spontaneously singing along and enjoying soft background music that enhances your study space the same way as good lighting and pleasant décor. Some people can study better with low-volume instrumental music that relaxes them and does not intrude on their thinking, while others can concentrate only in silence. And some people are so used to being immersed in music and the sounds of life that they find *total* silence more distracting—such people can often study well in places where people are moving around. The key thing is to be honest with yourself: if you're *actively* listening to music while you're studying, then you're likely not studying as well as you could be. It will take you longer and lead to less successful results.

3.3 Family and Roommate Issues

Sometimes going to the library or elsewhere for studying is just not practical , and then you have to find a way to cope in a shared space.

Part of the solution is time management. Talk to others in your shared space and agree to reserve certain times for studying; agree to keep the place quiet, not to have guests visiting, and to prevent other distractions. You can do this with a roommate, spouse, or older children. If there are younger children in your household and you have child-care responsibility, it may be more complicated. You may have to schedule your studying during their nap time or find quiet activities for them to enjoy while you study. Try to spend some time with your kids before you study, so they don't feel like you're ignoring them (more tips later in this chapter).

The key is to plan ahead. You don't want to find yourself, the night before an exam, in a place that offers no space for studying.

Finally, accept that sometimes you'll just have to say no. If your roommate or a friend starts talking to you or suggests doing something else when you need to study, just say no. Learn to be firm but polite as you explain that you just *really* have to get your work done first. Students who live at home may also have to learn how to say no to parents or family members—just be sure to explain the importance of the studying you need to do! Remember, you can't be everything to everyone all the time.

FIGURE 2.3

Multitasking makes studying much less effective.

© *Thinkstock*

KEY TAKEAWAYS

- Where you study can have a huge impact on the effectiveness of your study efforts. Choose and organize your space to your advantage.
- Control your study space to prevent or manage distractions, especially those caused by other people or your personal technology.
- Trying to multitask while studying lowers the quality of your studying and results in a loss of time.

CHECKPOINT EXERCISES

1. For each of the following statements, circle T for true or F for false:

T	F	Your bed is usually a good place to study if you can keep the room quiet.
T	F	To study well, go to the most drab, boring place you can find.
T	F	An empty classroom can be a good place to get some studying done if you happen to have an hour free between classes.
T	F	To maintain a clear focus while studying, limit the time you spend checking for e-mail and text messages to every ten minutes or so. Put your cell phone on vibrate mode and keep it in your pocket where you can more easily ignore it.
T	F	It's OK to have the television or radio on while you study as long as you don't give it your full attention.
T	F	The key to avoiding interruptions and distractions from family members or roommates is to plan ahead for when and where you'll study.

2. Class discussion exercise: Share stories about distractions caused by roommates and others that you and other students have experienced. Brainstorm together how to handle similar situations next time they arise.

4.   ORGANIZING YOUR TIME

LEARNING OBJECTIVES

1. **Discover your time personality and know what you do with your time.**
2. **Understand the basic principles of time management and planning.**
3. **Learn and practice time management strategies to help ensure your academic success.**
4. **Know how to combat procrastination when it threatens getting your academic work done.**
5. **Use a calendar planner and daily to-do list to plan ahead for study tasks and manage your time effectively.**
6. **Learn effective time management techniques for students who work, students with family, and student athletes.**

This is the most important part of this chapter. When you know what you want to do, why not just sit down and get it done? Millions of people who complain frequently about "not having enough time" would love it if it were that simple!

Time management isn't actually difficult, but you do need to learn how to do it well.

4.1   Time and Your Personality

People's attitudes toward time vary widely. One person seems to be always rushing around but actually gets less done than another person who seems unconcerned about time and calmly goes about the day. Since there are so many different "time personalities," it's important to understand yourself and how you approach time. Start by trying to figure out how you spend your time during a typical week, using Activity 2. (You can download and print out Activity 2 below.)

ACTIVITY 2: WHERE DOES THE TIME GO?

See if you can account for a week's worth of time. For each of the activity categories listed, make your best estimate of how many hours you spend in a week. (For categories that are about the same every day, just estimate for one day and multiply by seven for that line.)

Category of activity	Number of hours per week
Sleeping	
Eating (including preparing food)	
Personal hygiene (i.e., bathing, etc.)	
Working (employment)	
Volunteer service or internship	
Chores, cleaning, errands, shopping, etc.	
Attending class	
Studying, reading, and researching (outside of class)	
Transportation to work or school	
Getting to classes (walking, biking, etc.)	
Organized group activities (clubs, church services, etc.)	
Time with friends (include television, video games, etc.)	
Attending events (movies, parties, etc.)	
Time alone (include television, video games, surfing the Web, etc.)	
Exercise or sports activities	
Reading for fun or other interests done alone	
Talking on phone, e-mail, Facebook, etc.	
Other—specify: _____	
Other—specify: _____	

Now use your calculator to total your estimated hours. Is your number larger or smaller than 168, the total number of hours in a week? If your estimate is higher, go back through your list and adjust numbers to be more realistic. But if your estimated hours total fewer than 168, don't just go back and add more time in certain categories. Instead, ponder this question: *Where does the time go?* We'll come back to this question.

Think about your time analysis in Activity 2. People who estimate too high often feel they don't have enough time. They may feel anxious about time and often frustrated. People at the other extreme, who often can't account for how they use all their time, may have a more relaxed attitude. They may not actually have any more free time, but they may be wasting more time than they want to admit with less important things. Yet they still might complain about how much time they spend studying, as if there's a shortage of time.

People also differ in how they respond to schedule changes. Some go with the flow and accept changes easily, while others do well only when following a fixed schedule. If you do not react well to an unexpected disruption in your schedule, plan extra time for catching up if something throws you off. This is all part of understanding your time personality.

Another aspect of your time personality involves time of day. If you really need to concentrate, such as when writing a class paper, are you more alert and focused in the morning, afternoon, or evening? Do you concentrate best when you look forward to a relaxing activity later on, or do you study better when you've finished everything else? Do you function well if you get up early—or stay up late—to accomplish a task? How does that affect the rest of your day or the next day? Understanding all this will help you better plan your study periods.

While you may not be able to change your "time personality," you *can* learn to manage your time more successfully. The key is to be realistic. How accurate are the numbers of hours you wrote down in Activity 2? The best way to know how you spend your time is to record what you do all day in a time log, every day for a week, and then add that up. Make copies of the time log in Figure 2.4 and carry it with you. (You can download and print out the time log below.) Every so often, fill in what you have been doing. Do this for a week before adding up the times; then enter the total hours in the categories in Activity 2. You might be surprised that you spend a lot more time than you thought just hanging out with friends—or surfing the web or playing around with Facebook or any of the many other things people do. You might find that you study well early in the morning even though you thought you are a night person, or vice versa. You might learn how long you can continue at a specific task before needing a break.

FIGURE 2.4 Daily Time Log

AM		PM	
5:00		5:00	
5:15		5:15	
5:30		5:30	
5:45		5:45	
6:00		6:00	
6:15		6:15	
6:30		6:30	
6:45		6:45	
7:00		7:00	
7:15		7:15	
7:30		7:30	
7:45		7:45	
8:00		8:00	
8:15		8:15	
8:30		8:30	
8:45		8:45	
9:00		9:00	
9:15		9:15	
9:30		9:30	
9:45		9:45	
10:00		10:00	
10:15		10:15	
10:30		10:30	
10:45		10:45	
11:00		11:00	
11:15		11:15	
11:30		11:30	
11:45		11:45	
PM		**AM**	
12:00		12:00	
12:15		12:15	
12:30		12:30	
12:45		12:45	
1:00		1:00	
1:15		1:15	
1:30		1:30	
1:45		1:45	
2:00		2:00	
2:15		2:15	
2:30		2:30	
2:45		2:45	
3:00		3:00	
3:15		3:15	
3:30		3:30	
3:45		3:45	
4:00		4:00	
4:15		4:15	
4:30		4:30	
4:45		4:45	

If you have work and family responsibilities, you may already know where many of your hours go. Although we all wish we had more time, the important thing is what we do with the time we have. Time management strategies can help us better use the time we do have by creating a schedule that works for our own time personality.

4.2   Time Management

Time management for successful college studying involves several factors:

- Determine how much time you need to spend studying
- Know how much time you actually have for studying and increase that time if needed
- Be aware of the times of day you are at your best and most focused
- Use effective long- and short-term study strategies
- Schedule study activities in realistic segments
- Use a system to plan ahead and set priorities
- Stay motivated to follow your plan and avoid procrastination

For every hour in the classroom, college students should spend, on average, about two hours on that class, counting reading, studying, writing papers, and so on. If you're a full-time student with fifteen hours a week in class, then you need another thirty hours for rest of your academic work. That forty-five hours is similar to a full-time job. If you work part time, time management skills are even more essential—and still more important for part-time college students who work full time and commute or have a family. To succeed in college, virtually everyone has to develop effective strategies for dealing with time.

Look back at the number of hours you wrote in Activity 2 for a week of studying. Did you include two hours of study time for every hour in class? Many students begin college not knowing this much time is needed, so don't be surprised if you wrote down fewer hours. Remember this is just an average amount of study time—you may need more or less for your own courses. To be safe, and to help ensure your success, add another five to ten hours a week for studying.

To reserve this study time, you may need to adjust how much time you spend in other activities. Activity 3 will help you figure out what your typical week should look like. (You can download and print out Activity 3 below.)

ACTIVITY 3: WHERE *SHOULD* YOUR TIME GO?

Plan for the ideal use of a week's worth of time. Fill in your hours in this order:

1. Hours attending class
2. Study hours (2 times the number of class hours plus 5 or more hours extra)
3. Work, internships, and fixed volunteer time
4. Fixed life activities (sleeping, eating, hygiene, chores, transportation, etc.)

Now subtotal your hours so far and subtract that number from 168. How many hours are left?
_____ Then portion out the remaining hours for "discretionary activities" (things you don't have to do for school, work, or a healthy life).

Category of activity	Number of hours per week
Attending class	
Studying, reading, and researching (outside of class)	
Working (employment)	
Volunteer service or internship	
Sleeping	
Eating (including preparing food)	
Personal hygiene (i.e., bathing, etc.)	
Chores, cleaning, errands, shopping, etc.	
Transportation to work or school	
Getting to classes (walking, biking, etc.)	
Subtotal:	
Discretionary activities:	
Organized group activities (clubs, church services, etc.)	
Time with friends (include television, video games, etc.)	
Attending events (movies, parties, etc.)	
Time alone (include television, video games, surfing the Web, etc.)	
Exercise or sports activities	
Reading for fun or other interests done alone	
Talking on phone, e-mail, Facebook, etc.	
Other—specify: _____	
Other—specify: _____	

Note: If you find you have almost no time left for discretionary activities, you may be overestimating how much time you need for eating, errands, and the like. Use the time log in Figure 2.4 to determine if you really have to spend that much time on those things.

procrastinates

To intentionally (often habitually) put something off until another day or time.

Activity 3 shows most college students that they do actually have plenty of time for their studies without losing sleep or giving up their social life. But you may have less time for discretionary activities than in the past. *Something, somewhere has to give.* That's part of time management—and why it's important to keep your goals and priorities in mind. The other part is to learn how to use the hours you do have as effectively as possible, especially the study hours. For example, if you're a typical college freshman who plans to study for three hours in an evening but then **procrastinates**, gets caught up in a conversation, loses time to checking e-mail and social media, and listens to loud music while reading a textbook, then maybe you actually spent four hours "studying" but got only two hours of actual work done. So you end up behind and feeling like you're still studying way too much. The goal of time management is to actually get three hours of studying done in three hours and have time for your life as well.

Special note for students who work. You may have almost *no* discretionary time at all left in Activity 3 after all your "must-do" activities. If so, you may have overextended yourself—a situation that inevitably will lead to problems. You can't sleep two hours less every night for the whole school year, for example, without becoming ill or unable to concentrate well on work and school. It is better to recognize this situation now instead of setting yourself up for a very difficult term and possible failure.

If you cannot cut the number of hours for work or other obligations, see your academic advisor right away. It is better to take fewer classes and succeed than to take more classes than you have time for and risk failure.

Time Management Strategies for Success

Following are some strategies you can begin using immediately to make the most of your time:

- **Prepare to be successful.** When planning ahead for studying, think yourself into the right mood. Focus on the positive. "When I get these chapters read tonight, I'll be ahead in studying for the next test, and I'll also have plenty of time tomorrow to do X." *Visualize* yourself studying well!

- **Use your best—and most appropriate—time of day.** Different tasks require different mental skills. You might be able to start some kinds of studying first thing in the morning as you wake, while others need your most alert moments at another time.

- **Break up large projects into small pieces.** Whether it's writing a paper for class, studying for a final exam, or reading a long assignment or full book, students often feel daunted at the beginning of a large project. It's easier to get going if you break it up into stages that you schedule at separate times—and then begin with the first section that requires only an hour or two.

- **Do the most important studying first.** When two or more things require your attention, do the more crucial one first. If something happens and you can't complete everything, you'll suffer less if you've done the most crucial work.

- **If you have trouble getting started, do an easier task first.** Like large tasks, complex or difficult ones can be daunting. If you can't get going, switch to an easier task you can accomplish quickly. That will give you momentum, and often you feel more confident tackling the difficult task after being successful in the first one.

- **If you're feeling overwhelmed and stressed because you have too much to do, revisit your time planner.** Sometimes it's hard to get started if you keep thinking about other things you need to get done. Review your schedule for the next few days and make sure everything important is scheduled, then relax and concentrate on the task at hand.

- **If you're really floundering, talk to someone.** Maybe you just don't understand what you should be doing. Talk with your instructor or another student in the class to get back on track.

- **Take a break.** We all need breaks to help us concentrate without becoming fatigued and burned out. As a general rule, a short break every hour or so helps recharge your study energy. Get up and move around to get your blood flowing, clear your thoughts, and work off stress.

- **Use unscheduled times to work ahead.** You've scheduled that hundred pages of reading for later today, but you have the textbook with you as you're waiting for the bus. Start reading now, or flip through the chapter to get a sense of what you'll be reading later. Either way, you'll save time later. You may be amazed how much studying you can get done during downtime throughout the day.

- **Keep your momentum.** Prevent distractions, like multitasking, that will only slow you down. Check for messages, for example, only at scheduled break times.

- **Reward yourself.** It's not easy to sit still for hours of studying. When you successfully complete the task, feel good and give yourself a small reward. A healthy snack, a quick video game session, or social activity can help you feel even better about your successful use of time.

- **Just say no.** Always tell others nearby when you're studying, to reduce the chances of being interrupted. Still, interruptions happen, and if you are in a situation where you are frequently interrupted by a family member, spouse, roommate, or friend, it helps to have your "no" prepared in advance: "No, I *really* have to be ready for this test" or "That's a great idea, but let's do it tomorrow—I *just can't* today." You shouldn't feel bad about saying no—especially if you told that person in advance that you needed to study.

- **Have a life.** Never schedule your day or week so full of work and study that you have no time at all for yourself, your family and friends, and your larger life.

- **Use a calendar planner and daily to-do list.** We'll look at these time management tools in the next section.

4.3 Battling Procrastination

Procrastination is a way of thinking that lets you put off doing something that you should do now. This can happen to anyone at any time. It's like a voice inside your head keeps coming up with these brilliant ideas for things to do right now other than studying: "I really ought to get this room cleaned up before I study" or "I can study anytime, but tonight's the only chance I have to do X." That voice is also very good at rationalizing: "I really don't need to read that chapter now; I'll have plenty of time tomorrow at lunch...."

Procrastination is very powerful. Some people have to battle it daily, others only occasionally. Most college students procrastinate often, and about half say they need help avoiding procrastination. Procrastination can threaten your ability to do well on an assignment or test.

People procrastinate for different reasons. Some people are too relaxed in their priorities, seldom worry, and easily put off responsibilities. Others worry constantly, and that stress keeps them from focusing on the task at hand. Some procrastinate because they fear failure; others procrastinate because they are so perfectionist that they don't want to let themselves down. Some are daydreamers. Many different factors are involved, and there are different styles of procrastinating.

Just as there are different causes, there are different possible solutions for procrastination. Different strategies work for different people. The time management strategies described earlier can help you avoid procrastination. But because this is a psychological issue, some psychological strategies can also help:

- Since procrastination is usually a habit, accept that and work on breaking it as you would any other bad habit: one day at a time. Know that every time you overcome procrastination, the habit becomes weaker—and eventually you'll have a new habit of being able to start studying right away.

- Schedule times for studying using a daily or weekly planner. Carry it with you and look at it often. Just being aware of the time and what you need to do today can help you get organized and stay on track.

- If you keep thinking of something else you might forget to do later (making you feel like you "must" do it now), write yourself a note about it for later and get it out of your mind.

- Counter a negative with a positive. If you're procrastinating because you're not looking forward to a certain task, try to think of the positive future results of doing the work.

- Counter a negative with a worse negative. If thinking about the positive results of completing the task doesn't motivate you to get started, think about what could happen if you keep procrastinating. You'll have to study tomorrow instead of doing something fun you had planned. Or you could fail the test. Some people can jolt themselves right out of procrastination.

- On the other hand, fear causes procrastination in some people—so don't dwell on thoughts of failing. If you're studying for a test, and you're so afraid of failing it that you can't focus on studying and you start procrastinating, try to put things in perspective. Even if it's your most difficult class and you don't understand everything about the topic, that doesn't mean you'll fail, even if you may not receive an A or a B.

- Study with a motivated friend. Form a study group with other students who are motivated and won't procrastinate along with you. You'll learn good habits from them while getting the work done now.

- Keep a study journal. At least once a day write an entry about how you have used your time and whether you succeeded with your schedule for the day. If not, identify what factors kept you from doing your work. (Use the form at the end of this chapter.) This journal will help you see your own habits and distractions so that you can avoid things that lead to procrastination.

- Get help. If you really can't stay on track with your study schedule, or if you're always putting things off until the last minute, see a college counselor. They have lots of experience with this common student problem and can help you find ways to overcome this habit.

4.4 Calendar Planners and To-Do Lists

Calendar planners and to-do lists are effective ways to organize your time. Many types of academic planners are commercially available (check your college bookstore), or you can make your own. Some people like a page for each day, and some like a week at a time. Some use computer calendars and planners. Almost any system will work well if you use it consistently.

Digital vs. Paper Planners

Younger students who have grown up with digital technology may gravitate naturally toward using a calendar planner app on their smartphone. Many different apps are available for both Apple and Android devices, offering widely varying features. In addition to almost always having your calendar with you, the app or software typically syncs across all your devices, so that a change on your phone calendar shows up on your laptop as well. Because of these two benefits, students often assume a digital planner is better than an old-fashioned paper daily or weekly calendar.

On the other hand, digital calendar apps are often not as efficient as a paper planner for student work. Using the small screen of a smartphone, particularly when it comes to jotting notes to yourself, often requires considerable zooming in and out, flipping through various screens, and lots of screen taps when modifying a calendar entry or moving information from one date/time slot to another. Many students end up switching back to an old-fashioned paper planner where it's easy to cross things out and jot in new notes. Since you're likely already carrying a backpack with books and notebooks, it's no burden to carry along a paper planner. Another advantage, as you'll see in a later illustration, is that you can take in a whole day's or week's schedule in one quick glance.

Working with Your Planner

Some college students think they don't need to actually write down their schedule and daily to-do lists. They've always kept it in their head before, so why write it down in a planner now? Some first-year students were talking about this one day in a study group, and one bragged that she never used a calendar because she never forgot dates. Another student reminded her how she'd forgotten a preregistration date and missed taking a course she really wanted because the class was full by the time she went online to register. "Well," she said, "except for that time, I never forget anything!" Of course, none of us ever forgets anything—until we do.

Calendars and planners help you look ahead to important dates and deadlines so you don't forget. But it's just as important to use the planner to schedule *your own time,* not just deadlines. For example, the most effective way to study for an exam is to study in several short periods over several days. You can easily plan to do this by choosing time slots in your weekly planner over several days. You don't need to fill every time slot, or to schedule every single thing that you do, but the more carefully and consistently you use your planner, the more successfully will you manage your time.

But don't try to time-plan every single thing for your day. We'd go crazy if we tried to schedule every telephone call, every e-mail, every bill to pay, every trip to the grocery store. For things like that, use a to-do list on a separate page in your planner.

Check the example of a weekly planner form in Figure 2.5. (You can download that page below and use it to begin your schedule planning. By using this format first, you'll soon see if the time slots in a weekly planner are big enough for you to write in or whether you'd prefer a separate daily planner page day.) As an exercise, fill in this page for your next week. First write in all your class meeting times; your work or volunteer schedule; and your usual hours for sleep, family activities, and any other activities at fixed times. Don't forget time needed for transportation, meals, and so on. Your first goal is to find all the blocks of "free time" that are left over.

Next, check the syllabus for each of your courses and write important dates in the planner. If you are using a planner with pages for the whole term, write in all exams and deadlines for papers or other assignments. Use red ink or a highlighter for these key dates. If you're using the one-week planner page offered here, write any deadlines for your second week in the margin to the right. You need to know what's coming *next* week to help schedule how you're studying *this* week.

FIGURE 2.5 Weekly Planner

HOURS	Sun.	Mon.	Tue.	Wed.	Thu.	Fri.	Sat.
6–7 AM							
7–8							
8–9							
9–10							
10–11							
11–12 PM							
12–1							
1–2							
2–3							
3–4							
4–5							
5–6							
6–7							
7–8							
8–9							
9–10							
10–11							
11–12 AM							
12–1							
1–2							
2–3							
3–4							
4–5							
5–6							

Remember that for every hour spent in class, plan an average of two hours studying outside of class. These are the time periods you now want to schedule in your planner. These study times will change from week to week, with one course requiring more time in one week because of a paper due at the end of the week and a different course requiring more the next week because of a major exam. Make sure you block out enough hours in the week for what you need to do. As you choose your study times, consider what times of day you are at your best and what times you prefer to use for social or other activities.

Don't try to micromanage your schedule. Don't try to estimate exactly how many minutes you'll need two weeks from today to read a chapter in a textbook. Instead, just choose the blocks of time you will use for your studies. Don't yet write in the exact study activity—just reserve the block. Next, look at the major deadlines for projects and exams that you wrote in earlier. Estimate how much time you may need for each and work backward on the schedule from the due date. For example:

> *You have a short paper due on Friday. You determine that you'll spend ten hours total on it, from initial brainstorming and planning through to drafting and revising. Since you have other things also going on that week, you want to get an early start; you might choose to block an hour a week ahead on Saturday morning, to brainstorm your topic and jot down some preliminary notes. Monday evening is a good time to spend two hours on the next step or prewriting activities. Since you have a lot of time open Tuesday afternoon, you decide that's the best time to reserve to write the first draft; you block out three or four hours. You make a note on the schedule to leave time open that afternoon to see your instructor during office hours in case you have any questions on the paper; if not, you'll finish the draft or start revising. Thursday, you schedule a last block of time to revise and polish the final draft due tomorrow.*

If you're surprised by this amount of planning, you may be the kind of student who used to think, "The paper's due Friday—I have enough time Thursday night, so I'll write it then." What's wrong with that? First, college work is more demanding than many first-year students realize, and the instructor expects higher-quality work than you can churn out quickly without revising. Second, if you are tired on Thursday because you didn't sleep well Wednesday night, you may be much less productive than you hoped—and without a time buffer, you're forced to turn in a paper that is not your best work.

Figure 2.6 shows what one student's schedule looks like for a week. This is intended only to show you one way to block out time—you'll quickly find a way that works best for you.

FIGURE 2.6 Example of a Student's Weekly Planner Page with Class Times and Important Study Sessions

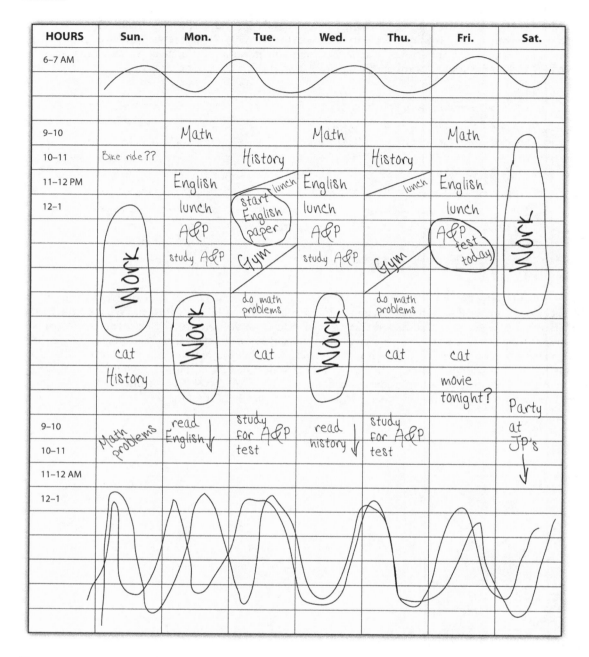

Here are some more tips for successful schedule planning:

- Studying is often most effective immediately after a class meeting. If your schedule allows, block out appropriate study time after class periods.
- Be realistic about time when you make your schedule. If your class runs to four o'clock and it takes you twenty minutes to wrap things up and reach your study location, don't figure you'll have a full hour of study between four o'clock and five o'clock.
- Don't overdo it. Few people can study four or five hours nonstop, and scheduling extended time periods like that may just set you up for failure.
- Schedule social events that occur at set times, but just leave holes in the schedule for other activities. Enjoy those open times and recharge your energies!
- Try to schedule some time for exercise at least three days a week.
- Plan to use your time between classes wisely. If you have the same hour free between two classes three days a week, what should you do with those three hours? Maybe you need to eat, walk across campus, or run an errand. But say you have an average forty minutes free at that time on

each day. Instead of just frittering the time away, use it to review your notes from the previous class or for the coming class or to read a short assignment. Over the whole term, that forty minutes three times a week adds up to a lot of study time.

- If a study activity is taking longer than you had scheduled, look ahead and adjust your weekly planner to prevent the stress of feeling behind.

- If you maintain your schedule on your computer or smartphone, it's still a good idea to print and carry it with you. Don't risk losing valuable study time if you're away from the device.

- If you're not paying close attention to everything in your planner, use a colored highlighter to mark the times blocked out for really important things.

- When following your schedule, pay attention to starting and stopping times. If you planned to start your test review at four o'clock after an hour of reading for a different class, don't let the reading run long and take time away from studying for the test.

- Finally, listen to what other college students have learned about time management techniques. Here are two videos made by college students who have developed successful strategies.

Time Management Tips for College

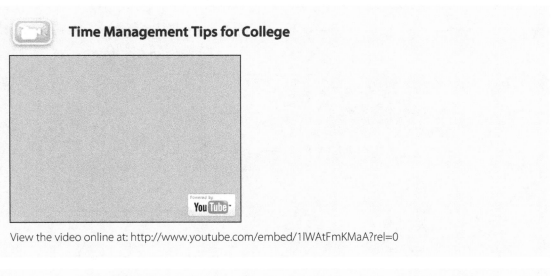

View the video online at: http://www.youtube.com/embed/1lWAtFmKMaA?rel=0

View the video online at: http://www.youtube.com/embed/HUjsEFkFyYs?rel=0

Your Daily To-Do List

People use to-do lists in different ways, and you should find what works best for you. As with your planner, consistent use of your to-do list will make it an effective habit.

Some people prefer not to carry their planner everywhere but instead copy the key information for the day onto a to-do list. Using this approach, your daily to-do list starts out with your key scheduled activities and then adds other things you hope to do today.

Some people use their to-do list only for things not on their planner, such as short errands, phone calls or e-mail, and the like. This still includes important things—but they're not scheduled out for specific times.

Although we call it a daily list, the to-do list can also include things you may not get to today but don't want to forget about. Keeping these things on the list, even if they're a low priority, helps ensure that eventually you'll get to it.

Start every day with a fresh to-do list written in a special small notebook or on a clean page in your planner. Check your planner for key activities for the day and check yesterday's list for items remaining.

Some items won't require much time, but other activities such as assignments will. Include a time estimate for these so that later you can do them when you have enough free time. If you finish lunch and have twenty-five minutes left before your next class, what things on the list can you do now and check off?

Finally, use a system to prioritize things on your list. Some students use a 1, 2, 3 or A, B, C rating system for importance. Others simply highlight or circle items that are critical to get done today. Figure 2.7 shows two different to-do lists—each very different but each effective for the student using it.

FIGURE 2.7 Examples of Two Different Students' To-Do Lists

Use whatever format works best for you to prioritize or highlight the most important activities.

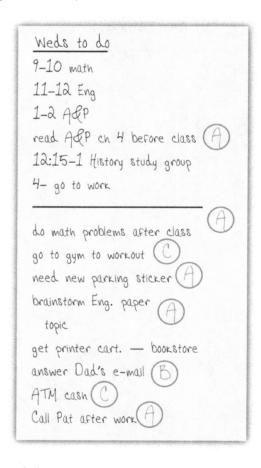

Here are some more tips for effectively using your daily to-do list:

- Be specific: "Read history chapter 2 (30 pages)"—not "History homework."
- Put important things high on your list where you'll see them every time you check the list.
- Make your list at the same time every day so that it becomes a habit.
- Don't make your list overwhelming. If you added *everything* you eventually need to do, you could end up with so many things on the list that you'd never read through them all. If you worry you might forget something, write it in the margin of your planner's page a week or two away.
- *Use* your list. Lists often include little things that may take only a few minutes to do, so check your list any time during the day you have a moment free.
- Cross out or check off things after you've done them—doing this becomes rewarding.
- Don't use your to-do list to procrastinate by looking for some minor thing you just "have" to do instead of studying!

4.5   Time Management Tips for Students Who Work

If you're both working and taking classes, you probably don't have large blocks of free time. Avoid the temptation to stay up very late studying, because losing sleep can lead to a downward spiral in performance at both work and school. Instead, try to follow these guidelines:

- If possible, adjust your work or sleep hours so that you don't spend your most productive times of day at work. If your job offers flex time, arrange your schedule to be free to study at times when you perform best.
- Try to arrange your class and work schedules to minimize commuting time. If you are a part-time student taking two classes, taking classes back-to-back two or three days a week uses less time than spreading them out over four or five days. Working three 5-hour days rather than five 3-hour days reduces time lost to travel, getting ready for work, and so on.
- If you can't arrange an effective schedule for classes and work, consider online courses that allow you to do most of the work on your own time.
- Use your daily and weekly planner conscientiously. Any time you have thirty minutes or more free, schedule a study activity.
- Consider your "body clock" when you schedule activities. Plan easier tasks for those times when you're often fatigued and reserve alert times for more demanding tasks.
- Look for any "hidden" time potentials. Maybe you prefer a thirty-minute drive to work over a forty-five-minute train ride. But if you can read on the train, that can be a gain of ninety minutes for every round trip at the cost of thirty minutes longer travel time. An hour a day can make a huge difference in your studies.
- Can you do quick study tasks during slow times at work? Take your class notes with you and use even five minutes of free time wisely.
- Remember your long-term goals. You need to work, but you also want to finish your college program. If you have the opportunity to volunteer for some overtime, consider whether it's really worth it. Sure, the extra money would help, but could the extra time put you at risk for not doing well in your classes?
- Be as organized on the job as you are academically. Use your planner and to-do list for work matters, too. The better organized you are at work, the less stress you'll feel—and the more successful you'll be as a student also.
- If you have a family as well as a job, your time is even more limited. In addition to the previous tips, try some of the strategies that follow.

4.6   Time Management Tips for Students with Family

Living with family members often involves additional time stresses. You may have family obligations that require careful time management. Use all the strategies described earlier, including family time in your daily plans the same as you would hours spent at work. Don't assume that you'll be "free" every hour you're home, because family events may occur at unexpected times. Schedule your important academic work well ahead and in blocks of time you control. See also the earlier suggestions for controlling your space: you may need to use the library or another space to ensure you are not interrupted or distracted during important study times.

Students with their own families are likely to feel time pressures. After all, you can't just tell your partner or kids that you'll see them in a couple years when you're not so busy with job and college! In addition to all the planning and study strategies discussed so far, you need to manage your family relationships and time spent with family. While there's no magical solution for making more hours in the day, even with this added time pressure there are ways to balance your life well:

- Talk everything over with your family. If you're going back to school, your family members may not have realized how life will be different. Don't let them be shocked by sudden household changes. Keep communication lines open so that your partner and children feel they're together with you in this new adventure. Eventually you will need their support.
- Work to enjoy your time together, whatever you're doing. You may not have as much time together as before, but cherish the time you do have—even if it's just washing dishes together or cleaning house. If you've been studying for two hours and need a break, spend the next ten minutes with family instead of checking e-mail or watching television. Ultimately, the important thing is *being together*, not going out to movies or dinners or the special things you used to do when you had more time. Look forward to being with family and appreciate every moment you are together, and they will share your attitude.

FIGURE 2.8

Make the most of your time with family, since you'll also need time alone for studying.

© Thinkstock

- Combine family activities to get the most out of time. Don't let your children watch television or play video games off by themselves while you're cooking dinner, or you may find you have only twenty minutes of family time together while eating. Instead, bring the family together in the kitchen and give everyone something to do. You can have a lot of fun together and share the day's experiences, and you won't feel so bad then when you have to go off and study by yourself.

- Share the load. Even children who are very young can help with household chores to give you more time. Attitude is everything: try to make it fun, the whole family pulling together—not something they "have" to do and may resent because Mom or Dad went back to school. (Remember, your kids will reach college age someday, and you want them to have a good attitude about college.) As they get older, they can do their own laundry, cook meals, and get themselves off to school, and older teens can run errands and do the grocery shopping. They will gain in the process by becoming more responsible and independent.

- Schedule your study time based on family activities. If you face interruptions from young children in the early evening, use that time for something simple like reviewing class notes. When you need more quiet time for concentrated reading, wait until they've gone to bed.

- Be creative with child care. Usually options are available, maybe involving extended family members, sitters, older siblings, cooperative child care with other adult students, as well as child-care centers. After a certain age, you can take your child along to campus when you attend an evening course, if there is somewhere the child can quietly read. At home, let your child have a friend over to play with. Network with other older students and learn what has worked for them. Explore all possibilities to ensure you have time to meet your college goals. And don't feel guilty: "day care babies" grow up just as healthy psychologically as those raised in the home full time.

4.7 Time Management Tips for Student Athletes

Student athletes often face unique time pressures because of the amount of time required for training, practice, and competition. During some parts of the year, athletics may involve as many hours as a full-time job. The athletic schedule can be grueling, involving weekend travel and intensive blocks of time. You might be exhausted after workouts or competitions, affecting how well you can concentrate on studies thereafter. Students on athletic scholarships often feel their sport is their most important reason for being in college, and this priority can affect their attitudes toward studying. For all of these reasons, student athletes face special time management challenges. Here are some tips for succeeding in both your sport and academics:

- Realize that even if your sport is more important to you, you risk everything if you don't also succeed in your academics. Failing one class in your first year won't get you kicked out, but you'll have to make up that class—and you'll end up spending more time on the subject than if you'd studied more to pass it the first time.

- It's critical to plan ahead. If you have a big test or a paper due the Monday after a big weekend game, start early. Use your weekly planner to plan well in advance, making it a goal, for example, to have the paper done by Friday—instead of thinking you can magically get it done Sunday night after a victory celebration. Working ahead will also free your mind to focus better on your sport.

- Accept that you have two priorities—your sport and your classes—and that both come before your social life. That's just how it is—what you have accepted in your choice to be a college athlete. If it helps, think of your classes as your job; you have to "go to study" the same as others "go to work."

- Use your planner to take advantage of any downtime you have during the day between classes and at lunch. Other students may seem to have the luxury of studying during much of the afternoon when you're at practice, and maybe they can get away with hanging out between classes, but you don't have that time available, at least not during the season. You need to use all the time you can find to keep up with your studying.

- Stay on top of your courses. If you let yourself start slipping behind, maybe telling yourself you'll have more time later on to catch up, just the opposite will happen. Once you get behind, you'll lose momentum and find it more difficult to understand what's going on the class. Eventually the stress will affect your athletic performance also.

- Get help when you need it. Many athletic departments offer tutoring services or referrals for extra help. But don't wait until you're at risk for failing a class before seeking help. A tutor won't take your test or write your paper for you—they can only help you focus in to use your time productively in your studies. You still have to want to succeed.

KEY TAKEAWAYS

- People "use" time very differently. To develop strategies for managing your time, discover your time personality and observe how much time you spend in different activities in the course of a week.
- Plan your schedule with two hours of study time for each hour in class. Use your most alert times of day, break up large tasks into smaller pieces and stages, take breaks to help you stay focused, avoid distractions, and reward yourself for successful accomplishments.
- Procrastination is a problem for most students. Different techniques can help you battle procrastination so you can get the job done.
- Use a weekly calendar planner to block out study times and plan well ahead for examinations and key assignments to achieve success in school.
- Use a daily to-do list along with your weekly planner to avoid overlooking anything and to make the most of your time throughout the day.
- Students who work, live with family, or are athletes often face significant time pressures and must make a special effort to stay organized and plan ahead for efficient studying.

CHECKPOINT EXERCISES

1. What time(s) of day are you at your most alert?

   _____

   What time(s) of day are you at your least alert?

   _____

2. What category of *discretionary* activity (not sleeping, working, studying, etc.) represents your largest use of time?

   _____

   Can you reduce the time you spend in that activity if you need more time for your coursework?

   _____

3. For each of the following statements about time management, circle T for true or F for false:

T	F	Think yourself into a positive mood before starting to study.
T	F	Always study just before going to sleep so that you'll dream about the topic.
T	F	Break up larger projects into smaller parts and stages.
T	F	Get everything done on your to-do list before studying so that you're not distracted.
T	F	When feeling stressed by a project, put it off until tomorrow.
T	F	Talk with your instructor or another student if you're having difficulty.
T	F	Try to study at least three hours at a time before taking a break.
T	F	Reward yourself for successfully completing a task.
T	F	Avoid studying at times not written in on your weekly planner; these are all free times just for fun.
T	F	Whenever interrupted by a friend, use that opportunity to take a break for up to thirty minutes.
T	F	Turn off all electronic devices when reading an assignment except for your laptop if you use it to take notes.
T	F	Since people procrastinate when they're distracted by other things that need doing, it's best to delay studying until you've done everything else first.
T	F	Studying with a friend is a sure way to waste time and develop poor study habits.
T	F	Use a study journal to observe how you use your time and determine what things are keeping you from getting your work done.
T	F	There's no reason to keep a weekly calendar if all your instructors have provided you with a syllabus that gives the dates for all assignments and tests.
T	F	Studying for a particular class is most effective immediately after that class meets.

4. Without looking at your planner, to-do list, or anything else in writing, quickly write a list of everything you need to do in the next few days. Then look through your planner, to-do list, and any other class notes for anything you missed. What might you have forgotten or delayed if you weren't keeping a planner and to-do list?

5. Without looking at your weekly or daily schedule, think about your typical week and the times you have free when not in class, working, studying, eating, socializing, and so on. List at least three "downtimes" when you don't usually study that you can use for coursework when necessary.

   _____

   _____

   _____

   _____

5. CHAPTER ACTIVITIES

Chapter Takeaways

- It's important to have short-, mid-, and long-term goals that are specific, realistic, time oriented, and attainable. Goals help you set priorities and remain motivated and committed to your college success.

- Attitude is the largest factor determining success in college. Work to stay positive and surround yourself with positive people, and you'll find you are motivated to do what you need to do to succeed in your courses.

- Planning ahead, and then following your plan, is the essence of time management. Organize both your space and your time to develop the best study habits. Learning strategies to stay on track, avoid distractions of people and technology, and to prevent procrastination will pay off not only in college but also later in your career.

- Plan your use of time based on your "time personality" after assessing how you typically use your free time. Then use a planner to schedule blocks of time most efficiently. Start well ahead of deadlines to prevent last-minute stresses and problems completing your work.

- Because many college students have major time commitments with work, family, athletics, or other activities, time management techniques are among the most important skills you can learn to help ensure your success.

CHAPTER REVIEW

1. Describe the characteristics of well-written goals.

   _____

   _____

2. List four or five things you can do to develop a positive attitude.

   _____

   _____

   _____

   _____

   _____

3. What have you personally found that helps motivate you to sit down and start studying?

   _____

   _____

4. Describe the most important characteristics of an effective study space.

   _____

   _____

   _____

   _____

5. How can you prepare for unplanned interruptions while studying?

   _____

   _____

6. After you have analyzed how you typically spend time and have blocked out study periods for the week, you may still have difficulty using that study time well. List additional time management strategies that can help you make the most of the time that you do have.

   _____

   _____

   _____

   _____

   _____

   _____

   _____

7. If you find yourself procrastinating, what can you do to get back on track?

   _____

   _____

   _____

   _____

8. What can go wrong if you try to micromanage every minute of the day?

   _____

   _____

   What should you do, instead?

   _____

   _____

9. Realizing that any action repeated consistently and frequently will soon become a habit, what should you do with your academic planner every day and every week to establish a strong habit that will help ensure your success in all your college courses to come?

   _____

   _____

   _____

   _____

OUTSIDE THE BOOK

Download and print out seven copies of the "Study Journal" page below. Near the end of the day, every day for the next week, spend a few minutes reviewing your day and write answers to those questions. At the end of the week, review your written notes and summarize what you observe about your study tendencies by answering these questions:

1. Did you usually get as much, more, or less schoolwork done as you had scheduled for the day?
   _____
   If you got less done, was the problem due to scheduling more time than you actually had, or not making effective use of your scheduled blocks of time?
   _____
   _____

2. List steps you will take to make your scheduling process work better next week.
   _____
   _____
   _____

3. What other things did you do repeatedly during the week when you should have been studying?
   _____
   _____
   _____

4. What were the most common distractions (people or other interruptions) during the week when you were studying? _____
   _____
   _____

5. List ways you can control your study space to avoid these activities and prevent these distractions next week. _____
   _____
   _____

6. Do you see a pattern in the activities you least enjoyed and had difficulty getting started on?
   _____
   _____
   _____

7. Review Section 3 and Section 4 for specific strategies to use to stay focused and motivated. Make a list here of five or more things you will do differently next week if studying becomes difficult or less enjoyable.
   _____
   _____
   _____
   _____
   _____
   _____
   _____
   _____

Study Journal for Date: _____

a. My daily planner had scheduled _____ hours of academic time today (not counting time in class). It turned out that I actually spent about _____ hours on my studies.
   At some times I was scheduled to study or do academic work, I was doing this instead:
   _____
   _____

b. The academic time I most enjoyed today was doing _____
   _____
   I enjoyed this most because
   _____
   _____

c. The academic time I least most enjoyed today was doing _____
   _____
   I enjoyed this least because
   _____
   _____

d. I had the most difficulty getting started on this study activity:

Why? _____

_____

e. I did my studying and other academic work in these places:

_____

_____

f. During the time I was studying, I was interrupted by these people:

_____

_____

Other interruptions included the following (phone calls, e-mail, etc.):

_____

_____

MAKE AN ACTION LIST

Goals

I have not yet set realistic, specific, and time-oriented goals for the following:

_____

_____

In the coming weeks and months, I will think about and clarify these goals:

_____

_____

Planning Ahead

Too often in the past, I have not started early enough on these kinds of school assignments and studying:

_____

_____

To ensure I successfully plan ahead to complete all work on time in the future, I will do the following:

_____

_____

Attitude

I have most difficulty maintaining a positive attitude at the following times:

_____

_____

I can do the following things to "adjust" my attitude at these times to help ensure my success:

_____

_____

Focus and Motivation

When I'm not feeling motivated to work on my studies, I often do these things instead:

_____

_____

I will try to use these strategies to keep motivated and focused on my studies in the future:

_____

_____

Study Space

I have the following problems with the places where I usually study now:

_____

_____

I will make the following changes in my study space (or I will try these new places) to help prevent distractions:

_____

_____

Time Management

I often feel I don't have enough time for my college work for the following reasons:

_____

_____

I will start using these techniques to make sure I use my available time well:

_____

_____

CLASS DISCUSSION QUESTIONS

1. When you really don't feel like studying but know you should, what ways have you found to motivate yourself to sit down and get started? (Encourage students to share what works best for them.)

2. Where do you think you study best? Where is it hardest to study? (Compare answers among students.)

3. Where is the strangest place (or time) you've studied or reviewed class notes? Examples: in the line for a movie, while washing dishes, on exercise equipment at the gym. (Encourage students to share tips for "making" time.)

Thinking about Thought

FIGURE 3.1

© *Thinkstock*

Where Are You Now?

Assess your present knowledge and attitudes.

	Yes	Unsure	No
1. I am a good problem solver.			
2. My friends consider me creative.			
3. I have good judgment.			
4. I find it easy to make decisions quickly.			
5. My decisions usually turn out to be good.			
6. I like to think things through before speaking.			
7. I am not shy about asking questions when I don't understand something.			
8. I enjoy good discussions and arguments.			
9. I regularly practice an art form (music, acting, painting, etc.)			
10. I enjoy hearing other people's points of view, even when I disagree with them.			
11. I usually question information presented as fact on the Internet or television.			

Where Do You Want to Go?

Think about how you answered the questions above. Be honest with yourself. On a scale of 1 to 10, how would you rate your level of thinking skills at this time?

Poor thinking skills   **Excellent thinking skills**

1   2   3   4   5   6   7   8   9   10

In the following list, circle the three most important areas in which you think you can improve:

- Applying information
- Analyzing information
- Thinking critically
- Asking questions about information
- Evaluating information
- Coming up with new ideas
- Solving problems
- Making decisions
- Identifying weaknesses in ideas
- Choosing sources for research

Are there other areas in which you can improve your thinking skills? Write down other things you feel you need to work on.

_____

_____

_____

How to Get There

Here's what we'll work on in this chapter:

- Understanding what makes thinking in college different from thinking in high school
- Learning how to think
- Knowing the types of thinking
- Recognizing why all types of thinking are important
- Understanding what critical thinking is
- Recognizing and avoiding logical fallacies and faulty assumptions

- Establishing critical thinking habits
- Researching and thinking critically
- Understanding what creative thinking is
- Developing creative thinking habits
- Solving problems
- Making decisions
- Brainstorming

1. IT'S ALL IN YOUR HEAD

Throughout earlier chapters we have said that college is really quite different from high school. Sure, the social life is different, and there are different pressures in college, perhaps a family to support or a job schedule to coordinate with studies. But the two most fundamental differences involve expectations of you as a college student: the expectation that you will be independent and take responsibility for your actions, and the expectation that you will think for yourself.

Remember the heavy "thinking" you did in high school? Most of it was recalling facts or information you had memorized. Perhaps in some courses you were asked to support a statement or hypothesis using content from your textbook or class. Your thinking in high school was very structured and often tied closely to reflecting what was taught in class.

In college, you are expected to think for yourself; to access and evaluate new approaches and ideas; to contribute to your knowledge; and to develop or create new, fresh ideas. You will be required to develop and use a variety of thinking skills—higher-order thinking skills—which you may not have used in high school. In college, your instructors' goal is not only to supply new information and ideas. Instead, good instructors will challenge you to stretch your skills and knowledge through critical and creative thinking. Much of their teaching involves questioning you, not just giving you directions. Your success in college—and in life beyond college—is directly linked to becoming a better thinker. This requires mastering some new skills and practicing them.

2. TYPES OF THINKING

LEARNING OBJECTIVES

1. **Understand that there are different types of thinking.**
2. **Identify how each type of thinking contributes to learning.**

So what are these types of thinking skills, and what kind of things are we doing when we apply them? In the 1950s, Benjamin Bloom developed a classification of thinking skills that is still helpful today; it is known as **Bloom's taxonomy**. He lists six types of thinking skills, ranked in order of complexity: knowledge, comprehension, application, analysis, synthesis, and evaluation. Figure 3.2 outlines each skill and what is involved in that type of thinking, as updated by Lorin Anderson and David Krothwohl.[1]

Bloom's taxonomy

A classification of thinking skills developed by Benjamin Bloom. In order of increasing complexity, they are knowledge, comprehension, application, analysis, synthesis, and evaluation.

FIGURE 3.2 Types of Thinking Skills

Thinking Skill	What It Involves
1. Remembering and Recalling	Retrieving or repeating information or ideas from memory. This is the first and most basic thinking skill you develop (starting as a toddler with learning numbers, letters, and colors).
2. Understanding	Interpreting, constructing meaning, inferring, or explaining material from written, spoken, or graphic sources. Reading is the most common understanding skill; these skills are developed starting with early education.
3. Applying	Using learned material or implementing material in new situations. This skill is commonly used starting in middle school (in some cases earlier).
4. Analyzing	Breaking material or concepts into key elements and determining how the parts relate to one another or to an overall structure or purpose. Mental actions included in this skill are examining, contrasting or differentiating, separating, categorizing, experimenting, and deducing. You most likely started developing this skill in high school (particularly in science courses) and will continue to practice it in college.
5. Evaluating	Assessing, making judgments, and drawing conclusions from ideas, information, or data. Critiquing the value and usefulness of material. This skill encompasses most of what is commonly referred to as critical thinking; this skill will be called on frequently during your college years and beyond. Critical thinking is the first focus of this chapter.
6. Creating	Putting parts together or reorganizing them in a new way, form, or product. This process is the most difficult mental function. This skill will make you stand out in college and is in very high demand in the workforce. Creative thinking is the second focus of this chapter.

All of these thinking skills are important for college work (and life in the "real world," too). You've likely already had much experience with the lower-level thinking skills (remembering and understanding). You will get a lot of practice with the mid-level skills (applying and analyzing) in college, and you may be well on your way to mastering them already. The higher-level thinking skills (evaluating and creating) are the most demanding, and most students need to work to develop them.

EXERCISE: THOUGHT INVENTORY

Think about Figure 3.2. Are you using all six thinking skills now in college? Reflect on your studies in the past three weeks and identify specific examples where you used each of the thinking skills. Use the comment column in this exercise to write notes about the skills you know you now have and those you would like to develop further.

Skill Set	How You Used It in the Past Three Weeks	Comments
Remembering and Recalling		
Understanding		
Applying		
Analyzing		
Evaluating		
Creating		

Look at the things you wrote that you have done in the last three weeks. Notice that certain verbs generally apply to each skill set. When you see those verbs as a prompt in an assignment or an exam, you will know what kind of thinking the instructor expects from you. Table 3.1 lists some of the most common verbs associated with each thinking skill.

TABLE 3.1   Thinking Verbs

Skill Set	Verbs
1. Remembering and Recalling	Bookmark, count, describe, draw, enumerate, find, google, identify, label, list, match, name, quote, recall, recite, search, select, sequence, tell, write
2. Understanding	Blog, conclude, describe, discuss, explain, generalize, identify, illustrate, interpret, paraphrase, predict, report, restate, review, summarize, tell, tweet
3. Applying	Apply, articulate, change, chart, choose, collect, compute, control, demonstrate, determine, do, download, dramatize, imitate, implement, interview, install (as in software), participate, prepare, produce, provide, report, role-play, run (software), select, share, show, solve, transfer, use
4. Analyzing	Analyze, break down, characterize, classify, compare, contrast, debate, deduce, diagram, differentiate, discriminate, distinguish, examine, infer, link, outline, relate, research, reverse-engineer, separate, subdivide, tag
5. Evaluating	Appraise, argue, assess, beta test, choose, collaborate, compare, contrast, conclude, critique, criticize, decide, defend, "friend/de-friend," evaluate, judge, justify, network, post, predict, prioritize, prove, rank, rate, review, select, support
6. Creating	Adapt, animate, blog, combine, compose, construct, create, design, develop, devise, film, formulate, integrate, invent, make, model, modify, organize, perform, plan, podcast, produce, program, propose, rearrange, remix, revise, rewrite, structure

Throughout this book, we give tips that will help you develop your thinking skills. You have read about the learning cycle and the importance of *applying* your knowledge. You will learn tips for *remembering* information from your notes and classes. Preparing for class requires you to *analyze* what you know and what you need to learn. The sections on listening and reading will help you develop your *understanding* skills. Look for those tips and practice them.

In this chapter, we will focus on critical thinking (evaluating) and creative thinking. These skills deserve some discussion because it is likely that you have least practice with them. These are the skills most helpful for success in college and the work world. Creative thinking will help you come up with possible solutions for problems and new ideas. Critical thinking will help you decide what ideas and solutions have most merit and deserve to be implemented.

KEY TAKEAWAYS

- We use different types of thinking skills in different situations; these skills are classified in Bloom's taxonomy.
- You have been using many thinking skills since childhood.
- Two very important thinking skills for success in college and life are critical (evaluative) thinking and creative thinking.

CHECKPOINT EXERCISES

1. List three verbs that are associated with application skills.

   _____

   _____

   _____

2. What is another name for "evaluation" thinking skills?

   _____

3. Which thinking skills are associated with each of the following?

   a. Compose, design: _____

   b. Tweet, describe: _____

   c. Break down, discriminate: _____

   d. Rank, conclude: _____

   e. Enumerate, search online: _____

3. IT'S CRITICAL

LEARNING OBJECTIVES

1. **Understand what critical thinking is and why it's important.**
2. **Identify logical pitfalls.**
3. **Discover assumptions and biases.**
4. **Practice problem solving and decision making.**
5. **Know the power of questions.**
6. **Evaluate information (on and off the Internet).**

Americans Have Access to...

- 1 million *new* books each year
- 5,500 magazines
- 10,500 radio stations
- 65,000 iPhone apps
- 1,000,000,000,000 web pages[2]

Today it is not as critical as in the past to "know" a great deal of information. The list above shows how much information anyone can easily access. If anything, the sheer abundance of information may be the greater challenge. In our world today success depends more on what you can do with the information than just what you know. How we filter and use all this data is one reason critical thinking is so important.

Critical thinking is the ability to discover the value of an idea, a set of beliefs, a claim, or an argument. Critical thinking requires using logic and reasoning to evaluate evidence or information to make a decision or reach a conclusion. Critical thinking is all these:

- A foundation for effective communication
- The principal skill used in effective decision making
- At the core of creating new knowledge
- A way to uncover bias and prejudices

3.1   The Critical Thinking Process

The critical thinking process begins with asking the right questions to understand a problem or issue and then gathering the data you need to complete the decision or take sides on an issue.

What is the problem or issue really about? Understanding this is key to successful critical thinking. What is your objective? Take a position? Make a decision? Are you deciding which candidate in an election will do a better overall job, or are you looking to strengthen the political support for a particular cause? Are you really against something your dad recommends, or are you using the issue to assert your independence?

Do you understand all the terms used to describe the issue? Do you agree with the proponent's definitions? For example, if you are evaluating a politician's statement about the health care system when reading background materials while writing a paper, your first thought might be whether to quote that statement or not—but before you can make that decision you need to understand what the person is really saying. If a term like "family values" is used, for example, does it refer to direct relations or some extended family? Does it include gay and lesbian couples? What does that speaker *really* mean by valuing families?

What are my options? What choices are available to you (if you are making a decision), or what are the "sides" (in an argument) you might choose to agree with? What are their differences? What are the likely consequences of each option? When making a decision, it's helpful to ask what is the worst thing that might happen in each scenario. Examining different points of view is very important; there may be dozens of alternative viewpoints to a particular issue—and the validity of each can change depending on circumstances. A position that is popular or politically correct today may not have been a year ago, and there is no guarantee it will be right in the future. Likewise, a solution to a personal problem that was successful for your roommate may not apply to you. Remember also that sometimes the best option might be a combination of the options you initially identified.

What do I know about each option? Make sure you have full information about each option. Do you have all the information to support each of your likely options? What may still be missing? Where can you get the information you need? Keep an open mind and don't dismiss information that supports any position before you evaluate it carefully.

How good is the information? Now it's time to evaluate the quality of information used to support each option or point of view. Evaluate the strengths and the weaknesses of each piece of supporting evidence. Are all the relevant facts presented? Are any facts presented in misleading ways? Are enough examples presented to support the premise? Consider the source of the supporting information. Who is the expert presenting the facts? That "expert" may have a vested interest in the position. Consider any expert's possible **bias** to help understand the point of view—don't simply accept or reject it. Consider also your own opinions (especially when working with emotional issues): are you so emotional about a particular point of view that you may not be thinking clearly about it because of your own biases? Are there any errors or fallacies in your logic? (See Table 3.2.)

Fallacies are defects in logic that weaken arguments. You should learn to identify them in the arguments of others and in your own thinking, so you can strengthen your own positions and arguments.

Critical thinking

The ability to discover the value of an idea, a set of beliefs, a claim, or an argument. It requires you to use logic and reasoning to evaluate evidence or information to make a decision or reach a conclusion.

bias

A personal inclination that may prevent unprejudiced consideration of a question.

Fallacies

Defects in logic that weaken arguments.

TABLE 3.2 Fallacies and How to Avoid Them

Fallacy	Description	Examples	How to Avoid It in Your Own Thinking
Generalizations	Making assumptions about a whole group of people (or data) based on an inadequate sample.	Engineering students are nerds. My economics class is boring, and my friend says her economic class is boring, too—therefore all economics classes are boring.	What kind of sample are you using? Is it large enough to support the conclusions? You may want to increase your sample size or draw a more modest conclusion by using the word "some" or "many."
False Cause	Drawing improper conclusions through sequencing. If A comes before B, then A causes B.	A large asteroid struck the earth long ago. The dinosaurs became extinct not long after. Therefore the asteroid caused the extinction of dinosaurs.	When making causal statements, be sure you can explain the process through which A causes B beyond their mere sequence.
Personalizations	Also known by their Latin names (*ad hominem*, or "against the man," and *tu quoque*, or "you too"). Inserting personalities inappropriately into an argument. Common in political arguments.	*Against the man:* I won't support Senator Smith's education bill. He was just caught having an extramarital affair. *You too:* A parent explains the evidence of the risks of binge drinking. The child rejects the arguments, saying, "When you were my age, you drank too."	Focus on the merits and supporting data of an argument, not on the personality or behavior of the people making the arguments.
Everyone Does It	Also known by its Latin name (*ad populum*, or "against many"). Justifying an issue based solely on the number of people involved.	It's healthy to drink sugary soft drinks; millions of American kids do.	The popular position is not always the right one. Be wary of arguments that rely exclusively on one set of numbers.
Appealing to Authority	Using an endorsement from someone as a primary reason for supporting a point of view.	We should oppose higher taxes; Curt Schilling does. (Pitcher Curt Schilling may be a credible authority on baseball, but is he an authority on taxes?)	Quoting authorities is a valuable tool to build an argument, but make sure the authorities you quote are truly subject matter experts on the issue you are discussing.
Weak Analogy	Using irrelevant similarities in two objects to draw a conclusion.	Cars and motorcycles are both driven at high speeds on the highway. Car drivers aren't required to wear helmets, so motorcycle riders shouldn't have to either.	You can draw an analogy between just about any two objects or ideas. If you are using an analogy, make sure you identify the properties relevant to the argument you are making and see if both share those properties. (In the example, the motorcycle does not provide protection to the rider, but the car does. Equating the two vehicles based on traveling speed is not relevant to the argument.)
False Dichotomy	Setting up a situation in which it looks like there are only two possible options. If one option is discredited, the other must be accepted.	A classic example: "That's the way it is in America—love it or leave it."	Examine your own thinking. Are there really only two options? Look for a third or even fourth option. If you were asked to develop a compromise between the two positions, what would it look like? What would its strengths and weaknesses be?

You will need to use critical thinking throughout your college years and beyond. Here are some common critical thinking situations and the kinds of questions you should ask to apply critical thinking. Note that critical thinking applies in almost everything discussed in this book.

■ **Personal choices.** Examples include "What should I major in?" and "Should I buy a new car?" What do you know about each of your options? What is the quality of that information? Where can you get more (reliable) information? How do those options relate to your financial and emotional needs? What are the pros and cons of each option? Are you open to the points of view of other people who may be involved? (See Chapter 11 and Chapter 12.)

- **Reading, listening, note taking, and studying.** What are the core messages of the instructor or author? Why are they important? How do these messages relate to one another or differ? What evidence do they provide in support of these messages? (This is covered in much more detail in Chapter 4 and Chapter 5.)
- **Research papers.** What evidence do you need to support your thesis? What sources are available for that evidence? Are they reliable sources? Are there any fallacies in how you build and support your argument? (This is covered in more detail in Chapter 8.)
- **Essay questions on exams.** What is the professor really asking you to do? What do you know about the question? What is your personal belief about the subject? What are the beliefs or biases of the professor or authors you've read? What are the arguments against your point of view? What are the most important pieces of evidence you should offer to support your answer? (This covered in more detail in Chapter 6.)

Tips for Critical Thinking

- Consider all points of view; *seriously* consider more than two (look for grey areas).
- Keep an open mind.
- Answer three questions about your supporting data:
    1. Is it enough support?
    2. Is it the right support?
    3. Is it credible?
- Look for evidence that contradicts your point of view. Pretend to disagree with the position you are supporting. What parts of your argument are weak? Do you have the supporting facts to overcome that evidence?
- Create a set of criteria you will use to evaluate the strength of information you want to use to support your argument. Ask questions like these:
    - What is the source of this information?
    - Is the author well respected in the field?
    - When was this information developed? Is that important? Why?
    - Does the author or publisher have an agenda for publishing the information? How might that agenda affect the credibility of the information?
- List your main points on a piece of paper; then for each one, list the evidence you have to support it. This method can help you visually identify where you have weak evidence and any points that actually lack evidence.
- Be willing to admit that you lack information to support a point of view or make a decision. Ask questions or do some more research to get the support you still need.
- Make sure that your assumptions and points of view are supported by facts, not opinions.
- Learn what types of fallacies you use habitually, and then be on the lookout for them. Student writers often rely on certain types of arguments as a matter of habit. Review some of your old papers to identify which fallacies you need to avoid.
- Question how you characterize others. Are those authorities truly competent in the area you are considering? Are you attacking opponents of your point of view rather than attacking their arguments?
- Be careful of broad generalizations. Claims that use absolute words like "all," "none," "always," "never," "no one," and "everyone" require much more proof than claims that use words like "most," "some," "often," "rarely," "sometimes," and so on.

If you're not sure exactly what is involved in critical thinking, watch this short video, which explains the core concepts more fully and offers tips for using critical thinking in college.

Critical Thinking in College

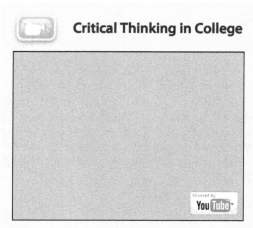

View the video online at: http://www.youtube.com/embed/W9IjF6aqy_E?rel=0

URL

An Internet address; URL stands for "uniform resource locator."

Where Did That Come From?

Often in your college work you'll need to use critical thinking when considering the value of research materials and deciding what to use and how. Between your college library and the Internet, you have access to an almost unlimited amount of data, and you must choose what to use carefully. Here are some guidelines for evaluating why you find online:

1. Look at the **URL**, the webpage address. It can give you important information about the reliability and intentions of the site. Have you heard of this source before, and would others consider it a reliable source? Now consider the domain type in the URL: ".com" and ".biz" are used by commercial enterprises, ".org" is normally used by nonprofit organizations, and ".edu" is reserved for educational institutions. None of these is necessarily bad or good, but they may give you a sense behind the motivation for publishing this material. Are you dealing with a company or an individual's website—and how might that affect the quality of the information on that site? For example, might information about heart attacks be more reliable from the American Heart Association (.org) or Harvard Medical School (.edu) than one person's blog (.com) or a drug manufacturer (.com)?

2. What can you learn from poking around the website with navigation tabs or buttons? Look for a tab labeled "About Us" or "Biography."

3. Consider what the site says about its sources of information. Does the site provide sources and references?

4. Is the information consistent with what you already know from other sources?

5. Ask yourself why the website was written. (To inform? To provide data or facts? To sell something? To promote a cause? To parody?)

Based on what you learned, ask yourself if the information from this website is reliable for your needs. These steps are covered in more detail in Chapter 5.

KEY TAKEAWAY

- Critical thinking involves evaluating the strength of your arguments, data, and information.
- Three questions to ask about the support for an argument or position:
    1. Is there enough support?
    2. Is it the right support?
    3. Is the support credible?
- Weaknesses in arguments are most commonly logical fallacies. Recognizing them will help you evaluate the strength of an argument effectively.

CHECKPOINT EXERCISES

FIGURE 3.3   Crossword: Full of Fallacies

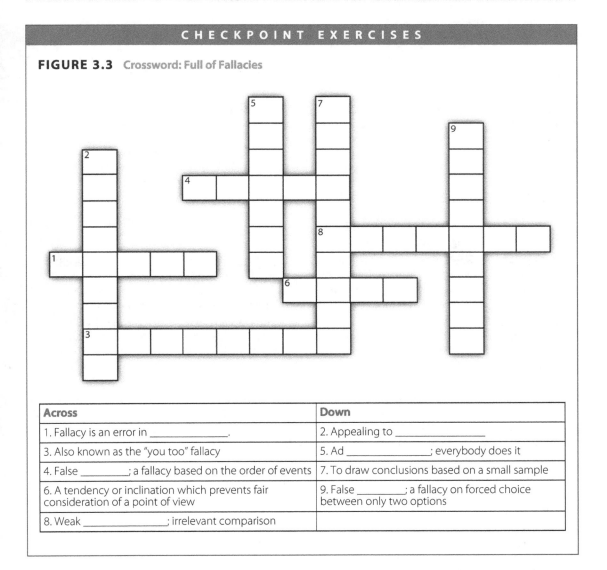

Across	Down
1. Fallacy is an error in _____.	2. Appealing to _____
3. Also known as the "you too" fallacy	5. Ad _____; everybody does it
4. False _____; a fallacy based on the order of events	7. To draw conclusions based on a small sample
6. A tendency or inclination which prevents fair consideration of a point of view	9. False _____; a fallacy on forced choice between only two options
8. Weak _____; irrelevant comparison	

4. SEARCHING FOR "AHA!"

LEARNING OBJECTIVES

1. Use creative thinking: the competitive advantage in the twenty-first century.
2. Understand the difference between creative thinking and free-form thinking.
3. Practice guidelines for creating ideas.
4. Use rules and directions to create effectively.
5. Understand group creativity: how to conduct effective brainstorming.

America still has the right stuff to thrive. We still have the most creative, diverse, innovative culture and open society—in a world where the ability to imagine and generate new ideas with speed and to implement them through global collaboration is the most important competitive advantage.
  - Thomas Friedman[3]

Let's face it: many jobs within American companies are outsourced. The more menial or mechanical the job, the greater the likelihood that someone overseas will do the job for a lot less pay. But generating new ideas, fostering innovation, and developing processes or plans to implement them cannot be easily farmed out, and these are strengths of the American collegiate education. Businesses want problem solvers, not just doers. Developing your creative thinking skills will position you for lifelong success in whatever career you choose.

Creative thinking is the ability to look at things from a new perspective, to come up with fresh solutions to problems. It is a deliberate process of thinking in ways that improve the likelihood of generating new ideas or thoughts.

Let's start by killing a couple of myths:

- **Creativity is an inherited skill.** Creativity is not something people are born with but is a skill that is developed over time with practice. It can be argued that people you think were "born" creative because their parents were also creative are creative more because they have been practicing creative thinking since childhood, stimulated by their parents' questions and discussions.

- **Creativity is free-form thinking.** While you may want to free yourself from all preconceived notions, creative thinking has a recognizable structure. Rules and requirements do not limit creative thinking—they provide the scaffolding on which truly creative solutions can be built. Free-form thinking often lacks direction or an objective, while creative thinking is aimed at producing a defined outcome or solution.

Creative thinking involves coming up with new ideas; it involves a process of seeing the same things others see but seeing them differently. You use skills such as examining associations and relationships, flexibility, elaboration, modification, imagery, and metaphorical thinking. In the process, you will stimulate your curiosity, come up with new approaches to things, and have fun!

4.1 Tips for Creative Thinking

- **Feed your curiosity.** Read. Read books, newspapers, magazines, blogs—anything at any time. When surfing the web, follow links just to see where they will take you. Go to the theater or movies. Attend lectures. Creative people make a habit of gathering information, because they never know when they might put it to good use. Creativity is often as much about rearranging known ideas as it is about creating a completely new concept. The more "known ideas" you have been exposed to, the more options you'll have for combining them into new concepts.

- **Develop your flexibility** by looking for a second right answer. Throughout school we have been conditioned to come up with *the* right answer, but in reality there is often more than one "right" answer. Examine all the possibilities. For example, look at the items in Figure 3.4. Which is different from all the others?

Creative thinking

The ability to look at things from a new perspective, to come up with fresh solutions to problems. It is a deliberate process that allows you to think in ways that increase the likelihood of generating new ideas or thoughts.

If you chose C, you're right; you can't eat a board. But maybe you chose D; that's right, too—clams are the only animal on the chart. And B is right too, as it's the only item you can make oil from, and A can also be right; it's the only red item.

FIGURE 3.4

a. Apple

b. Olives

d. Clams

c. Board

Each option can be right depending on your point of view. Life is full of multiple answers, and if we go along with only the first most obvious answer, we are in danger of losing the context for our ideas. The value of an idea can be determined only by comparing it with another. Multiple ideas also help you generate new approaches by combining elements from a variety of "right" answers. In fact, the greatest danger to creative thinking is to have only one idea. Always ask yourself, "What's the *other* right answer?"

- **Combine old ideas in new ways.** When King C. Gillette registered his patent for the safety razor, he built on the idea of disposable bottle caps, but his venture didn't become profitable until he toyed with a watch spring and came up with the idea of how to manufacture inexpensive (therefore disposable) blades. Bottle caps and watch springs are far from shaving materials, but Gillette's genius was in combining those existing but unlikely ideas. Train yourself to think "outside the box." Ask yourself questions like, "What is the most ridiculous solution I can come up with for this problem?" or "If I were transported by a time machine back to the 1930s, or forward to the 2050s, how would I solve this problem?"

- **Think metaphorically.** Metaphors are useful to describe complex ideas; they are also useful in making problems more familiar and in stimulating possible solutions. For example, if you were a partner in a company about to take on outside investors, you might use the pie metaphor to clarify your options (a smaller slice of a bigger pie versus a larger slice of a smaller pie). If an organization you are a part of is lacking direction, you may search for a "steady hand at the tiller," communicating quickly that you want a consistent, nonreactionary, calm leader. Based on that ship-steering metaphor, it will be easier to see which of your potential leaders you might want to support. Your ability to work comfortably with metaphors takes practice. When faced with a problem, take time to think about metaphors to describe it and the desired solution. Observe how metaphors are used throughout communication and think about why those metaphors are effective. Have you ever noticed that the financial business uses water-based metaphors (cash *flow*, *frozen* assets, *liquidity*) and that meteorologists use war terms (*fronts*, wind *force*, storm *surge*)? What kinds of metaphors are used in your area of study?

- **Ask.** A creative thinker always questions the way things are: Why are we doing things this way? What were the objectives of this process and the assumptions made when we developed the process? Are they still valid? What if we changed certain aspects? What if our circumstances changed? Would we need to change the process? How? Get in the habit of asking questions—lots of questions.

Here's a website (http://99u.com/articles/7160/test-your-creativity-5-classic-creative-challenges) where you can learn more about creative thinking while you have some fun solving some creativity problems and puzzles. Just stretching your mind with exercises like this gets you started in learning to think more creatively.

KEY TAKEAWAYS

- Creative thinking is a requirement for success.
- Creative thinking is a deliberate process that can be learned and practiced.
- Creative thinking involves, but is not limited to, curiosity, flexibility, looking for the second right answer, combining things in new ways, thinking metaphorically, and questioning the way things are.

CHECKPOINT EXERCISES

1. **Feed your curiosity.** List five things you will do in the next month that you have never done before (go to the ballet, visit a local museum, try Moroccan food, or watch a foreign movie). Expand your comfort "envelope." Put them on your calendar.

    a. _____

    b. _____

    c. _____

    d. _____

    e. _____

2. **How many ways can you use it?** Think of as many uses for the following common items as possible. Can you name more than ten?

Peanut Butter (PBJ counts as one, regardless of the flavor of jelly)	Paper Clips	Honors Level: Pen Caps

3. **A metaphor for life.** In the movie *Forrest Gump*, Forrest states, "Life is like a box of chocolates; you never know what you're gonna get." Write your own metaphor for life and share it with your classmates.

    _____

4. **He has eyes in the back of his head.** What if we really had eyes in the backs of our heads? How would life be different? What would be affected? Would we walk backward? Would we get dizzy if we spun in circles? Would it be easy to put mascara on the back eyes? Generate your own questions and answers; let the creative juices flow!

    _____

    _____

    _____

    _____

5. PROBLEM SOLVING AND DECISION MAKING

LEARNING OBJECTIVES

1. **Learn to understand the problem.**
2. **Learn to combine creative thinking and critical thinking to solve problems.**
3. **Practice problem solving in a group.**

Much of your college and professional life will be spent solving problems; some will be complex, such as choosing a career, and will require time and effort to come up with a solution. Others will be small, such as deciding what to eat for lunch, and will allow you to make a quick decision based entirely on your own experience. But, in either case, when coming up with the solution and deciding what to do, follow the same basic steps.

- **Define the problem.** Use your analytical skills. What is the real issue? Why is it a problem? What are the root causes? What kinds of actions do you expect will help to solve the problem? What are some of the key characteristics that will make a good choice: Timing? Resources? Availability of tools and materials? For more complex problems, it helps to actually write out the problem and your answers to these questions. Can you clarify your understanding of the problem by using metaphors to illustrate the issue?

- **Narrow the problem.** Many problems are made up of a series of smaller problems, each requiring its own solution. Can you break the problem into different facets? What aspects of the current issue are "noise" that should not be considered in the solution? (Use critical thinking to separate facts from opinion in this step.)

- **Generate possible solutions.** List all your options and imagine how each will solve the problem. Use your creative thinking skills in this phase. Did you come up with the second "right" answer, and the third or the fourth? Can any of these answers be combined into a stronger solution? What past or existing solutions can be adapted or combined to solve this problem?

Brainstorming

A process of generating ideas for solutions in a group of people.

GROUP THINK: EFFECTIVE BRAINSTORMING

Brainstorming is a process of generating ideas for solutions in a group. This method is often very effective because ideas from one person will trigger additional ideas from another. The following guidelines make for an effective brainstorming session:

- Decide who should moderate the session. That person may participate, but his or her main role is to keep the discussion flowing.
- Define the problem to be discussed and the time you will allow to consider it.
- Write all ideas down on a board or flip chart for everyone to see.
- Encourage everyone to speak.
- Do not allow criticism of ideas. *All* ideas are good during a brainstorm. Suspend disbelief until after the session. Remember a wildly impossible idea may trigger a creative and feasible solution to a problem.

- **Choose the best solution.** Use your critical thinking skills to select the most likely choices. List the pros and cons for each of your selections. How do these lists compare with the requirements you identified when you defined the problem? If you still can't decide between options, you may want to seek further input from your brainstorming team.

5.1 Decisions, Decisions

You will be called on to make many decisions in your life. Some will be personal, like what to major in, or whether or not to get married. Other times you will be making decisions on behalf of others at work or for a volunteer organization. Occasionally you will be asked for your opinion or experience for decisions others are making. To be effective in all circumstances, it is helpful to understand some principles about decision making.

First, define who is responsible for solving the problem or making the decision. In an organization, this may be someone above or below you on the organization chart but is often whoever is responsible for implementing the solution. Choosing an academic major should be your decision, because *you* will have to follow the course of study. Deciding on the boundaries of a sales territory is usually done by the sales manager who supervises the territories, because he or she will be responsible for the results. Once you define who is responsible for making the decision, everyone else falls into one of two roles: giving input, or in rare cases, approving the decision.

Understanding the role of input is very important for good decisions. You seek input from someone with experience, knowledge, or expertise, but it is up to you to weigh the input and decide whether and how to use it. Input should be based on facts, or if a person is offering an opinion, it should be clearly stated as such. Finally, the person who gave the input should support the final decision, whether or not the input is actually used.

Consider a team working on a project for a science course. The team assigns you the responsibility of analyzing and presenting a large set of complex data. Others on the team will set up the experiment to test the hypothesis, prepare the class presentation, and write the paper summarizing the results. As you consider the data, you go to the team to seek input about how much data detail you should consider in your analysis. Perhaps the person doing the experiment setup thinks you should be very detailed, because then it will be easy to compare experiment results with the data. However, maybe the person preparing the class presentation wants to use only high-level data because that will make for a clearer presentation. If the whole team does not clearly understand the decision-making process, each of you may think the decision is yours to make because it influences the output of your work—and the team will experience conflict and frustration. But if the decision maker is clearly defined upfront, and the input is thoughtfully given and considered, a good decision can be made (perhaps a creative compromise?) and the team can get behind the decision and work together to complete the project.

Finally, approval has a role in decisions. This is very common in business decisions but often occurs in college work as well. For example, the professor may need to approve the theme of the team project. In business, approval decisions are usually based on availability of resources, legality, history, or policy.

KEY TAKEAWAYS

- Effective problem solving involves critical and creative thinking.
- There are four steps to effective problem solving:
    1. Define the problem
    2. Narrow the problem
    3. Generate solutions
    4. Choose the solution
- Brainstorming is a good method for generating creative solutions.
- Understanding the difference between the roles of deciding and providing input makes for better decisions.

CHECKPOINT EXERCISES

1. Gather a group of three or four friends and have three short brainstorming sessions (ten minutes each) to generate ideas for alternate uses for peanut butter, paper clips, and pen caps. Compare the results of the group brainstorming with your own ideas before you began. Be sure to follow the brainstorming guidelines. Did you generate more ideas as a group? Did the quality of the ideas improve? Were the group ideas more innovative? Which was more fun? Write your conclusions here.

   _____
   _____
   _____
   _____
   _____

2. Using the steps outlined earlier for problem solving, write a plan for the following problem: You are in your second year of studies in computer animation in a community college. You and your wife both work, and you would like to start a family in the next year or two. You want to become a video game designer and can benefit from more advanced work in programming. Should you plan to go on a university to complete a four-year degree?

   a. Define the problem: What is the core issue? What are related issues? Are there any requirements to a successful solution? Can you come up with a metaphor to describe the issue?

   _____
   _____
   _____
   _____
   _____

   b. Narrow the problem: Can you break down the problem into smaller manageable pieces? What are they?

   _____
   _____
   _____
   _____
   _____

   c. Generate solutions: What are at least two "right" answers to each of the problem pieces?

   _____
   _____
   _____
   _____
   _____

   d. Choose the right approach: What do you already know about each solution? What do you still need to know? How can you get the information you need? Make a list of pros and cons for each solution.

   _____
   _____
   _____
   _____
   _____

6. CHAPTER ACTIVITIES

Chapter Takeaways

- Your ability to think critically and creatively is a key to your success in college and in life. Work to develop and practice these skills.
- Bloom's taxonomy describes the many kinds of thinking we need to do. Up to this point, you probably have practiced most of the lower-level thinking skills but may not have much experience with the higher-level skills (critical thinking and creative thinking).

- Critical thinking involves evaluating the strength of ideas or concepts by asking questions about them. Critical thinking will also allow you to identify and weed out logical fallacies that weaken an academic argument.
- Creative thinking is the process of generating new ideas, concepts, or solutions. This often involves adapting existing ideas or combining them in new ways to create a new solution.
- Problem solving is effectively achieved by applying both critical thinking and creative thinking to generate viable solutions and decisions.

CHAPTER REVIEW

1. List the six levels of thinking described in Bloom's taxonomy.
   _____
   _____
   _____
   _____
   _____
   _____

2. Which thinking skill is most important for short answer quizzes? Why?
   _____
   _____

3. List five verbs that describe the application level of thought.
   _____
   _____

4. What thinking skills are you using if you are blogging? How do you use each one?
   _____
   _____
   _____
   _____

5. What is critical thinking?
   _____
   _____

6. Why is it important to pose some questions about the source of the material you read? What kinds of questions should you ask?
   _____
   _____
   _____
   _____

7. What is a logical fallacy? Give an example for each of two types.
   _____
   _____
   _____

8. List six words that signal a broad generalization, and provide an alternative that resolves that problem of each.
   _____
   _____
   _____
   _____
   _____
   _____

9. What are some ways in which you can feed your curiosity?
   _____
   _____

10. Why is brainstorming often more effective at generating new ideas than individual work?
   _____
   _____

11. List the four steps of problem solving.
   a. _____
   b. _____
   c. _____
   d. _____

12. How do you use critical thinking and creative thinking in solving problems?
   _____
   _____

MAKE AN ACTION LIST

Two things I will do to practice	Action	By when I expect to take the action	The expected results of that action
My critical thinking	1.		
	2.		
My creative thinking	1.		
	2.		
My problem solving	1.		
	2.		

CLASS DISCUSSION QUESTIONS

1. When an instructor asks a question to students in the class, how can you tell if he or she is expecting you to repeat back what you heard in the lecture or reading or if you're really supposed to give your own ideas in answer? (Hint: think of different verbs that are used with different types of thinking.)

2. Say you are researching a new phenomenon and you discover that the two leading experts in the field make opposing statements about what causes that phenomenon. How would you handle that when writing a paper on the topic? What kinds of words and phrases might you use?

3. Sometimes people value creativity above all else—and work hard to be "original" and say very different things from everyone else. When can that cause trouble? When can it be beneficial?

ENDNOTES

1. L. W. Anderson and David R. Krathwohl, eds., *A Taxonomy for Learning, Teaching, and Assessing: A Revision of Bloom's Taxonomy of Educational Objectives* (Boston, MA: Allyn & Bacon, 2001).

2. Scott McLeod and Karl Fisch, "Did You Know? 4.0," video, http://www.youtube.com/watch?v=6ILQrUrEWe8 (accessed January 10, 2010).

3. Thomas L. Friedman, "Time to Reboot America," *New York Times*, December 23, 2008, http://www.nytimes.com/2008/12/24/opinion/24friedman.html?_r=2 (accessed January 14, 2010).

CHAPTER 4
Listening, Taking Notes, and Remembering

FIGURE 4.1

© Thinkstock

Where Are You Now?

Assess your present knowledge and attitudes.

	Yes	Unsure	No
1. I am satisfied with my grades.			
2. I usually feel well prepared for classes.			
3. I usually understand what is going on in class.			
4. I find it easy to stay focused in class.			
5. I am not shy or self-conscious about asking questions in class.			
6. I learn from recorded lectures and podcasts.			
7. I take useful notes in class.			
8. I go to the instructor's office when I have a question about an assignment.			
9. I can successfully study for a test from the notes I have taken.			
10. I use different note-taking methods in different classes.			
11. I do not have trouble remembering facts and ideas.			
12. I retain useful information after an exam.			

Where Do You Want to Go?

Think about how you answered the questions above. Be honest with yourself. On a scale of 1 to 10, how would you rate your level of academic achievement on these issues at this time?

A poor student					An excellent student				
1	2	3	4	5	6	7	8	9	10

In the following list, circle the three most important areas in which you think you can improve:

- Preparing for class
- Taking notes on your laptop
- Listening in class
- Using different systems for note taking
- Using seat selection to your advantage
- Remembering facts and figures
- Listening to podcasts
- Remembering ideas and concepts
- Asking good questions
- Choosing a memory method that's right for you
- Taking notes on paper
- Using a memory system

Are there other areas in which you can improve your academic performance in these areas? Write down other things you feel you need to work on.

_____

_____

_____

_____

How to Get There

Here's what we'll work on in this chapter:

- Setting yourself up for success by following the learning cycle
- Listening actively in class
- Asking good questions
- Taking effective notes
- Learning the principal note-taking methods
- Modifying your note-taking methods to meet your learning style and your instructor's approach to the material
- Understanding how your memory works
- Using your memory effectively
- Learning memory-building tips

1.   THIS IS NOT LIKE HIGH SCHOOL; THIS IS NOT LIKE WORK

As you embark on your college career, you have found yourself in an environment like no other. Consider some of the differences between college classes and what you likely were used to in high school. These differences are important because they demand you change your behavior if you want to be a successful student.

TABLE 4.1   Differences between High School and College Classes

In High School	In College
Your teacher guided you and let you know when you were falling behind.	You are expected to take responsibility for your academic success.
Your teacher took attendance and reported you when you were absent; the teacher helped you make up the material you missed.	Your instructor may rarely take attendance but expects you to be in class and understand the material.
Your teacher wrote assignments on the board and reminded you to complete them.	It is up to you to read, save, and follow the course syllabus and to know what material you must read and understand and by when. Since the syllabus makes this clear, instructors may rarely remind you of assignment due dates.
Each class typically met three to five times each week with minimal homework each night.	Each class meets less frequently but requires much more work. Count on doing two to three hours of studying for each hour of class. Take responsibility for budgeting your time and not falling behind. In college it is much harder to catch up if you do get behind.
High school teachers are passionate about guiding their students and teaching them to learn.	College instructors are often more passionate about their subject matter than they are about their teaching. But you can tap into their passion for their subject and guide your own learning by asking questions, seeking advice during office hours, and participating in class discussions.
Daily homework assignments and unit quizzes contributed heavily to your grade. Often a teacher offered extra-credit opportunities to give students a chance to make up for lapses along the way.	Your grade in a course may be determined primarily by one or two exams and a long-term project or paper. A poor performance on a single exam or paper can really drag your grade down. Identify the assignments on the syllabus and get to work on them early and consistently. Don't put off assignments or studying for tests until the last minute. In college, extra credit is not an option to fall back on!
You were told what you should study and when. You followed a predetermined curriculum set by state and local officials. Likely your parents and guidance counselors had a major say in your "elective" choices.	You determine what you want to learn. It is your education—not someone else's. Find your passion and follow it! You will be a much better student if you do.

2. SETTING YOURSELF UP FOR SUCCESS

1. **Identify the roles of listening and note taking in the learning cycle.**

Too many students try to get the grade just by going to class, maybe a little note taking, and then cramming right before an exam. Sound familiar? This approach may have worked for you in high school where tests and quizzes were more frequent and teachers prepared study guides for you, but colleges require you to take responsibility for your learning and to be better prepared.

Many students simply have not learned how to study and don't understand how learning works. As we discussed in Chapter 1, learning is actually a cycle of four steps: preparing, absorbing, capturing, and reviewing. When you get in the habit of paying attention to this cycle, it becomes relatively easy to study well. But you must use all four steps.

This chapter focuses on **listening**, a key skill for learning new material, and note taking, the most important skill in the capturing phase of the cycle. These skills are closely related. Good listening skills make you a better note taker, and taking good notes can help you listen better. Both are key study skills to help you do better in your classes.

listening

Purposefully focusing on what a speaker is saying with the objective of understanding.

FIGURE 4.2 The Learning Cycle

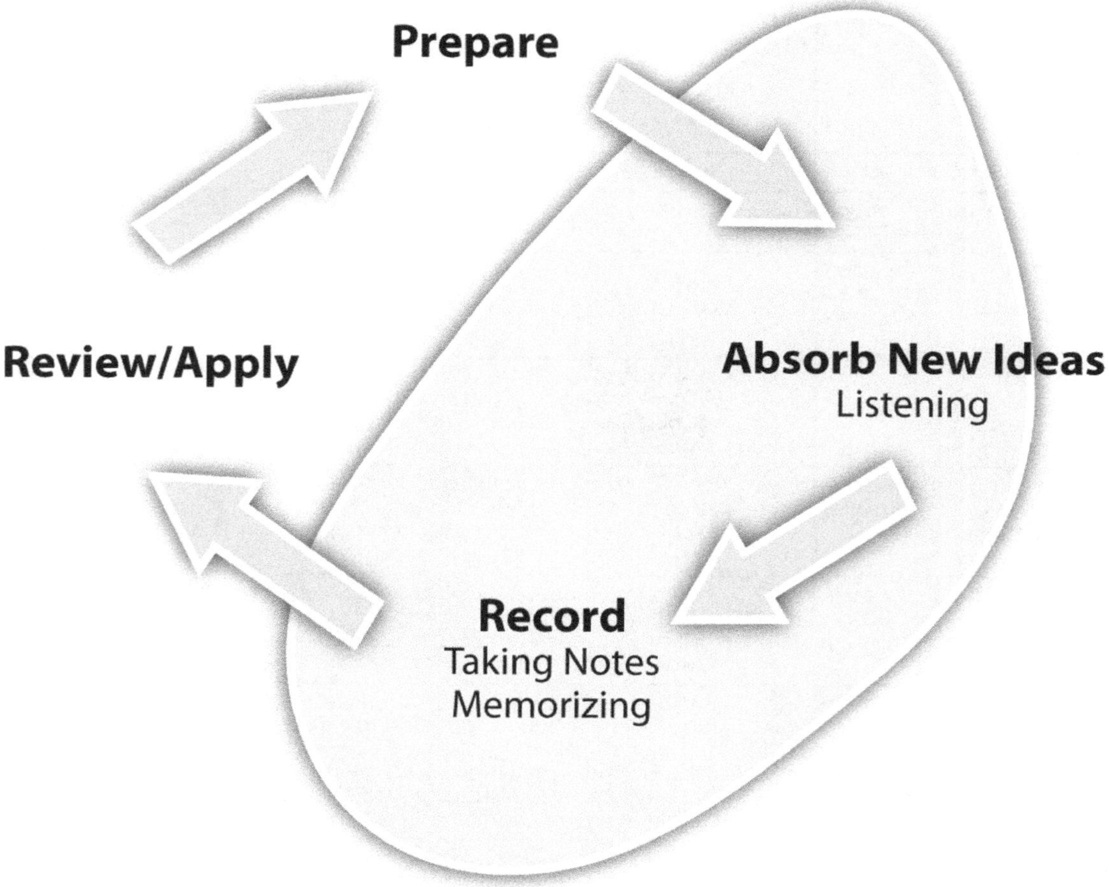

Prepare

Review/Apply

Absorb New Ideas
Listening

Record
Taking Notes
Memorizing

KEY TAKEAWAYS

- College is very different from high school.
- You must take personal responsibility for your learning.
- Time management is crucial.
- Learning is a cycle of four steps: preparing, absorbing, capturing, and reviewing.

3. ARE YOU READY FOR CLASS?

LEARNING OBJECTIVES

1. Prepare for listening in class and taking notes.
2. Use a syllabus.
3. Work through pre-class exercises suggested or required by the instructor.

A professional athlete wouldn't take the field without warming up first. An effective student won't go to a class without preparing for it first. To get the most out of a class, you need to get yourself in the right frame of mind. This does not take a lot of time, but it greatly increases your ability to listen actively and take good notes.

Like a good athlete, first you need to get psyched. Clearly visualize your goals. Thinking about the following questions may help:

- What do I want to get out of the class?
- What is the main idea the class will cover?
- How will today's class help me do better in this course?

Go to class with confidence. The best way to achieve this is to start early and be sure you've completed any assignment the instructor gave you in the last class. Think about how today's material will tie into what you've already learned. You should also review the course **syllabus** to see what the instructor expects to cover in the class and how it relates to what you have learned so far.

Be physically prepared, too:

- Make sure you are getting enough sleep and eating nutritious meals, including breakfast. It's hard to focus on learning when you're hungry.
- Make sure you have all materials you'll need for class (paper, pens, laptop, books, etc.).
- Be punctual. Give yourself plenty of time to get into your seat and organize your space. If you are late, you'll struggle to get into the right mindset for listening, and you won't feel in control of your learning as you try to catch up with the class. If you're tardy, you also create a distraction for your classmates—and the instructor, who will take notice!
- Clear away all other distractions before the instructor starts. Remember that putting your cell phone on "vibrate" may still distract you—so turn it off, all the way off.

Now, take a deep breath, focus on the instructor, and listen and learn!

syllabus

An outline of the course from the instructor, which covers the course objectives, the material to be covered in each class, and often assignments.

3.1 Pre-Class Exercises: The "Flipped Class"

In the old-fashioned approach once used in many college courses, particularly large lecture courses, the instructor made a reading assignment before class and then lectured on that material. Some students invariably figured out that tests were based more on the lecture material than on the reading, and some didn't even bother to read the assigned chapter, thinking that if "it's on the test," the instructor would cover it in class. And indeed, many of these students were able to pass the test without doing the reading, although they seldom achieved a very high grade that way. But this approach is now the exception rather than the rule.

Increasingly common these days are what is often called the "flipped class" or model. Instead of the instructor lecturing to less prepared students on new topics or simply assigning a chapter that might not be read, the instructor expects students to be well prepared before class—to already *know* the material. Then the instructor uses class time to answer questions and pursue other learning activities, such as group work, to build on the learning that should have occurred before class. This model of teaching "flips" the traditional lecture model to put the responsibility on students to actively engage in learning rather than passively "receiving" knowledge via a lecture.

What this means, of course, is that it's absolutely essential to do the reading and work through assigned exercises—before class! You can't sneak by, skipping the reading and hoping the instructor will tell you what's on the test. In fact, you'll likely be very confused during the class time if you haven't done the expected work first. The flipped class may also have a strong online component: you may need to log in the night before, do reading online and perhaps watch associated video, and answer questions or do other online exercises. Most online systems also tell the instructor whether you did in fact log in, how much time you spent on the reading and other assignments, and how you performed on exercises. There's no way a lazy student can coast through this approach.

But take heart: this educational approach has been shown to be not only more effective for learning but also more fun than sitting and listening to a lecture. All that's really required is that you put in the effort to keep up and plan ahead in your studying so that you are in fact truly prepared in advance for the class time.

KEY TAKEAWAYS

- To get the most out of a class, get yourself in the right frame of mind.
- Clearly visualize your goals and approach the class with confidence.
- Be physically prepared: rested, punctual, and not distracted.
- Always do assigned reading and exercises in advance of class.

4. ARE YOU REALLY LISTENING?

LEARNING OBJECTIVES

1. **Listen actively in social situations and in class environments.**
2. **Apply strategies that make listening more effective.**
3. **Ask good questions.**

Are you a good listener? Most of us like to think we are, but when we really think about it, we realize that often we're only half listening. We're distracted, thinking about other things, or formulating what we are going to say in reaction to what we are hearing before the speaker has even finished. Effective listening is one of the most important learning tools you can have in college. And it is a skill that will benefit you on the job and help your relationships with others. Listening should purposefully focus on what a speaker is saying with the objective of understanding.

That definition is straightforward, but it deserves a closer look. "Purposefully focusing" implies that you are actively processing what the speaker is saying, not just letting the sounds of their voice register in your senses. "With the objective of understanding" means that you will learn enough about what the speaker is saying to be able to form your own thoughts about the speaker's message. Listening is an active process, as opposed to hearing, which is passive.

You listen to others in many situations: to interact socially, to get instructions for a task, or to learn new material. In some listening situations you can interact freely with the speaker (everyday conversations, small discussion classes, business meetings), while in others interaction is limited (lectures, webcasts, etc.).

In interactive situations, you should apply the basic principles of **active listening** (next section). These are not hard to understand, but they can be hard to implement and require practice.

active listening

A strategy for listening effectively in interactive situations by focusing on what is being said, confirming that you heard the right message, asking for any needed clarification, watching for nonverbal messages, and listening for requests.

Principles of Active Listening

1. Focus on what is being said. Give the speaker your undivided attention. Clear your mind of anything else. Don't prejudge. You want to understand what the person is saying; you don't need to agree with it.
2. Repeat what you just heard. Confirm with the speaker that what you heard is what he or she said.
3. Ask the speaker to expand or clarify. If you are unsure you understand, ask questions; don't assume.

4. Look for nonverbal signals as well as hearing the words. Nonverbal messages come from facial expressions, body positioning, arm gestures, and tone of voice. Confirm these body language messages just as you would verbal messages by saying, for example, "You seem very excited about this idea."

5. Listen for requests. A speaker will often hide a request as a statement of a problem. If a friend says, "I hate math!" this may mean, "Can you help me figure out a solution to this problem?"

ACTIVITY: LISTENING WITH YOUR WHOLE BODY

Think of someone you consider an excellent listener. Picture that person clearly in your mind. Focus on what the person does, not what he or she is saying. Describe what actions and postures show he or she is listening. Put this list on the left-hand side of the page.

Think of a person you consider a poor listener. Picture that person clearly in your mind. Focus on what the person does, not what he or she is saying. Describe what actions and postures show he of she is not listening. Put this list on the right-hand side of the page.

Now compare these lists with your own behavior. How many of the body language signals from each side do you think others may see in you? How can you add more of the left column's attitudes and actions to your own behaviors? How can you control those behaviors you recognize in yourself from the right column?

Listening in a classroom or lecture hall to learn can be challenging because you are limited by how—and how much—you can interact with the instructor during the class. The following strategies help make listening at lectures more effective and learning more fun.

1. **Get your mind in the right space.** Prepare yourself mentally to receive the information the speaker is presenting by following the preparation guidelines presented earlier and by doing your assignments (instructors build upon work presented earlier).

2. **Get yourself in the right space.** Sit toward the front of the room where you can make eye contact with the instructor easily. Most instructors read the body language of the students in the front rows to gauge how they are doing and if they are losing the class. Instructors also believe students who sit near the front of the room take their subject more seriously and are more willing to give them help when needed or to give them the benefit of the doubt when making a judgment call while assigning grades.

3. **Focus on what is being said.** Eliminate distractions. Turn your cell phone off and put it away. If you are using your laptop for notes, close all applications except the one that you use to take notes. Clear your mind and keep quiet. Listen for new ideas. Think like an investigative reporter: you don't just want to accept what is being said passively—you want to question the material and be convinced that it makes sense.

4. **Look for signals.** Each instructor has a different way of telling you what is important. Some repeat or paraphrase an idea; others raise (or lower) their voices; still others write related words on the board. Learn what signals your instructors tend to use and be on the lookout for them. When they use that tactic, the idea they are presenting needs to go in your notes and in your mind—and don't be surprised if it appears on a test or quiz!

5. **Listen for what is *not* being said.** If an instructor doesn't cover a subject, or covers it only minimally, this signals that that material is not as important as other ideas covered in greater length.

6. **Sort the information.** Decide what is important and what is not, what is clear and what is confusing, and what is new material and what is review. This mental organizing will help you remember the information, take better notes, and ask better questions.

7. **Take notes.** Taking notes is covered in detail later in this chapter, but for now think about how taking notes can help recall what your instructor said and how notes can help you organize your thoughts for asking questions.

8. **Ask questions.** Asking questions is one of the most important things you can do in class. Obviously it allows you to clear up any doubts you may have about the material, but it also helps you take ownership of (and therefore remember) the material. Good questions often help instructors expand on their ideas and make the material more relevant to students. Thinking through the material critically in order to prepare your questions helps you organize your new knowledge and sort it into mental categories that will help you remember it.

A note about tape-recording lectures: You may want to record a lecture to later review or check what you heard in class, but it's usually not a good idea. Depending on a recording may lead you to listen less effectively and think less actively while in the room. Many instructors do not allow students to record their lectures.

4.1 Dealing with Special Listening Challenges

What to Do If…

- **Your instructor speaks too fast.** Crank up your preparation. The more you know about the subject, the more you'll be able to pick up from the instructor. Exchange class notes with other students to fill in gaps in your notes. Visit the instructor during office hours to clarify areas you may have missed. You might ask the instructor—very politely, of course—to slow down, but habits like speaking fast are hard to break!

- **Your instructor has a heavy accent.** Sit as close to the instructor as possible. Make connections between what the instructor seems to be saying and what is presented on the board or screen. Ask questions when you don't understand. Visit the instructor during office hours; the more you speak with the instructor the more likely you will learn to understand the accent.

- **Your instructor speaks softly or mumbles.** Sit as close to the instructor as possible and try to hold eye contact as much as possible. Check with other students if they are having problems listening, too; if so, you may want to bring the issue up with the instructor. It may be that the instructor is not used to the lecture hall your class is held in and can easily make adjustments.

Now That's a Good Question…

Are you shy about asking questions? Do you worry that someone might ridicule you for asking a "dumb" question? Students sometimes feel this way because they have never been taught how to ask questions. Practice the following steps, and soon you'll be on your way to customizing each course to meet *your* needs and letting the instructor know you value the course.

- **Be prepared.** Doing your assignments for a class or lecture will give you a good idea about the areas you are having trouble with and will help you frame some questions ahead of time.

- **Position yourself for success.** Sit near the front of the class. It is easier to make eye contact with the instructor as you ask the question. Also, you won't be intimidated by a class full of heads turning to stare at you as you ask your question.

- **Don't wait.** Ask your questions as soon as the instructor has finished a thought. Being one of the first students to ask a question also helps ensure that your question is given the time it deserves and won't be cut short by the end of class.

- **In a lecture class, write your questions down.** Jot your questions down as they occur to you, before you forget. Some may be answered in the course of the lecture, but if the instructor asks you to hold your questions until the end of class, you'll be glad you have a list of the items you need the instructor to clarify or expand on.

- **Ask specific questions.** "I don't understand" is a statement, not a question. The instructor needs to know specifically what you are having trouble with. "Can you clarify how to use the formula to calculate velocity?" is a better way of asking for help. If you ask your question at the end of class, give the instructor some context for your question by referring to the part of the lecture that triggered the question. For example, "Professor, you said the Union troops were emboldened by Lincoln's leadership. Was this throughout the Civil War, or only after Gettysburg?"

- **Don't ask questions just for the sake of asking questions.** If your question is not thought out, or if it appears that you are asking the question to try to look smart, instructors will see right through you!

KEY TAKEAWAYS

- In all interactive learning situations, apply the basic principles of active listening.
- Focus on what is being said, confirm that you heard the right message, ask for any clarification you need, watch for nonverbal messages, and listen for requests.
- Specific strategies improve listening in a lecture hall.
- Be ready to compensate if your instructor speaks too fast, has a heavy accent that makes understanding difficult for you, or speaks too softly.
- Don't be shy about asking questions. Asking questions is easier when you are prepared and positioned for success.

CHECKPOINT EXERCISES

1. List two things you should do before the class to prepare yourself for active listening.

   _____

   _____

2. Where should you sit in the classroom? Why?

   _____

   _____

3. What are some of the ways instructors signal important material?

   _____

   _____

   _____

5. GOT NOTES?

LEARNING OBJECTIVES

1. **Explain why taking notes is important.**
2. **Use the four primary methods of note taking: lists, outlines, concept maps, and the Cornell method.**
3. **Describe the pros and cons of using a digital note taking method.**
4. **Define which note-taking methods support your learning style and the instructor's teaching style.**
5. **Apply strategies to make note taking more effective.**
6. **Use some effective strategies if you happen to miss a class.**
7. **Organize your notes into effective study guides.**
8. **Use teacher handouts to complement your notes.**
9. **Determine what to do with your notes after the course.**

Everybody takes notes, or at least everybody claims to. But if you take a close look, many who are claiming to take notes on their laptops are actually surfing the Web, and paper notebooks are filled with doodles interrupted by a couple of random words with an asterisk next to them reminding you that "This is important!" In college, these approaches don't work. In college, your instructors expect *you* to make connections between class lectures and reading assignments; they expect *you* to create an opinion about the material presented; they expect *you* to make connections between the material and life beyond college. Your notes are your road maps for these thoughts. Do you take good notes? After learning to listen, note taking is the most important skill to ensure your success in a class.

Effective note taking is important because it

- Supports your listening efforts
- Allows you to test your understanding of the material
- Helps you remember the material better when you write key ideas down

- Gives you a sense of what the instructor thinks is important
- Creates your "ultimate study guide"

There are various ways to take notes, and which you choose depends on both your personal style and the instructor's approach to the material. Each can be used in a notebook, index cards, or in a digital form on your laptop. No one type is good for all students and all situations, so we recommend that you develop your own style, but you should also be ready to modify it to fit the needs of a specific class or instructor. To be effective, all of these methods require you to listen actively and to think; merely jotting down words the instructor is saying will be of little use to you.

TABLE 4.2 Note-Primary Taking Methods

Method	Description	When to Use
Lists	A sequential listing of ideas as the instructor presents them. Lists may be short phrases or complete paragraphs describing ideas in more detail.	This method is what most students use as a fallback if they haven't learned other methods. This method typically requires a lot of writing, and you may find that you are not keeping up with the professor. It is not easy for students to prioritize ideas in this method.
Outlines	The outline method places most important ideas along the left margin, which are numbered. Supporting ideas to these main concepts are indented and are noted with capital letters. Under each idea, further detail can be added, designated with a number, a lowercase letter, and so forth.	A good method to use when the material presented by the instructor is well organized. Easy to use when taking notes on your computer.
Concept Maps	When designing a concept map, place a central idea in the center of the page and then add lines and new circles in the page for new ideas. Use arrows and lines to connect the various ideas.	Great method to show relationships among ideas. Also good if the instructor tends to hop from one idea to another and back.
Cornell Method	The Cornell method uses a two-column approach. The left column takes up a third of the page and is often referred to as the "cue" or "recall" column. The larger right column is used for taking notes using any of the methods described above or a combination of them. After class or completing the reading, review your notes and write the key ideas and concepts or questions in the left column. You may also write a summary of the class or reading in your own words at the bottom of the page.	The Cornell method can include any of the methods above and provides a useful format for calling out key concepts, prioritizing ideas, and organizing review work. Most colleges recommend using some form of the Cornell method.

5.1   The List Method

FIGURE 4.3   The List Method of Note Taking

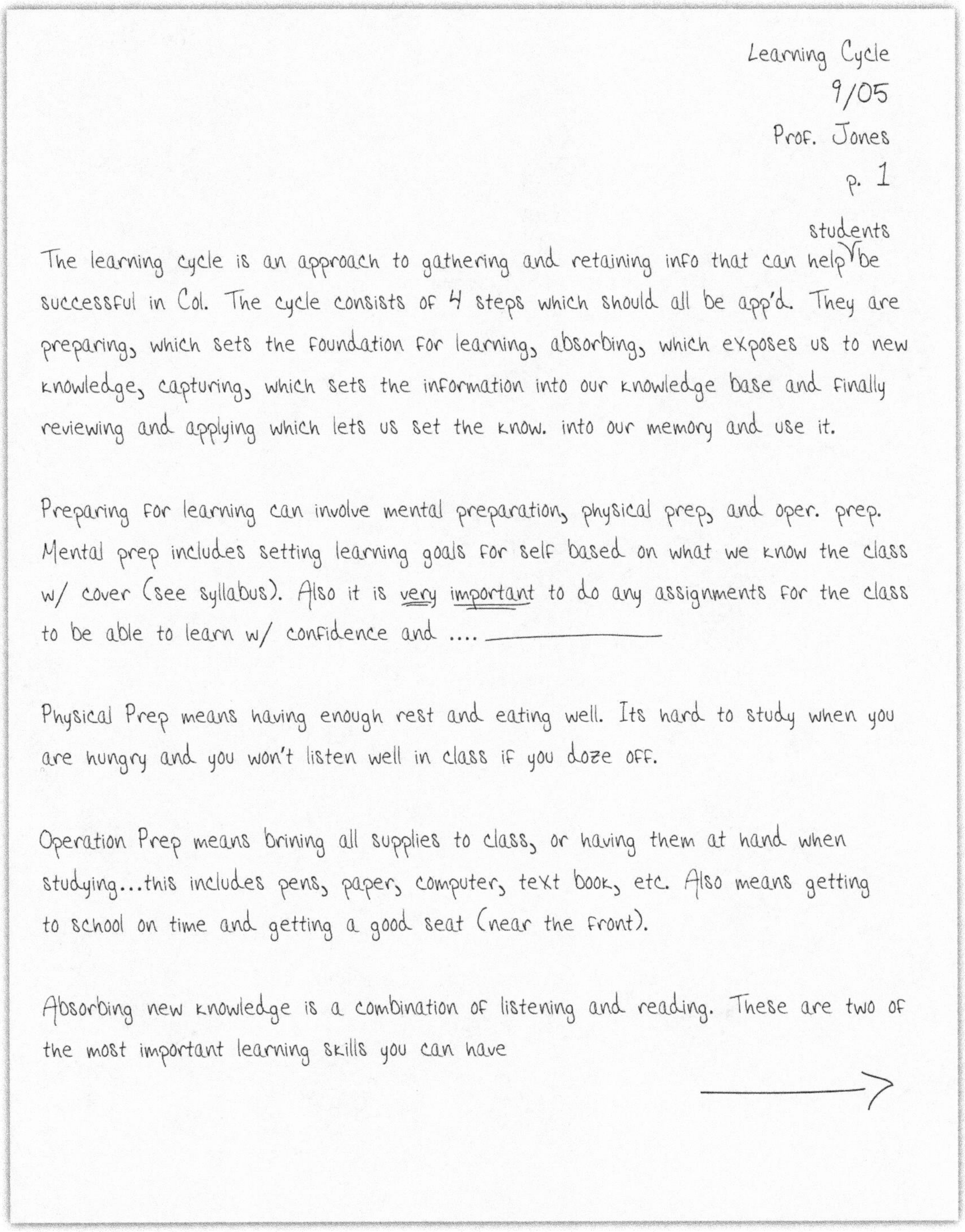

Learning Cycle
9/05
Prof. Jones
p. 1

The learning cycle is an approach to gathering and retaining info that can help be students
successful in Col. The cycle consists of 4 steps which should all be app'd. They are
preparing, which sets the foundation for learning, absorbing, which exposes us to new
knowledge, capturing, which sets the information into our knowledge base and finally
reviewing and applying which lets us set the know. into our memory and use it.

Preparing for learning can involve mental preparation, physical prep, and oper. prep.
Mental prep includes setting learning goals for self based on what we know the class
w/ cover (see syllabus). Also it is very important to do any assignments for the class
to be able to learn w/ confidence and .... _____

Physical Prep means having enough rest and eating well. Its hard to study when you
are hungry and you won't listen well in class if you doze off.

Operation Prep means brining all supplies to class, or having them at hand when
studying...this includes pens, paper, computer, text book, etc. Also means getting
to school on time and getting a good seat (near the front).

Absorbing new knowledge is a combination of listening and reading. These are two of
the most important learning skills you can have

———————⟶

The list method is usually not the best choice because it focuses exclusively on capturing as much of what the instructor says as possible, not on processing the information. Many students who have not learned effective study skills use this method, because it's easy to think that this is what note taking is all about. Even if you are skilled in some form of shorthand, you should probably also learn one of the other methods described here, because they are all better at helping you process and remember the material. You may want to take notes in class using the list method, but transcribe your notes to an outline or concept map method after class as a part of your review process. Always try to review your notes as soon as possible after class and write a summary of the class in your own words.

5.2 The Outline Method

FIGURE 4.4 The Outline Method of Note Taking

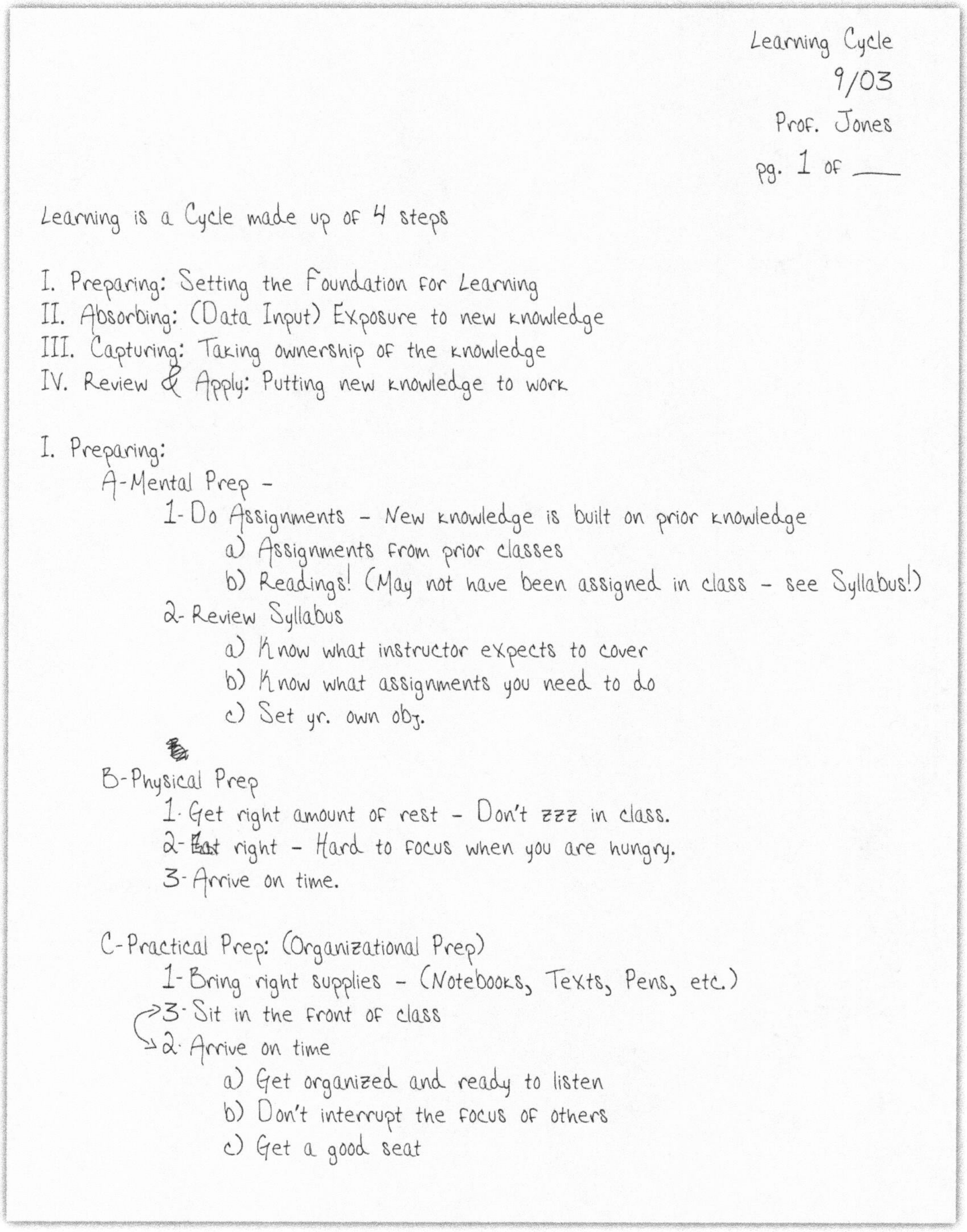

Learning Cycle
9/03
Prof. Jones
pg. 1 of ___

Learning is a Cycle made up of 4 steps

I. Preparing: Setting the Foundation for Learning
II. Absorbing: (Data Input) Exposure to new knowledge
III. Capturing: Taking ownership of the knowledge
IV. Review & Apply: Putting new knowledge to work

I. Preparing:
    A- Mental Prep -
        1- Do Assignments - New knowledge is built on prior knowledge
            a) Assignments from prior classes
            b) Readings! (May not have been assigned in class - see Syllabus!)
        2- Review Syllabus
            a) Know what instructor expects to cover
            b) Know what assignments you need to do
            c) Set yr. own obj.

    B- Physical Prep
        1· Get right amount of rest - Don't zzz in class.
        2- Eat right - Hard to focus when you are hungry.
        3- Arrive on time.

    C- Practical Prep: (Organizational Prep)
        1- Bring right supplies - (Notebooks, Texts, Pens, etc.)
        3· Sit in the front of class
        2· Arrive on time
            a) Get organized and ready to listen
            b) Don't interrupt the focus of others
            c) Get a good seat

The advantage of the outline method is that it allows you to prioritize the material. Key ideas are written to the left of the page, subordinate ideas are then indented, and details of the subordinate ideas can be indented further. To further organize the ideas, you can use the typical outlining numbering scheme (starting with roman numerals for key ideas, moving to capital letters on the first subordinate level, Arabic numbers for the next level, and lowercase letters following, as shown in the illustration.) At first you may have trouble identifying when the instructor moves from one idea to another. This takes practice and experience with each instructor, so don't give up! In the early stages, try using your syllabus to determine what key ideas the instructor plans to present. Your reading assignments before class can also give you guidance in identifying the key ideas.

If you're using your laptop computer for taking notes, a basic word processing application (like Microsoft Word) is very effective. Format your document by selecting the outline format from the format bullets menu. Use the increase or decrease indent buttons to navigate the level of importance you want to give each item. The software will take care of the numbering for you! (See later section on Digital Note-Taking.)

After class be sure to review your notes and then summarize the class in one or two short paragraphs using your own words. This summary will significantly affect your recall and will help you prepare for the next class (and future tests!).

5.3 The Concept Map Method

FIGURE 4.5 The Concept Map Method of Note Taking

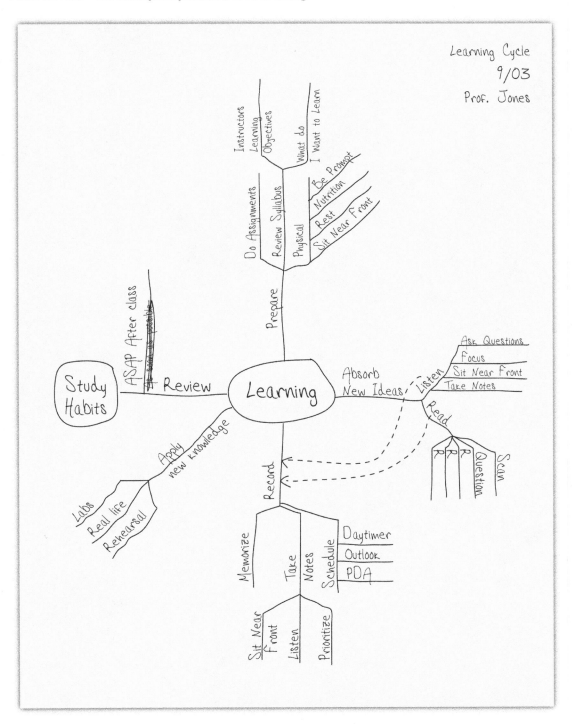

This is a very graphic method of note-taking that is especially good at capturing the relationships among ideas. Concept maps harness your visual sense to understand complex material "at a glance." They also give you the flexibility to move from one idea to another and back easily, so they are helpful if your instructor moves freely through the material.

To develop a concept map, start by using your syllabus or assigned reading to rank ideas to be covered that day in class by level of detail (from high-level or abstract ideas to detailed facts). Put the overriding idea (high level) it in a circle in the middle of the page. Then create branches off that circle for more detailed information from the lecture, creating additional limbs as you need them. Arrange the branches with others that are interrelated. When a new high-level idea is presented, create a new circle with its own branches. Link together related circles or concepts. Use arrows and symbols to capture relationships between ideas. For example, an arrow may be used to illustrate cause or effect, a double-pointed arrow for dependence, or a dotted arrow for impact or effect.

As with all note-taking methods, you should summarize the chart in one or two paragraphs of your own words after class.

5.4   The Cornell Method

FIGURE 4.6   The Cornell Method of Note Taking

The **Cornell method** was developed in the 1950s by Professor Walter Pauk at Cornell University. Many colleges recommend it because of its usefulness and flexibility. This method is simple to use for capturing notes, is helpful for defining priorities, and is a very helpful study tool.

The Cornell method follows a very specific format that consists of four boxes: a header, two columns, and a footer (see illustration).

The header is a small box across the top of the page. Here you write identification information like the course name and class date. Beneath the header are two columns: a narrow one on the left (a third of the page) and a wide one on the right. The wide column, called the "notes" column, takes up most of the page and is used to capture your notes using any of the methods outlined earlier. The left column,

Cornell method

A classic method of taking organized class notes using a two-column approach that highlights key ideas.

known as the "cue" or "recall" column, is used to jot down main ideas, keywords, questions, clarifications, and other notes. Use the left column both during class and when reviewing your notes after class. Finally, use the box in the footer to write a summary of the class in your own words. This will help you make sense of your notes in the future and is a valuable tool to aid with recall and studying.

Using Index Cards in the Cornell Method

Some students like to use index cards to take notes, and they work well with the Cornell method. Use the lined side of the card to write notes in class. Use one card per key concept. Use the unlined side of the card for the left hand "cue" column. Use it after class to write keywords, comments, or questions related to the notes on the other side. When you study, use the cards as flash cards with questions on one side and answers on the other. Write a summary of the class on a separate card and place it on the top of the deck as an introduction for that day's class.

I used to tape my lecture classes so I could fill in my sketchy notes afterward. Now that I'm using the Cornell system, my notes are complete and organized in much less time. And my regular five-minute reviews make learning almost painless. No more taping and listening twice.
- a student at Southern Methodist University

All note-taking methods end with the same step: reviewing your notes as soon as possible after class. Any review of your notes is helpful (reading them, copying them into your computer, or even recasting them using another note-taking method). But *think* during this activity—make your review of notes thoughtful, not a mindless process. When you review your notes, think about questions you still have and determine how you will get the answers. (From the next class? Studying with a friend? Looking up material in your text or on the net?) Consider how the material is related to other tings you've learned in the course; make connections with notes from other class sessions, with material in your text, and with class discussions. Finally, it's fun to think about how the material in your notes can apply in real life: "What does this mean to me in relation to what I want to do with my life?" and even "Is there anything cool here I can work into a conversation with my friends?"

5.5 Digital Note Taking

Some students naturally want to use their laptop, tablet, or smartphone for taking notes and feel more comfortable with a keyboard than paper and pencil. As mentioned earlier, it is easy to take notes in a word processing program like Microsoft Word, using the outline function. In addition, many note-taking apps are available for smartphones and tablets. In some cases these apps may be useful, but they also involve risks for learning. Think about your habits carefully before deciding to take notes digitally.

First, any device can easily distract you from what is taking place in the class. Once you have your laptop or phone in hand, it's tempting to switch over to another app "just for a second" to check Facebook or read an arriving text or email. It can take a lot of will power to avoid such distractions, and even if you're somewhere else for only a few seconds, it can be hard to get back into lecture mode without losing the thread of what's being said.

Even if you stay focused and avoid other distractions on your device, the app or software itself can become a distraction. The small screen of a smartphone makes it very difficult to view much content at a time, and you may find yourself scrolling up and down looking for previously written notes to add something more if the instructor circles back to comment further. It also takes more time to delete something digitally than to simply cross out something you've written. It takes even more time to put something in boldface, circle it, or highlight it with color. It is also difficult to use special notations (scientific and math formulas, for example) in apps or software. Virtually any use of such formatting options can distract you from the flow of the class.

Finally, consider what your instructor is seeing when you are looking down at your device. The instructor may think you're doing something else and ignoring the lecture, even if you're not, and that's a strike against you. Indeed, many instructors (and some colleges as a whole) forbid the use of electronic devices during class, and breaking that rule can have serious consequences. In all, even if you can use your keyboard much faster than you write on paper, for most students it's generally still better to take class notes on paper.

5.6 Instructor Handouts

Some instructors hand out or post their notes or PowerPoint slides from their lectures. *Never* consider these handouts a substitute for taking notes in class. They are a very useful complement and will help you confirm the accuracy of your notes, but they do not involve you in the process of learning as well as your own notes do. After class, review your notes using a highlighter and mark keywords and ideas in your notes. This will help you write the summary of the class in your own words.

5.7   General Tips on Note Taking

Regardless of what note-taking method you choose, work on developing these note-taking habits for all your courses:

1. **Be prepared.** Make sure you have the tools you need to do the job. If using a notebook, be sure you have it with you along with enough paper. Make sure to have your pen (as well as a spare) and perhaps another with different colored ink to use for emphasis.

2. **Write on only one side of the paper.** This will allow you to integrate your reading notes with your class notes.

3. **Label, number, and date all notes at the top of each page.** This will help you keep organized.

4. **Don't try to capture everything that is said.** Listen for the big ideas and write them down. Make sure you can recognize the instructor's emphasis cues and write down all ideas and keywords the instructor emphasizes. Listen for clues like "the four causes were…" or "to sum up…."

5. **Copy anything the instructor writes on the board.** It's probably important.

6. **Leave space between ideas.** This lets you add related notes later (e.g., notes on the answer to a question you or one of your classmates asked).

7. **Use symbols and abbreviations.** Which ones you use is up to you, but be consistent so you will know exactly what you mean by "att." when you review your notes. You may find it useful to keep a key to your abbreviations in your notebook.

8. **Use some method for identifying your own thoughts and questions to keep them separate from what the instructor or textbook author is saying.** Some students use different color ink; others box or underline their own thoughts. Do whatever works for you.

9. **Create a symbol to use when you fall behind** or get lost in your note taking. Jot down the symbol, leave some space, and focus on what the instructor is covering now. Later you can ask a classmate or the professor to help you fill in what you missed, or you can find it in your textbook.

10. **Review your notes as soon after class as possible (the same day is best).** *This is the secret to making your notes work!* With the Cornell method, use the recall column to call out the key ideas and organize facts. Fill in any gaps in your notes and clean up or redraw hastily drawn diagrams.

11. **Write a summary of the main ideas of the class in your own words.** This process is a great aid to recall. Be sure to include any conclusions from the lecture or discussion.

JOURNAL ENTRY

Choose one of your classes where you normally take notes. Use the Cornell method with either the outline or concept map method for taking your notes. Follow as many steps listed previously as possible. Now compare these notes with those you took in the previous class. Are your new notes more useful? What did you like about taking notes this way? What are some of the things you need to work on improving? (Remember this will get much easier with more practice.) Write your thoughts here.

_____

_____

_____

_____

_____

_____

5.8 What If You Miss Class?

Clearly the best way to learn class material is to be at the class and to take your own notes. In college, regular attendance is expected. But life happens, and sometimes you may have to miss a class or lecture. When this happens, take steps to make up for it:

- Check with the instructor to see if there is another section of the class you can attend. Never ask the instructor "Did I miss anything important?" (Think about what that's saying and you'll see it's rather insulting.)

- If the instructor posts his or her lectures as a podcast, listen to the lecture online and take notes. If the instructor uses PowerPoint slides, request a copy (or download them if posted) and review them carefully, jotting down your own notes and questions. Review your notes with a classmate who did attend.

- You may want to borrow class notes from a classmate. If you do, don't just copy them and put them in your notebook. They will not be very helpful. When you borrow notes from a classmate, make a copy you can mark up with your own notes and questions as you review them carefully. Use your textbook to try to fill in any gaps. Finally, schedule a study session with the person who gave you the notes to review the material and confirm your understanding. (See studying with others in Chapter 6.)

- If none of these options is available for you, use the course syllabus to determine what was covered in the class, then write a short paper (two pages or so) on the material using the class readings and reliable online sources. See your instructor during office hours to review your key findings and to answer any questions you still may have.

5.9 Keeping Your Notes

Class is over, and you have a beautiful set of notes in your spiral notebook or saved in your laptop. You have written the summary of the class in your own words. Now what?

Start by organizing your notes. A three-ring binder often works best for each of your subjects. Print your notes if you used a computer. If you used note cards, insert them in plastic photo holders for your binder. Group all notes from a class or unit together in a section, including class notes, reading notes, and instructor handouts. You might also want to copy the instructor's syllabus for the unit on the first page of the section.

Next, spend some time linking the information across the various notes. Use the recall column in your notes to link to related information in other notes (e.g., "See class notes date/page").

If you have had a quiz or test on the unit, put it in your binder too, but be sure to write out the correct answer for any item you missed. Link those corrections to your notes, too.

Now is a good time to write "notes on your notes." Review your summary to see if it still is valid in light of your notes on the reading and any handouts you may have added to your notes package.

You don't need to become a pack rat with your notes. It may be safe to discard them after the end of a course *except* in the following cases:

1. If the course you took is a prerequisite for another course, or is part of a standard progression of courses that build upon each other (this is very common in math and science courses), keep them as a reference and review them before the next course.

2. If the course may pertain to your future major, keep your notes. You may not realize it now, but they may have future value when you study similar topics or even the same topics in more depth.

3. If you are very interested in the course subject and would like to get into the material through a more advanced course, independent study, or even research, keep your notes as a prep tool for further work.

KEY TAKEAWAYS

- After effective listening, good note taking is the most important skill for academic success.
- Choose the note-taking style that works best for you and modify it to meet the needs of a specific class or instructor.
  - List notes are generally less effective and not prioritized.
  - Outlines work well for taking notes on a laptop when the instructor is well organized.
  - Concept map notes are good for showing the relationships among ideas.
  - The Cornell method is effective for calling out key concepts and organizing notes for review.
- Instructor handouts and PowerPoint presentations help with—but do not replace the need for—personal note taking.
- If you miss a class, explore your options for replacing your missing notes.
- Keep your notes organized in a way that makes it easy to study for tests and other uses in the future.

CHECKPOINT EXERCISES

1. Name two advantages of the Cornell system over the list method of note taking.

   _____

   _____

2. Describe the benefits of—and potential problems with—taking class notes on a laptop or other digital device.

   _____

   _____

   _____

   _____

3. List at least three ways to make up for missing notes because you miss a class.

   _____

   _____

   _____

   _____

6.   REMEMBERING COURSE MATERIALS

LEARNING OBJECTIVES

1. **Identify what is important to remember.**
2. **Understand the difference between short- and long-term memory.**
3. **Use a variety of strategies to build your memory power.**
4. **Identify four key types of mnemonic devices.**
5. **Use mnemonics to remember lists of information.**

So far we have covered how to capture material in your notes. The rest of this chapter looks at strategies for remembering ideas and facts.

6.1   The Role of Memorization in Learning

Have you ever gone into an exam you have studied for and drawn a blank on a particular question? Have you ever walked into a room only to forget for a moment why you went there? Have you ever forgotten where you left your keys? How about finding yourself in a conversation with someone whose name you can't remember? The fact is, memory fails everyone from time to time. It is not surprising that students, with a huge amount of information they must commit to memory, are often frustrated by their memory.

Let's start by taking off some of the pressure. You will not be required to memorize everything your instructor says in a class—nor should you try to. There is way too much to capture. People speak at a rate of 100 to 150 words per minute. An average 50-minute lecture may contain well over 5,000 words. When you are listening effectively and taking notes, your job is to distill the main ideas and a few keywords. *These* are the things you should choose to memorize.

In your early and high school education, memorization was a key aspect of learning. You memorized multiplication tables, the names of the states, vocabulary words. Memorized facts ensured your success on multiple-choice questions. In college, however, most of your work is focused on understanding the material in depth. Remembering the year of the 9/11 attack (2001) is far less important than grasping the impact of that attack on American foreign policy. Understanding themes and ideas and being able to think critically about them is really the key to your success in college learning. (For more on critical thinking skills, see Chapter 3.) Although memorization is seldom the primary key to success, having a good memory is important to capture ideas in your mind, and it helps tremendously in certain subjects like sciences and foreign languages.

6.2 How Memory Works

Memory is the process of storing and retrieving information. There are two types of memory: short-term or active memory, and long-term or passive memory. As its name suggests, short-term or active memory is made up of the information we are processing at any given time (such as listening in class) as well as information retrieved from passive memory for doing complex mental tasks (such as thinking critically and drawing conclusions). But short-term memory is limited and suffers with the passing of time and lack of use. We begin to forget data within thirty seconds of not using it, and interruptions (such as phone calls or distractions) require us to rebuild the short-term memory structure—to get "back on task." (Learn more about multitasking in Chapter 6.) To remember information, we must either keep using it or place it into our long-term memory (much like saving a document on your computer).

How we save information in our long-term memory affects our ability to retrieve it when we need it at a later date. Our mind "saves" information by creating a complex series of links to the data. The stronger the links, the easier it is to recall. You can strengthen these links by using the following strategies. Notice how closely these strategies relate to good listening and note-taking strategies.

- **Make a deliberate decision to remember the specific data.** Specifically thinking "I need to remember Richard's name" creates stronger links than just wishing you had a better memory for names.

- **Link the information to your everyday life.** Ask yourself, "Why is it important that I remember this material?"—and answer it.

- **Link the information to other information you already have "stored,"** especially the key themes of the course, and you will recall the data more easily. Ask yourself how something new is related to other information you already have. Look for ways to tie items together. Are they used in similar ways? Do they have similar meanings? Do they sound alike?

- **Mentally group similar individual items into "buckets."** By doing this, you are creating links, for example, among terms to be memorized. For example, if you have to memorize a vocabulary list for a Spanish class, group the nouns together with other nouns, verbs with verbs, and so forth. Or you may group vocabulary words by making sentences of them.

- **Use visual imagery.** Picture the concept vividly in your mind. Make those images big, bold, and colorful—even silly! Pile concepts on top of each other or around each other; exaggerate their features like a caricature; let your imagination run wild. Humor and crazy imagery can help you recall key concepts.

- **Use the information.** Studies have generally shown that we retain only 5% of what we hear, 10% of what we read, 20% of what we see in multimedia, and 30% of what is demonstrated to us. But we retain 50% of what we discuss, 75% of what we practice by doing, and 90% of what we teach others or use immediately in a relevant activity. Review your notes, participate in class, and study with others.

- **Break information down into manageable "chunks."** Memorizing the ten-digit number "3141592654" seems difficult, but breaking it down into smaller sets of digits, like a phone number—(314) 159-2654—makes it easier to remember. (Congratulate yourself if you recognized that series of digits: with a decimal point after the three, that's the value of pi to ten digits. Remember your last math class?)

- **Work from general information to the specific.** People usually learn best when they get the big picture first, and then look at the details.

- **Eliminate distractions.** Every time you have to "reboot" your short-term memory, you risk losing data points. Multitasking—listening to music or chatting on Facebook while you study—will play havoc with your ability to memorize because you will need to reboot your short-term memory each time you switch mental tasks.

- **Repeat, repeat, repeat.** Hear the information; read the information; say it (yes, out loud), and say it again. The more you use or repeat the information, the stronger the links to it. Some studies have shown you have to repeat some kinds of information as often as seven times before you'll remember it. The more senses you use to process the information, the stronger the memorization. Write information on index cards to make flash cards and use downtime (when waiting for the subway or during a break between classes) to review key information.

- **This is a test.** Test your memory often. Try to write down everything you know about a specific subject, from memory. Then go back and check your notes and textbook to see how you did. Practicing retrieval in this way helps ensure long-term learning of facts and concepts.

- **Location, location, location.** There is often a strong connection between information and the place where you first received that information. Associate information to learning locations for stronger memory links. Picture where you were sitting in the lecture hall as you repeat the information in your mind.

- **Stay healthy.** Like your brain as a whole, your memory functions best when you are physically healthy. Eating well provides nutrients needed for optimum brain function, exercise stimulates nerve cell functions, and a good night's sleep enhances learning and strengthens connections among brain cells.

To remember and use these and other memory tips, download and print the following attachment and post it where you study.

JUST FOR FUN

Choose a specific fact or piece of information from each of your classes on a given day. Now find a way of working that information into your casual conversations during the rest of the day in a way that is natural. Can you do it? What effect do you think that will have on your memory of that information?

EXERCISE YOUR MEMORY

Read the following list for about twenty seconds. After you have read it, cover it or scroll away and then write down all the items you remember.

Arch		Pen
Chowder		Maple
Airplane		Window
Kirk		Scotty
Paper clip		Thumb drive
Column		Brownies
Oak		Door
Subway		Skateboard
Leia		Cedar
Fries		Luke

How many were you able to recall? Most people can remember only a fraction of the items.

Now read the following list for about twenty seconds, cover it, and see how many you remember.

Fries		Skateboard
Chowder		Subway
Brownies		Luke
Paper clip		Leia
Pen		Kirk
Thumb drive		Scotty
Oak		Column
Cedar		Window
Maple		Door
Airplane		Arch

Did your recall improve? Why do you think you did better? Was it easier? Most people take much less time doing this version of the list and remember almost all the terms. The list is the same as the first list, but the words have now been grouped into categories. Use this grouping method to help you remember lists of mixed words or ideas.

6.3 Using Mnemonics

Mnemonics

Tricks for memorizing lists and data.

acronym

A word formed from the initial letters of words in a phrase or series of words, such as "USA" for "United States of America."

What do the names of the Great Lakes, the order of the planets, and the number of days in a month have in common? They are easily remembered by using mnemonic devices. **Mnemonics** (pronounced neh-MA-nicks) are tricks for memorizing lists and data. They create artificial but strong links to the data, making recall easier. The most commonly used mnemonic devices are acronyms, acrostics, rhymes, and jingles.

Acronyms are words or phrases made up by using the first letter of each word in a list or phrase. Need to remember the names of the Great Lakes? Try the acronym HOMES using the first letter of each lake:

- **H**uron
- **O**ntario
- **M**ichigan
- **E**rie
- **S**uperior

To create an acronym, first write down the first letters of each term you need to memorize. Then rearrange the letters to create a word or words. You can find acronym generators online (just search for "acronym generator") that can help you. Acronyms work best when your list of letters includes vowels as well as consonants and when the order of the terms is not important. If no vowels are available, or if the list should be learned in a particular order, try using an acrostic instead.

Acrostics are similar to acronyms in that they work off the first letter of each word in a list. But rather than using them to form a word, the letters are represented by entire words in a sentence or phrase. If you've studied music, you may be familiar with "Every Good Boy Deserves Fudge" to learn the names of the notes on the lines of the musical staff: E, G, B, D, F. The ridiculous and therefore memorable line "My Very Educated Mother Just Served Us Nine Pizzas" was used by many of us to remember the names of the planets (at least until Pluto was downgraded):

acrostic
A mnemonic method in which words in a sentence or phrase work as memory aids for something beginning with the same first letters in the acrostic.

My	Mercury
Very	Venus
Educated	Earth
Mother	Mars
Just	Jupiter
Served	Saturn
Us	Uranus
Nine	Neptune
Pizzas	Pluto

(Now that Pluto is is no longer considered a planet, try ""My Very Educated Mother Just Served Us Nectarines"—see how it easy it is to come up with an acrostic!)

To create an acrostic, list the first letters of the terms to be memorized in the order in which you want to learn them (like the planet names). Then create a sentence or phrase using words that start with those letters.

Rhymes are short verses used to remember data. A common example is "In fourteen hundred and ninety-two, Columbus sailed the ocean blue." Need to remember how many days a given month has? "Thirty days hath September, April, June, and November…," and so forth. Writing rhymes gets easy with practice. To start, keep your rhymes short and simple. Define the key information you want to remember and break it down into a series of short phrases. Look at the last words of the phrases: can you rhyme any of them? If they don't rhyme, can you substitute or add a word to create the rhyme? (For example, in the Columbus rhyme, "ninety-two" does not rhyme with "ocean," but adding the word "blue" completes the rhyme and creates the mnemonic.)

Rhymes
Short verses used to remember data.

Jingles are phrases set to music, and the music helps trigger your memory. Jingles are commonly used by advertisers to get you to remember their product or product features. Anytime you add rhythm to the terms you want to memorize, you are activating your auditory sense, and the more senses you use for memorization, the stronger the memory links. To create a jingle for your data, start with a familiar tune and try to create alternate lyrics using the terms you want to memorize. Another approach you may want to try is reading your data aloud in a hip-hop or rap music style.

Jingles
A phrase that is set to music and is easy to remember.

CREATIVE MEMORY CHALLENGE

Create an acrostic to remember the noble gasses in the Periodic Table of the Elements: helium, neon, argon, krypton, xenon, and radon.

Create an acronym to remember the names of the G8 group of countries: France, the United States, the United Kingdom, Russia, Germany, Japan, Italy, and Canada. (Hint: Sometimes it helps to substitute terms with synonyms—"America" for the United States or "England" for the United Kingdom—to make the acronym easier.)

Create a jingle to remember the names of the Seven Dwarfs: Bashful, Doc, Dopey, Grumpy, Happy, Sleepy, and Sneezy.

Mnemonics are good memory aids, but they aren't perfect. They take a lot of effort to develop, and they also take terms out of context because they don't focus on the meaning of the words. Since they lack meaning, they can also be easily forgotten later on, although you may remember them through the course.

Other Ways to Understand and Remember

Finally, sometimes the issue isn't simply that we forget something but that we don't remember it because we didn't understand it very well to begin with. If our understanding of some information is fuzzy, the memory will be fuzzy—or worse, nonexistent. You've checked your notes, you've looked back at the chapter you read, and something still isn't clear. Maybe you don't have time to go see your instructor to ask for clarification. What to do?

Many students turn frequently to Wikipedia, which can be helpful. Sometimes you just need to read the information again in different words, and then you understand it and can remember it. But often it helps to switch gears, such as by watching a good educational video. Of course you need to be careful: YouTube has a lot of misleading or simply wrong information mixed in with quality videos. Look for material put up by professors and colleges—but be aware that if you start a classroom lecture, you might have to sift through an entire long lecture just to find the one section you need help with.

One highly recommended source of instructional videos useful for beginning college students is the Khan Academy, which has posted videos on more than 4,000 college topics. Search YouTube for "Khan Academy Algebra," for example, to find about a hundred short videos—and then locate the specific one you need to understand a specific problem. Similar searches work in all the basic sciences, history, business, and many other fields of study. In fact, there's even a good video to help you learn the memory tips described in this chapter:

Memory Encoding Strategies

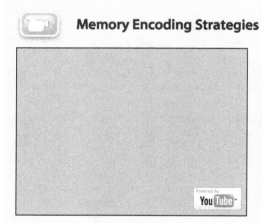

View the video online at: http://www.youtube.com/embed/pMMRE4Q2FGk?rel=0

KEY TAKEAWAYS

- Understanding ideas is generally more important in college than just memorizing facts.
- To keep information in our memory, we must use it or build links with it to strengthen it in long-term memory.
- Key ways to remember information include linking it to other information already known; organizing facts in groups of information; eliminating distractions; and repeating the information by hearing, reading, and saying it aloud.
- To remember specific pieces of information, try creating a mnemonic that associates the information with an acronym or acrostic, a rhyme or a jingle.

CHECKPOINT EXERCISE

1. For each of the following statements, circle T for true or F for false:

T	F	Preparing for class is important for listening, for taking notes, and for memory.
T	F	Multitasking enhances your active memory.
T	F	If you listen carefully, you will remember most of what was said for three days.
T	F	"Use it or lose it" applies to information you want to remember.
T	F	Mnemonics should be applied whenever possible.

7. CHAPTER ACTIVITIES

Chapter Takeaways

Listening

- Learning involves following a cycle of preparing, absorbing, recording, and reviewing.
- The most important difference between high school learning and college learning is that colleges expect you to take full responsibility for your learning. Many of the support mechanisms you had in high school do not exist in college.
- Listening takes place in two primary situations: open interaction with the speaker (social conversation, small group discussions, business meetings, and small classes) and limited interaction with the speaker (lectures, online courses).
- In situations where interaction can occur, active listening principles work well.
- In lecture situations, additional strategies are required, including physical preparation, seating for listening, eliminating distractions, thinking critically about the material as it is presented, taking notes, and asking appropriate questions.
- Prepare for listening by completing all assignments for the class and reviewing the syllabus. Ask yourself what you expect to gain from the class and how that ties in to the rest of the course material.
- Think critically about what you are listening to. Do you agree with what the instructor is saying? How does it tie to the rest of the material in the course? What does this new material mean to you in "real" life?

Note Taking

- There are four primary ways of taking notes (lists, outlines, concept maps, and the Cornell method).
- Select the note-taking method that best serves your learning style and the instructor's teaching style. Remember that methods may be combined for maximum effect.
- Completing assignments and reviewing the syllabus can help you define the relative importance of the ideas the instructor presents.
- Don't expect to capture everything the instructor says. Look for keywords and central ideas.
- Anything the instructor writes on the board is probably important.
- Review your notes as soon as possible after the class, to annotate, correct, complete, and summarize.

Memory

- The two types of memory are short-term memory, which allows you to apply knowledge to a specific task, and long-term memory, which allows you to store and recall information.
- The brain commits information to long-term memory by creating an intricate system of links to that information. Strength, number, and variety of links all lead to better recall.
- To create strong links, start by making a conscious decision to want to commit something specific to memory. Link the information to real life and other data from the course. Group like information to create links among the terms you want to remember.
- Use the information. The more you use the information, the more you will activate the links in your brain.
- Eliminate distractions. Every time you are diverted from your task, you need to reboot your short-term memory, weakening the links.

CHAPTER REVIEW

1. Describe the four steps of active listening.
   _____
   _____
   _____
   _____

2. How is active listening defined?
   _____
   _____
   _____

3. List three things you should do to prepare to listen in class.
   _____
   _____
   _____

4. Where should you sit in a class? Why?
   _____
   _____
   _____

5. What should you do with your notes soon after each class?
   _____
   _____

6. Why do you think the Cornell method of note taking is recommended by so many colleges?
   _____
   _____
   _____

7. How do short-term and long-term memory differ?
   _____
   _____
   _____

8. List three ways in which you can create links to help remember ideas.
   _____
   _____
   _____

9. Why is multitasking dangerous to memorization?
   _____
   _____

10. What is a mnemonic?
   _____
   _____

MAKE AN ACTION LIST

Two things I will do to improve	Action	By when I expect to take the action	How I will know I accomplished the action
My listening	1.		
	2.		
My note taking	1.		
	2.		
My memory	1.		
	2.		

CLASS DISCUSSION QUESTIONS

1. When you are sitting in a large lecture hall, what things could distract you from listening carefully to the instructor? For each, what can you do to avoid the distraction?

2. What kinds of notes did you take in high school or former classes? How does that method compare with the Cornell Method described in this chapter?

3. Without looking back at the earlier reading in this chapter, how many memory tips do you now remember? If less than all of them, why? (Print out the list of tips and post it where you can see it as you study.)

CHAPTER 5
Reading to Learn

FIGURE 5.1

Where Are You Now?

Assess your present knowledge and attitudes.

	Unsure	No	Yes
1. I am a good reader and like to read for pleasure.			
2. I feel overwhelmed by the amount of reading I have to do for classes.			
3. I usually understand what is written in textbooks.			
4. I get frustrated by difficult books.			
5. I find it easy to stay focused on my reading.			
6. I am easily bored reading for classes.			
7. I take useful notes when I read.			
8. I can successfully study for a test from the notes I have taken.			
9. I use a dictionary when needed while reading.			
10. I have trouble reading long passages on the computer screen.			

Where Do You Want to Go?

Think about how you answered the questions above. Be honest with yourself. On a scale of 1 to 10, how would you rate your level of academic reading at this time?

Poor reader   **Excellent reader**

1   2   3   4   5   6   7   8   9   10

In the following list, circle the three most important areas in which you think you can improve:

- Preparing for reading
- Understanding what you read
- Staying focused while reading
- Selecting the best location for reading
- Selecting the best time for reading assignments
- Breaking down assignments into manageable pieces
- Working my way through a difficult text
- Setting priorities for reading assignments
- Reading faster
- Taking notes while reading
- Finding strategies for highlighting and marginal notes
- Reading primary source documents
- Improving my vocabulary

Are there other ways in which you can improve your reading? Write down other things you feel you need to work on.

_____
_____
_____
_____

How to Get There

Here's what we'll work on in this chapter:

- Understanding why reading is so important for college success
- Learning how reading fits into the learning cycle
- Learning how reading in college is different from reading in high school

- Discovering the principles of reading to learn (active reading)
- Knowing where, when, and how long to read
- Discovering the anatomy of a textbook
- Learning tips for reading textbooks in specific subjects
- Learning tips for reading primary sources
- Learning tips for reading digital texts
- Building your vocabulary

1. READING TO LEARN

Sure you can read. After all, that's what you are doing now, at this moment. But reading to learn is an active form of reading, a process that involves much more than passively moving your eyes over a block of text. Reading is a process that you will use for gathering much of the new information you get in school—and in life.

Does the following sound familiar? You've had a full day of classes and work, so you go to the gym to get some exercise. Afterward, you run into a friend who suggests going out for a quick bite; you get back to your place around eight o'clock and settle in to read your assignment, a chapter from your sociology text entitled "Stratification and Social Mobility." You jump right in to the first paragraph, but the second paragraph seems a bit tougher. Suddenly you wake up and shake your head and see your clock says 11:15 p.m. Oh no! Three hours down the drain napping, and your book is still staring back at you at the beginning of the chapter, and you have a crick in your neck.

Now, picture this: You schedule a series of shorter reading periods at the library between classes and during the afternoon. You spend a few minutes preparing for what you are going to read, and you get to work with pen and paper in hand. After your scheduled reading periods, by 5:30 p.m. you have completed the assignment, making a note for a possible paper topic comparing social mobility in India with that of the United States. You reward yourself with a workout and dinner with a friend. At 8 p.m., you return to your room and review your notes, feeling confident that you are ready for the next class.

The difference between these two scenarios is **active reading**. Active reading is a planned, deliberate strategy to engage with a text with the purpose of increasing your understanding. This is a key skill you need to master for college. Along with listening, reading is the primary method for absorbing new ideas and information in college. But active reading also involves the other steps of the learning cycle; it is critical for preparing, capturing, and reviewing, too.

active reading

A conscious process in which the reader chooses to create an interaction with the written word, with the objective of increasing understanding.

FIGURE 5.2   The Role of Reading in the Learning Cycle

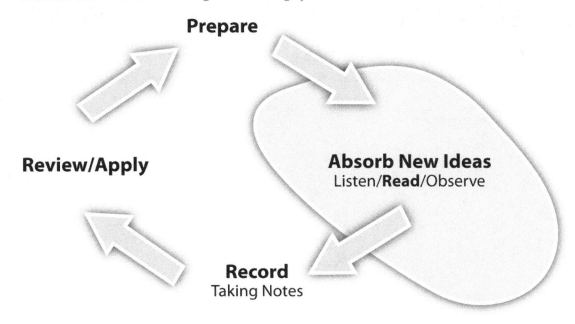

Prepare

Review/Apply

Absorb New Ideas
Listen/**Read**/Observe

Record
Taking Notes

In this chapter, you will learn the basics of active reading. Follow all the recommended steps, even if at first it seems to take longer than just reading as you always have. In the end, you will be able to cut your reading time while increasing what you learn from reading. Read on!

2. ARE YOU READY FOR THE BIG LEAGUES?

LEARNING OBJECTIVES

1. **Explain how reading in college is different from high school and casual reading.**
2. **Understand the importance of reading for college learning.**

Think back to a high school history or English class—probably the classes in which you had the most reading. You were assigned a chapter, or a few pages in a chapter, and then discuss the reading assignment in class. The teacher usually guided you and other students through a review of the reading and asked questions to keep the discussion moving. The teacher usually was a key part of how you learned from your reading.

If you have been away from school for some time, your reading has probably been mostly casual. While time spent with a magazine or newspaper can be important, it's not the sort of concentrated reading needed in college. And no one will ask you to write in response to a magazine piece you've read or quiz you about a newspaper article.

In college, reading is much different. First, you are expected to read much more. For each classroom hour, you are expected to spend two or more hours studying between classes, and most of that involves reading. Assignments are usually longer (a couple of chapters is common, compared with perhaps only a few pages in high school) and much more difficult. College textbooks often use technical terms and include complex ideas. Many college textbooks include research, and some have a style you may find very dry. You may also read a variety of sources: your textbook, **ancillary materials**, **primary sources**, academic journals, periodicals, and online postings—and be expected to bring all this information together in a meaningful way.

In college, most instructors do not spend much time reviewing the reading assignment in class. Rather, they expect that you have done the assignment before coming to class and understand the material. The class lecture or discussion is often based on that expectation, and tests as well. This is why active reading is so important—it's up to you to do the reading and comprehend what you read.

Note: It may not always be clear on an instructor's syllabus, but a reading assignment listed on any given class date should be read *before* the class on that date.

ancillary materials

Additional or supplemental reading materials beyond a standard course textbook. These may include journal articles and academic papers.

primary sources

Documents, letters, diaries, newspaper reports, financial reports, lab reports, and records that directly report or offer new information or ideas, rather than secondary sources (like many textbooks) that collect information that originated in primary sources.

KEY TAKEAWAYS

- College reading is very different from high school reading.
- You must take personal responsibility for understanding what you read.
- Expect to spend about two or more hours on homework, most of it reading, for every hour you spend in class.
- Reading is a primary means for absorbing ideas in the learning cycle, but it is also very important for the other three aspects of the learning cycle.

3.   HOW DO YOU READ TO LEARN?

LEARNING OBJECTIVES

1. **Understand the four steps of active reading.**
2. **Develop strategies to help you read effectively and quickly.**

The four steps of active reading are almost identical to the four phases of the learning cycle—and that is no coincidence! Active reading is learning through reading the written word, so the learning cycle naturally applies. Here are the steps:

1. Preparing
2. Reading
3. Capturing the key ideas
4. Reviewing

Let's take a look at how to use each step when reading.

3.1   Preparing to Read

Start by thinking about why your instructor has chosen this text. Has the instructor said anything about the book or the author? Look at the table of contents; how does it compare with the course syllabus? What do you learn about the author in the book's **front matter**? The table of contents and author define the focus of the book and point toward what is most important in the text. Doing this with each of your textbooks will give you insight throughout the course.

Next, develop a plan of attack for your assignment. Your first step is to understand the context of what you are about to read. Consider the large themes or goals the instructor has spelled out for the class. Remember that you are not merely reading—you are reading for a purpose. What parts of a reading assignment should you pay special attention to? As mentioned earlier, you will do a considerable amount of reading in college, and you will not get through it all by reading each and every word with a high level of focus and mental intensity. This is why it is so important to learn to define where to invest your efforts.

Now open your text to the assigned pages. What is the chapter title? Is the chapter divided into sections? What are the section titles? Which sections are longer? Are there any illustrations, and what are they about? Illustrations in books cost money, so chances are the author and publisher thought these topics were particularly important. How about tables: what kinds of information do they show? Are certain terms put in boldface or a special color? Do you already know these terms, or are they new to you? Are you getting a sense for what is important in the chapter? Use the critical thinking skills discussed in Chapter 3 as you make these observations. Why did the author choose to cover certain ideas and to emphasize specific ideas? What does all this tell you about what is most important for your course? What do you think your instructor wants you to get out of the assignment? Why?

front matter

A publishing term used to describe the first parts of the book that are not part of the actual text. The front matter may include a preface, a foreword, an introduction, biographical profiles of the authors, and the table of contents.

Anatomy of a Textbook

Good textbooks are designed to help you learn, not just to present information. They differ from other academic publications that present research findings, advance new ideas, or deeply examine a specific subject. Textbooks have many features worth exploring because they can help you learn more effectively when reading. In your textbooks, look for the elements listed in the Anatomy of a Textbook table.

TABLE 5.1 Anatomy of a Textbook

Textbook Feature	What It Is	Why You Might Find It Helpful
Preface or Introduction	A section at the beginning of a book in which the author outlines its purpose and scope, acknowledges individuals who helped prepare the book, and perhaps outlines the features of the book.	You will gain perspective on the author's point of view, what the author considers important. If the preface is written with the student in mind, it will also explain how to "use" the textbook and its features.
Foreword	A section at the beginning of the book, often written by an different expert, endorsing the author's work and explaining why the work is significant.	A foreword can give you an idea about what makes this book different from others in the field. It may provide hints as to why your instructor selected the book for your course.
Author Profile	A short biography of the author, suggesting the author's credibility in the subject.	This will help you understand the author's perspective and what the author considers important.
Table of Contents	A listing of all the chapters in the book and often the primary sections within chapters.	The table of contents is an outline of the entire book. It can help you establish links among the text, the course objectives, and the syllabus.
Chapter Preview or Learning Objectives	A section at the beginning of each chapter where the author outlines what is covered in the chapter and what you should expect to know or be able to do at the end of the chapter.	These sections tell you what to pay special attention to. Be sure to compare these outcomes with the objectives stated in the course syllabus.
Introduction	The first paragraph(s) of a chapter, often stating the chapter's key themes. An introduction is also common at the beginning of primary chapter sections.	Introductions to chapters or sections are "must reads" because they give you a road map to the material you are about to read, pointing you to what is truly important in the chapter or section.
Applied Practice Elements	Exercises, activities, or drills designed to let you apply your knowledge gained from the reading. Some features may be accessed via a website that supplements the text.	These features give you a great way to confirm your understanding of the material. If you have trouble with them, go back and reread the section. They also improve your recall of the material.
Chapter Summary	A section at the end of a chapter that confirms key ideas presented in the chapter.	It is a good idea to read this section before reading the body of the chapter. It helps you strategize where to invest your reading effort.
Review Material	A section at the end of the chapter that includes additional practice exercises, review questions, and suggestions for further reading.	Review questions help you confirm your understanding of the material.
Endnotes and Bibliographies	Formal citations of sources used to prepare the text.	These help you infer the author's biases and are important if doing further research on the subject for a paper.

Now, before actually starting to read, try to give your reading still more direction. Are you ever bored when reading a textbook? Students sometimes feel that about some of their textbooks. To prevent this, create a purpose or quest for your reading, which will help you become more actively engaged and less bored.

Start by checking your attitude: if you are unhappy about the reading assignment and complaining that you even have to read it, you *will* have trouble with the reading. You need to get yourself psyched for the assignment. Stoke your determination by setting a reasonable time to do the reading, and schedule some short breaks. Approach the reading with a sense of curiosity and thirst for new understanding. Think of yourself more as an investigator looking for answers than a student doing a homework assignment.

Take out your notebook for the class. Remember the Cornell method of note taking described in Chapter 4 Use the same format here for reading, with a narrow column on the left and a wide column on the right. With reading, taking notes is slightly different. In the Cornell method used for class notes, you took notes in the right column and wrote in questions and comments in the left column after class as you reviewed your notes. When using this system with reading, write your questions about the reading first in the left column (spacing them well apart so that you have plenty of room for notes in the right column while you read). From your preliminary scanning of the pages, as described above, you should already have questions at your fingertips.

Using critical thinking, question what the author is saying. Turn the title of each major section in the chapter into a question and write it in the left column of your notes. For example, if the section title is "The End of the Industrial Revolution," you might write, "What caused the Industrial Revolution to end?" If the section title is "The Chemistry of Photosynthesis," you might write, "What chemical reactions take place to cause photosynthesis, and what are the outcomes?" Note that your questions are related to the topics you are hearing about in class, and they usually require not a short answer but a thoughtful, complete understanding. Ideally, you should not already know the answer to the questions you are writing! (Even if you are familiar with the topic already, look forward to learning something new in your reading .) Finally, also in the left column, jot down any keywords that appear in boldface. You will want to discover their definitions and the significance of each as you read.

ACTIVITY: TRY IT NOW!

Time to take a break from reading this chapter. Choose a textbook in which you have a current reading assignment. Scan the assigned pages, looking for what is really important, and write down your questions using the Cornell method.

Now answer the following questions with a journal entry.

- Do you feel better prepared to read this assignment? How?
- Do you feel more confident?
- Do you feel less overwhelmed?
- Do you feel more focused?

_____

_____

_____

_____

_____

_____

_____

_____

_____

Alternative Approaches for Preparing to Read

In Chapter 4 you may have learned that you are more comfortable with the outline or concept map methods of note taking. You can use either of these methods also with reading. With the outline method, start with the chapter title as your primary heading, then create subheadings for each section, rephrasing each section title in terms of a question.

If you are more comfortable using the concept map method, start with the chapter title as your center and create branches for each section within the chapter. Make sure you phrase each item as a question.

3.2 Now Read

Now you are ready to start reading actively. Take another look at your notes; they are your road map. What is the question you would like to answer in the first section? Before you start reading, reflect on what you already know about the subject. Even if you don't know anything, this step helps put you in the right mindset to accept new material. Now read through the entire section with the goal to understand it. Follow these tips while reading, but do not yet start taking notes or highlighting text at this point:

- Look for answers to the questions you wrote.
- Pay particular attention to the first and last lines of each paragraph.
- Think about the relationships among section titles, boldface words, and graphics.
- Skim quickly over parts of a section that are not related to your key question.

After reading the section, can you answer the section question you earlier wrote in your notes? Did you discover additional questions that you should have asked or that were not evident from the title of the section? Write them down now in your notes. Can you define the keywords used in the text? If you can't do both of these things, go back and reread the section.

3.3 Capture the Key Ideas

Once you can answer your questions effectively and can define the keywords, commit these concepts to your notes and to your memory. Start by writing the answers to your questions in your notes in the right column. Also define the keywords you found in the reading.

Now is also the time to go back and reread the section with your highlighter or pencil to call out key ideas and words and make notes in the margins. Marking up your book may go against what you were told in high school, when the school owned the books and expected to use them year after year. In college, *you* bought the book. Make it truly yours. Although some students may tell you that you can get more cash by selling a used book that is not marked up, this should *not* be a concern at this time—that's not nearly as important as understanding the reading and doing well in the class!

The purpose of marking your textbook is to make it your personal studying assistant with the key ideas called out in the text. Most readers tend to highlight too much, however, hiding key ideas in a sea of color. When it comes to highlighting, less is more. Think critically before you highlight. Your choices will have a big impact on what you study and learn for the course. Make it your objective to highlight no more than 10% of the text.

Use your pencil also to make annotations in the margin. Use a symbol like an exclamation mark (!) or an asterisk (*) to mark an idea that is particularly important. Use a question mark (?) for anything you don't understand or are unclear about. Box new words, then write a short definition in the margin. Use "TQ" (for "test question") or some other shorthand or symbol to signal key things that may appear in test or quiz questions. Write personal notes where you disagree with the author. Don't feel you have to use the symbols listed here; create your own if you want, but be consistent. Your notes won't help you if you later think, "I wonder what I meant by that?"

If you are reading an essay from a magazine or an academic journal, remember that such articles are typically written in response to other articles. In Chapter 4, you learned to be on the lookout for signal words when you listen. This applies to reading, too. You'll need to be especially alert to signals like "according to" or "Jones argues," which make it clear that the ideas came from another author. Be sure to note when an author is quoting someone else or summarizing another person's position. Sometimes students hurrying through a complicated article don't clearly distinguish the author's ideas from the ideas the author argues against. Other words like "yet" or "however" indicate a turn from one idea to another. Words like "critical," "significant," and "important" signal ideas to look at closely.

After annotating, you are ready to read the next section.

3.4 Reviewing What You Read

When you have completed each of the sections for your assignment, review what you have read. Start by answering these questions: "What did I learn?" and "What does it mean?" Next, write a summary of your assigned reading, in your own words, in the box at the base of your notepaper. Working with your notes, cover up the answers to your questions and answer each of your questions aloud. (Yes, out loud. Remember from Chapter 4 that memory is improved by using as many senses as possible.) Think about how each idea relates to material the instructor is covering in class. Think about how this new knowledge may be applied in your next class.

If the text has review questions at the end of the chapter, answer those, too. Talk to other students about the reading. Merge your reading notes with your class notes and review both together. How does your reading increase your understanding of what you have covered in class, and vice versa?

3.5 Strategies for Textbook Reading

The four steps of active reading are a proven approach for effective learning. Here are some strategies you can use to enhance your reading even further:

- **Pace yourself.** Figure out how much time you have to complete the assignment. Divide the assignment into smaller blocks rather than trying to read the entire assignment in one sitting. If you have a week for an assignment, for example, divide the work into five daily blocks, not seven; that way you won't be behind if something comes up to prevent you from doing your work one day. If everything works out on schedule, you'll end up with an extra day for review.

- **Schedule your reading.** Set aside blocks of time, preferably at the time of the day when you are most alert, to do your reading assignments. Don't just leave them for the end of the day after other assignments.

- **Get yourself in the right space.** Read in a quiet, well-lit space. Your chair should be comfortable but provide good support. Libraries were designed for reading—they should be your first option! Don't use your bed for reading textbooks, since it reading in bed is likely associated with going to sleep soon. The combination of the cozy bed, comforting memories, and dry text is sure to invite some shut-eye!

- **Avoid distractions.** Active reading takes place in your short-term memory. Every time you move from task to task, you have to "reboot" your short-term memory and you lose the continuity of active reading. Multitasking—listening to music or texting while you read—will cause you to lose your place and force you to start over again. Every time you lose focus, you cut your effectiveness and increase the amount of time you need to complete the assignment.

- **Avoid reading fatigue.** Read for about fifty minutes, and then give yourself a break for five to ten minutes. Put down the book, walk around, get a snack, stretch, or do some deep knee bends. Short physical activity will do wonders to help you feel refreshed.

- **Read your most difficult assignments early** in your reading time, when you are freshest.

- **Make your reading interesting.** Try connecting the material you are reading with class lectures or other chapters. Ask yourself where you disagree with the author. Approach finding answers to your questions like an investigative reporter. Carry on a mental conversation with the author.

KEY TAKEAWAYS

- Consider why the instructor chose this particular text. Map the table of contents to the course syllabus.
- Understand how the textbook is put together and what features might help you with your reading.
- Plan your reading by scanning the reading assignment first, and then create questions based on the section titles. These help you focus and prioritize your reading.
- Use the Cornell method for planning your reading and recording key ideas.
- Don't try to highlight your text as you read the first time through. At that point, it is hard to tell what is really important.
- At the end of your reading time, review your notes.
- Pace yourself and read in a quiet space with minimal distractions.

CHECKPOINT EXERCISES

1. List the four steps of active reading. Which one do you think will take most time? Why?

   _____
   _____
   _____
   _____

2. Think of your most difficult textbook. What features can you use to help you understand the material better?

   _____
   _____

3. What things most commonly distract you when you are reading? What can you do to control these distractions?

   _____
   _____

4. List three places on your campus or at home that work well for you to do your reading. Which is best suited? What can you do to improve that reading environment?

   _____
   _____
   _____

4. DEALING WITH SPECIAL TEXTS

While the active reading process outlined earlier works well for most assignments, consider additional strategies for reading assignments in certain special subjects.

4.1 Mathematics Texts

Mathematics texts have unique challenges because they have many formulas, charts, sample problems, and exercises. Follow these guidelines:

- Do not skip over these special elements as you work through the text.
- Read the formulas and make sure you understand what all factors and variables are.
- Substitute actual numbers for variables and work through the formula.
- Make formulas real by applying them to real-life situations.
- Do all exercises within the assigned section of text to make sure you understand it.
- Since mathematical learning builds on prior knowledge, do not go on to the next section until you have mastered the material in the current section.
- Seek help from the instructor or teaching assistant during office hours if need be.

Reading Graphics

You read earlier about noticing graphics in your text as a signal of important ideas. But it is equally important to understand what the graphics intend to convey. Textbooks contain tables, charts, maps, diagrams, illustrations, photographs, and the newest form of graphics—Internet URLs for accessing text and media material. Many students are tempted to skip over graphic material and focus only on the reading. Don't. Take the time to read and understand your textbook's graphics. They will increase your understanding, and because they engage different comprehension processes, they will create different kinds of memory links to help you remember the material.

To get the most out of graphic material, use your critical thinking skills and question why each illustration is present and what it means. Don't just glance at the graphics; take time to read the title, caption, and any labeling in the illustration. In a chart, read the data labels to understand what is being shown or compared. Think about projecting the data points beyond the scope of the chart; what would happen next? Why?

Table 5.2 shows the most common graphic elements and notes what they do best. This knowledge may help guide your critical analysis of graphic elements.

TABLE 5.2 Common Uses of Textbook Graphics

Table	Most often used to present raw data. Understand what is being measured. What data points stand out as very high or low? Why? Ask yourself what might cause these measurements to change.
Bar Chart	Used to compare quantitative data or show changes in data over time. Also can be used to compare a limited number of data series over time. Often an illustration of data that can also be presented in a table.
Line Chart	Used to illustrate a trend in a series of data. May be used to compare different series over time.
Pie Chart	Used to illustrate the distribution or share of elements as a part of a whole. Ask yourself what effect a change in distribution of factors would have on the whole.

Map	Used to illustrate geographic distributions or movement across geographical space. In some cases can be used to show concentrations of populations or resources. When encountering a map, ask yourself if changes or comparisons are being illustrated. Understand how those changes or comparisons relate to the material in the text.
 Effect of Postwar Suburban Development City of Oak Hills	
Photograph 	Used to represent a person, a condition, or an idea discussed in the text. Sometimes photographs serve mainly to emphasize an important person or situation, but photographs can also be used to make a point. Ask yourself if the photograph reveals a biased point of view.
Illustration 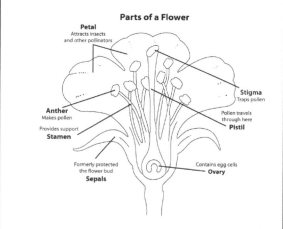	Used to illustrate parts of an item. Invest time in these graphics. They are often used as parts of quizzes or exams. Look carefully at the labels. These are vocabulary words you should be able to define.

Flowchart or Diagram	Commonly used to illustrate processes. As you look at diagrams, ask yourself, "What happens first? What needs to happen to move to the next step?"
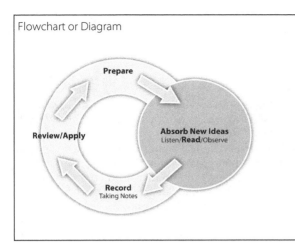	

4.2   Scientific Texts

Science occurs through the experimental process: posing an hypothesis, and then using experimental data to prove or disprove it. When reading scientific texts, look for hypotheses and list them in the left column of your notes pages. Then make notes on the proof (or disproof) in the right column. In scientific studies these are as important as the questions you ask for other texts. Think critically about hypotheses and the experiments used to prove or disprove them. Think about questions like these:

- Can the experiment or observation be repeated? Would it reach the same results?
- Why did these results occur? What kinds of changes would affect the results?
- How could you change the experiment design or method of observation? How would you measure your results?
- What are the conclusions reached about the results? Could the same results be interpreted in a different way?

In scientific texts you also often encounter theories. A theory is a supposition or a system of ideas intended to explain something, often a natural phenomenon being observed. Again, think critically and ask yourself these questions:

- Is the theory being described the author's or is the author reporting a previous or historic theory? If not the author's own, does the author agree with the theory or argue against it?
- What is the nature of the evidence offered in support of the theory? How strong does it appear to be? What evidence in the future might disprove this theory or require revising it?
- Is an explanation being offered or described actually a theory? Or accepted by science as fact?

4.3   Social Sciences Texts

Social sciences texts, such as those read in history, economics, and political science classes, often involve interpretation where the authors' points of view and theories are as important as the facts they present. Put your critical thinking skills into overdrive when you are reading these texts. As you read, ask yourself questions such as the following:

- Why is the author using this argument?
- Is it consistent with what we're learning in class?
- Do I agree with this argument?
- Would someone with a different point of view dispute this argument?
- What key ideas would be used to support a counterargument?

Record your reflections in the margins and in your notes.

Social science courses often require you to read primary source materials. Primary sources include documents, letters, diaries, newspaper reports, financial reports, lab reports, and records that provide firsthand accounts of the events, practices, or conditions you are studying. Start by understanding the author(s) of the document and their agenda. Infer their intended audience. What response did the authors hope to get from their audience? Do you consider this a **bias**? How does that bias affect your thinking about the subject? Do you recognize personal biases that affect how you might interpret the

bias

A personal inclination that may prevent unprejudiced consideration of a question.

document? If the source is historic rather than recent, have things changed over time that affect how you interpret an idea or argument made in the source document?

4.4 Foreign Language Texts

Reading texts in a foreign language is particularly challenging—but it also provides you with invaluable practice and many new vocabulary words in your "new" language. It is an effort that really pays off. Start by analyzing a short portion of the text (a sentence or two) to see what you do know. Remember that all languages are built on **idioms** as much as on individual words. Do any of the phrase structures look familiar? Can you infer the meaning of the sentences? Do they make sense based on the context? If you still can't make out the meaning, choose one or two words to look up in your dictionary and try again. Look for longer words, which often are the nouns and verbs that will give you meaning sooner. Don't rely on a dictionary (or an online translator); a word-for-word translation does not always yield good results. For example, the Spanish phrase "Entre y tome asiento" might be translated word for word as "Between and drink a seat," which means nothing, rather than its actual meaning, "Come in and take a seat."

Reading in a foreign language is hard and tiring work. Make sure you schedule significantly more time than you would normally allocate for reading in your own language and reward yourself with more frequent breaks. But don't shy away from doing this work; the best way to learn a new language is to practice, practice, practice.

Note to English-language learners: Every book you are assigned to read may feel like a foreign language. If you struggle with the high reading level required of college students, check for college resources that may be available to ESL (English as a second language) learners. Never feel that those resources are only for weak students. As a second-language learner, you have a rich linguistic background that many American-born students should envy. You simply need to address the difficulties you'll face and (like anyone learning a new language) practice, practice, practice.

4.5 Integrating Reading with Your Family Life

If you are a parent of young children, you know how hard it is to study with them around. You might want to consider some of these strategies.

- Don't expect that you will often have long periods of uninterrupted time for reading. Find or create short periods of time to do things like scanning the assignment and preparing your questions.
- Schedule your heavy reading for early in the morning or late at night when the children are sleeping. Don't use that precious uninterrupted time for watching television or washing the dishes; those can be done when the kids are awake.
- Read to your children and then tell them it's time for everybody to read their own book. (Even very young children like to "read" books by looking at the pictures.) You'll be surprised how long kids will read, especially when they see Mommy and Daddy reading, too.
- Take your reading with you. You can get a lot of reading done while waiting for your children after soccer practice or while you wait to pick them up at school.
- Share child-care responsibilities with other students who also have children. This can buy an additional big block of reading time for each of you.

4.6 Reading Web Pages

When accessing materials online, you should ask additional questions in order to fully understand the assignment. The Internet provides access to virtually endless numbers of articles on just about any subject. The following steps help you understand the "story behind the story" in online materials and also evaluate the reliability of the material, especially if this is a reading you selected yourself for research or independent work.

1. Look at the **URL**, the web address, which can give you important information about the reliability and intentions of the site. Start with the publisher—do you consider it a reliable source for the kind of material you are about to read? For example, you might happen upon an article about cholesterol from http://www.americanheart.org. This is the website of the American Heart Association, a reputable source of health information. Also consider the domain type: ".com" and ".biz" are used by commercial enterprises, ".org" is normally used by nonprofit organizations, and ".edu" is used by educational institutions. No domain is necessarily bad or good, but it may

give you a sense of the motivation for publishing this material. For example, a different article about cholesterol on a pharmaceutical company's website might be biased toward treatment of high cholesterol with a drug the company makes.

2. With an unfamiliar site, consider whether it comes from a company or an individual—and how that might affect the quality of the information. What can you learn from poking around with navigation tabs or buttons: what do they tell you about the objective of the Web site? Look for a tab labeled "About Us" or "Biography"; those pages will give you additional background on the writer.

3. Check the quality of the information. Based on what you learned earlier, ask yourself if the information from this Web site is reliable for your needs. If the material you are reading was originally published elsewhere, was that publication reputable, such as an academic or peer-reviewed journal or a well-known newspaper? Does the author reference reliable sources? What other websites does the author link to? Are they active and reputable?

4. What are your impressions about the material? You have recently been exposed to related material in your class and textbooks. What does your "gut" say about the material? Ask yourself why the website was written. (To inform and provide data or facts? To sell something? To promote a cause? To parody?) If you are unsure of the quality of the information, don't use it or check first with your instructor or college librarian before you do.

Tips for Studying Websites

Students often discover they do not naturally learn as effectively when reading online materials. Part of this has to do with the nature of the medium: it just may not be as easy to concentrate on screen text as on a book held in one's hands, and certainly it's not as easy to take notes on your reading (even when cutting and pasting key points from the web page to a document file for later use. When the web reading is really important, try printing it out instead and mark it up the same way as described earlier for a textbook, and keep the pages in your textbook or notebook. If the web page has a lot of extraneous material that would clutter up the printout and waste paper and ink to print, look for an add-on for your browser that allows you to print out only what you want (such as "Nuke Anything Enhanced" or "Readability" for the Firefox browser).

A second difficulty with studying web pages has to do with links to other pages. When you click a link in the original page to access more information on a particular point, often that link opens in the same tab, and if you click another link there, you may eventually have difficulty getting back to where you started or be so distracted by shifting your attention that you have to start the original document all over. There's an easy solution, however, involving a little self-discipline. Most browsers let you right-click links to open them in new tabs while you stay on the original page in the working tab. When you see an interesting link you want to check, go ahead and open it—but do it in a new tab and keep it waiting until you finish reading the present section of the original page. Make sure you understand the main points of the main article before changing tabs to read the extra material. Keeping focused this way is much better than jumping all over following links.

Tips for Studying Websites

Students often discover they do not naturally learn as effectively when reading online materials. Part of this has to do with the nature of the medium: it just may not be as easy to concentrate on screen text as on a book held in one's hands, and certainly it's not as easy to take notes on your reading (even when cutting and pasting key points from the web page to a document file for later use. When the web reading is really important, try printing it out instead and mark it up the same way as described earlier for a textbook, and keep the pages in your textbook or notebook. If the web page has a lot of extraneous material that would clutter up the printout and waste paper and ink to print, look for an extension for your browser that allows you to print out only what you want (such as

Additional Resources

University of California Berkeley Library. http://www.lib.berkeley.edu/TeachingLib/Guides/Internet/Evaluate.html

Cornell University Olin and Uris Libraries. http://guides.library.cornell.edu/evaluating_Web_pages

Reading Online Texts

Finally, another special type of textbook is an online text, or e-textbook, read on a computer or tablet rather than from the printed page. (You may be reading this chapter digitally right now.) For many reasons digital texts are becoming more popular in college classes: they are less expensive and more portable than heavy physical books, are more easily updated with new material than a printed book typically updated only every few years, and often include additional materials from embedded videos to links to web pages to interactive exercises. But it is usually a very different experience studying a digital text, compared to a printed book, often requiring students to make some adjustments. Follow these guidelines:

- Follow the same guidelines as given earlier for preparing to read. Get yourself in the right mindset, set up a page for note taking, analyze the major sections of the chapter you're about to read, and pay attention to illustrations, carts, graphs, and key terms.
- Capture key ideas in your notes and review the reading afterwards. Make sure you can answer your questions about the content.
- Follow the guidelines above for reading web pages: complete the reading of a section before following links to other content or multimedia.
- Learn and use the system offered by the online program for taking notes on the page or highlighting important information. (Different e-texts have different functions for interacting with the text and other components; use the system's capabilities fully.
- Watch out for tendencies to multitask while reading; it may be very tempting to switch over to check email or social media, but after any distraction you'll have to "reboot" back into studying the reading.

KEY TAKEAWAYS

- Do all the exercises in math textbooks; apply the formulas to real-world situations.
- Each type of graphic material has its own strength; those strengths are usually clues about what the author wants to emphasize by using the graphic.
- Look for statements of hypotheses and theories when reading science texts.
- History, economics, and political science texts are heavily influenced by interpretation. Think critically about what you are reading.
- Working with foreign language texts requires more time and more frequent breaks. Don't rely on word-for-word translations.
- If you need to read with children around, don't put off your reading until you have a large block of time; there is much you can do with short reading periods.
- Online materials offer endless possibilities, but select websites for information carefully to ensure reliability and currency.
- Take extra steps to avoid distractions when reading e-textbooks and other online materials, taking notes as usual.

CHECKPOINT EXERCISE

Go online and find an article about something you are reading about in a textbook. (Use the earlier steps to evaluate the article.) Scan both the web page and the equivalent textbook section and list your questions for both. Are the questions different, or are many similar? How does each author answer those questions? Which do you think is better written and more authoritative? Why?

5. BUILDING YOUR VOCABULARY

LEARNING OBJECTIVES

1. **Recognize the importance of building your vocabulary.**
2. **Master techniques for building your vocabulary.**

In real life as in education, leaders inspire people to take action by choosing their words carefully and using them precisely. A good vocabulary is essential for success in any role that involves communication, and just about every career and role in life requires good communication skills. And communication is at the very essence of college success. We include this section on vocabulary in this chapter on reading because of the connections between vocabulary building and reading. Building your vocabulary will make your reading easier, and reading is the best way to build your vocabulary.

Learning new words can be fun and does not need to involve tedious rote memorization of word lists. The first step, as always in the learning cycle, is to prepare yourself to learn. Consciously decide that you want to improve your vocabulary; decide you want to be a student of words. Work to become more aware of the words around you: the words you hear, the words you read, the words you say, and those you write.

Do you have a lazy vocabulary? Wake it up with the "lazy speech" exercise:

ACTIVITY: LAZY SPEECH

Recruit a friend you spend a lot of time with. Give them an index card with the following words written on it and ask them to keep a tally of the number of times you say these words sometime when you are together for an hour or more. If practical, ask them to use a recording app on their phone to record you at a time you are not aware of it.

- Ummm or Uhh
- Like
- Well
- You know
- OK
- Yeah
- Ohmigod

Include in this list any other "filler" words, including expletives, that you may be using without thinking.

Are there words you constantly overuse? Were you surprised at how often you used some of these expressions? Now that you are aware of how often you use certain expressions, what can you do to avoid them or substitute more articulate and expressive words?

Building a stronger vocabulary starts with a strong foundation of healthy word use. Just as you can become aware of your overuse of certain words, as in the previous activity, think about the kinds of words you should be using more frequently. You can teach yourself to use stronger, more precise words rather than commonly used informal phrases. For example, many students say he or she "goes" instead of he or she "says"—and often there are still more accurate word choices. Perhaps, he "claims" or she "argues." Maybe he "insists" or "assumes." Or maybe she "believes" or she "suggests." This may seem a small point, but it's important to distinguish among the different meanings. And you can develop greater awareness by bringing some of these words into your speech.

You can develop such habits more easily as you gain a stronger vocabulary. Try these tips:

- **Be on the lookout for new words.** Most will come to you as you read, but they may also appear in an instructor's lecture, a class discussion, or a casual conversation with a friend. They may pop up in random places like billboards, menus, or online ads.

- **Write down the new words you encounter, along with the sentences in which they were used.** Do this in your notes with new words from a class or reading assignment. If a new word does not come from a class, you can write it on just about anything, but make sure you write it. Many word lovers carry a small notepad or a stack of index cards specifically for this purpose.

- **Infer the meaning of the word.** The context in which the word is used may give you a good clue about its meaning. Do you recognize a common word root in the word? (Check Table 5.3 for common roots.) What do you think it means?

- **Look up the word in a dictionary.** Do this as soon as possible (but only after trying to infer its meaning). When you are reading, you should have a dictionary at hand for this purpose. In other situations, do this within a couple hours, definitely during the same day. How does the dictionary definition compare with what you inferred?

- **Write the word in a sentence, ideally one that is relevant to you.** If the word has more than one definition, write a sentence for each.

- **Say the word out loud** and then say the definition and the sentence you wrote.

- **Use the word.** Find occasion to use the word in speech or writing over the next two days.

- **Schedule a weekly review** with yourself to go over your new words and their meanings.

TABLE 5.3 Common Latin and Greek Word Roots

Root	Meaning	Examples
auto	self	automatic, automobile
bi	two	bicycle, biplane
bio	life	biography, biology
chrono	time	synchronize, chronicle
dict	say	predict, dictate
gen	give birth	generate, genetic
geo	earth	geology, geography, geometry
log	thought	biology, logic, pathology
manu	hand	manufacture, manual
phil	love	philosophy, anglophile
port	carry	transport, portable
sub	under	submarine, subtract
vac	empty	vacuum, evacuate

Where Have You Been All My Life?

Here are some fun ways to find new words:

- Read.
- When you look up a word in the dictionary, look at other interesting words on the same page.
- Solve crossword puzzles.
- Play word games like Scrabble, Boggle, or Pictionary.
- Watch movies.
- Listen to speeches and attend lectures.
- Go to comedy clubs.
- Have discussions (not just casual conversations) with friends.
- Read some more.

KEY TAKEAWAYS

- The best way to build your vocabulary is to read, and a stronger vocabulary makes it easier and more fun to read.
- Be aware of your own lazy vocabulary and try to avoid those words and expressions.
- Look for new words everywhere, not just in class readings.
- Before you look up a word in the dictionary, try to infer its meaning based on the context and its roots.
- After you look up a word in the dictionary, write your own sentence using the new word. Say the word and definition out loud.
- Use the new word as soon as possible.

CHECKPOINT EXERCISES

1. Which words do you habitually overuse? Do your friends overuse the same words? How can you collaborate to correct that overuse?

   _____

   _____

   _____

2. During the course of the day, find five new words in five different places. What were those words, and where did you uncover them?

   _____

   _____

   _____

   _____

   _____

3. What do the words "manuscript," "scribe," and "scribble" have in common? Can you detect the same root in these words?

   _____

4. What do you think the root means?

   _____

6. CHAPTER ACTIVITIES

Chapter Takeaways

Reading

- Reading, like learning, involves a cycle of preparing, absorbing, recording, and reviewing.
- In college, you are expected to do much reading; it is not unusual to do two or more hours of reading for every hour you spend in class. In college, you are also expected to think critically about what you read.
- Active reading involves four steps:
  1. Prepare for reading by scanning the assignment and developing questions for which you want to discover answers through your reading.
  2. Read the material and discover the answers to your questions.
  3. Capture the information by highlighting and annotating the text as well as by taking effective notes.
  4. Review the reading by studying your notes, integrating them with your class notes, and discussing the reading with classmates.
- Before you read, learn as much as you can about the author and his or her reason for writing the text. What is his or her area of expertise? Why did the instructor select this text?
- When scanning a reading, look for clues to what might be important. Read the section titles, study illustrations, and look for keywords and boldface text.
- Do not highlight your text until you have read a section completely to be sure you understand the context. Then go back and highlight and annotate the text during a second read-through.
- Think critically about what you are reading. Do you agree with what the author is saying? How does it relate to the rest of the material in the course? What does this new material mean to you in "real life"?

Special Texts and Situations

- Do all the exercises in math textbooks; apply the formulas to real-world situations.
- Practice "reading" illustrations. Each type of graphic material has its own strength or purpose.
- Look for statements of hypotheses and theories when reading science texts.
- History, economics, and political science texts heavily involve interpretation. Think critically about what you are reading.
- Working with foreign language texts requires more time and more frequent breaks. Don't rely on word-for-word translations.
- If you need to read with children around, don't put off your reading until you have a large block of time; learn to read in short periods as available.

- When reading on the Internet, be extra diligent to evaluate the source of the material to decide how reliable that source may be.
- Reading an e-text requires special attention; be sure to use system tools to take notes, and work all exercises.
- If English is your second language, seek out resources that may be offered on campus. Be patient with the process of mastering college-level English. And remember that what feels like a disadvantage in one situation can be a great gift in another situation.

Vocabulary

- Reading and vocabulary development are closely linked. A stronger vocabulary makes reading easier and more fun; the best way to build a vocabulary is to read.
- Look for new words everywhere, not just in class.
- When you encounter a new word, follow these steps:

    1. Write it down and the sentence in which it was used.
    2. Infer its meaning based on the context and word roots.
    3. Look it up in a dictionary.
    4. Write your own sentence using the word.
    5. Say the word, its definition, and your sentence out loud.
    6. Find an opportunity to use the word within two days.

CHAPTER REVIEW

1. Describe the four steps of active reading.
   _____
   _____
   _____
   _____

2. What part of a textbook should you compare with the class syllabus? Why?
   _____
   _____

3. Why is it important to know something about a textbook's author?
   _____
   _____

4. What time of the day should you plan to do your reading? Why?
   _____
   _____

5. What is the difference between using the Cornell method for taking class notes and using the Cornell method for reading notes?
   _____
   _____

6. Why do you think it is important to pose some questions about the material before you read?
   _____
   _____

7. What should you do if you are getting tired when reading?
   _____
   _____

8. List three requirements for a good reading location.
   _____
   _____
   _____

9. Can you multitask while doing a reading assignment? Why or why not?
   _____
   _____
   _____

10. Describe the process of evaluating a web-based or e-text reading selection.
    _____
    _____
    _____

MAKE AN ACTION LIST

Two things I will do to improve	Actions	By when I expect to take the action	How I will know I accomplished the action
My reading comprehension/ understanding	1.		
	2.		
My reading speed	1.		
	2.		
My vocabulary	1.		
	2.		

CLASS DISCUSSION QUESTIONS

1. When you read a work of fiction or poetry, the meaning is often open to interpretation, and two students can have very different ideas about the meaning without one being more "right" than the other. Is the same true of reading a chapter in a college textbook? Why or why not?

2. Why is it important not to skip over illustrations in an assigned reading? What can they bring to the chapter's meaning that might otherwise be lost?

3. If you have read an online or e-text assignment on your computer, what was different about the experience compared to reading a physical book? Did you find it easier or more difficult? Were you distracted in any way? What would you advise a brand-new student about how to transition to reading online?

CHAPTER 6
Preparing for and Taking Tests

FIGURE 6.1

© *Thinkstock*

Where Are You Now?

Assess your present knowledge and attitudes.

	Usually	Sometimes	Seldom
1. I do well on exams.			
2. Exams make me very nervous and anxious.			
3. I usually study for exams at the last minute.			
4. I feel confident going into tests or exams.			
5. When we get pop quizzes, I do OK.			
6. I remember what I've studied long after studying for an exam.			
7. I am overwhelmed by the amount of material I have to study for an exam.			
8. I run out of time when taking exams.			
9. I write good responses to essay questions.			
10. I "draw a blank" during an exam on material I know.			
11. I have trouble understanding what the instructor is looking for on a test.			
12. I lose points for stupid mistakes.			

Where Do You Want to Go?

Think about how you answered the questions above. Be honest with yourself. On a scale of 1 to 10, how would you rate your preparation for tests at this time?

Prepare for tests poorly					Prepare for tests well				
1	2	3	4	5	6	7	8	9	10

On a scale of 1 to 10, how would you rate your test-taking skills at this time?

A poor tester					An excellent tester				
1	2	3	4	5	6	7	8	9	10

In the following list, circle the three most important areas in which you think you can improve:

- Reducing my test anxiety
- Cramming for exams
- Using my study time more effectively
- Feeling confident for an exam
- Staying focused while studying
- Using my time effectively during an exam
- Selecting the right things to study
- Answering multiple-choice questions
- Selecting the best time and place to study
- Answering short answer questions
- Working in effective study groups
- Answering essay questions
- Studying from my notes
- Taking oral exams/giving presentations as exams
- Studying from my text
- Taking online exams

Are there other areas in which you can improve your test preparation and test taking? Write down other things you feel you need to work on.

_____

_____

How to Get There

Here's what we'll work on in this chapter:

- Knowing what exams really are and why the right attitude about them is important for success in college
- Discovering how studying for and taking tests fit in to the learning cycle
- Dealing with test anxiety
- Learning when, where, and how to study most effectively
- Recognizing types of tests and types of test questions
- Learning tips for multiple-choice, true-or-false, fill-the-blank, matching, short answer, and essay questions
- Applying general strategies for tests and exams
- Applying strategies for math and science tests

1. TESTED AT EVERY TURN

Testing is a part of life. Have you ever participated in an athletic event? Completed a crossword puzzle? Acted in a play? Cooked dinner? Answered a child's question? Prepared a cost estimate? All of these are forms of tests because they measure how much we know about a specific subject at a single point in time. Alone, tests are not good measurements about how smart or gifted you are—they show only how much you know or can do at that moment. We can learn from how we have performed, and we can think about how to apply what we have learned to do even better next time. We can even have fun measuring our progress.

Many of our daily activities are measurements of progress toward mastery of skills or knowledge. But when our academic activities are measured by tests, we often dread them. In reality, however, academic tests are like measurements of our knowledge and skills we experience almost everyday:

- They help us measure our progress toward mastery of a particular skill.
- They do not represent how smart, talented, or skilled we are but rather measure only what we know about a specific subject at a specific point in time.
- They are extraordinary learning opportunities.

Tests in college are usually different from those you took in high school. College instructors expect to see much more of *you* in an exam: your thoughts, your interpretations, your thinking process, your conclusions. High school teachers often look for your ability to repeat what you read in your text or heard in your class. Success on high school tests relies much more on memorization than on understanding the material. This is why you need to modify your study habits and your strategies for taking exams in college.

Take a look again at the learning cycle in Figure 6.2 In this chapter, we will cover reviewing and applying the material you learn. This will help you prepare for and take exams more successfully.

FIGURE 6.2   The Learning Cycle: Review and Apply

The end and the beginning of the learning cycle are both involved in test taking, as we'll see. We will discuss the best study habits for reviewing and strategies for applying your knowledge in tests and exams. Finally, we will cover how these review and application processes help prepare you for additional learning.

Let's start at the top of the cycle. You have invested your time in preparing for class, you have been an active listener in class, and you have asked questions and taken notes. You have summarized what you learned and have looked for opportunities to apply the material. You have completed your reading assignments and compared your reading notes with your class notes. And now you're about to face an exam on this material.

Many students then feel a sense of dread. You may worry about the exam and what might be on it. You may stay up all night trying to work through the volumes of material covered so far. Learning or remembering it all may seem hopeless. You may find yourself staring at the same paragraph in your text over and over again, but you just don't seem to get it. As the exam looms closer, you may even feel your understanding of the material is slipping away. You show up to the exam and the first questions look familiar, but then you may draw a blank—you're suffering from test anxiety.

2.   TEST ANXIETY AND HOW TO CONTROL IT

LEARNING OBJECTIVES

1. Learn what test anxiety really is.
2. Gain strategies for controlling anxiety.

Take the true-or-false quiz below (circle T for true or F for false). There are no wrong answers.

ACTIVITY: TESTING YOUR TEST ANXIETY

T	F	I have a hard time starting to study for a test.
T	F	When studying for an exam, I feel desperate or lost.
T	F	When studying for an exam, I often feel bored and tired.
T	F	I don't sleep well the night before an exam.
T	F	My appetite changes the day of the exam. (I'm not hungry and skip meals or I overeat—especially high-sugar items like candy or ice cream.)
T	F	When taking an exam, I am often confused or suffer mental blocks.
T	F	When taking an exam, I feel panicky and my palms get sweaty.
T	F	I'm usually in a bad mood after taking an exam.
T	F	I usually score lower on exams than on papers, assignments, and projects.
T	F	After an exam, I can remember things I couldn't recall during the exam.

If you answered true to any of the statements above, you have suffered some of the symptoms of test anxiety. Most of us have experienced this. It is normal to feel stress before an exam, and in fact, that may be a good thing. Stress motivates us to study and review, generates adrenaline to help sharpen our reflexes and focus while taking the exam, and may even help us remember some of the material. But suffering too many stress symptoms or suffering any of them severely will impede your ability to show what you have learned. **Test anxiety** is a psychological condition in which a person feels distress before, during, or after a test or exam to the point of causing poor performance. Anxiety during a test interferes with your ability to recall knowledge from memory as well as your ability to use higher-level thinking skills well. To learn more about critical thinking and study skills, see Chapter 3 and Chapter 4

Try these steps if you find that stress is getting in your way:

- **Be prepared.** A primary cause of test anxiety is not knowing the material. If you take good class and reading notes and review them regularly, you'll feel less stress. You should be confident going into your exam (but not overconfident).

- **Bounce bad vibes.** Your own negative thoughts—"I'll never pass this exam" or "I can't figure this out, I must be really stupid!"—may in themselves cause enough anxiety to block your best efforts when you're studying for a test. When you feel you are brewing a storm of negative thoughts, stop what you are doing and clear your mind. Let yourself daydream a little; visualize yourself in pleasant surroundings with good friends. Don't go back to work until you feel the tension release. Sometimes it helps to take a deep breath and silently shout "STOP!" and then proceed with clearing your mind. Once your mind is clear, repeat a reasonable affirmation to yourself—"I know this stuff"—before continuing your studying.

- **Visualize success.** Picture what it will feel like to get an A on the test. Translate that vision into specific, reasonable study goals and work toward each individual goal. Take one step at a time and reward yourself for each goal you complete.

- **It's all about you!** Don't waste your time comparing yourself to other students in the class, especially during the exam. Keep focused on your own work and your own plan. Exams are not a race, so it doesn't matter who turns in their paper first. Certainly you have no idea how they did on their exam, so a thought like "Kristen is already done, she must have aced it, I wish I had her skills" is counterproductive and will only cause additional anxiety.

- **Have a plan and follow it.** As soon as you know that an exam is coming, develop a plan for studying. And as soon as you get your exam paper, you should develop a plan for the exam itself. We'll discuss this more later in this chapter. Don't wait to cram for an exam at the last minute; the pressure you put on yourself and the late night will cause more anxiety, and you won't learn or retain much.

- **Make sure you eat well and get a good night's sleep before the exam.** Hunger, poor eating habits, energy drinks, and lack of sleep all contribute to test anxiety.

- **Chill!** You perform best when you are relaxed, so learn some relaxation exercises you can use during exams. Before you begin your work, take a moment to listen to your body. Which muscles are tense? Move them slowly to relax them. Tense them and relax them. Exhale, then continue to exhale for a few more seconds until you feel that your lungs are empty. Inhale slowly through your nose and feel your rib cage expand as you do. This helps oxygenate your blood and reenergize your mind. Chapter 10 has more tips for dealing with stress.

Test anxiety

A psychological condition in which a person feels distress before, during, or after a test or exam to the point where stress causes poor performance.

EXERCISE: TALKING BACK TO BOOGIE TALK

You've learned how negative thoughts contribute to test anxiety and keep you from doing as well as you can. Take some time to disarm your most common negative thoughts. From the following list, select three negative thoughts that you have experienced (or write your own). Then fill in the second and third columns for each statement, as shown in the example.

- I don't know anything... what's the matter with me?
- If I fail this test, I'll flunk the course.
- I should have studied more... I'll never make it through.
- I just can't think... why did I ever take this course?
- I know everyone's doing better than I am.
- If I fail this test, my dad (or husband/wife, boyfriend/girlfriend, teacher) will be mad. I don't know how I can face them again.
- I'm going to be the last one done again... I must really be stupid.
- I'm getting really tense again; my hands are shaking... I can't even hold my pen.
- I can't remember a thing... this always happens to me... I never do well on anything.

My boogie statement	How rational is this thought? Do you have any evidence that it is true?	Reasonable reinforcing or affirmation statements you can use to replace it.
Example: I'm drawing a blank... I'll never get the answer... I must really be stupid.	I've missed questions on things that I studied and knew before.	I studied this and know it. I'll visualize where it's written in my notes to help me trigger my memory.

KEY TAKEAWAYS

- Some stress before a test or exam is normal and can be beneficial.
- Test anxiety is stress that gets in the way of performing effectively.
- The most common causes of test anxiety are lack of preparation and negative attitudes.
- The key to combating test anxiety is to try to reduce the causes to a manageable level rather than try to eliminate them totally.

CHECKPOINT EXERCISES

1. List three things you should do before a test or exam to combat test anxiety.

   _____
   _____
   _____

2. List three things you can do during an exam to reduce stress.

   _____
   _____
   _____

3. STUDYING TO LEARN (NOT JUST FOR TESTS)

LEARNING OBJECTIVES

1. Face tests with confidence, not anxiety.
2. Learn how to use class and reading notes to learn the material, not just to pass tests.
3. Gain key strategies for effective studying.
4. Form and participate in study groups.

You have truly learned material when you can readily recall it and actually use it—on tests or in real-life situations. Effective studying is your most important tool to combat test anxiety, but more important, effective studying helps you truly master the material and be able to apply it as you need to, in school and beyond.

In Chapter 4 and Chapter 5 we set the foundation for effective learning. You learned how to listen and how to take notes. You learned some tricks for improving your memory. You learned how to read actively and how to capture information from written sources. Now we'll follow up on those ideas and take the learning cycle to its conclusion and a new beginning.

The reviewing and applying stage of the learning cycle involves studying and using your course materials. Recall that in Chapter 4 and Chapter 5 we emphasized the importance of reviewing your notes soon after the class or assignment. This review is largely what studying is all about.

Effective studying is an ongoing process of reviewing. **First and most important, studying is not something you do a few days before an exam.** To be effective, studying is something you do as part of an ongoing learning process, throughout the duration of the term.

FIGURE 6.3

Late-night cramming is not an effective studying strategy!

© Thinkstock

3.1 Studying Every Day

Studying begins after each class or assignment when you review your notes. Each study session should involve three steps:

1. **Gather your learning materials.** Take time to merge your class notes with your reading notes. How do they complement each other? Stop and think. What do the notes tell you about your material? What aspects are you unsure about? Do you need to reread a part of your text? Write down any questions you have for your instructor and pay a visit during office hours. It is better to clear up any misconceptions and get your questions answered soon after you are exposed to the material rather than waiting, for two reasons: (1) the question or doubt is fresh in your mind and you won't forget about it and (2) instructors usually build their lessons on material already presented. If you don't take these steps now, you are setting yourself up for problems later in the course.

2. **Apply or visualize.** What does this material mean to *you*? How will *you* use this new knowledge? Try to find a way to apply it in your own life or thoughts. If you can't use the knowledge right away, visualize yourself using the knowledge to solve a problem or visualize yourself teaching the material to other students.

3. **Cement your knowledge.** If you use the two-column note-taking method, cover up the right side of your notes with a piece of paper. Test yourself on the questions in the left column by trying to answer your questions without referring to your notes. How did you do? If you are unsure about anything, look up the answer and write it down right away. Don't let a wrong answer be the last thing you wrote on a subject, because you will most likely continue to remember the wrong answer.

3.2 Studying in Course Units

At the end of each unit, or at least every two weeks or so, use your notes and textbook to write an outline or summary of the material in your own words. (Remember the paragraphs you wrote to summarize each class or reading? They'll be very helpful to you here.) After you have written the summary or outline, go back and reread your outline from the prior unit followed by the one you just wrote. Does the new one build on the earlier one? Do you feel confident you now understand the material?

3.3   Studying before the Exam

At least a week before a major exam, ask yourself these questions: What has the instructor said about what is included on the exam? Has the instructor said anything about what types of questions will be included? If you were the instructor, what questions would you ask on an exam? Challenge yourself to come up with some really tough open-ended questions, and think about how you might answer them. Be sure to go to any review sessions the instructor or your section leader holds.

Now go back and review your outlines. Do they cover what the instructor has suggested might be on the exam? After reviewing your outlines, reread the sections of your notes that are most closely associated with expected exam questions. Pay special attention to those items the instructor emphasized during class. Read key points aloud and write them down on index cards. Make flash cards to review in downtimes, such as when you're waiting for a bus or for a class to start.

3.4   Studying for the Type of Exam

When an exam is approaching, be sure you know what kinds of questions will be on it. If the instructor (or syllabus) has not already clarified the types of test questions will be on the exam, ask. The types of questions give you important clues about what to expect and how to study.

For example, an exam in a large lecture class may be all multiple-choice questions—in part simply because such a test is easier to grade when one instructor has a large number of students. Multiple-choice questions often (but not always) tend to focus more on recalling information and facts; there is usually only one "right" answer to such questions. Multiple-choice questions can also involve higher-level thinking, such as how information can be applied in specific circumstances. If the instructor tells you the exam is primarily short-answer and essay questions, however, this will be a very different sort of test, and you should study somewhat differently. In this case the larger ideas and themes in the material are likely more important than specific facts and information. You will probably be asked to explain such larger concepts, and how *you* think about them may be more important than just recalling what the textbook author wrote. Of course facts and specific information are still important, since you will need to cite specifics to build a larger argument or to explain an idea, but *you* will be able to choose what information to include in your answers rather than needing to be prepared with the specifics for all likely multiple-choice questions.

A later section in this chapter discusses different types of test questions in more detail and offers tips for how to answer each type when you're actually in the test. But knowing the question types ahead of time helps also. In your studying and in study groups, practice answering the types of questions that will be on the exam.

3.5   More Tips for Success

- **Schedule a consistent study-review time for each course at least once a week**, in addition to your class and assignment time. Keep to that schedule as rigorously as you do your class schedule. Use your study time to go through the steps outlined earlier, but not as a substitute for your assignment time.

- **Get yourself in the right space.** Choose to study in a quiet, well-lit space. Your chair should be comfortable but provide good support. Remember that libraries were designed for reading and should be your first option.

- **Minimize distractions.** Turn off your cell phone and get away from Facebook, television, other activities, and chatty friends, roommates, or family members. All of these can cut into the effectiveness of your study efforts. Multitasking and studying don't mix.

- **If you will be studying for a long time, take short breaks at least once an hour.** Get up, stretch, breathe deeply, and then get back to work. (If you keep up with your daily assignments and schedule weekly review sessions for yourself—and keep them—there should be almost no need for long study sessions.)

3.6   Studying in Groups

Study groups are a great idea—as long as they are thoughtfully managed. A study group can give you new perspectives on course material and help you fill in gaps in your notes. Discussing course content will sharpen your critical thinking related to the subject, and being part of a group to which you are accountable will help you study consistently. In a study group, you will end up "teaching" each other the material, which is the strongest way to retain new material. But remember, working together in a group doesn't mean there will be less work for you as an individual; your work will just be much more effective.

Here are some tips for creating and managing effective study groups:

FIGURE 6.4

A study group that is too large is more likely to digress into casual conversation.

© *Thinkstock*

- **Think small.** Limit your study group to no more than three or four people. A larger group would limit each student's participation and make scheduling of regular study sessions a real problem.

- **Go for quality.** Look for students who are doing well in the course, who ask questions, and who participate in class discussions. Don't make friendship your main reason for choosing group members. Meet up with your friends instead during "social time"—study time is all about learning.

- **Look for complementary skills and learning styles.** Complementary skills make for a good study group because your weaknesses will be countered by another student's strengths. When a subject requires a combination of various skills, strengths in each of those skills is helpful (e.g., a group with one student who is really good at physics and another at math would be perfect for an engineering course). Finally, a variety of learning styles is helpful because each of you pick up differing signals and emphases from the instructor that you can share with each other, so you will not likely miss important points.

- **Meet regularly.** When you first set up a study group, agree to a regular meeting schedule and stick to it. Moving study session times around can result in nonparticipation, lack of preparation, and eventually the collapse of the study group. Equally important is keeping your sessions to the allotted times. If you waste time and regularly meet much longer than you agreed to, participants will not feel they are getting study value for the invested time .

- **Define an agenda and objectives.** Focus your study sessions so that you don't get sidetracked. Based on requests and comments from the group, the moderator should develop the agenda and start each session by summarizing what the group expects to cover and then keep the group to task.

- **Include some of the following items on your agenda:**
  - Review and discuss class and assignment notes since your last meeting.
  - Discuss assigned readings.
  - Quiz each other on class material.
  - "Reteach" any aspects of the material that team participants are unsure of.
  - Brainstorm possible test questions and responses.
  - Review quiz and test results and correct misunderstandings.
  - Critique each other's ideas for paper themes and approaches.
  - Define questions to ask the instructor.

- **Assign follow-up work.** If any work needs to be done between meetings, make sure that all team members know specifically what is expected of them and agree to do the work.

- **Rotate the role of moderator or discussion leader.** This helps ensure "ownership" of the group is spread equally across all members and ensures active participation and careful preparation.

KEY TAKEAWAYS

- Effective studying happens over time, not just a few days before an exam. Consistent and regular review time helps you learn the material better and saves you time and anguish as exam time approaches.
- The following are three steps to follow in each study session:
  - Gather your knowledge.
  - Apply or visualize your knowledge.
  - Cement your knowledge.
- Study groups are a great idea—provided they are thoughtfully managed.

CHECKPOINT EXERCISES

1. What do we mean by "gathering your knowledge"?

   _____
   _____

2. What study habits recommended in this section do you want to develop or improve? What specific steps will you take to start working on them?

   _____
   _____
   _____
   _____

3. Think of your toughest course. Which students in that class would you want to include in a study group? Why?

   _____
   _____
   _____
   _____

4. TAKING TESTS

LEARNING OBJECTIVES

1. **Understand the kinds of tests you will take in college and how you can learn from them.**
2. **Learn general strategies to apply when taking tests and quizzes.**

4.1 Types of Tests

formative assessments

A test or quiz used to determine a student's basic understanding of material before taking on more challenging ideas.

summative assessments

A test or exam used by an instructor to determine if a student has mastered the material sufficiently to get credit for the course.

All tests are designed to determine how much you know about a particular subject at a particular point in time. But you should be aware of differences in types of tests because this will help guide how you prepare for them. Two general types of tests are based on how they are intended to be used: **formative assessments** and **summative assessments**.

Formative assessments include quizzes, unit tests, pop quizzes, and review quizzes from a textbook or its online components. Their main objective is to make sure you know the fundamental material before moving on to more challenging topics. Because such quizzes usually don't count as much toward your final grade, many students think they are not very important. In fact, these quizzes are very important, particularly to you; they can help you to identify what you know and what you still need to learn to be successful in the course and to apply the material as the course progresses. A poor result on a quiz may not negatively affect your final grade much—but learning from its results and correcting your mistakes *will* affect your final grade, on the positive side, when you take the midterms and final! This is discussed more in Section 7

Summative assessments include midterms and finals. They are used by the instructor to determine if you have mastered a large portion of course material, and as such, they usually carry a heavy weight toward your final course grade. Because of this, they often cause test anxiety and require more studying.

In addition to this classification by objective, tests can also be grouped into various categories based on how they are delivered. Each type has its own peculiar strategies.

- **Paper tests** are still the most common type of test, requiring students to write answers on the test pages or in a separate test booklet. They are typically used for in-class tests. Neatness and good grammar count, even if it's not an English exam. Remember that the instructor will be reading lots of test papers and will not want to spend time trying to figure out your handwriting. (For machine-scored tests, be sure your pencil marks are done correctly.)

- **Open-book tests** allow the student to consult their notes, textbook, or both while taking the exam. Instructors may give this type of test to see your thoughts and critical thinking more than your memory power. Be prepared to expose and defend your own viewpoints. When preparing for such a test, know where key material is present in your book and notes; create an index for your notes and use sticky notes to flag key pages of your textbook before the exam. Be careful when copying information or formulas to your test answers, because nothing looks worse in an open-book exam than misusing the material at your disposal.

- **Take-home tests** are like open-book tests except you have the luxury of time on your side. Be clear about when the test is due and make sure you submit it on time. (Some instructors will ask you to e-mail your exam to them by a specific time.) Know what the instructor's expectations are for the content of your answers. The instructor will likely expect more detail and more complete work because you are not under a strict time limit and because you have access to reference materials. Also find out if the instructor allows or expects you to collaborate with classmates. Be sure to type your exam and don't forget to spell-check!

- **Presentations and oral tests** are the most complete means for instructors to evaluate students' mastery of material, because the evaluation is highly interactive. The instructor can (and likely will) probe you on certain points, question your assumptions, or ask you to defend your point of view. Make sure you practice your presentation many times with and without an audience (your study group is good for this). Have a clear and concise point of view and keep to the allotted time. (You don't want to miss delivering a killer close if your instructor cuts you off because you lost track of time!) Chapter 7 covers public speaking and class presentations in more detail. Use the same strategies in oral exams.

4.2 Digital Tests

Digital tests are more commonly being used in college courses, including online tests taken by computer in the classroom or out of class as well as other forms of electronic testing. The main advantage of online tests is that they can be computer graded, providing fast feedback to the student (with formative tests) and grading hundreds of exams easily for the instructor (with summative assessments). Since digital tests are computer graded, the instructor's judgment is not involved. Your answers will be either right or wrong; there is no room for partially correct responses.

As always with computer technology, be aware of the chances of a glitch happening. With an exam that you take on your own time, don't wait until the last minute to take the test. Should you have technical problems, you want to have time to resolve the issues. What if your wifi cuts out? What if you're in the library and your battery dies and you forgot your charger? To avoid any conflicts with the testing software, close all other software applications before beginning the testing software.

Like other tests, digital tests maybe timed or not and may allow use of your textbook and notes or not. Digital exams may also use any of the types of test questions mentioned so far or covered in the next section. But digital tests are different when it comes to actual testing experience and what the test system allows you to do, or not do, during the test.

For example, with a paper test, when you first begin, you can easily and quickly flip through the whole test to see how many questions there are, what types of questions are coming, and how to budget your time. For example, if you have 50 minutes and the test has 30 multiple-choice questions followed by an essay question, you might read the essay question first for a sense of how much time you will need for writing; you might, for example, tell yourself to work through the multiple-choice questions in 20 minutes to allow 30 minutes for writing. With a digital test, depending on the system being used, it may be more difficult to quickly see what the whole test looks like. You may be able to see section two only after finishing section one, for example. With digital tests it is especially important to listen in advance to what your instructor says about the size and shape of the test so that you can budget your time in advance.

Another possible difference in digital tests is the ease of changing your answers. You may answer an early question a certain way, but then later on in the test a different question suddenly jars your memory and you realize you need to go back to the earlier question and change your answer. On a paper test this is usually a quick process. You might quickly find the earlier question simply by remembering where it was placed physically on the page. On a digital test you usually can change an answer (but sometimes not after you've completed that section of the test)—but you have to find it first, and that's more time consuming if you have a long series of questions to scroll through. The first time you take a digital test in the system used in a given course, it is crucial to read all operating instructions carefully and understand what you can and cannot do, and take the test accordingly. You can't go whining to an instructor later saying "The computer wouldn't let me change my answer after I clicked the Submit Answers button!"

Digital testing is increasingly being used within larger online "learning systems" that may include reading digital text, experiencing multimedia, working exercises, and finally taking a quiz or test on the material covered. As with other digital tests, many different systems (software) are in use, and the large textbook publishers have developed several different systems for instructor use. This area of education is evolving so quickly that we can't offer specific advice on how to use any one digital system because it will likely have changed before you read this. One thing is certain, however: always take the time to learn everything you can about how the system works and how the instructor is using it. When in doubt, assume your laptop is just like your instructor sitting in front of you: the system knows how long you spend reading a section, it knows whether you clicked a link for an optional video presentation, it knows how much time you spent taking the test—and more. The system may be calculating a "participation grade" for you based on these variables. Newer systems are pushing further still, such as using your webcam to prove it is actually you taking that test at home or to see if you're looking at notes or other things during the test. It can seem creepy to think of "Big Brother" watching you during a test or even just when studying! The key thing, however, is to realize that if you're motivated to do well and are doing the work as your instructor expects, the technology won't get in the way but becomes just another tool to master.

4.3 Tips for Taking Tests

You've reviewed the material for a test and feel confident that you will do well. You have brought your test anxiety under control. What else can you do to ensure success on a test? Learn and apply these top ten test-taking strategies:

1. **Learn as much as you can about the test.** What has the instructor told you about the test? Will it be open book? What types of questions will be on it? Are some parts of the test worth more points than others? Will it be cumulative or just cover the most recent material? Will you have choices about which questions to answer?

2. **Try to foresee the questions likely to be on the test.** What kinds of questions would you include if you were the instructor? Brainstorm possible questions with your study group. Look for possible questions in your notes. Review past quizzes and tests to see what kinds of questions the instructor likes to ask. Above all, take it seriously whenever your instructor warns, "This will be on the test."

3. **Don't be tempted to stay up late cramming. Get some exercise and watch what you eat.** Cramming is not a substitute for doing assignments and studying consistently over time. It is far more important to get a good night's sleep and face your test fresh and well rested. A good workout the day before an exam will help you be fresh and stay focused during the exam (provided you already like to work out; if not, find time to take a long walk). A healthy diet the night before and on the day of the exam will give you energy and concentration to do well on the exam. Include "brain foods," such as those rich in omega-3 oils, and avoid "heavy" foods that are rich in fat and sugar.

4. **Get to the test site early.** Take out all your allowable tools (pencils, pens, calculator, etc.). Turn off your cell phone (all the way off, not on vibrate) to disconnect from your everyday world. Do some of the relaxation exercises described earlier for controlling test anxiety.

5. **Create a test plan.** Listen carefully to the instructor's opening instructions. When you receive your test, scan the entire test first. Evaluate the importance of each section. Then create a time allocation plan. Decide how much time you should dedicate to each section. You don't want to spend 80% of your time on a question worth 10% of the grade.

6. **Write it down.** Take a couple minutes to write down key facts, dates, principles, statistics, and formulas on a piece of scratch paper or in the margin of the exam paper. Do this while you are still fresh and aren't yet feeling time pressure (when it will be harder to remember them). Then you can refer to these notes as you take the exam.

7. **Read the question directions carefully.** Then reread them. Do you understand what is expected of you? If not, ask the instructor to be sure you are clear. Too many students lose points simply by not following directions completely!

8. **Do the easy questions first.** By getting the easy questions out of the way, you'll feel more confident about the test and have more time to think about the tougher questions. Start with the

objective sections of the exam first (multiple choice, true or false, and matching questions). As you answer these questions, keep an eye out for facts or concepts you may want to use later in an essay question.

9. **Keep an eye on the time.** Keep as close to your plan as possible. If you see that you are running out of time, don't panic. Move to those questions you think you can still answer accurately within the remaining time.

10. **Check your work.** This doesn't mean going through all your calculations again. Start by ensuring that you have *complete* answers according to the directions. Then look for other common mistakes, such as a misplaced decimal point, dropped words (especially those that can modify the answer, like "not"), and any incomplete or incomprehensible phrases.

Strategies for Math and Science Exams

Math tests require some special strategies because they are often based on problems rather than questions.

Do the following before the test:

- Attend all classes and complete all assignments. Pay special attention to working on all assigned problems. After reviewing problems in class, take careful notes about what you did incorrectly. Repeat the problem and do a similar one as soon as possible. It is important that the last solution to a problem in your mind is a correct solution.

- Think about how each problem solution might be applied in a real-world situation. This helps make even the most complex solutions relevant and easier to learn.

- In your study group, take turns presenting solutions to problems and observing and correcting everyone's work.

- If you are having difficulty with a concept, get help right away. Remember that math especially builds new material on previous material, so if you are having trouble with a concept now, you are likely to have trouble going forward. Make an appointment with your instructor, your teaching assistant, or a skilled classmate. Check with your college's academic support office to see about a tutor. Don't be shy about asking for a tutor—tutoring is not just for students needing remedial help; many successful students seek them out, too.

Do this during the test:

- Review the entire test before you start and work the problems you feel most confident with first.

- Approach each problem following three distinct steps:

  1. Read the problem through twice: first to get the full concept of the question, and second, to draw out pertinent information. After you read the problem the first time, ask yourself, "What is this problem about?" and "What is the answer likely to look like?" The second time through, consider these questions: "What facts do I have available?" "What do I know?" "What measurable units must the answer be in?" Think about the operations and formulas you will need to use. Try to estimate a ballpark answer.

  2. Calculate your answer. First, eliminate as many unknowns as possible. You may need to use a separate formula for each unknown. Work through algebraic formulas as far as you can before plugging in actual numbers; that will make it easier to cancel and combine factors. Remember that you may need two or more tries before you come up with the answer.

  3. Check your work. Start by comparing your actual answer to the estimate you made when you first read the problem. Does your final answer sound likely? Check your arithmetic by opposite operations: use multiplication to check division and addition to check subtraction, and so on.

Try using these three steps with any math problems, not just when you get problems on tests.

Science tests also are often based on problems, but they also generally use the scientific method. This is why science tests may require some specific strategies.

- Before the test, review your lab notes, class notes, and assignments. Many exam questions build on lab experience, so pay close attention to your notes, assignments, and labs. Practice describing the experimental process.

- Read the question carefully. What does the instructor expect you to do? Prove a hypothesis? Describe an experiment? Summarize research? Underline the words that state the objective of the question.

■ Look carefully at any diagrams given with the question. What do they illustrate? Why are they included with the question? Are there elements on the diagram you are expected to label?

■ Many science questions are based on the scientific method and experimental model. When you read the test question, identify any hypothesis involved in the problem; be prepared to describe an experimental structure to prove a hypothesis. When you check your work, make sure the hypothesis, experimental steps, and a summary of results (or expected results) are clear. Some of these elements may be part of the question, while others you may need to provide in your answer.

KEY TAKEAWAYS

- There is no such thing as an unimportant quiz.
- In addition to studying, prepare for exams and quizzes by getting plenty of rest, eating well, and getting some exercise the day before the exam.
- Cramming is seldom a good strategy.
- Before the exam, learn as much as you can about the kinds of questions on it and the specific material that will be covered.
- The first step to a successful exam is to browse the entire exam and develop a plan (including a "time budget") for completing the exam.
- Read questions carefully. Underline keywords in questions, particularly in essay questions and science questions.

5. THE SECRETS OF THE Q AND A'S

LEARNING OBJECTIVES

1. **Understand the five main types of questions.**
2. **Gain specific strategies for addressing each type of question.**

You will have even more confidence in your test-taking abilities when you understand the different kinds of questions an instructor may ask and apply the following proven strategies for answering them. Most instructors use various conventional types of questions. Here are some tips for handling the most common types.

5.1 Multiple-Choice Questions

■ Read the instructions carefully to determine if there may be more than one right answer. If there are multiple right answers, does the instructor expect you to choose just one, or do you need to mark all correct options?

■ Read each question carefully and try to answer it in your head *before* reading the answer options. Then consider *all* the options. Eliminate first the options that are clearly incorrect. Compare the remaining answers with your own answer before choosing one.

■ Look for clue words that hint that certain option answers might be correct or incorrect. Absolute words like "never," "always," "every," or "none" are rarely found in a correct option. Less absolute words like "usually," "often," or "rarely" are regularly found in correct options.

■ Be on the lookout for the word "not" in the stem phrase and in answer choice options; it is an easy word to miss if you are reading too quickly, but it completely changes the meaning of the possible statements.

■ Unless points are deducted for a wrong answer, it pays to make an educated guess—don't just leave a question unanswered.

5.2 True-or-False Questions

■ Most of the tips for multiple-choice questions apply here as well. Be particularly aware of the words "never," "always," "every," "none," and "not" because they can make an answer choice incorrect.

- Answer the questions that are obvious to you first. Then go back to statements that require more thought.

- If the question is stated in the positive, restate it to yourself in the negative by adding the word "not" or "never." Does the new statement sound truer or more false?

- If you still are unsure whether a statement is true or false and must guess, choose "true" because most tests include more true statements than false (but don't guess if a wrong answer penalizes you more than one left blank).

5.3   Matching Columns

- Start by looking at the two columns to be matched. Is there an equal number of items in both columns? If not equal, do you have to match some items in the shorter column to two or more items in the longer column, or can you leave some items unmatched? Read the directions to be sure.

- If one column has a series of single words to be matched to phrases in the other column, read all the phrases first, then all the single words before trying to make any matches. Now go back and read each phrase and find the word that best suits the phrase.

- If both columns have single words to be matched, look to cut down the number of potential matches by grouping them by parts of speech (nouns with nouns, verbs with verbs, etc.).

- As always, start by making the matches that are obvious to you, and then work on the ones that require more thought. Mark off all items you have already used so you can easily see which words or phrases still remain to be matched.

5.4   Short Answer Questions

- Short answer questions are designed for you to recall and provide some very *specific* information (unlike essay questions, which also ask you to apply critical thinking to that information). When you read the question, ask yourself what exactly the instructor wants to know. Keep your answers short and *specific*.

5.5   Essay Questions

- Essay questions are used by instructors to evaluate your thinking and reasoning applied to the material covered in a course. Good essay answers are based on *your* thoughts, supported by examples from classes and reading assignments.

- Careful planning is critical to answering essay questions effectively. Note how many essay questions you have to answer and how difficult each question seems. Then allocate your time accordingly.

- Read the question carefully and underline or circle keywords. Watch for words that reveal the instructor's expectations for your response (see Table 6.1).

- If time allows, organize your thoughts by creating a quick outline for your essay. This helps ensure that you don't leave out key points, and if you run out of time, it may pick up a few points for your grade. Jot down specific information you might want to use, such as names, dates, and places. Chapter 8 discusses outlining and other aspects of the writing process in more detail.

- Introduce your essay's main idea, but get right to the point. Remember that the instructor will be grading dozens of papers and avoid "filler" text that does not add value to your answer. For example, rather than writing, "In our study of the Civil War, it is helpful to consider the many facets that lead to conflict, especially the economic factors that help explain this important turning point in our nation's history," write a more direct and concise statement like this: "Economic factors help explain the start of the Civil War."

- Write neatly and watch your grammar and spelling. Allow time to proofread your essay. You want your instructor to want to read your essay, not dread it. Remember that grading essays is largely subjective, and a favorable impression can lead to more favorable grading.

- Be sure to answer all parts of the question. Essay questions often have more than one part. Remember, too, that essay questions often have multiple acceptable answers.

FIGURE 6.5

An essay test requires careful planning of what you want to write.

© Thinkstock

TABLE 6.1 Words to Watch for in Essay Questions

Word	What It Means	What the Instructor Is Looking For
Analyze	Break concept into key parts	Don't just list the parts; show how they work together and illustrate any patterns.
Compare	Show similarities (and sometimes differences) between two or more concepts or ideas	Define the similarities and clearly describe how the items or ideas are similar. Give examples. Do these similarities lead to similar results or effects? Note that "compare" is often combined with "contrast." If so, make sure you do both.
Contrast	Show differences between two or more concepts or ideas	Define the differences and clearly describe how the items or ideas are different. Give examples. How do these differences result in different outcomes? Note that "contrast" is often combined with "compare." If so, make sure you do both.
Critique	Judge and analyze	Explain what is wrong—and right—about a concept. Include your own judgments, supported by evidence and quotes from experts that support your point of view.
Define	Describe the meaning of a word, phrase, or concept	Define the concept or idea as your instructor did in class—but use your own words. If your definition differs from what the instructor presented, support your difference with evidence. Keep this type of essay short. Examples can help illustrate a definition, but remember that examples alone are *not* a definition.
Discuss	Explain or review	Define the key questions around the issue to be discussed and then answer them. Another approach is to define pros and cons on the issue and compare and contrast them. In either case, explore all relevant data and information.
Explain	Clarify, give reasons for something	Clarity is key for these questions. Outline your thoughts carefully. Proofread, edit, proofread, and proofread again! Good explanations are often lost in too many words.
Illustrate	Offer examples	Use examples from class material or reading assignments. Compare and contrast them to other examples you might come up with from additional reading or real life.
Prove	Provide evidence and arguments that something is true	Instructors who include this prompt in an exam question have often proven the hypothesis or other concepts in their class lectures. Think about the kind of evidence the instructor used and apply similar types of processes and data.
Summarize	Give a brief, precise description of an idea or concept	Keep it short, but cover all key points. This is one essay prompt where examples should not be included unless the instructions specifically ask for them. (For example, "Summarize the steps of the learning cycle and give examples of the main strategies you should apply in each one.")

CHECKPOINT EXERCISE

Test your test knowledge.

FIGURE 6.6 Crossword

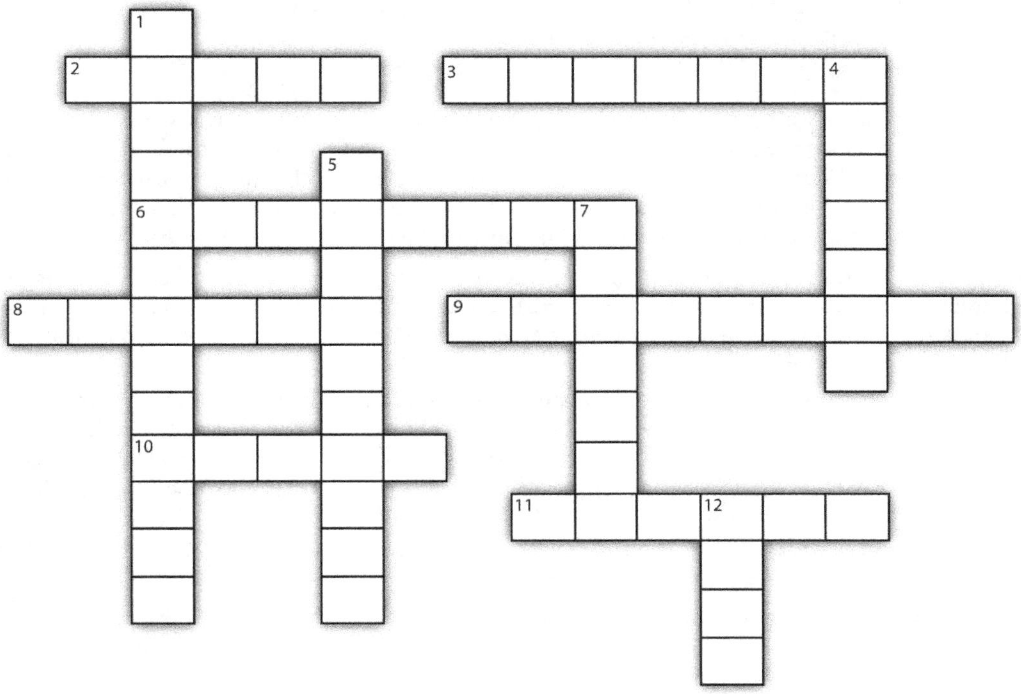

Across	Down
2. "Always," "never," and "every" are words that usually indicate the statement is _____.	1. It helps to group words in matching columns by _____ ___ _____.
3. A way to organize your thoughts for an essay	4. Clarify, give reasons for something
6. Short answer questions require a _____ answer.	5. Essay questions often have more than one _____ answer.
8. Describe the meaning of a word	7. Show similarities and differences
9. Give a brief, precise description of an idea or concept	12. Most common answer in true and false questions
10. Type of question used to evaluate thinking and reasoning	
11. Since instructors need to read many essays, it is important to write _____.	

6. THE HONEST TRUTH

LEARNING OBJECTIVES

1. **Understand the importance of academic integrity and the consequences of dishonesty.**
2. **Identify the most common types of academic dishonesty.**

academic dishonesty

Cheating or using any unauthorized or unacceptable material in academic activities such as assignments and tests; turning in work that is not your own under your name.

Throughout this book we have focused on the process of *active learning*, not just how to get good grades. The attitude of some students that grades are the end-all in academics has led many students to resort to **academic dishonesty** to try to get the best possible grades or handle the pressure of an exam or writing assignment. Although you may be tempted when you hear people say, "Everybody does it," or "It's no big deal at my school," you should be mindful of the consequences of cheating:

- **You don't learn as much.** Cheating may get you the right answer on a particular exam question, but it won't teach you how to apply knowledge in the world after school, nor will it give you a foundation of knowledge for learning more advanced material. When you cheat, you cheat yourself out of opportunities.

- **You risk failing the course or even expulsion from school.** Academic dishonesty generally means cheating, plagiarism, and fabrication or falsification. The exact details of what is allowed or not allowed vary somewhat among different colleges and even instructors, so you should be sure to check your college's website and your instructor's guidelines to see what rules apply. Ignorance of the rules is seldom considered a valid defense.

- **Cheating causes stress.** Fear of getting caught will cause you stress and anxiety; this will get in the way of performing well with the information you *do* know.

- **You're throwing away your money and time.** Getting a college education is a big investment of money and effort. You're simply not getting your full value when you cheat, because you don't learn as much.

- **You are trashing your integrity.** Cheating once and getting away with it makes it easier to cheat again, and the more you cheat, the more comfortable you will feel with giving up your integrity in other areas of life—with perhaps even more serious consequences.

- **Cheating lowers your self-esteem.** If you cheat, you are telling yourself that you are simply not smart enough to handle learning. It also robs you of feeling satisfied with genuine success.

FIGURE 6.7

Resist the temptation to cheat by using material from the Internet.

© *Thinkstock*

Technology has made it easier to cheat. Your credit card and an Internet connection can procure a paper for you on just about any subject and length. You can copy and paste for free from various websites. Students have made creative use of texting and video on their cell phones to gain unauthorized access to material during exams. But be aware that technology has also created ways for instructors to easily detect these forms of academic dishonesty. For example, programs can detect whether a piece of writing came from somewhere on the web even if a student modifies it somewhat. Most colleges make these tools available to their instructors. Instructors are also modifying their testing approaches to reduce potential academic misconduct by using methods that are harder to cheat at (such as in-class essays that evaluate *your* thinking and oral presentations).

If you feel uneasy about doing something in your college work, trust your instincts. Confirm with the instructor that your intended form of research or use of material is acceptable. Cheating just doesn't pay.

Examples of Academic Dishonesty

Academic dishonesty can take many forms, some of which are even accidental, and you should be careful to avoid them. The following list from Northwestern University is a clear and complete compilation of what most institutions will consider unacceptable academic behavior.

1. **Cheating:** using unauthorized notes, study aids, or information on an examination; altering a graded work after it has been returned, then submitting the work for regrading; allowing another person to do one's work and submitting that work under one's own name; submitting identical or similar papers for credit in more than one course without prior permission from the course instructors.

2. **Plagiarism:** submitting material that in part or whole is not entirely one's own work without attributing those same portions to their correct source.

3. **Fabrication:** falsifying or inventing any information, data or citation; presenting data that were not gathered in accordance with standard guidelines defining the appropriate methods for collecting or generating data and failing to include an accurate account of the method by which the data were gathered or collected.

4. **Obtaining an Unfair Advantage:** (a) stealing, reproducing, circulating or otherwise gaining access to examination materials prior to the time authorized by the instructor; (b) stealing, destroying, defacing or concealing library materials with the purpose of depriving others of their use; (c) unauthorized collaboration on an academic assignment; (d) retaining, possessing, using or circulating previously given examination materials, where those materials clearly indicate that they are to be returned to the instructor at the conclusion of the examination; (e) intentionally obstructing or interfering with another student's academic work; or (f) otherwise undertaking activity with the purpose of creating or obtaining an unfair academic advantage over other students' academic work.

5. **Aiding and Abetting Academic Dishonesty:** (a) providing material, information, or other assistance to another person with knowledge that such aid could be used in any of the violations stated above, or (b) providing false information in connection with any inquiry regarding academic integrity.

6. **Falsification of Records and Official Documents:** altering documents affecting academic records; forging signatures of authorization or falsifying information on an official academic document, grade report, letter of permission, petition, drop/add form, ID card, or any other official University document.

7. **Unauthorized Access** to computerized academic or administrative records or systems: viewing or altering computer records, modifying computer programs or systems, releasing or dispensing information gained via unauthorized access, or interfering with the use or availability of computer systems or information.[1]

KEY TAKEAWAYS

- Being dishonest can have major consequences that can affect not only your college career but also your life beyond college.
- "Everybody does it" and "It's no big deal at my school" are not valid excuses for cheating.
- When you cheat, you are primarily cheating yourself.

CHECKPOINT EXERCISES

1. What are the most common forms of academic dishonesty you have heard about at your school? What should be done about them?

   _____

   _____

   _____

2. What resources do you have on campus to learn about correct forms of referencing other people's work in your own?

   _____

   _____

   _____

7. USING TEST RESULTS

L E A R N I N G   O B J E C T I V E S

1. **Effectively evaluate your test results and correct your mistakes.**
2. **Use your test results as a study guide.**

So far, we have focused on how to study for and take tests effectively. This section discusses how to *use* your test results later on to their greatest benefit. Some of your most important learning begins when your graded test is returned to you. Your first reaction, of course, is to see what grade you received and wonder how you did compared with your classmates. This is a natural reaction.

Make sure you listen to the instructor as the tests are returned. What does the instructor say about the test? Is there a particular point everyone had trouble with? Does the instructor generally think everyone did well? The instructor's comments at this point may give you important information about what you should study more, about the value of review sessions, and even about possible questions for the next exam.

Although you may be tempted to throw away the exam, don't. It is a very helpful tool for the next phase of preparing for learning. This involves a three-step process, beginning with evaluating your results.

7.1 Evaluating Your Test Results

When you receive your test back, sit quietly and take a close look at it. What questions did you get wrong? What kind of mistakes were they? (See Table 6.2) Do you see a pattern? What questions did you get right? What were your strengths? What can you learn from the instructor's comments?

Now think about how you prepared for the exam and the extent to which you applied the exam strategies described earlier in this chapter. Were you prepared for the exam? Did you study the right material? What surprised you? Did you read the entire test before starting? Did your time allocation work well, or were you short of time on certain parts of the exam?

TABLE 6.2 Exam Errors and How to Correct Them

Type of Error	Examples	Corrective Steps
Study and Preparation Errors	I did not study the material for that question (enough).	Practice predicting possible questions.
	I ran out of time.	Join a study group.
	I did not prepare enough.	Read the entire test before starting. Allocate your time.
Focus Errors or Carelessness	I did not read the directions carefully.	Allocate exam time carefully.
	I confused terms or concepts that I actually know well.	Give yourself time to read carefully and think before answering a question.
	I misread or misunderstood the question.	
Content Errors	I studied the material but couldn't make it work with the question	Seek additional help from the instructor.
	I didn't understand what the instructor wanted.	Go to all classes, labs, and review sessions.
	I confused terms or concepts.	Join a study group.
		Check and practice your active reading and listening skills.
		Schedule regular study time for this course.
Mechanical Errors	The instructor misread my writing.	Slow down! Don't rush through the exam. Take the time to write clearly.
	I didn't erase a wrong answer completely (on a computer-graded answer sheet).	
	I forgot to go back to a question I had skipped over.	
	I miscopied some calculations or facts from my worksheet.	

Based on your analysis of your test results, identify what corrective steps to take to improve your learning and test performance. Implement those steps as you begin your preparation for your next class. If you don't learn from your mistakes, you are doomed to repeat them; if you don't learn from your successes, it will be harder to repeat them.

7.2   Correcting Your Mistakes

The second step in making your test work for you is to correct your wrong answers. The last time you wrote the information (when you took the test), you created a link to wrong information in your memory, so that must be corrected.

- For multiple-choice questions, write out the question stem with the correct answer to form a single correct sentence or phrase.
- For true-or-false questions, write the full statement if it is true; if it is false, reword it in such a way that it is true (such as by inserting the word "not"). Then write the new statement.
- For math and science questions involving calculations, redo the entire solution with the calculations written out fully.
- You need not rewrite an entire essay question if you did not do well, but you should create a new outline for what would be a correct answer. Make sure you incorporate any ideas triggered by your instructor's comments.
- When you have rewritten all your answers, read them all out loud before incorporating your new answers in your notes.

7.3   Integrating Your Test into Your Study Guide

Your corrected quizzes and exams are an important study tool for the course final exam. Make sure you file them with your notes for the study unit. Take the time to annotate your notes based on the exam. Pay particular attention to any gaps in your notes on topics that appeared in the quiz or exam. Research those points in your text or online and complete your notes. Review your exams throughout the term (not just before the final) to be sure you cement the course material into your memory.

When you prepare for the final exam, start by reviewing your quizzes and other tests to predict the kinds of questions the instructor may ask on the final. This helps focus your final studying when you have a large amount of coursework to cover.

7.4   If You Don't Get Your Test Back

If your instructor does not return tests to students, make an appointment to see the instructor soon after the test to review it and your performance. Take notes on what you had trouble with and the correct answers. Add these notes into your study guide. Make sure you don't lose out on the opportunity to learn from your results.

KEY TAKEAWAYS

- The meaning of an exam does not end when your instructor hands back your graded test.
- Quizzes and midterms are reliable predictors of the kind of material that will be on the final exam.
- When evaluating your test performance, don't look only at the content you missed. Identify the types of mistakes you commonly make and formulate plans to prevent these mistakes in future assessments.

CHECKPOINT EXERCISES

1. Take time to examine your notes for each course you are now taking. Are your past exams and quizzes part of that package? If not, include them now. Review them this week.

2. Compare your exams across two or three courses. What kinds of mistakes do you make on a regular basis? Is there a trend you need to correct?

_____

_____

_____

_____

8. CHAPTER ACTIVITIES

CHAPTER REVIEW I

1. What is test anxiety? What are the three causes of test anxiety you would like to work on controlling?

     _____

     _____

     _____

     _____

2. When should you start studying for an exam?

     _____

3. Can you multitask while studying? Why or why not?

     _____

     _____

4. What are some of the most common distractions to your studying?

     _____

     _____

5. Describe the characteristics of a successful study group.

     _____

     _____

6. What are the two types of assessment? Which of these might be called the "student's assessment"? Why?

     _____

     _____

     _____

7. Why would an instructor assign an open-book exam? What types of things should you pay attention to if you are taking an open-book exam?

     _____

     _____

     _____

     _____

8. How might you predict the kinds of questions that will be on an exam?

     _____

     _____

     _____

9. What should you do right after the instructor hands out the exam?

     _____

     _____

10. List five words to watch for in multiple-choice and true-or-false questions.

     _____

     _____

11. List five words to watch for in essay questions.

     _____

     _____

12. What forms of academic dishonesty are most prevalent on your campus? What can you do to avoid them in your own academic career?

     _____

     _____

     _____

13. List the five most common types of errors made on exams.

     _____

     _____

     _____

14. What should you do with your exam after is has been graded and returned to you?

     _____

     _____

CHAPTER REVIEW II

The following test will allow you to practice the strategies for each question type outlined in Chapter Review I:

I. Multiple-choice section (10 points)

1. All actions on this list are examples of academic dishonesty except

    a. copying from a classmate
    b. using another author's words without appropriate credit
    c. chewing gum in class
    d. creating fictitious data to support a point

2. To avoid running out of time on a test, you should

    a. write quickly, even if it's not so neat
    b. stick with a difficult question until you get a right answer so that you don't have to come back to it later
    c. spend time reviewing the entire test before you start to budget your time
    d. frequently ask your instructor to tell you how much time is left

II. True-or-false section (10 points)

1. _____ You should never use examples when an essay question asks you to illustrate.
2. _____ Beds are a good place to study because they are comfortable and quiet.
3. _____ It's smart to schedule a specific and consistent time for studying for each course.
4. _____ In true-or-false questions, it is safer to mark true than false if you don't know the answer.
5. _____ One advantage of studying in a group is that students can encourage each other to do their best work.

III. Matching column section (10 points)

_____ 1. Define	A. A type of formative assessment
_____ 2. Study group	B. To describe pros and cons and compare them
_____ 3. Weekly quiz	C. To describe the meaning of a word, phrase, or concept
_____ 4. Discuss	D. Your own personalized study guide
_____ 5. Class and assignment notes	E. Three or four students from a class who meet regularly to review class material and encourage each other

IV. Short answer section (15 points)

1. List three things you should do before a test to prepare your brain to perform effectively.

    _____
    _____
    _____

2. Name at least three characteristics of successful study groups.

    _____
    _____
    _____

3. List at least four steps you should take before you start writing the answer to an essay question.

    _____
    _____
    _____
    _____

V. Essay section (Choose one; 55 points)

1. Compare and contrast effective studying and cramming.
2. Discuss academic dishonesty and its consequences.

MAKE AN ACTION LIST

Two things I will do to...	Actions	By when I expect to take each action	How I will know I accomplished each action
Reduce my test anxiety	1.		
	2.		
Improve my study effectiveness	1.		
	2.		
Improve my performance on exams	1.		
	2.		

CLASS DISCUSSION QUESTIONS

1. At this point in the current academic term, are you feeling more or less anxious about quizzes and tests than you did at the beginning of the term? Why or why not? Do your feelings about taking tests affect your overall attitude about college?

2. Have you used a study group in any of your courses so far this term? What was the best part of studying in a group? The worst? How could you make a study group more effective?

3. Review the list of 10 tips for taking tests, presented earlier in this chapter. Is there anything here that you don't usually do? Think of some examples of problems that might occur if you *never* do this.

ENDNOTES

1. Undergraduate Academic Conduct Committee of Northwestern University, "Definitions of Academic Violations," http://www.northwestern.edu/uacc/defines.html (accessed July 13, 2010).

CHAPTER 7
Interacting with Instructors and Classes

FIGURE 7.1

© Thinkstock

Where Are You Now?

Assess your present knowledge and attitudes.

	Often	Sometimes	Seldom
1. I talk with my college instructors outside of class.			
2. I participate in class discussions, ask questions in class, and volunteer to answer the instructor's questions.			
3. I go to all my classes except when prevented by illness or an emergency.			
4. I prepare for classes and make an active effort to pay attention and get the most from class lectures.			
5. During lecture classes, I sometimes read other materials, check for phone messages or e-mail, and talk with friends.			
6. I don't sign up for classes when I hear other students say the instructor is boring or difficult.			
7. I talk to my instructors in their offices only if I have a problem with a specific assignment.			
8. I write effective, professional e-mails to my instructors when appropriate.			
9. I am comfortable giving presentations in class and know how to prepare successfully.			
10. When assigned a group presentation, I take the lead and help ensure everyone works together well in his or her specific roles.			

Where Do You Want to Go?

Think about how you answered the questions above. Be honest with yourself. On a scale of 1 to 10, how would you rate your interactions with your instructors and other students at this time?

Not very effective   **Very successful**

1   2   3   4   5   6   7   8   9   10

In the following list, circle the three most important areas in which you think you can improve:

- Attending classes
- Networking and studying with other students
- Going to classes fully prepared
- Interacting with instructors through e-mail and telephone calls
- Paying attention in lecture classes
- Resolving a problem with an instructor
- Asking questions in class
- Interacting with the instructor and students in an online course
- Answering questions in class
- Giving presentations in front of the class
- Participating in class discussions
- Creating and using visual aids in a presentation
- Speaking with instructors outside of class
- Working with a student group to give a presentation

Are there other areas also in which you can improve how you interact with instructors and other students to get the most out of your college education? Write down other things you feel you need to work on.

_____

_____

_____

How to Get There

Here's what we'll work on in this chapter:

- Understanding why it is so important to interact well with your instructors and participate in class
- Understanding why it is essential to attend classes and actively engage in the learning process
- Preparing for and being comfortable participating in class
- Discovering the best communication practices for asking and answering questions in class
- Staying active in lecture classes to increase your learning
- Adapting your learning style when an instructor has a different teaching style
- Building a relationship with an instructor outside of class and finding a mentor
- Writing professional e-mails to instructors and others
- Interacting with the instructor of an online course
- Preparing for and delivering a successful class presentation
- Working with other students on a group presentation

1.   INTERACTING WITH THE COLLEGE EXPERIENCE

Throughout this text you have been reading about how success in college depends on your active participation in the learning process. Much of what you get out of your education depends on what you put into it. This chapter considers how to engage in the learning process through interactions with your instructors and other students. Students who actively interact with others are much more successful than passive students who do not.

Yet relatively few college students consistently interact with their instructors and other students in class. Why is that? If you're just too shy, you can learn to feel comfortable participating.

Interacting with instructors and participating in class discussions is among the most important steps you can take to succeed in college. The essence of a college education is not just absorption of knowledge and information but learning a way of thinking that involves actively responding to the ideas of others. Employers seek graduates who have learned how to think critically about situations and ideas, to solve new problems, and to apply their knowledge in new circumstances. These characteristics come from active participation in the learning process.

1.1   Differences from High School

To understand why interaction is so important in college, let's look again at some typical differences between high school and college instructors:

- **Many college classes focus more on how one thinks about a subject than on information about the subject.** While instructors in some large lecture classes mostly present information, as you take more classes in your major and other smaller classes, you'll find that simply giving back facts or information on tests or in assigned papers means much less. You are expected to develop your own ideas and communicate them well. Doing that successfully usually requires talking with others, testing out your thoughts against those of others, responding to instructors' questions, and other interactions.
- **Instructors are usually very actively involved in their fields.** While high school teachers often are most interested in *teaching*, college instructors are often more interested in their own fields. They may be passionate about their subject and want you to be as well. They can become excited when a student asks a question that shows a deeper understanding of something in the field.

academic freedom

The concept present in almost all colleges that instructors are free, within the boundaries of laws and ethics, to pursue studies and to teach topics they deem appropriate within their field, without interference from administrators, officials, or others.

- **College instructors give *you* the responsibility for learning.** Many high school teachers monitor their students' progress and reach out if they see a student not doing well. In college, however, students are considered adults in charge of their own learning. Miss some classes, turn in a paper late, do poorly on an exam—and you will get a low grade, but the instructor likely won't come looking for you to offer help. But if *you* ask questions when you don't understand and actively seek out your instructor during office hours, then you'll get the help you need.

- **Academic freedom is very important in college.** High school instructors often have a set curriculum and little freedom to choose what—or how—to teach. College instructors have **academic freedom**, however, allowing them to teach controversial topics and express their own ideas—and they may expect you to partake in this freedom as well. They have more respect for students who engage in the subject and demonstrate their thinking skills through participation in the class.

2. WHY ATTEND CLASSES AT ALL?

LEARNING OBJECTIVES

1. **Describe why it is important to attend classes.**
2. **Know what to do if you must miss a class.**
3. **Explain the benefits of participating in class for both students and instructors.**

podcast

An audio or video recording, such as of a class lecture, made available online; so named because podcasts were originally developed to be downloaded and played on iPods.

Among the freedoms in college is the choice not to attend classes. Most college instructors do not "grade" attendance, and some students develop an attitude that if you can get class notes from someone else, or watch a **podcast** of a lecture, there's no reason to go to every class. What's wrong with that?

True, you don't have to attend every single class of every course to get a good grade. But thinking only in terms of grades and how much one can get away with is a dangerous attitude. The real issue is whether you're trying to get the most out of your education. Let's compare students with different attitudes toward their classes:

Carla wants to get through college, and she knows she needs the degree to get a decent job, but she's just not that into it. She has trouble paying attention in those big lecture classes, which mostly seem pretty boring. She's pretty sure she can pass all her courses as long as she takes the time to study before tests. It doesn't bother her to skip classes when she's studying for a test in a different class or for another reason. She makes it through her freshman year with passing grades. Then she fails the midterm exam in her first sophomore class. Depressed, she skips the next couple classes, then feels guilty and goes to the next. It's even harder to stay awake because now she has no idea what they're talking about. Even a hard night of studying before the final isn't enough to pass the course. She just barely passes another course. She is starting to think that maybe she'll drop out for now.

Karen wants to have a good time in college and still do well enough to get a good job in business afterward. Her sorority keeps a file of class notes for her big lecture classes, and from talking to others and reviewing these notes, she's discovered she can skip lots of classes and still get a B or C on the tests. She stays focused on her grades, and because she has a good memory, she's able to get by. She never talks with instructors outside class because she can always find out what she needs from another student. In her senior year, she starts working on her résumé and asks other students which instructors write the best letters of recommendation. She's sure her college degree will land her a good job.

Alicia enjoys her classes, even when she has to get up early after working or studying late the night before. Often she asks the instructor questions after class. In class discussions, she enjoys arguing her ideas. In her sophomore year, unsure of what to major in, she talks things over with one of her favorite instructors, whom she has gotten to know through office visits. The instructor gives her some insights into careers in that field and helps her explore her interests. She takes two more courses with this instructor over the next year, and she's comfortable in her senior year going to him to ask for a job reference. When she does, she's thrilled when he urges her to apply for a high-level paid internship with a company in the field that happens to be run by a friend of his.

Think about the differences in the attitudes of these three students and how they approach their classes—and the different results when they graduate. One's attitude toward learning, toward going to class, and toward the whole college experience is a huge factor in college success. Make it your goal to attend every class—don't even think about not going. Going to class is the first step in engaging in your education by interacting with the instructor and other students. Here are some reasons why it's important to attend every class:

- Miss a class and you'll miss *something*, even if you never know it. Even if a friend gives you notes for the class, they cannot contain *everything* said or shown by the instructor or written on the board for emphasis or questioned or commented on by other students. What you miss might affect your grade or your enthusiasm for the course. Why go to college at all if you're not going to *go* to college?

- While some students may say that you don't have to go to every class to do well on a test, that is often simply wrong. Do you want to take that risk?

- Your final grade often reflects how you think about course concepts, and you will think more often and more clearly when engaged in class discussions and hearing the comments of other students. You can't get this by borrowing class notes from a friend.

- Research shows there is a correlation between absences from class and lower grades.

- Your instructor will note your absences—even in a large class. You'll make a poor impression, and you can't just go up to the instructor the next time and ask the insulting question, "Did I miss anything important?"

- You might be tempted to skip a class because the instructor is "boring," but it's more likely that you found the class boring because you weren't very attentive or didn't appreciate how the instructor was teaching.

- You paid a lot of money for your tuition. Get your money's worth!

Attending the first day of class is critical. There you'll get the syllabus and other handouts, learn the instructor's policies for the class, and often take notes in an opening lecture.

If You Must Miss a Class...

- If you know that you will miss a class, take steps in advance. Ask your instructor if he or she teaches another section of the course that you might attend instead. Ask about any handouts or special announcements.

- Ask another student whose judgment you trust if you can see their notes. Then talk to them after you've read their notes to go over things that may be unclear to you.

- It may not be necessary to see your instructor after missing a lecture class, and no instructor wants to give you fifty minutes of office time to repeat what was said in class. But if you are having difficulty after the *next* class because of something you missed earlier, stop and see your instructor and ask what you can do to get caught up. But remember the worst thing you can say to an instructor: "I missed class—did you talk about anything important?"

2.1   The Value of Interaction in Class

While there are many good reasons to attend every class, it's not enough just to *be* there—you need to interact with the instructor and other students for the full experience:

FIGURE 7.2

In a large class, your instructor will still notice if you are paying attention.

© *Thinkstock*

FIGURE 7.3

In a small class, it's easy to interact with the instructor.

© Thinkstock

- Participating in class discussions is a good way to meet other students. You may form a study group, borrow class notes if you miss a class, or team up with other students on a group project. You may meet students with whom you form a lasting relationship, developing your network of contacts for other benefits in the future, such as learning about internships or jobs.

- Asking the instructor questions, answering the instructor's questions in class, and responding to other students' comments makes a impression on your instructor. The instructor will remember you as an engaged student—and this matters if you later need extra help or even a potential mentor.

- Paying close attention and thinking critically about what the instructor is saying makes the class more enjoyable. You'll notice things you'd miss if you're feeling bored and may discover your instructor is much more interesting than you first thought.

- Students actively engaged in their class learn more and thus get better grades. When you speak out in class and answer the instructor's questions, you are more likely to remember the discussion.

2.2 Use Podcasts and Recordings Instead of Attending Class?

Why not just listen to a recording or watch a video of the lecture instead of going to class? Why not sleep late and "go" to this class whenever it's convenient for you? What could be wrong with that?

Educators have discussed this issue much after many colleges and universities began videotaping class lectures and making them available for students online or in podcasts. Would students would stop coming to class and simply watch the podcasts instead? In fact, some students do cut class, as some always have, but better students learned to use podcasts and recordings to review material they were unsure about. A video podcast doesn't offer the opportunity to ask questions or participate, and even if you pay close attention to watching a video, it's still a passive experience from which you're likely to learn much less.

KEY TAKEAWAYS

- The benefits of attending every class include not missing important material, thinking more clearly about course topics, developing a better relationship with the instructor, and being better prepared for tests.
- When possible, prepare in advance for missing a class by speaking with the instructor and arranging to borrow and discuss someone's notes.
- Students benefit in many ways from class interaction, including more actively engaging in learning, developing a network with other students, and forming a relationship with the instructor.
- Podcasts, lecture videos, and similar methods can supplement lectures but cannot replace all the benefits of attending class in person.

CHECKPOINT EXERCISES

1. Why is it more important to interact with your instructors in college than it was in high school?

    _____

    _____

    _____

2. Give an example of something important you may miss in a class if you are absent—even if you read a friend's notes and hear a recording of the lecture.

    _____

    _____

3. List at least three potential benefits of forming a network with other students.

    _____

    _____

    _____

4. What can you do as a student to be more engaged during a lecture if you are finding it boring?

    _____

    _____

3. PARTICIPATING IN CLASS

LEARNING OBJECTIVES

1. **Understand how to prepare for successful participation in class.**
2. **List guidelines for effectively asking and answering questions in class.**
3. **Describe how to interact successfully with an instructor in a large lecture class.**
4. **Explain what to do if your learning style is different from your instructor's teaching style.**

Even though participating in class has many benefits, not everyone naturally feels comfortable speaking out. Following are general guidelines to make it easier.

3.1   Guidelines for Participating in Classes

Smaller classes generally favor discussion, but instructors in lecture classes also often make some room for participation.

A fear of speaking in public is common. If you feel afraid to speak out in class, take comfort from the fact that many others do as well—and that anyone can learn how to speak in class without much difficulty. Try these guidelines to help you prepare and communicate.

- Set yourself up for success by coming to class fully prepared. Complete assigned reading. Review your notes on the reading and previous class. If there is something you don't understand well, start formulating your question now.
- Sit up front with a good view of the instructor, board or screen, and visual aids. In a lecture hall, this helps you hear better and pay better attention, and it makes a better impression on the instructor. Don't sit with friends—socializing isn't what you're there for.
- Remember your body language. Sit up and look alert, with a pleasant expression on your face, and make good eye contact with the instructor. Show some enthusiasm.
- Pay attention to the instructor's **body language** too. How the instructor moves and gestures, and the looks on his or her face, adds meaning and cues you when it's a good time to ask a question or stay silent.
- Take good notes, but don't write obsessively—and never page through your textbook (or browse on a laptop). Don't eat or play with your cell phone. Except when writing brief notes, keep your eyes on the instructor.
- Follow class protocol for making comments and asking questions. In a small class, the instructor may encourage students to ask questions at any time, while in lecture classes the instructor may ask for questions only at the end. In this case, jot down your questions so that you don't forget them later.
- Don't say or ask anything just to try to impress your instructor. Most instructors immediately recognize insincere flattery—and the impression this makes is just the opposite of what you want.
- Pay attention to how the instructor thinks. Does this instructor emphasize theory more than facts, wide perspectives over specific ideas, abstractions more than concrete experience? Try to think in a similar way when participating in class.
- It's fine to disagree with your instructor. Many instructors invite challenges. Before speaking up, however, be sure you can explain why you disagree and give supporting evidence or reasons. Be respectful.
- Pay attention to your communication style. Use **standard English**, not slang. Avoid sarcasm and joking around. Show confidence in your ideas while being respectful of the ideas of others.
- When your instructor asks a question to the class:
    - Raise your hand and make eye contact, but don't call out or wave your hand all around.
    - Before speaking, take a moment to gather your thoughts and take a deep breath. Don't just blurt it out—speak calmly and clearly.

body language

Another term for forms of nonverbal communication, including gestures, postures, and facial expressions.

standard English

Use of relatively formal English language with correct grammar and syntax, avoiding slang, colloquialisms, and irregular phrasings and word meanings that may be common to a particular cultural group but that differ from those generally accepted by the larger culture.

When your instructor asks you a question directly:

- Be honest and admit it if you don't know the answer or are not sure. Don't try to fake it or make excuses. If asked for your opinion about something, it's fine to explain that you haven't decided yet, such as when weighing two opposing ideas or actions.
- Organize your thoughts to give a sufficient answer. Instructors seldom want a yes or no answer. Give your answer and provide reasons or evidence in support.

- When you want to ask the instructor a question:

  - Don't ever feel a question is "stupid." If you have been paying attention in class and have done the reading and you still don't understand something, you have every right to ask.
  - Ask at the appropriate time. Don't interrupt the instructor or jump ahead and ask a question about something the instructor may be starting to explain. Wait for a natural pause and a good moment to ask.
  - Don't ask a question just because you weren't paying attention. If you drifted off and then realize that you don't really understand what the instructor is talking about, don't ask a question about something that was already covered.
  - Don't ask a question that is really a complaint. You may be thinking, "Why would so-and-so believe that? That's just crazy!" Take a moment to think about what you really need to know. It's better to say, "I'm having some difficulty understanding what so-and-so is saying here. What evidence did he use to argue for that position?"
  - Avoid dominating a discussion. Sometimes you can make a follow-up comment, but avoid trying to have a one-on-one conversation with the instructor.

Lecture Hall Classes

FIGURE 7.4

Don't use your cell phone during class time.

© Thinkstock

Even in large lecture classes participation is important. The instructor often provides an opportunity to ask questions. Be ready with your question or comment when the opportunity arises—and don't be shy about raising your hand first.

Listen carefully to the lecture before asking a question. You don't want to ask a question when the lecture already answered it. Organize your thoughts and choose your words carefully. Be specific. Don't say something like, "I don't understand the big deal about whether the earth revolves around the sun or the sun around the earth. So what?" Instead, you might ask, "When they discovered that the earth revolves around the sun, was that such a disturbing idea because people were upset to realize that maybe they weren't the center of the universe?" The first question suggests you haven't thought much about the topic, while the second shows that you are beginning to grasp the issue and want to understand it more fully.

Here are some more guidelines for asking good questions:

- Ask a question or two early in the term, even on the first day of class. Once the instructor has noticed you, you are more likely to be recognized again when you have a question. You won't be lost in the crowd.
- Speak deliberately and professionally, using standard English.

- If you're very shy about public speaking or worried you'll say the wrong thing, write down your question before asking. Rehearse it in your mind.
- When questions are allowed in class, ask then rather than saving a question for after class. A private conversation with the instructor is more appropriate about a paper or other project you are working on for the course.

A note on lecture hall technology. Technology is present in many lecture halls. Students may use an electronic "clicker" to provide instant feedback to the instructor during the class. The classroom may have wifi and the instructor may encourage students to use their laptops to communicate with the instructor in "real time" during the lecture. Be serious in the use of such technology even if you have anonymity. Don't be one of those who think it's funny to send irrelevant, disruptive, or insulting messages.

3.2 Teaching Style versus Learning Style

As you learned in Chapter 1 students have different **learning styles**. In the same way different instructors have different teaching styles.

When the teaching style matches your learning style, it is easier to be attentive in class and you may feel you are learning better. But what happens if your instructor has a style very different from your own? For example, an instructor may give lectures, speak rapidly, and seldom use visuals, and may talks in large abstract ideas and almost never give examples. Maybe you are a visual learner who learns more effectively with visual aids and concrete examples. So maybe you find it hard to pay attention in class and follow the lectures. What can you do?

- Capitalize on your learning strengths, as you learned in Chapter 1 For example, you could use a visual style of note taking, such as concept maps, during lectures. And see if *you* can supply examples of the ideas as you listen.
- Form a study group with other students. You can gain what they have learned through their styles while you contribute what you have learned through yours.
- Use ancillary study materials. Many courses have online resources or additional learning materials. These may review course material in ways that may better fit your learning style.
- Communicate with your instructor to bridge the gap. If the instructor is speaking in abstractions and general ideas you don't understand, ask the instructor for an example.
- You can also communicate with the instructor privately during office hours. For example, you can explain that you are having difficulty understanding lectures because so many things are said so fast.

learning styles

A person's preferred approach to or way of learning most effectively.

KEY TAKEAWAYS

- To prepare for class participation, come to class ready, sit in front, and pay attention to the instructor's words and body language.
- Use good communication techniques when asking or answering questions in class.
- Take advantage of all opportunities to interact with your instructors, even in lecture classes.
- If your learning style does not match the instructor's teaching style, adapt your learning and study with other students to stay actively engaged.

CHECKPOINT EXERCISES

1. For each of the following statements about class participation, circle T for true or F for false:

T	F	To avoid having to answer a question in class when you don't know the answer, sit in the back row and avoid making eye contact with the instructor.
T	F	If you haven't finished a reading assignment before coming to a lecture class, bring the book along and try to finish during the lecture.
T	F	Although it is OK to disagree with something in your textbook, never disagree with something the instructor says in a lecture.
T	F	If you are asked a question but don't know the answer, be honest and admit it.
T	F	Before raising your hand to ask a question, take a moment to consider whether maybe it's a stupid question.
T	F	Because you don't want your instructor to form a poor impression of you, wait a week or two into the term before starting to ask questions in class.
T	F	If you're shy, it's best never to speak up in class at all.
T	F	If you are struggling with a class during the first two weeks of the term, drop the class immediately because the situation won't improve.

2. List two things you can do if you are having difficulty understanding what your instructor is talking about.

_____

_____

4. COMMUNICATING WITH INSTRUCTORS

LEARNING OBJECTIVES

1. **Describe additional benefits for interacting with your instructor.**
2. **List guidelines for successfully communicating individually with an instructor.**
3. **Write e-mail messages to instructors and others that are polite, professional, and effective.**
4. **Know how to graciously resolve a problem, such as a grade dispute, with an instructor.**
5. **Understand the value of having a mentor and how interactions with instructors, your academic advisor, and others may gain you a mentor.**
6. **Explain what is needed to succeed in an online course and how to interact with an instructor online.**

In addition to class participation, students gain benefits from communicating directly with instructors. Learn best practices for communicating with your instructors during office hours and through e-mail.

4.1 Additional Benefits of Talking with Your Instructors

College students are sometimes surprised to discover that instructors like students and enjoy getting to know them. The human dimension of college really matters, and as a student you are an important part of your instructor's world. Most instructors are happy to see you during their office hours or to talk a few minutes after class.

Talking with your instructors often leads to benefits beyond simply doing well in that class:

Networking

The process of engaging others in helping reach an objective.

- Talking with instructors helps you feel more comfortable and connected in college. Students who talk to their instructors are less likely to become disillusioned and drop out.
- Talking with instructors is a valuable way to learn about an academic field or a career. Don't know for sure what you want to major in, or what people with a degree in your chosen major actually *do* after college? Most instructors will share information and insights with you.
- You may need a reference or letter of recommendation for a job or internship application. Getting to know some of your instructors puts you in an ideal position to ask when you need one in the future .
- Because instructors are often well connected within their field, they may know of a job, internship, or research possibility you might not know about. An instructor who knows you is a valuable part of your network. **Networking** is important for future job searches and other opportunities. In fact, most jobs are found through networking, not through job postings.
- Think about what it truly means to be "educated": how one thinks, understands society and the world, and responds to problems and new situations. Much of this learning occurs outside the classroom. Talking with your instructors can be among your most meaningful experiences in college.

4.2 Guidelines for Communicating with Instructors

Getting along with instructors and communicating well begins with attitude. As experts in their field, they deserve your respect. As you get to know your instructors better, you'll learn their personalities and find appropriate ways to communicate. Here are some guidelines for getting along with your instructors:

- **Prepare before going to the instructor's office.** Go over your notes and write down specific questions. You'll feel more comfortable, and the instructor will appreciate your being organized.

- **Don't forget to introduce yourself.** Don't assume your instructor has learned everyone's names and don't make him or her have to ask you. Unless the instructor has already asked you to address him or her as "Dr. _____," "Ms. _____" or Mr. _____," or something similar, it's appropriate to say "Professor _____."

- **Respect the instructor's time.** College instructors sit on committees, do research and other professional work, and have personal lives. Don't show up two minutes before the end of an office hour and expect the instructor to stay late.

- **Realize that the instructor will recognize you from class—even in a large lecture hall.** If you were joking around with friends in the back row, don't think you can show up during office hours to find out what you missed while you weren't paying attention.

- **Don't try to fool an instructor.** Insincere praise or making excuses for not doing an assignment won't make it in college. To earn your instructor's respect, come to class prepared, do the work, participate genuinely in class, and show respect—and the instructor will be happy to see you when you come to office hours or need some extra help.

- **Try to see things from the instructor's point of view.** Imagine that you spent a couple hours making PowerPoint slides and preparing a class lecture on something you find very stimulating and exciting. Standing in front of a full room, you are gratified to see faces smiling and heads nodding as people understand what you're saying—they really get it! And then a student after class asks, "Is this going to be on the test?" How would *you* feel?

- **Be professional.** You can be cordial and friendly, but keep it professional. Come to office hours prepared with your questions—not just to chat. (Don't wear sunglasses or earphones in the office or check your cell phone for messages.) Be prepared to accept criticism in a professional way, without taking it personally or complaining.

- **Use your best communication skills.** In Chapter 9 you'll learn the difference between assertive communication and passive or aggressive communication.

FIGURE 7.5

Your instructor can often help explain course topics.

© *Thinkstock*

Part-Time and Returning Students

Students who are working or who have other responsibilities may have special issues interacting with instructors. Sometimes an older student feels a little out of place and may even feel "the system" is designed for younger students.

But participation and communication with instructors is very important for all students—and may be even more important for "nontraditional" students. Getting to know your instructors is crucial for feeling at home in college. Instructors enjoy talking with older and other nontraditional students—even when, as sometimes happens, a student is older than the instructor. Nontraditional students are often highly motivated and eager to learn. If you can't make the instructor's office hours because of your work schedule, ask for an appointment at a different time—your needs will be respected.

Part-time students, especially in community colleges where they may be taking evening courses, often have greater difficulty meeting with instructors. In addition, the instructor may teach part-time and be on campus only at limited times. But it is just as critical for part-time students to engage in learning and have a sense of belonging on campus. With effort, you can usually find a way to talk with your instructors. Don't hesitate to ask for an appointment at another time or to meet with your instructor over a cup of coffee after class before driving home. Don't give up or feel defeated; talk with your instructor to arrange a time to meet, and make the most of your time together. Use e-mail to communicate when you need to and contact your instructor when you have any question you can't raise in person.

4.3   E-mail Best Practices

E-mail has become an important way to communicate with instructors. Virtually all younger college students have grown up using e-mail, although some have developed poor habits from using e-mail principally with friends. Some older college students may not yet understand the importance of e-mail and other computer skills in college (see "Getting Started with E-mail"). Especially when it is difficult to see an instructor during office hours, e-mail can be an effective form of interaction with instructors. E-mail is also an effective way to collaborate with other students on group projects or when studying.

Getting Started with E-mail

- If you don't have your own computer, find out where on-campus computers are available for student use, such as at the library or student center.
- Set up a free web-based e-mail account at Google, Yahoo, or other sites. Then you can use e-mail from any computer connected to the Internet.
- If you don't have enough computer experience to set up your own e-mail, ask a friend for help or check at your library or student services office.
- Once you have your account set up, give your e-mail address to instructors who request it and to other students with whom you study or maintain contact. E-mail is a good way to contact another student if you miss a class.
- Once you begin using e-mail, remember to check it regularly for messages. Most people view e-mail like a telephone message and expect you to respond fairly soon.
- Be sure to use good e-mail etiquette when writing to instructors.

If your instructor gives you his or her e-mail addresses, use e-mail rather than the telephone unless instructed otherwise. Using e-mail respects other people's time, allowing them to answer at a time of their choosing, rather than interrupting them with a telephone call. Generally it's best not to text-message an instructor unless invited to do so.

As a written form of communication, e-mail should be professional. Avoid shortcuts you might use with friends, such as not spelling out full words, ignoring capitalization and punctuation, and not bothering with grammar or full sentences. Instructors expect a more professional quality of writing. Write in full sentences, correctly spell words, and use good grammar. Follow these guidelines:

- Use a professional e-mail name. If you have a funny name you use with friends, create a different account with a professional name for use with instructors, work supervisors, and others.
- Use the subject line to label your message effectively at a glance. "May I make an appointment?" says something; "In your office?" doesn't.
- Address e-mail messages as you do a letter, beginning "Dear Professor ____." Include your full name if it's not easily recognizable in your e-mail account.
- Get to your point quickly and concisely. Don't make the reader scroll down a long e-mail to see what you want to say.
- Don't try to be funny, ironic, or sarcastic. Write as you would in a paper for class. In a large lecture class or an online course, your e-mail voice may be the primary way your instructor knows you, and emotionally charged messages can be confusing or give a poor impression.
- Don't use capital letters to emphasize. All caps look like SHOUTING.
- Avoid abbreviations, nonstandard spelling, slang, and emoticons like smiley faces.
- Don't make demands or state expectations such as "I'll expect to hear from you soon" or "If I haven't heard by 4 p.m., I'll assume you'll accept my paper late."
- When you reply to a message, leave the original message with yours. The reader may not recall what he or she said in the original message.
- Be polite. End the message with a "Thank you" or something similar.
- Proofread your message before sending it.
- With any important message to a work supervisor or instructor, it's a good idea to wait and review the message later before sending it. You may have expressed an emotion or thought that you will think better about later. Many problems occur when people send messages too quickly without thinking.

4.4 Resolving a Grade Issue with an Instructor

Students often feel an instructor has given them a grade lower than they think they deserve—especially new students not yet used to the higher standards of college. It's depressing to get a low grade, but it's not the end of the world. Don't be too hard on yourself—or on the instructor. Make sure you know what to do better next time, as discussed in Chapter 6.

If you genuinely believe you deserved a higher grade, you can talk with your instructor. *How* you communicate in that conversation, however, is very important. Instructors are used to hearing students complain about grades and having to explain their standards for grading. Most instructors seldom change grades. Yet it can still be worthwhile to talk with the instructor because of what you will learn from the experience.

Follow these guidelines to talk about a grade or resolve any other disagreement with an instructor:

- Review the requirements for the paper or test and the instructor's comments. Be sure you actually have a reason for discussing the grade—not just that you didn't do well. Be prepared with specific points to go over.
- Make an appointment with your instructor during office hours or another time. Don't try to talk about this before or after class or with e-mail.
- Begin by politely explaining that you thought you did better on the assignment or test and that you'd like to go over it to better understand the result.
- Allow the instructor to explain his or her comments on the assignment or grading of the test. Don't complain or whine; instead, show your appreciation for the explanation. Raise any specific questions or make comments at this time. For example, you might say, "I really thought I was being clear here when I wrote...."
- Use good listening skills. Whatever you do, don't argue!
- Ask what you can do to improve grade, if possible. Can you rewrite the paper or do any extra-credit work to help make up for a test score? Make it clear that you're willing to put in the effort and that you want to *learn more*, not just get the higher grade.
- If there is no opportunity to improve on this specific project, ask the instructor for advice on what you might do on the next assignment or when preparing for the next test. You may receive good study advice, and your instructor will respect your willingness to make the effort as long as it's clear that you're more interested in learning than simply getting the grade.

Tips for Success: Talking with Instructors

- When you have a question, ask it sooner rather than later.
- Be prepared and plan your questions and comments in advance.
- Be respectful but personable, and communicate professionally.
- Be open minded and ready to learn. Avoid whining and complaining.
- There is no such thing as a "stupid question."

Controlling Anger over Grades

If you're going to talk with an instructor about your grade or any other problem, control any anger you may be feeling. The GPS LifePlan project of the Minnesota State Colleges and Universities System offers some insights into this process:

- Being upset about a grade is good because it shows you care and that you have passion about your education. But anger prevents clear thinking, so rein it in first.
- Since anger involves bodily reactions, physical actions can help you control anger: try some deep breathing first.
- Try putting yourself in your instructor's shoes and seeing the situation from their point of view. Try to understand how grading is not a personal issue of "liking" you—that they are really doing something for your educational benefit.
- It's not your life that's being graded. Things outside your control can result in not doing well on a test or assignment, but the instructor can grade only on what you actually did on that test or assignment—not what you *could have done* or *are capable of doing*. Understanding this can help you accept what happened and not take a grade personally.[1]

4.5 Finding a Mentor

A **mentor** is someone who is usually older and more experienced than you who becomes your trusted guide, adviser, and role model. A mentor is someone you may want to be like in your future career or profession—someone you look up to and whose advice and guidance you respect.

Finding a mentor can be one of the most fulfilling aspects of college. As a student, you think about many things and make many decisions, large and small, almost daily: What do you want to do in the future? How can you best balance your studies with your job? What should you major in? Should you take this course or that one? What should you do if you feel like you're failing a course? How can you be a better student? The questions go on and on. We talk about things like this with our friends and

mentor

A trusted individual, often an older and wiser role model, who provides guidance and advice.

often family members, but often they don't have the experience or background to help us as a mentor can.

Most important, a mentor is someone who is willing to help you, to talk with you about decisions you face, to support you when things become difficult, and to guide you when you're feeling lost. A mentor can become a valuable part of your future network but also can help you in the here and now.

Many different people can become mentors: other students, family members, people you know through work, your boss. As a college student, your best mentor likely is someone involved in education. Finding a mentor is another reason to develop good relationships with your instructors, starting with class participation and communication outside of class.

A mentor is not like a good friend, exactly—you don't invite your instructor to a movie—but it does involve a form of friendship. Nor is a mentor a formal relationship: you don't ask an instructor to become your mentor. The mentor relationship evolves slowly, often without actively looking for a mentor. Here's an example of how one student "found" a mentor:

As a freshman taking several classes, Miguel particularly admired one of his instructors, Professor Canton. Miguel spoke up more in Canton's class and talked with him sometimes during office hours. When considering classes for the next term, Miguel saw that Canton was teaching another course he was interested in, so he asked him about that course one day during office hours. Miguel was pleased when Professor Canton said he'd like to have him in his class next term. By the end of his first year, Miguel knew Canton better than any of his other instructors and felt very comfortable talking with him outside of class. One day after talking about a reading assignment, Miguel said he was enjoying this class so much that he was thinking about majoring in the subject and asked Professor Canton what he thought about it. Canton suggested that he take a few more classes before making a decision, and he invited Miguel to sit in on his seminar with upper-level students. In his second year, Miguel's interests turned in another direction as he began to think about future job possibilities, but by then he felt comfortable enough talking with Canton that he occasionally he stopped by the professor's office even though he was not taking a class with him. Sometimes he was surprised how much Professor Canton knew about other departments and other faculty, and Canton often shared insights about other courses he might be interested in. When Miguel learned about a summer internship in his field and was applying, Canton not only volunteered to write him a letter of recommendation but even offered to help Miguel with the essay part of the application if he wanted.

Some colleges have mentoring programs, and you should become involved in one if you have this opportunity, but often a mentoring relationship occurs informally as you get to know an instructor or someone else over time. In your first year, you don't go searching frantically for a mentor, but you should begin interacting with your instructors and other students in ways that may lead, over time, to developing that kind of relationship.

Similarly, your academic advisor or a college counselor might become a mentor if you share interests and you look up to that person as a role model and trusted guide. Your advisor is so important for your college success that if you feel you are not getting along well, you should ask the advising department to switch you to a different advisor. Take the time to build a good relationship with your advisor, the same as with instructors.

4.6 Relating to an Instructor of an Online Course

While online learning once focused on students at a distance from campus, now many students enrolled in regular classes also take some courses online. Online courses pose special issues related to how students interact with other students and the instructor.

Some online courses do involve "face time" or live audio connections with the instructor and other students, via webcasts or webinars, but many are self-paced and asynchronous, meaning that you experience the course on your own time and communicate with others via messages back and forth rather than communicating in real time. All online courses include opportunities for interacting with the instructor, typically through e-mail or a bulletin board where you may see comments and questions from other students as well.

Two important differences affect how online interaction occurs and how successful it is for engaging students in learning. Most communication is written, with no or limited opportunity to ask questions face to face or during office hours, and students must take the initiative to interact beyond required online assignments.

Some students who are reluctant to speak in class communicate more easily in writing and are happy in online courses. But other students may have less confidence in their writing skills or may never initiate interaction at all and end up feeling lost. Depending on your learning style, an online course may feel natural to you or more difficult than a classroom course. Online courses generally have higher dropout and failure rates due to some students feeling isolated and unmotivated.

Success in an online course requires commitment and motivation. Follow these guidelines:

- **Make sure you have the technology.** If you're not comfortable reading and writing on a computer, don't rush into an online course. If you have limited access to a computer or high-speed Internet connection, you may have difficulty with the course.

- **Accept that you'll have to motivate yourself and take responsibility for your learning.** It's actually harder for some people to sit down at the computer on their own than to show up at a set time. Be sure you have enough time in your week for all course activities, and try to schedule regular times online and for assignments. Evaluate the course requirements carefully before signing up.

- **Work on your writing skills.** If you are not comfortable writing, you may want to avoid online courses until you have had more experience with college-level writing. When communicating with the instructor of an online course, follow the guidelines for effective e-mail outlined earlier.

- **Use critical thinking skills.** Most online courses involve assignments requiring problem solving and critical thinking. It's not as simple as watching video lectures and taking multiple-choice tests. You need to actively engage with the course material.

- **Take the initiative to ask questions and seek help.** Remember, your instructor can't see you to know if you're confused. You must take the first step to communicate your questions.

- **Be patient.** When you ask a question or seek help with an assignment, you have to wait for the instructor's reply, and you may need to continue working ahead before you receive it. If the instructor is online at scheduled times for direct contact, take advantage of those times for immediate feedback and answers.

- **Use any opportunity to interact with other students in the course.** If you can interact with other students online, do it. Ask questions of other students and monitor their communications. If you know someone taking the same course, try to synchronize your schedules so that you can study together and talk over assignments. Students who feel they are part of a learning community always do better than those who feel isolated and on their own.

Other Digital Interaction

As we discussed in Chapter 6, many courses now use some type of online learning system in which students interact with course materials, other students, and the instructor via their computers even within traditional classroom courses. As noted in the earlier chapter, such systems often monitor student performance in a variety of ways. Even if the instructor seems not to be directly involved, for example, the system may be reporting to him or her the amount of interaction you are having with the online content and with other students. Be aware of the impression you are making, even if it is not "required" that you complete every exercise or interaction. For example, you may have the option to post questions or comments that other students will see, and you may have the option to comment on their posts as well. Here's a chance for you to stand out from the crowd by going the extra mile when many other students do only what is required. Take advantage of such opportunities, not only because the instructor may receive a report of the extent of student activities but because such interactions will increase your learning as well. Follow all the guidelines given earlier for effective communication.

FIGURE 7.6

Online courses let you study when you want, where you want.

© *Thinkstock*

KEY TAKEAWAYS

- Additional benefits of getting to know and networking with instructors include receiving references and academic advice.
- Interacting with college instructors contributes to the intellectual growth that is part of what it means to be educated.
- Prepare in advance before meeting with an instructor, and communicate respectfully, honestly, and sincerely.
- It is especially important for part-time and nontraditional students to make the effort to interact with instructors.
- Be professional in your use use of e-mail with instructors.
- It is worthwhile speaking with an instructor when you disagree about a grade because of what you will learn in this interaction.
- Finding a mentor can be one of the most fulfilling college experiences. Getting to know your instructors may be the first step toward find a mentor.
- In online courses, make the effort to interact with the instructor and other students in a way that encourages your success.

CHECKPOINT EXERCISES

1. Name three benefits of talking with an instructor that you might experience weeks or months after the course has ended.

   _____

   _____

   _____

2. What should you do before going to see your instructor during office hours?

   _____

   _____

3. For each of the following statements, circle T for true or F for false:

T	F	The instructor of a large lecture course will recognize you even if you sit in the back and try not to be noticed.
T	F	Instructors appreciate it when you talk to them in the kind of language you use with your best friends.
T	F	Whining and complaining is the best way to convince an instructor to change your grade.
T	F	It is acceptable to ask an instructor if you can rewrite a paper or do extra-credit work to help make up for a poor grade.

4. Write an appropriate opening for an e-mail to an instructor.

   _____

5. Think for a few minutes about instructors you have had. Would you like to get to know any of them better, perhaps as a mentor? What personality traits does this person have that would make him or her a good mentor? (If no instructor you have met so far is your idea of a perfect mentor, write down the traits you hope to find in an instructor in the future.)

   _____

   _____

   _____

5. PUBLIC SPEAKING AND CLASS PRESENTATIONS

LEARNING OBJECTIVES

1. **Know how to overcome nervousness and anxiety associated with public speaking and giving class presentations.**
2. **Effectively use a six-step process to prepare for and deliver a class presentation.**
3. **Create effective visual aids for use in class presentations.**
4. **Work with a group to successfully plan and deliver a class presentation.**

Public speaking—giving an oral presentation before a class or another group of people—is a special form of interaction common in education. You will likely be asked to give a presentation in one of your classes at some point, and your future career may also involve public speaking. It's important to develop skills for this form of communication.

Public speaking is like participating in class—sharing your thoughts, ideas, and questions with others in the group. In other ways, however, public speaking is very different. You stand in front of the class to speak, rather than from your usual seat—and for most students, that changes the psychology of the situation. You also have time outside of class to prepare your presentation, allowing you to plan it carefully—and, for many, giving more time to worry about it!

5.1 Overcoming Anxiety

Although a few people seem to be natural public speakers, most of us feel some stage fright or anxiety about having to speak to a group, at least at first. This is completely normal. We feel like everyone is staring at us and seeing our every flaw, and we're sure we'll forget what we want to say or mess up somehow. Take comfort from knowing that almost everyone else dreads giving class presentations the same as you! But you can learn to overcome your anxiety and prepare in a way that not only safely gets you through the experience but also leads to success in your presentation. Following are proven strategies for overcoming anxiety when speaking in public:

- **Understand anxiety.** Since stage fright is normal, don't deny feeling anxious. A little anxiety can help motivate you to prepare and do your best. Accept this and work to overcome it. Anxiety is usually worst just before you begin and but eases up once you've begun.
- **Understand that your audience actually wants you to succeed.** They're not looking for faults or hoping you'll fail. Other students and your instructors are on your side, not your enemy. They likely won't even see your anxiety.
- **Reduce anxiety by preparing and practicing.** The next section discusses the preparation process in more detail. The more fully you prepare and the more often you practice, the more your anxiety will go away.
- **Focus on what you're saying, not how you're saying it.** Keep in mind that you have ideas to share, and this is what your classmates and instructors are interested in. Don't obsess about speaking, but focus on the content of your presentation. Think how easily you share your ideas with a friend or family member, as you naturally speak your mind. The same can work with public speaking if you focus on the ideas themselves.
- **Develop self-confidence.** As you prepare, you will make notes you can refer to during the presentation. You're not going to forget what you want to say. The more you practice, the more confident you'll become.

5.2 Guidelines for Presentations

Preparing and delivering a presentation in class (or in business or other settings) is a process very similar to the learning process discussed in Chapter 4, Chapter 5, and Chapter 6 and the writing process discussed in Chapter 8. The process breaks down into six basic steps:

1. Analyze your audience and goals
2. Plan, research, and organize your content
3. Draft and revise the presentation
4. Prepare speaking notes

5. Practice the presentation

6. Deliver the presentation

Step 1: Analyze Your Audience and Goals

Who will see and hear your presentation—and why? Obviously, other students and the instructor. Think about what they already know, and don't know, about your topic. If your topic relates to subject matter in class lectures and readings, consider what background information they already have and don't give a boring recap of things they already know. It may be important, however, to show how your specific topic fits in with subjects that have been discussed already in class, especially in the beginning of your presentation, but be sure to focus on your new topic.

New terms and concepts may become familiar to you while doing your research and preparation, but remember to define and explain them to other students. Consider how much explanation or how many examples are needed for your audience to grasp your points. If your topic involves anything controversial or may provoke emotion, consider your audience's attitudes and choose your words carefully. Thinking about your audience will help you find ways to get their attention and keep them interested.

Be sure you are clear about the goals for the presentation. Are you primarily presenting new information or arguing for a position? Are you giving an overview or a detailed report? Review the assignment and talk to your instructor if you're unsure. Your goals guide everything in the presentation: what you say, how much you say, what order you say it in, what visual aids you use, whether you use humor or personal examples, and so forth.

Step 2: Plan, Research, and Organize Your Content

Starting with the assignment and your goals, brainstorm your topic. Jot notes on specific important topics. If you're doing reading or research to gather more information, take notes as you would with any reading. As you research the topic, don't worry at first about how much content you are gathering. It's better to know too much and then pick out the most important things to say than to rush ahead to drafting the presentation and then realize you don't have enough material.

Organizing a presentation is similar to organizing topics in a class paper and uses the same principles. Introduce your topic and state your main idea (thesis), go into more detail about specific ideas, and conclude your presentation. Look for a logical order for the specifics in the middle. Some topics work best in chronological (time) order or with a compare-and-contrast organization. If your goal is to persuade the audience, build up to the strongest reason. Put similar ideas together and add transitions between different ideas.

While researching your topic and outlining your main points, think about visual aids that may help the presentation.

Also start thinking about how much time you have for the presentation, but don't limit yourself yet in the outline stage.

Step 3: Draft and Revise the Presentation

Unless required by the assignment, you don't need to actually write out the presentation in full sentences and paragraphs. How much you write depends on your own speaking style. Some students speak well from brief phrases written in an outline, while other students find it easier to write sentences out completely. There's nothing wrong with writing the presentation out fully like a script if that helps you be sure you will say what you intend to—just so you don't actually get up and read from the script.

You can't know for sure how long a presentation will last until you rehearse it later, but you can estimate the time while drafting it. On average, it takes two to three minutes to speak is written on a standard double-spaced page—but with visual aids, pauses, and audience interaction, it may take longer. While this is only a rough guide, you can start out thinking of a ten-minute presentation as the equivalent of a three- to four-page paper.

Never wait until the last minute to draft your presentation. Plan your time to complete the first draft early and then come back to it a day or two later to ask these questions:

- Am I going on too long about minor points? Could the audience get bored?
- Do I have good explanations and reasons for my main points? Do I need more data or better examples? Where would visual aids be most effective?
- Am I using the best words for this topic and this audience? Should I be more or less informal in the way I talk?
- Does it all hold together and flow well from one point to the next? Do I need a better introduction or transition when I shift from one idea to another?

Visual Aids in Presentations

Except for very short informal presentations, most presentations gain from visuals—and visual aids are often expected. If allowed to include visuals in your presentation, plan to do so. Consider all possible types:

- Charts or graphs
- Maps
- Photos or other images
- Video clips
- Handouts (only when necessary—they can be distracting)

Use the available technology, whether it's an overhead projector, **PowerPoint** slides, a flip chart, or posters. (Talk to your instructor about resources and software for designing your visuals.) Follow these guidelines:

- Design your visuals carefully. Follow these basic rules:
  - Use a simple, neutral background. A light-colored background with text in a dark color works best for words; a dark background used like matting works best for photos.
  - Minimize the amount of text in visuals—more than eight words per slide is usually too much. Don't simply presenting word outlines of what you are saying. Make sure text is large enough for the audience to read.
  - Don't use more than two pictures in a slide, and use two only to make a direct comparison. Montages are hard to focus on and distract the viewer from what you're saying. Use images only when they support your presentation; don't use clip art just as decoration.
  - Try to avoid tables of numbers in a visual aid. If you need to illustrate numerical data, use a graph. (Microsoft Excel can make them for you easily.)
  - Don't use sound effects. Use a very brief recording only if directly related to your main points.
  - Don't use visual special effects such as dissolves, spins, box-outs, or other transitions. They are distracting. Use animation sparingly and only if it helps make a point.
- Don't use so many visuals or move through them so quickly that the audience gives all its attention to them rather than to you.
- Practice your presentation using your visual aids, because they affect your timing.
- Explain visuals when needed but not when they're obvious.
- Keep your eyes on your audience, only briefly glancing at visuals to stay in sync with them.
- Don't hand out a printout of your visuals. Your audience should keep their eyes on you instead of fiddling around with paper.

PowerPoint
The name of a specific software presentation program (within Microsoft Office) used in many educational and business settings to produce and deliver "slides" containing text and graphics to a group via a projected computer screen.

Step 4: Prepare Speaking Notes

As mentioned earlier, don't read your presentation from a written page. To keep your audience's attention, make eye contact with them and to use a normal speaking voice—and you can't do this if you keep your eyes on a written script.

Speaking notes are a brief outline for your presentation. You can write them on index cards or sheets of paper. Include important facts and data as well as keywords for your main ideas, but don't write too much. (If you forget things later when you start practicing, you can always add more to your outline then.) Be sure to number your cards or pages to prevent a last-minute mix-up.

Think especially about how to open and close your presentation, because these two moments have the most impact. Use the opening to capture the audience's attention, but be sure it is appropriate for your audience and the goals. Here are some possibilities for an opening:

- A striking fact or example (illustrating an issue or a problem)
- A brief interesting or humorous anecdote (historical, personal, or current event)
- A question to the audience
- An interesting quotation

Then relate the opening to your topic and your main point and move into the body of the presentation.

Your closing mirrors the opening. Transition from your last point to a brief summary that pulls your ideas together. You might end with a challenge to the audience, a strong statement about your topic, or a personal reflection on what you have been saying. Just make sure you have a final sentence planned so that you don't end up uncomfortably fumbling around at the end and saying something like "Well, I guess that ends my presentation."

Step 5: Practice the Presentation

Practice may be the most important step. It is also the best way to get past stage fright and gain confidence.

Practice first in an empty room where you imagine people sitting, so that you can move your eyes around the room to this "audience." The first time through, focus on putting your outlined notes into full sentences in your natural speaking voice. Don't read your notes aloud. Glance down at your notes only briefly and then look up immediately around the room. Practice two or three times just to find the right words to explain your points and feel more comfortable working with your notes. Time yourself, but don't obsess over your presentation being the exact length required. If your presentation is much too long, however, adjust it now in your notes so that you don't start memorizing things that you might accidentally still say later on even though you cut them from your notes.

Once you feel good speaking from your notes, practice to add some more polish to your delivery. You might want to record or videotape your presentation or ask a friend or roommate to watch it. Pay attention to these aspects of how you speak:

- Try to speak in your natural voice, not in a monotone as if you were just reading aloud. If you will be presenting in a large room without a microphone, you will need to speak louder than usual, but still try to use a natural voice.

- In usual conversation, we speed up and slow down and vary the intensity of our words to show how we feel about what we're saying. Practice changes in your delivery style to emphasize key points.

- Don't keep staring at your notes. It's fine if you use words that are different from those you wrote down—the more you rehearse without looking at your notes, the more natural sounding you will be.

- Be sure you can pronounce new words and technical terms correctly. Practice saying them slowly and clearly to yourself until you can say them naturally.

- Don't forget transitions. Listeners need a cue when you're moving to a new idea. Practice phrases such as "*Another* important reason for this is…" or "Now let's move on to *why* this is so.…"

- Watch out for all those little "filler" words people use so often, such as "like," "you know," "well," and "uh." They're very distracting to most audiences. Listen to or watch your tape to see if you are using these fillers or ask your friend to point it out.

- Pay attention to body language when practicing. Stand up straight and tall in every practice session so that you become used to it. Unless you have to stand at a podium to use a fixed microphone in your presentation, practice moving around while you speak; this helps keep the audience watching you. Use hand and arm gestures if they are natural for you, but don't try to make up gestures for the presentation because they will look phony. Most important, keep your eyes moving over the audience. Practice smiling and pausing at key points.

- Finally, it's a good idea to be ready in case of an accident. Your presentation will probably go smoothly, you'll stay on track with your notes, and your PowerPoint slides will work fine—but sometimes a mishap happens. Be ready to joke about it, rather than becoming flustered. If the computer fails and you lose your visuals, say something like, "Well, that's a shame, I had some really great photos to show you!" If you drop your index cards or notes, or accidentally skip ahead in your presentation and then have to backtrack, make a joke: "Sorry about that, I was so excited to get to my next point that I'm afraid I lost control there for a moment!" Let your audience laugh with you—they'll still be on your side, and you can defuse the incident and move on without becoming more nervous.

Step 6: Deliver the Presentation

Be sure to get enough sleep and eat a healthy breakfast. Don't drink too much caffeine or you may become hyper and nervous. Wear your favorite—and appropriate—clothing and comfortable shoes.

CHAPTER 7   INTERACTING WITH INSTRUCTORS AND CLASSES

Remember, your audience is on your side! If you're still nervous before your turn, take a few deep breaths. Rehearse your opening lines in your mind. Smile as you move to the front of the room, looking at your audience. You'll see some friendly faces smiling back encouragingly. As you start the presentation, move your eyes among those giving you a warm reception—and if you see some student looking bored or doing something else, just ignore them. But don't focus on any one person in the audience for too long, which could make them nervous or cause them to look away.

Don't keep looking at your watch or a clock: If your rehearsal times were close to your assigned time, your presentation will be also. If you do notice that you're running behind schedule, it may be that you're saying too much out of nervousness. Use your notes to get back on track and keep the pace moving. But it's better to deliver your presentation naturally and fluidly and be a bit long or short than to try to change your words and end up sounding unnatural.

At the closing, deliver your last line with confidence, sweeping your eyes over the audience. If appropriate, ask if there are any questions. When you're done, pause, smile, say "Thank you," and walk back to your seat.

Later on, ask other students and your instructor for comments. Be open minded—don't just ask for praise. If you hear a suggestion for improvement, file that in your memory for next time.

FIGURE 7.7

You may use computerized visual aids when you give a presentation to a class.

© *Thinkstock*

Group Presentations

You may be assigned to give a presentation in a small group. The six-step process works for group presentations too, although group dynamics often call for additional planning and shared responsibilities:

1. Schedule a group meeting right away to get started. Don't let another student put things off. Explain that you're too busy and won't have time at the last minute.

2. Begin by analyzing your audience and your goals together as a group to make sure everyone understands the assignment in the same way. Discuss who should do what. While everyone should talk about what content to include, each of you will have a specialized role. One or more may begin research and gathering information. Others who are good writers may volunteer to draft the presentation, while one or more others may develop the visual aids. Those who have public speaking experience may volunteer to do all or most of the speaking (unless the assignment requires everyone to have a speaking role). You also need a team leader to keep everyone on schedule, organize meetings, and so on. The best team leader is a student with good social skills, who can motivate everyone to cooperate.

3. Steps 2 and 3 can likely be carried out individually with assigned tasks, but group members should stay in touch. For example, the person developing the visuals should be talking to those doing the researching and drafting to see what visuals are needed and get started finding or creating them.

4. Before preparing notes in step 4, meet again to go over the content and plan for visuals. Everyone should be comfortable with the plan so far. Make final decisions about who will do each section of the presentation. Set the time for each segment. Then speakers should prepare their own speaking notes. Let someone with strong speaking skills open or close the presentation (or both), with others doing the other parts.

5. The whole group should participate in practice sessions in step 5, even if not everyone is speaking. Those not speaking should take notes and give feedback. If one student is doing most of the presenting, an alternate should be chosen in case the first choice is sick on the scheduled day. The alternate also needs to practice.

6. During the delivery, especially if using technology for visual aids, one student should manage the visuals while others do the presenting. If several students present different segments, plan the transition from one to another so that the presentation keeps flowing without pauses.

Additional Resources

For Class Presentations

Using PowerPoint. A series of illustrated tutorials for learning how to create effective visual presentations with PowerPoint. http://www.electricteacher.com/tutorial3.htm

"How to Give a Bad Talk." A humorous look (with some very good advice) on what *not* to do when preparing for and giving a class presentation. http://pages.cs.wisc.edu/~markhill/conference-talk.html#badtalk

Class presentations on YouTube. Search YouTube with the phrase "class presentation" and look for video examples of actual students giving class presentations. Critiquing the presentations of other students is a good way to get started preparing your own and learning from others. Here's a good example of a student group presentation on a topic we can all relate to (how body language works):

View the video online at: //www.youtube.com/embed/8zOniRgF330

In this presentation, take note of

- how students make good eye contact with the audience
- the first student's natural speaking voice and tone, and how she did not have to use her note cards very often (obviously she practiced well)
- some differences among these students
- the use of PowerPoint slides within the presentation (some better than others)
- the appropriate occasional use of humor
- the division of presentation responsibilities within the student group
- each presenter's interaction with the audience

KEY TAKEAWAYS

- Public speaking skills are important because you will likely give presentations in class and perhaps in a future job.
- Overcome anxiety about public speaking by preparing well and practicing your delivery, focusing on your subject.
- Follow a six-step process to prepare and deliver a presentation:
    1. Analyze your audience and goals
    2. Plan, research, and organize your content
    3. Draft and revise the presentation
    4. Prepare speaking notes
    5. Practice the presentation
    6. Deliver the presentation and seek feedback
- Use visual aids to support a presentation, creating visuals that are relevant, attractive, and powerful.
- The success of a group presentation depends on effective group meetings, successful division of roles, and repeated group practices.

CHECKPOINT EXERCISES

1. If you have given a class presentation in the past, what worked best for you? (If you have not given a presentation yet as a student, what aspect do you think will be most difficult for you?)

   _____

   _____

2. Name the two most important things you can do to reduce anxiety about a class presentation you will give.

   _____

   _____

3. For each of the following statements about class presentations, circle T for true or F for false:

T	F	Although you are delivering the presentation to the class, your real audience is your instructor, so you don't need to waste time defining terms and concepts he or she already knows.
T	F	Organizing a presentation or speech is similar to organizing topics in a paper you write for class.
T	F	When creating visual aids, put as many photos as you can in each PowerPoint slide to have the strongest impact.
T	F	In case your memory goes blank while giving a presentation, write the full presentation out so that you can read it aloud.

4. Describe how best to use body language (facial expressions, eye movements, gestures, etc.) when giving a presentation.

   _____

   _____

   _____

5. If you were assigned along with three other students to give a group presentation, what would be your preferred role in the preparation stages? Your least preferred role? If you had to take your least preferred role, what single thing would you want to work hardest on to make the presentation successful?

   _____

   _____

   _____

   _____

6. CHAPTER ACTIVITIES

Chapter Takeaways

- Actively engaging in your college education is essential for success, including attending classes, participating, and communicating with your instructors.
- Students benefit in many ways when they participate in class and feel free to ask questions.
- Successful participation in class and interaction with your instructor begin with preparing for class and working on communication skills.
- Networking with instructors has benefits for your future and may lead to finding a helpful mentor.
- Both impromptu speaking in class and class presentations help develop key skills.
- Learning to work well in a group is an element of college success.

CHAPTER REVIEW

1. List as many benefits of participating in class as you can think of.

   _____
   _____
   _____
   _____
   _____
   _____

2. Consider the instructors in your current classes. Which instructor have you spoken with *the least* (in or outside of class)?

   _____

   Are you hesitant to speak up in this class—or to see the instructor outside of class? Why?

   _____
   _____

   When you have a question for this instructor about an assignment or reading, which form of communication would be most appropriate?

   _____

3. List ways to be prepared if you have a question to ask in a large lecture class.

   _____
   _____
   _____
   _____

4. Think ahead about this: If you were to develop a mentoring relationship with one of your present instructors, what sorts of things might you still talk about in the future even after graduation?

   _____
   _____
   _____
   _____

5. Review the six stages for preparing and giving a class presentation. Which stage(s) do you feel you personally need to pay special attention to next time you are assigned a presentation?

   _____
   _____

   What specifically can you plan to do to ensure your success in those stages in your next presentation?

OUTSIDE THE BOOK

Choose your current class with the most students in it and decide to ask the instructor a question in the next class or during office hours. Prepare by carefully reviewing your notes and select a subject area that you do not feel confident you fully understand. Focus on a specific topic and write down a question whose answer would help you better understand the topic. Go to class prepared to ask that question if it is relevant to the day's discussion or lecture; if it is not relevant, visit your instructor during office hours and ask the question. If this is your first time talking with this instructor, remember to introduce yourself and explain your interest in the topic as you ask the question. Remember that your second goal is to begin establishing a relationship with this instructor.

MAKE AN ACTION LIST

Attending Class

I sometimes don't go to class because

_____

_____

I'll keep myself motivated to go to every class by

_____

_____

Participating in Class

I tend to participate most in this class:

_____

I need to make an effort to participate more in this class:

_____

I need to participate more because

_____

_____

I will take the following steps to be ready to ask a question:

_____

_____

Attending Lecture Classes

I tend to do these nonproductive things if I feel bored in a lecture:

_____

_____

I will work on staying more actively engaged in lectures in these ways:

_____

_____

Talking with Instructors Outside of Class

I have not yet spoken to this instructor outside of class:

_____

Within the next two weeks, I will stop by during office hours to talk about the following:

_____

_____

This instructor's office hours are

_____

Using E-mail

The following are my worst e-mail habits:

_____

_____

The following current instructors prefer student questions through e-mail:

_____

_____

I will follow these professional e-mail practices:

_____

_____

Speaking Publicly

I am nervous about giving class presentations because

_____

_____

I realize that the best way to overcome my anxiety about public speaking and succeed in class presentations is to

_____

_____

CLASS DISCUSSION QUESTIONS

1. You attend every class session of a course and take effective notes on both class lectures and the readings. After the second week of class, another student asks to borrow your notes after missing a class. He compliments you on the quality of your notes, then misses another class and again asks to borrow your notes. The next week he does it again. What might you say to this student?

2. One of your classes is a large lecture class in which the instructor does not seem to invite much interaction with students. You notice no one ever speaks with her after class, and she seems to quickly gather up her things and leave. Is it worthwhile to attempt to speak with this instructor, or should you just write off the chances of interaction in this case? If you do decide to speak with her, what approach would you take?

3. You are assigned to a group with three other students to give a presentation a week from now. You all agree to a meeting time to get started, but one of the others does not show up. What do you do? (If you message him to remind him, what happens if again he doesn't show up after he agrees to?)

ENDNOTES

1. Adapted from "How to Communicate and Problem Solve with Your Instructor," http://www.gpslifeplan.org/generic/pdf/how-to-communicate-with-professor.pdf (accessed December 27, 2009).

CHAPTER 8
Writing for Classes

FIGURE 8.1

© *Thinkstock*

Where Are You Now?

Assess your present knowledge and attitudes.

	Yes	Unsure	No
1. I enjoy writing and am a confident and effective writer.			
2. I know what my instructors expect in student writing.			
3. I understand the feedback I get from instructors and accept their criticism.			
4. I am comfortable sharing my writing with peers.			
5. I begin working on papers early and always revise my first draft before turning in the paper.			
6. I have a consistent approach to the writing process that works well for me.			
7. I understand what plagiarism is and always cite online and print sources appropriately.			
8. I seek out help whenever needed as I work on paper assignments.			
9. I try to write all my college papers as if they were written for my composition instructor.			

Where Do You Want to Go?

Think about how you answered the questions above. Be honest with yourself. On a scale of 1 to 10, how would you rate your level of confidence and your attitude about writing?

Not very strong					Very strong				
1	2	3	4	5	6	7	8	9	10

In the following list, circle the three areas you see as most important to your improvement as a writer:

- Using time effectively
- Using sources effectively and appropriately
- Understanding instructors' expectations
- Citing sources in the proper form
- Being productive with brainstorming and other prewriting activities
- Sharing my work in drafts and accepting feedback
- Organizing ideas clearly and transitioning between ideas
- Understanding the difference between proofreading and revision
- Developing ideas fully
- Drafting and redrafting in response to criticism
- Using correct sentence mechanics (grammar, punctuation, etc.)
- Using websites, reference books, and campus resources
- Developing an academic "voice"

Think about the three things you chose: Why did you choose them? Have you had certain kinds of writing difficulties in the past? Consider what you hope to learn here.

_____

_____

_____

How to Get There

Here's what we'll work on in this chapter:

- Understanding why writing is vital to your success in college
- Learning how writing in college differs from writing in high school
- Understanding how a writing class differs (and doesn't differ) from other classes with assigned writing
- Knowing what instructors in college expect of you as a writer
- Understanding the different types of writing assignments that are common in college
- Using the writing process to achieve your best work
- Identifying common errors and become a better editor of your own work
- Responding to an instructor's feedback on your work in progress and on your final paper
- Using sources appropriately and avoiding plagiarism
- Writing an in-class essay, for an online course, and in group writing projects

1. THE IMPORTANCE OF WRITING

Writing is one of the key skills all successful students must acquire. You might think your main job in a history class is to learn facts about events. So you read your textbook and take notes on important dates, names, causes, and so on. But however important these details are, they don't mean much if you can't explain them in writing. Even if you remember the facts well and believe you understand their meaning completely, if you can't express your understanding by communicating it—in college that almost always means in writing—then as far as others may know, you don't have an understanding at all.

In a way, then, learning history is learning to write about history. Think about it. Great historians don't just know facts and ideas. Great historians use their writing skills to share their facts and ideas effectively with others.

History is just one example. Consider a lab course—a class that's as much hands-on as any in college. At some point, you'll be asked to write a step-by-step report on an experiment. The quality of your lab work will not show if you cannot describe that work and state your findings well in writing. Even though many instructors in courses other than English classes may not comment directly on your writing, their judgment of your understanding will still be mostly based on what you write. This means that in all your courses, not just your English courses, instructors expect good writing.

In most college courses, writing is how ideas are exchanged. While the grade in some courses may be based mostly on class participation, oral reports, or multiple-choice exams, writing is by far the single most important form of assessment. Instructors expect you to learn by writing, and they will grade you on the basis of your writing.

If you find that a scary thought, take heart! By paying attention to your writing and learning and practicing basic skills, even those who never thought of themselves as good writers can succeed in college writing. As with other college skills, getting off to a good start is mostly a matter of being motivated and developing a confident attitude that you can do it.

As a form of communication, writing is different from oral communication. Instructors expect writing to be well thought out and organized and to explain ideas fully. In oral communication, the listener can ask for clarification, but in written work, everything must be clear within the writing itself. Guidelines for oral presentations are provided in Chapter 7

Note: Most college students take a writing course in their first year, often in the first term. Even if you are not required to take a class, it's a good idea for all students to learn more about college writing. This short chapter cannot cover even a small amount of what you will learn in a full writing course. Our goal here is to introduce some important writing principles, if you're not yet familiar with them, or to remind you of things you may have already learned. But always pay the most attention to what your instructor says—the terms of a specific assignment may overrule a tip given here!

2.   WHAT'S DIFFERENT ABOUT COLLEGE WRITING?

LEARNING OBJECTIVES

1. Define "academic writing."
2. Identify key differences between writing in college and writing in high school or on the job.
3. Identify different types of papers commonly assigned in college.
4. Describe what instructors expect from student writing.

Academic writing refers to writing produced in a college environment. Often this is writing that responds to other writing, such as to ideas that you read about in a course. While this definition sounds simple, academic writing may be very different from other types of writing you have done in the past. Often college students begin to understand what academic writing really means only after they have received negative feedback on some assignment. To become a strong writer in college, you need to achieve a clear sense of two things:

Academic writing

Analytical or informative nonfiction writing that is assigned by college instructors.

1. The academic environment
2. The kinds of writing you'll be doing in that environment

2.1   Differences between High School and College Writing

Students who struggle with writing in college often conclude that their high school teachers were too easy or that their college instructors are too hard. Usually neither explanation is fully accurate or fair. A student having difficulty with college writing usually just hasn't yet made the transition from high school writing to college writing—in fact, most beginning college students do not even know that there is a difference.

In high school, most students think of writing as the subject of English classes. Few teachers in other courses give much feedback on student writing; many do not even assign writing. This says more about high school than about the quality of teachers or about writing. High school teachers typically teach five courses a day and often have more than 150 students with a wide range of skill levels.

Many high school English instructors therefore focus on specific, limited goals. For example, they may teach the "five paragraph essay" as the right way to shape a paper because they want every student to have a clear idea of an essay's basic structure. They may give assignments on stories and poems because an English course is often a literature course. In classes other than English, many high school teachers must focus on their specific subject and may judge students using tests that measure only how much of this information they acquire. Often writing itself is not directly addressed in other classes.

This doesn't mean that you didn't learn a great deal in high school, but it's easy to see why some students think that writing is important only in English classes. Many students also graduate thinking that an academic essay must be five paragraphs long and that "school writing" is usually literary analysis.

Think about how college differs from high school. In many colleges, instructors teach fewer classes and have fewer students. In addition, the writing skills of college students are less variable than in an average high school class. College instructors may design their courses in unique ways, and they may teach specialized subjects. For all of these reasons, college instructors are much more likely than high school teachers to:

- assign writing
- respond in detail to student writing
- ask questions that cannot be dealt with easily in a fixed form like a five-paragraph essay

genre

A kind or type of essay; an approach or a specific form of organization; a compare-and-contrast essay, for example, is a genre often assigned by college instructors.

Your transition to college writing could be even more dramatic. The kind of writing you have done in the past may not translate at all into the kind of writing required in college. For example, you may at first struggle with having to write about very different kinds of topics, using different approaches. You may have learned only one kind of writing **genre** (a kind of approach or organization) and now find you need to master other types of writing as well.

2.2   What Kinds of Papers Are Commonly Assigned in College Classes?

Think about the topic "gender roles"—referring to expectations about differences in how men and women act. You might study gender roles in an anthropology class, a film class, or a psychology class. The topic itself may overlap from one class to another, but you would not write about this subject in the same way in these different classes. For example, in an anthropology class, you might be asked to describe how men and women in a particular culture behave differently. In a film class, you may be asked to analyze how a scene portrays gender roles enacted by the film's characters. In a psychology course, you might be asked to summarize the results of an experiment involving gender roles or compare and contrast the findings of two related research projects.

It would be simplistic to say that there are three, or four, or ten, or any number of types of academic writing that have unique characteristics, shapes, and styles. **Every assignment in every course is unique in some ways, so don't think of writing as a fixed form you need to learn.** On the other hand, there are certain writing *approaches* that do involve different kinds of writing. An approach is the way you go about meeting the writing goals for the assignment. The approach is usually signaled by the words instructors use in their assignments.

When you receive a writing assignment, pay attention first to key words in the assignment. These suggest how you may structure and develop your paper. Look for terms like these in the assignment:

- **Summarize.** To restate in your own words the main point or points of another's work.
- **Define.** To describe, explore, or characterize a key event, idea, or phenomenon.
- **Classify.** To group individual items by their shared characteristics, different from other groups of items.
- **Compare/contrast.** To explore significant likenesses and differences between two or more subjects.
- **Analyze.** To break something, a phenomenon, or an idea into its parts and explain how those parts fit or work together.
- **Argue.** To state a claim and support it with reasons and evidence.
- **Synthesize.** To bring together in a unified whole varied pieces or ideas from two or more sources.

Note how this list is similar to the words used in exam questions that involve writing, as discussed in Chapter 6. This overlap is not a coincidence, because essay exams are a form of academic writing such as a class paper.

Sometimes the key words listed above don't actually appear in the assignment, but usually one or more are implied by questions asked in the assignment. "What," "why," and "how" are common question words that require a certain kind of response. Look back at the list of key words and think about which approaches relate to "what," "why," and "how" questions.

- "What" questions usually prompt the writing of summaries, definitions, classifications, and sometimes compare-and-contrast essays. For example, "**What** does Jones see as the main elements of Huey Long's populist appeal?" or "**What** happened when you heated the chemical solution?"
- "Why" and "how" questions typically prompt analysis, argument, and synthesis essays. For example, "**Why** did Huey Long's brand of populism gain force so quickly?" or "**Why** did the chemical solution respond the way it did to heat?"

Successful academic writing starts with recognizing what the instructor asks you to do in the assignment, so pay close attention to the written instructions. When the instructor talks about an assignment in class, also listen for the key words that will help you understand what the instructor expects. If you feel the assignment instructions do not give you a sense of direction, seek clarification. Ask questions that will lead to helpful answers. For example, here's a short and very vague assignment:

Discuss the perspectives on religion of Rousseau, Bentham, and Marx. Papers should be four to five pages in length.

With an assignment like this, you could ask about the **scope (or focus)** of the assignment:

- Which of the assigned readings should I concentrate on?
- Should I read other works by these authors that haven't been assigned in class?
- Should I do research to see what scholars think about the way these philosophers view religion?
- Do you want me to pay equal attention to each of the three philosophers?

You can also ask about the approach the instructor would like you to take. You can use the keywords the instructor may not have used in the assignment:

- Should I just *summarize* the positions of these three thinkers, or should I *compare and contrast* their views?
- Do you want me to *argue* a specific point about the way these philosophers approach religion?
- Would it be OK if I *classified* the ways these philosophers think about religion?

Never just complain about a vague assignment. It is fine to ask questions like these. Such questions usually lead to a productive discussion with your instructor.

> **scope (or focus)**
>
> A deliberate and purposeful narrowing of coverage. Writers must define specific limitations to work within to narrow the scope or sharpen the focus of their subject.

KEY TAKEAWAYS

- Writing is crucial to college success because it is the single most important means of evaluation.
- Writing in college is generally very different from the kinds of writing assignments commonly done in high school English classes.
- Writers in college must pay close attention to the terms of an assignment.
- If an assignment is not clear, seek clarification from the instructor.

CHECKPOINT EXERCISES

1. What kind(s) of writing have you practiced most in your recent past?
   _____
   _____

2. Name two things that make academic writing in college different from writing in high school.
   _____
   _____

3. Explain how the word "what" asks for a different kind of paper than the word "why."
   _____
   _____
   _____
   _____

3. HOW CAN I BECOME A BETTER WRITER?

LEARNING OBJECTIVES

1. **Describe how a writing class can help you succeed in other courses.**
2. **Define what instructors expect of a college student's writing.**
3. **Explain why learning to write is an ongoing task.**
4. **Understand writing as a process.**
5. **Develop productive prewriting and revision strategies.**
6. **Distinguish between revision and editing.**
7. **Access and use available resources.**
8. **Understand how to integrate research in your writing.**
9. **Define plagiarism and explain how to avoid it.**

Students are usually required to take at least one writing course in their first year of college. But a writing course can help you only if you recognize how it connects to your other work in college. If you approach your writing course merely as another hoop you need to jump through, you may miss out on the main message: writing is vital to your academic success at every step toward your degree.

3.1 What Do Instructors Really Want?

Some instructors may say they have no particular expectations for student papers. This is partly true. When they assign a paper topic, college instructors do not usually have in mind one right answer or one right approach to take. They expect you to engage in critical thinking and decide for yourself what you are saying and how to say it. But in other ways college instructors do have expectations that you need to understand. Some expectations involve mastering the course material or demonstrating critical thinking. Other expectations involve specific writing skills. Here are general principles you should follow when writing essays or student papers. (Some may not be appropriate for specific formats such as lab reports.)

Title the paper to identify your topic. This may sound obvious, but it needs to be said. Some students think of a paper as an exercise and write something like "History 101 Assignment 2" on the title page. Such a title gives no idea about your topic or approach. Your title should prepare your reader for what your paper is about or what you will argue. (With essays, always consider your reader as an educated adult interested in your topic. An essay is not a letter written to your instructor.) Compare the following:

Ineffective: History 101 Assignment 2
Effective: Why the New World Was Not "New"

It is obvious which of these two titles prepares your reader for the paper itself. Similarly, don't the title of a work you are writing about as your own title. Instead, be sure your title signals an aspect of the work you are focusing on:

Ineffective: *Catcher in the Rye*
Effective: Family Relationships in *Catcher in the Rye*

Address the terms of the assignment. As discussed earlier, pay particular attention to words in the assignment that signal the expected approach. If the instructor asks you to "argue" a point, be sure your paper makes a statement that actually expresses *your idea* about the topic. The paper should include your reasons and evidence in support of the statement. Look for any signals in the assignment that help you focus or limit your approach. Since no paper can cover *everything* about a complex topic, what is it that your instructor wants you to cover?

Finally, pay attention to the little things. For example, if the assignment specifies "5 to 6 pages in length," write a five- to six-page paper. Don't try to stretch a short paper longer by enlarging the font (12 points is standard) or making your margins bigger than the normal one inch (or as specified by the instructor). If the assignment is due at the beginning of class on Monday, have it ready then or before. Do not assume you can negotiate a revised due date.

In your introduction, describe your topic and establish your approach or sense of purpose. Think of your introduction as an extension of your title. Instructors (like all readers) appreciate being oriented by a clear opening. They appreciate knowing that you have a purpose for your topic—that you have a reason for writing the paper. If they feel they've just been dropped into the middle of a paper, they may miss important ideas. They may not make connections you want them to make.

Build from a thesis or a clearly stated sense of purpose. Many college assignments require you to make some form of an argument. To do that, you generally start with a statement and build support for it. Your thesis is that statement; it is a guiding assertion for the paper. Be clear in your own mind of the difference between your topic and your thesis. The topic is what your paper is about; the thesis is what *you argue about* the topic. Some assignments do not require an explicit argument and thesis, but even then you should make clear at the beginning your main emphasis, your purpose, or your most important idea.

Develop ideas patiently. You might at first worry about boring your reader with too much detail or information, but college instructors will not be bored by carefully explained ideas, well-selected examples, and relevant details. College instructors, after all, are professionally devoted to their subjects. If your sociology instructor asks you to write about youth crime in rural areas, you can be sure he or she is interested in that subject.

In some respects, how you *develop* your paper is the most crucial part of the assignment. You'll win the day with detailed explanations and well-presented evidence—not big generalizations. For example, anyone can write something broad (and bland) like "The constitutional separation of church and state is a good thing for America"—but what do *you* really *mean* by that? Specifically? Are you talking about banning "Christmas trees" from government property—or calling them "holiday trees" instead? Are you arguing for eliminating the tax-free status of religious organizations? Are you saying that American laws should never be based on moral values? The more you really dig into your topic—the more time you spend thinking about the specifics of what *you* really want to argue and developing specific examples and reasons for your argument—the more *developed* your paper will be. It will also be much more interesting to your instructor as the reader. Remember, those grand generalizations we all like to make ("America is the land of the free") actually don't mean much at all until we develop the idea in specifics. (Free to do what? No laws? No restrictions like speed limits? Freedom not to pay any taxes? Free food for all? What do you *really* mean when you say American is the land of the "free"?)

Integrate—do not just "plug in"—quotations, graphs, and illustrations. As you outline or sketch out your material, you will think things like "This quotation can go here" or "I can put that graph there." Remember that a quotation, graph, or illustration does not make a point for you. *You* make the point first and then use such material to help back it up. Using a quotation, a graph, or an illustration involves more than simply sticking it into the paper. Always lead into such material. Make sure the reader understands why you are using it and how it fits in at that place in your presentation.

Build clear transitions at the beginning of every paragraph to link from one idea to another. A good paper is more than a list of good ideas. It also shows how the ideas fit together. As you begin the first sentence of any paragraph, think what the prior paragraph was about. The first sentence in any paragraph is a kind of bridge for the reader from what came before.

Document your sources appropriately. If your paper involves research of any kind, indicate clearly your use of outside sources. If you use those sources well, there is no reason to hide them. Careful research and the thoughtful application of the ideas and evidence of others is an essential part of most college writing. (We'll address the specifics about documentation later on.)

Carefully edit your paper. College instructors assume you will take the time to edit and proofread your essay. A misspelled word or an incomplete sentence may suggest you don't care much about your work. It may not seem fair to judge your seriousness based on little errors, but in all writing, impressions count. Since it is often hard to find small errors in our own writing, always print out a draft well before you need to turn in a paper. Ask a classmate or a friend to review it and mark any word or sentence that seems "off" in any way. Don't assume a spell-checker can catch everything. A spell-checker cannot tell if you have the *right* word. For example, these words are commonly misused or mixed up:

- there, their, they're
- its, it's
- effect, affect
- complement, compliment

Your spell-checker can't help with these. You also can't trust a "grammar checker" (like the one in the Microsoft Word spell-checker)—computers are still a long way from being able to fix your writing for you!

Turn in a clean hard copy. Some instructors accept or even prefer digital papers, but do not assume this. Most instructors want a paper copy and most definitely do *not* want to do the printing themselves. Present your paper in a professional (and unfussy) way, using a staple or paper clip on the left top to hold the pages together (unless the instructor specifies otherwise). Never bring your paper to class and ask the instructor, "Do you have a stapler?" Do not put your paper in a plastic binder unless the instructor asks you to.

3.2 The Writing Process

process

Discovery, exploration, development, and clarification through a series of steps or exercises.

product

The outcome or end result of a writing process; the finished paper you submit.

Writing instructors distinguish between **process** and **product**. The expectations described here all involve the "product" you turn in on the due date. The writing process focuses on how to get to that goal, how you work to actually write a paper. What do you do to get started? How do you organize your ideas? Why do you make changes along the way as you write? Thinking of writing as a process is important because writing is actually a complex activity. Even professional writers rarely sit down and write out an article beginning to end without stopping along the way to revise portions they have drafted, to move ideas around, or to revise their opening and thesis. Professionals and students alike often say they realized what they wanted to say only *after* they started to write. This is why many instructors see writing as a way to learn. Writing instructors often ask you to submit a draft for review before submitting a final paper. To roughly paraphrase a famous poem, you learn by doing what you have to do.

3.3 How Can I Make the Process Work for Me?

No single set of steps automatically works best for everyone when writing a paper, but most writers have some steps very helpful. Your job is to try out ways that your instructor suggests and discover what works for you. As you'll see in the following list, the process starts before you even write a word. There are three basic stages in the writing process:

1. Preparing before drafting (thinking, brainstorming, planning, reading, researching, outlining, sketching, etc.)—sometimes called "prewriting" (such as jotting notes)
2. Writing the draft
3. Revising and editing

Because writing is hard, procrastination is easy. Don't let yourself put off the task. Use the time management strategies described in Chapter 2. A good approach is to schedule short time periods over a series of days—rather than trying to accomplish it all in one long period. (Even professional writers can write only so much at a time.) Try these strategies to get started:

- **Discuss what you read, see, and hear.** Talking with others about your ideas is a good way to clarify ideas. Listening to others helps you understand what points need special attention.
- **Use e-mail to carry on discussions in writing.** An e-mail exchange with a classmate or your instructor might be the first step toward putting words on a page.
- **Brainstorm.** Jot down your thoughts as they come to mind. Just write away, not worrying at first about how those ideas fit together. (This is often called "free writing.") After writing notes or short blocks of sentences, pause and read them over. Take note of anything that stands out as particularly important. Think about how parts of your scattered notes might eventually fit together or how they might end up in a sequence in the paper you'll get to later on.
- **Ask and respond in writing to "what," "why," and "how" questions**. Good questions prompt a productive writing session. Again, "what" questions will lead to descriptions or summaries; "why" and "how" questions will lead you to analyses and explanations. Construct your own "what," "why," and "how" questions and then start answering them.
- **In your notes, respond directly to what others have written or said about a topic you are interested in.** Most academic writing engages the ideas of others. Academic writing carries on a conversation among people interested in the field. By thinking of how your ideas relate to those of others, you can clarify your sense of purpose and sometimes even discover a way to write your introduction.

All of these steps and actions so far are prewriting actions. Again, almost no one at the beginning just sits down and starts writing a paper—at least not a successful paper! The prewriting steps help you get going in the right direction. Once you are ready to start drafting your essay, keep moving forward in these ways:

revision

A critical reflection of an early draft that leads to significant changes.

- **Write a short statement of intent or outline your paper before your first draft.** This road map can be very useful, but don't assume you'll stick with your first plan. Once you start writing, you may discover a need for changes in your ideas or the order you'd planned for your essay. Such discoveries don't mean you made mistakes in the outline. They simply mean you are involved in a process that cannot be completely scripted in advance.
- **Write down on a card or a separate sheet of paper what you see as your paper's main point or thesis.** As you draft your essay, look back at that thesis statement. Are you staying on track? Or are you discovering that you need to change your main point or thesis? From time to time, check

the development of your ideas against what you started out saying you would do. Revise as needed and move forward.

- **Reverse outline your paper.** Outlining is usually a beginning point, a road map for the task ahead. But many writers find that outlining what they have already written in a draft helps them see more clearly how their ideas fit or do not fit together. This can reveal trouble spots that are harder to see in a full draft. Once you see those trouble spots, effective **revision** is easier.

- **Don't obsess over detail when writing the draft.** Remember, you have time for revising and editing later on. Now is the time to test out the plan you made and see how your ideas develop. The last things in the world you want to worry about now are the little things like grammar and punctuation—spend your time developing your material, knowing you can fix the details later.

- **Read your draft aloud.** Hearing your own writing often helps you see it more plainly. You may catch a gap or an inconsistency in an argument that you simply did not see in a silent reading. You may also catch sentence-level mistakes by reading your paper aloud.

3.4 What's the Difference between Revising and Editing?

Some students think of a first draft as something that they need only "correct" after writing. This is a big mistake. A good writer does not write fast. Good writers know that the task is complicated enough to demand some patience. *"Revision"* rather than "correction" suggests *seeing again* in a new light generated by all the thought that went into the first draft. Revising a draft usually involves significant changes including the following:

- Making organizational changes like the reordering of paragraphs (don't forget that new transitions will be needed when you move paragraphs)
- Clarifying the thesis or adjustments between the thesis and supporting points that follow
- Cutting material that is unnecessary or irrelevant
- Adding new points to strengthen or clarify the argument

Editing and proofreading are the last steps following revision. Correcting a sentence in the first draft may not be the best use of your time since you may cut the sentence entirely in revision. Editing and proofreading are focused, late-stage activities for style and correctness. Editing and proofreading a draft involve these steps:

Editing and proofreading
A close review of a revised draft that leads to stylistic refinements and sentence- or word-level corrections.

- Careful spell-checking, including the spelling of names.
- Attention to sentence-level issues. Be especially attentive to sentence boundaries, subject-verb agreement, punctuation, and pronoun referents. You can also try to improve style.

Remember to get started on a writing assignment early so that you complete the first draft well before the due date, allowing you needed time for genuine revision and careful editing.

3.5 What If I Need Help with Writing?

Writing is hard work. Most colleges provide resources that can help you from the early stages of an assignment through to completion. Your first resource may be a writing class. Most students are encouraged or required to enroll in a writing class in their first term, and it's a good idea for everyone. Use everything you learn there about drafting and revising in all your courses.

Tutoring services. Most colleges have a tutoring service. Look up and visit your tutoring center early in the term to learn what services are offered. Specifically check on the following:

1. Do you have to register in advance for help? If so, is there a registration deadline?
2. Are appointments required or encouraged, or can you just drop in?
3. Are regular standing appointments with the same tutor encouraged?
4. Are the number of sessions allowed per term limited?
5. Are small group workshops offered in addition to individual appointments?
6. Are specialists available for help with students who have learned English as a second language?

Three points about writing tutors are crucial:

1. Writing tutors are there for all student writers—not just for weak or inexperienced writers. Writing in college is *supposed* to be a challenge. Some students make writing even harder by working in isolation. But writing is a social act. A good paper should engage others.

2. Tutors are not there for you to "correct" sentence-level problems or polish your finished draft. They will help you identify and understand sentence-level problems so that you can achieve greater control over your writing. But their more important goals often are to address larger concerns like the paper's organization, the fullness of its development, and the clarity of its argument. So don't make your first appointment the day before a paper is due, because you may need more time to revise after discussing the paper with a tutor.

3. Tutors cannot help you if you do not do your part. Tutors respond only to what you say and write; they cannot magically jump you past the thinking an assignment requires. So do some thinking about the assignment before your meeting and be sure to bring relevant materials with you. For example, bring the paper assignment. You might also bring the course syllabus and perhaps even the required textbook. Most importantly, bring any writing you've already done related to the assignment (an outline, a thesis statement, a draft, an introductory paragraph). If you want to get help from a tutor, you need to give the tutor something to work with.

Teaching assistants and instructors. In a large class, you may have both a course instructor and a teaching assistant (TA). Seek help from either or both as you draft your essay. Some instructors offer only limited help. They may not, for example, have time to respond to a complete draft of your essay. But even a brief response to a draft introduction or to a question can be tremendously valuable. Remember that most TAs and instructors want to help you learn. View them along with tutors as part of a team that works with you to achieve academic success. Remember the tips you learned in Chapter 7 for interacting well with your instructors.

Writing websites and writing handbooks. Many writing websites and handbooks can help you along every step of the way, especially in the late stages of your work. You'll find lessons on style as well as information about language conventions and "correctness." Not only should you use the handbook your composition instructor assigns in a writing class, but you should not sell that book after the course. You will need it again for future writing. For more help, become familiar with a good website for student writers. There are many, but one we recommend is maintained by the Dartmouth College Writing Center at http://writing-speech.dartmouth.edu/learning/materials.

3.6 Writing Software and Apps

"There's an app for that!" These days it seems there are apps, software, and websites for practically everything—and of course writing is no exception. Many apps and software programs promise to speed up your writing process or help you improve your writing. And while various applications do in fact assist with some aspects of writing, college writing generally is much too variable and flexible for any magic solutions to the work involved.

Most of the software designed for helping students think up a topic, brainstorm ideas about it, and organize ideas into an effective shape were developed for younger writers, from elementary school through high school. Some are effective in helping teach writing, but generally they're pretty basic and tend to be formulaic—and therefore not very applicable to college writing. Some of the available more advanced software may be helpful for brainstorming, such as programs that develop mind maps or bubbles, but they may actually take more time to use than plain old pen and paper. Still, there are some other good tools to help you at different points when writing.

First, use a good word processing program. Microsoft Word has become in the standard in business and much of the academic world, and it has useful features for writing college essays. It is easy to outline an essay and move outline entries around and change how ideas are joined together or subordinated to other ideas. The "comment" feature in Word and other word processors is useful when you want to note something to come back to when writing or to give comments to other writers, as in a group project. The free LibreOffice and OpenOffice software suites are similar and effective for outlining, footnoting, spell-checking, and so on if you don't want to buy Word.

Other programs and apps are useful in the research stage. Note-taking programs such as Evernote and OneNote make it easy to clip information from websites and elsewhere, along with source citations, for later use when writing. Both of these can sync across devices, so that you can view information on your computer after clipping from a site on your tablet. Syncing can also be useful for sharing material in a group project.

Also useful in group projects are programs, such as Dropbox, that make it easy to share files that are too large to send by email, such as sharing large graphics files or PowerPoints among different members of a group. And if you want to share a document and allow various group members to work on it simultaneously, without having, for example, to send a Word document back and forth, you might use Google Docs. This maintains your working document in the cloud so that anyone in the group can access it and make revisions online at any time.

Finally, in case you've never developed your typing skills and are slow on a keyboard, invest some time in a program like RapidTyping Tutor, which will help you gain proficiency. If you are a slow typist it's worthwhile to spend the time now at the beginning of your college career, since you'll be doing a lot of keyboarding in your future!

3.7   Plagiarism—and How to Avoid It

Plagiarism is the unacknowledged use of material from a source. At the most obvious level, plagiarism involves using someone else's words and ideas as if they were your own. Copying another person's work is cheating, pure and simple. But plagiarism is not always so simple. Notice that our definition of plagiarism involves both "words and ideas." Let's break that down a little further.

Words. Copying the words of another is clearly wrong. If you use someone's words, those words must be in quotation marks, and you must tell your reader where those words came from. But you can't just change some words and call the material yours; close, extended paraphrase is not acceptable. For example, compare the two passages that follow. The first comes from *Murder Most Foul*, a book by Karen Halttunen on changing ideas about murder in nineteenth-century America; the second is a close paraphrase of the same passage:

> *The new murder narratives were overwhelmingly secular works, written by a diverse array of printers, hack writers, sentimental poets, lawyers, and even murderers themselves, who were displacing the clergy as the dominant interpreters of the crime.*

> *The murder stories that were developing were almost always secular works that were written by many different sorts of people. Printers, hack writers, poets, attorneys, and sometimes even the criminals themselves were writing murder stories. They were the new interpreters of the crime, replacing religious leaders who had held that role before.*

It is easy to see that the writer of the second version closely followed the ideas and even echoed some words of the original. This is a serious form of plagiarism. Even if this writer were to acknowledge the original author, there would still be a problem. To simply cite the source at the end would not excuse using so much of the source.

Ideas. Ideas are also a form of intellectual property. Consider this third version of the previous passage:

> *At one time, religious leaders shaped the way the public thought about murder. But in nineteenth-century America, this changed. Society's attitudes were influenced more and more by secular writers.*

This version summarizes the original. That is, it states the main idea in compressed form in language that does not come from the original. But it could still be seen as plagiarism if the source is not cited. Here's a way to fix that: *"Halttunen argues that at one time, religious leaders shaped...."*

This example may make you wonder if you can write anything without citing a source. To help you sort out what ideas need to be cited and what not, think about these principles:

Common knowledge. There is no need to cite **common knowledge**. Common knowledge does not mean knowledge everyone has. It means knowledge that everyone can easily access. For example, most people do not know the date of George Washington's death, but everyone can easily find that information. If the information or idea can be found in multiple sources and the information or idea remains constant from source to source, it can be considered common knowledge. This is one reason so much research is usually done for college writing—the more sources you read, the more easily you can sort out what is common knowledge: if you see an idea in multiple sources, none of which cite a source for it, then you can feel secure that idea is common knowledge.

Distinct contributions. One *does* need to cite ideas that are **distinct contributions**. A distinct contribution may have come from the work of one person. It is an insight that is not commonly expressed (not found in multiple sources) and is not universally agreed upon.

Disputable figures. Always remember that numbers, even when stated as fact, are only as good as the sources they come from. If you use numbers like attendance figures, unemployment rates, or demographic profiles—or any statistics at all—always cite your source of those numbers.

Everything said previously about using sources applies to all forms of sources. Some students mistakenly believe that material from the web, for example, need not be cited. Or that an idea from an

Plagiarism

The unacknowledged use of another writer's words or ideas.

common knowledge

Knowledge that is generally accepted as true and that can be found easily in various sources.

distinct contributions

Knowledge or an idea that may be disputed or that is not found in many sources.

instructor's lecture is automatically common property. You must evaluate all sources in the same way and cite them as necessary.

3.8 Forms of Citation

Your instructors will generally tell you what form of citation to use in your course papers. No one standard is used in all academic papers. Three major forms or styles are used in most any college writing handbook and on many websites for college writers:

- The Modern Language Association (MLA) system of citation is widely used in humanities courses, particularly literature courses.
- The American Psychological Association (APA) system of citation is most common in the social sciences.
- The Chicago Manual of Style is commonly in history and other courses.

Many college departments have their own style guides, which may be based on one of the above. Your instructor should tell you what guide to use, and be sure to ask if you don't know.

Checklists for Revision and Editing

When you revise your writing:

	Check the assignment: does your paper do what it's supposed to do?
	Check the title: does it clearly identify the overall topic or position?
	Check the introduction: does it set the stage and establish the purpose?
	Check each paragraph in the body: does each begin with a transition from the preceding?
	Check organization: does it make sense why each topic precedes or follows another?
	Check development: is each topic fully explained, detailed, supported, and exemplified?
	Check the conclusion: does it restate the thesis and pull key ideas together?

When you edit your writing:

	Read the paper aloud, listening for flow and natural word style.
	Check for any lapses into slang, colloquialisms, or nonstandard English phrasing.
	Check sentence-level mechanics: spelling, grammar, and punctuation (pay special attention to past writing problems).
	When everything seems done, run the spell-checker again and do a final proofread.
	Check physical layout and mechanics against instructor's expectations: Title page? Font and margins? End notes?

KEY TAKEAWAYS

- A writing course is central to all students' success in future courses.
- Writing is a process that involves a number of steps; the product will not be good if one does not allow time for the process.
- Seek feedback from classmates, tutors, and instructors during the writing process.
- Revision is not the same thing as editing.
- Many resources are available to college writers.
- Words and ideas from sources must be documented in a form required by the instructor.

CHECKPOINT EXERCISE

1. For each of the following statements, circle T for true or F for false:

T	F	Intellectual freedom means that college instructors have no specific expectations for student writing.
T	F	Since your instructor knows what you are writing about, you do not need to worry about titling your paper.
T	F	The writing process begins when you start writing the first paragraph of a paper.
T	F	If you discover at some point in the writing process that you have to make significant organizational changes or even change your thesis, then you must have misunderstood the assignment.
T	F	Copying directly from another's text is the only serious form of plagiarism.
T	F	The Internet is a free zone of information; web sources need not be cited.
T	F	All college instructors expect citations to be made in exactly the same way.

4. OTHER KINDS OF WRITING IN COLLEGE CLASSES

LEARNING OBJECTIVES

1. **Understand the special demands of specific writing situations, including these:**
   - **Writing in-class essays**
   - **Writing with others in a group project**
   - **Writing in an online class**

Everything we've said about college writing so far in this chapter applies in most college writing assignments. Some particular situations, however, deserve special attention. These include writing in-class essays, group writing projects, and writing in an online course.

4.1   Writing In-Class Essays

You might well think the whole writing process goes out the window when you have to write an essay in class. After all, you don't have much time to spend on the essay. You certainly don't have time for an extensive revision of a complete draft. You also don't have the opportunity to seek feedback at any stage along the way. Nonetheless, the best writers of in-class essays bring as much of the writing process as they can into an essay exam situation. Follow these guidelines:

- Prepare for writing in class by making writing a regular part of your study routine. Students who write down their responses to readings throughout a term have a huge advantage over students who think they can study by just reading the material closely. Writing is a way to build better writing, as well as a great way to study and think about the course material. Don't wait until the exam to start writing about things you have been studying throughout the term.

- Read the exam prompt or assignment very carefully before you begin to respond. Note key words in the exam prompt. For example, if the exam assignment asks for an argument, be sure to structure your essay as an argument. Also look for ways the instructor has limited the scope of the question and your response. Focus on what is highlighted in the exam question itself. See Chapter 6 for more tips for exam writing.

- Jot notes and sketch out a list of key points you want to cover before you jump into writing. If you have time, you might even draft an opening paragraph on scratch paper before committing yourself to a particular response. Too often, students begin writing before they have thought about the whole task before them. When that happens, you might find that you can't develop your ideas as fully or as coherently as you need to. Students who take the time to plan actually write longer in-class essays than those who begin writing their answers right after they have read the assignment. Take as much as a fourth of the total writing time allowed to plan.

- Use a consistent approach for in-class exams. Students who begin in-class exams with a plan that they have used successfully in the past are better able to control the pressure of the in-class exam.

Students who need to discover a new approach for each exam are far more likely to panic and freeze.

- Keep track of the time. Some instructors signal the passing of time during the exam period, but do not count on that help. Don't compulsively check the time every minute or two, look at your watch now and then.

- Save a few minutes at the end of the session for quick review of what you've written and for making small changes you note as necessary.

A special issue of in-class exams concerns handwriting. Some instructors allow students to write in-class exams on laptops, but the old-fashioned blue book is still the standard in many classes. For students used to writing on a keyboard, this can be a problem. Be sure you don't let poor handwriting hurt you. Your instructor will have many exams to read. Be courteous. Write as clearly as you can.

4.2   Group Writing Projects

College instructors sometimes assign group writing projects. These assignments vary greatly. Sometimes the instructor specifies roles for each member of the group, but often the group has to define everyone's role. Follow these guidelines:

- Get off to an early start and meet regularly through the process.

- Sort out your roles as soon as you can. You might divide the work in sections and then meet to pull those sections together. But you might also think more in terms of the specific strengths and interests each of you has. For example, if one group member is an experienced researcher, that person might gather and annotate materials for the assignment. You might also assign tasks that relate to the stages of the writing process. For example, one person for one meeting might construct a series of questions or a list of points to be addressed, to start a discussion about possible directions for the first draft. Another student might take a first pass at shaping the group's ideas with an outline or in a rough draft. And so on. Remember that whatever you do, you cannot likely keep each person's work separate from the work of others. You'll need to work together eventually to make the project successful.

- Be a good citizen. This is the most important point of all. If you are assigned a group project, be an active part of the group's work. Never try to ride on the skills of others or let others do more than their fair share. Don't let any lack of confidence you may feel as a writer keep you from doing your share. One of the great things about a group project is that you can learn from others. Another great thing is that you will learn more about your own strengths that others value.

- Complete a draft early so that you can collectively review, revise, and finally edit together.

- See the section on group presentations in Chapter 7 for additional tips.

4.3   Writing in Online Courses

All the principles discussed in this chapter apply also in online writing—and many aspects are even more important in an online course. In most online courses, almost everything depends on written communication. Discussion is generally written rather than spoken. Questions and clarifications take shape in writing. Feedback on assignments is given in writing. To succeed in online writing, apply the same writing process as fully and thoughtfully as with an essay or paper for any course.

With an online course, you might write as usual using a word processing program and then submit the final document within the course system. But in some cases you may be writing "in a box" within the system itself. Be especially careful with this approach, which may tempt you to do only first-draft work without revision (or even editing). Instead, use the full writing process to your advantage, as usual, and then paste the revised final draft into the system to submit it. Even with a timed writing exercise, like an in-class essay, take some time to plan and organize your thoughts.

Finally, you may learn that in some cases, the computer is grading your writing rather than the instructor reading it on the other end. Several such computer-grading systems have been developed for essays, and proponents argue they can be effective (while detractors argue that software cannot possibly fairly evaluate the written expression of ideas). In any case, if you learn that the grading is being done by computer, don't try to game the system. For example, some students may think the software will just look for identifiable facts or key terms in the essay—and then try to "beat the system" by just sticking every possible term and fact in their writing rather than coherently developing their ideas in an organized essay. Such an essay is not very likely to make good sense! In addition, even if the computer assigns a score, the instructor will likely read or at least skim some or all students' work, and attempts to game the system will be obvious.

KEY TAKEAWAYS

- Even in in-class essays, using an abbreviated writing process helps produce more successful writing.
- Group writing projects require careful coordination of roles and cooperative stages but can help students improve their writing.
- Writing for an online course puts your writing skills to the ultimate test, when almost everything your instructor knows about your learning must be demonstrated through your writing.

CHECKPOINT EXERCISES

1. List three ways in which a process approach can help you write an in-class essay.

   _____
   _____
   _____

2. Describe what you see as a strength you could bring to a group writing project.

   _____
   _____

3. Explain ways in which writing in an online course emphasizes the importance of writing skills.

   _____
   _____

5. CHAPTER ACTIVITIES

Chapter Takeaways

- Successful writers in all contexts think of writing as:
  - A process
  - A means to learn
  - A social act
- Paying close attention to the terms of the assignment is essential for understanding the writing approach the instructor expects and for shaping the essay.
- Using the writing process maximizes the mental processes involved in thinking and writing. Take the time to explore prewriting strategies before drafting an essay in order to discover your ideas and how best to shape and communicate them.
- Avoid the temptation, after writing a draft, to consider the essay done. Revision is almost always needed, involving more significant changes than just quick corrections and editing.
- Virtually all college writing builds on the ideas of others. In your writing, be sure you always make it clear in your phrasing and use of citations which ideas are your own or common knowledge and which come from other sources.
- College writing extends throughout the curriculum, from your first writing class through to your last term, including writing in class on examinations, group projects, and online courses. Through all this great variety of writing, the main principles of effective writing remain consistent. Work to develop your college writing skills at this early stage, and you will be well served throughout your education and into your career.

CHAPTER REVIEW

1. Complete this sentence:

   The main reason I am in college right now is

   _____

2. Look for abstract or general words in what you just wrote. (For example, if you wrote, "I want a better job," the key general word is "better." If you wrote, "I need a good education for my future," the general words are "good" and "education." Circle the general word(s) in what *you* wrote.

3. Write a sentence that gives your personal definition for each of your general words. (For example, if you wrote "I want a better job," what makes a job *better* to you personally?)

   _____

   _____

4. Now look at the *why* of what you've written. *Why* did you define your reason for being in college in the way that you did? Why this reason and not other reasons? Think about this for a minute, and then jot down a statement about why this is important to you.

   _____

   _____

   _____

5. Now look at the *what* involved in your reasoning. *What specifically* do you expect as a result of being in college? What are you gaining? Try to come up with at least three or four *specific examples* related to your reasoning so far.

   _____

   _____

   _____

   _____

6. Imagine you are assigned to write an essay for this prompt: "Argue for a particular benefit of a college education." Look back at what you've written so far—is it headed in this direction? Write down a tentative thesis statement for such an essay.

   _____

   _____

7. Look back at what you wrote for questions 5 and 6 to see if you have the beginning of a list of topics you might discuss in an assigned essay like this. Test out a possible outline by jotting down a few key phrases in the order in which you might discuss your ideas in the essay.

   _____

   _____

   _____

   _____

   _____

8. Think about what you have just been doing in the previous questions. If you took this exercise seriously and wrote out your responses, you might actually be ready to begin writing such an essay—at least you are as prepared as you might be for an in-class exam essay. You have just gone through the first step of the writing process, even if very quickly. If you spent a few minutes thinking about your ideas, clarifying your reasons, and thinking of developing your thesis through examples and explanations, you are in a better and stronger position to begin writing than if you'd started immediately with the prompt. Your essay will be much more successful.

OUTSIDE THE BOOK

1. Use this exercise for the next paper you write in any of your college classes. Your goal is not merely to write a great paper but to learn what writing process techniques work best for you. Plan to begin just as soon as you are given the assignment. Try to use each and every one of these strategies (review them in the chapter), even if some things seem repetitive. Your goal is to find out which techniques work best for you to stimulate the most thought and lead to the best writing.

   - Read the assignment and make sure you understand exactly what is expected.
   - Sit down with a piece of paper and jot some notes as you brainstorm about your topic.
   - Talk with another student in the class about what you're thinking about your topic and what you might say about it.
   - Write a journal entry, written strictly to yourself, about what you think you might do in your paper.
   - Write down some questions to yourself about what your paper will cover. Start your questions with "why," "how," and "what."
   - Send a classmate an e-mail in which you describe one of the points you'll make in your essay, asking them for their opinion about it.
   - When your classmate responds to your e-mail, think about what they said and prepare a written response in your notes.
   - Write a statement of purpose for the paper and a brief outline listing key points.
   - Show your outline to your instructor or TA and ask if you're on the right track for the assignment. (You can ask other questions, too, but try this step even if you feel confident and have no questions at all. You might be surprised by their response.)
   - Write a fuller outline—and then go ahead and draft the paper.

2. Return to this exercise after receiving the paper back from your instructor. If you feel the paper was successful, think back to the techniques you used and circle the steps above that you felt were particularly helpful and contributed to your success. If you are dissatisfied with the paper, it's time to be honest with yourself about what happened. When unhappy about a grade on a paper, most students admit they didn't spend as much time on it as they should have. Look back at the list above (and other writing strategies earlier in this chapter): what *should* you have done more fully or more carefully to make sure your paper got off to a good start?

MAKE AN ACTION LIST

Past Writing

My worst writing habits have been the following:

_____

_____

To overcome these bad habits in college, I will take these steps:

_____

_____

Sentence-Level Mechanics

I generally make the following specific errors (things my past teachers have marked):

_____

_____

I can learn to correct errors like these when proofreading and editing by

_____

_____

Writing Process

I generally rush through the following stage: (circle one)

- Prewriting
- Drafting
- Revising/proofreading

I will spend this much time on that stage in my next college paper:

_____

_____

I will use these strategies to ensure that I successfully move through that stage:

_____

_____

Seeking Help

I am most likely to need help in these areas of writing:

_____

_____

I will use these resources if I need help in these areas in my next paper:

_____

_____

CLASS DISCUSSION QUESTIONS

1. What was the most difficult writing assignment you have had so far this term? What specifically made it so hard? Based on what you have learned in this chapter, how would you do such an assignment differently next time?

2. Many great writers have said that one of the keys to their success was writing in the same place at the same time of day. How do you think that could contribute to successful writing?

3. This chapter does not directly discuss "writer's block," the difficulty getting started writing when faced by a blank page. What strategies discussed in this chapter can help ensure that you don't experience writer's block in your academic writing?

The Social World of College

FIGURE 9.1

© *Thinkstock*

Where Are You Now?

Assess your present knowledge and attitudes.

	Yes	Unsure	No
1. My interactions with students and others on campus will contribute to my academic success.			
2. I feel I would like to make more or different friends in college.			
3. I am sometimes shy about interacting with others in social settings or feel lonely when by myself.			
4. I make an effort to communicate well in social interactions, especially to listen actively when others are speaking.			
5. I use social networking websites to actively enhance social relationships.			
6. When I get in an argument with someone, I work to calm the situation and try to reach a compromise solution we can both live with.			
7. I am comfortable in situations interacting with people who are different from me in age, race, ethnicity, or cultural background.			
8. I make an effort to meet and learn about others different from me and to accept and respect their differences.			
9. When I see someone making a racist or sexist joke or comment, I speak out against prejudice.			
11. I am participating in some clubs and activities on campus that interest me.			

Where Do You Want to Go?

Think about how you answered the questions above. Be honest with yourself. On a scale of 1 to 10, how would you rate your college relationships and interactions with people from different backgrounds at this time?

Not very healthy					Very strong				
1	2	3	4	5	6	7	8	9	10

In the following list, circle the three most important areas of social interaction in which you think you can improve:

- Variety of friends and relationships
- Ability to interact comfortably with strangers
- Speaking skills
- Listening skills
- Assertive communication skills
- Use of online social networking
- Conflict resolution
- Comfort level around people of different race or ethnicity
- Interacting with people of different cultural backgrounds
- Ability to speak out against prejudice
- Knowledge of campus clubs and activities
- Participation in campus groups

Are there other areas in which you can improve your social relationships and interactions with others to improve your college experience? Write down other things you feel you need to work on.

_____

_____

_____

How to Get There

Here's what we'll work on in this chapter:

- Understanding why social interaction is such an important part of the college experience
- Developing new friendships on campus
- Improving communication skills for social interactions at all levels
- Knowing why and how to use online social networking
- Balancing your schoolwork and social life
- Resolving conflicts that may occur in social interactions
- Knowing what to do if you experience harassment
- Understanding the many kinds of diversity found on college campuses
- Celebrating the benefits of diversity for all students
- Dealing with prejudice and discrimination
- Discovering the value of participating in organized campus groups and activities

1. SOCIAL LIFE, COLLEGE LIFE

New college students may not immediately realize that they've entered a whole new world at college, including a world of other people possibly very different from those they have known before. This is a very important dimension of college—almost as important as the learning that goes on inside the classroom. How you deal with the social aspects and diversity of college world has a large impact on your academic success.

All the topics covered in this chapter relate to the social world of college. Here you will gain some insight into the value of making new friends and getting along with a wide variety of people encountered on campus. You will learn why and how a broad diversity of people enriches the college experience and better prepare you for the world after college.

Enter this new world with an open mind and you'll gain many benefits. Even if you are taking a course or two at night and do not spend much of your day on campus, try to make the most of this experience. You'll meet others who will challenge and stimulate you and broaden your thinking and emotional experiences.

2.   GETTING ALONG WITH OTHERS

LEARNING OBJECTIVES

1. Explain the benefits of social interactions with a variety of people in the college environment.
2. List personal characteristics and skills that contribute to one's ability to get along well with others.
3. Improve your communication skills.
4. Use online social networking beneficially.
5. Balance your social life with your studies.
6. Describe how to successfully resolve a conflict with another person.

2.1   Interdependence

Humans are social creatures—it's simply in our nature. We continually interact with other students and instructors, and we can learn much from these interactions that heighten the learning process. This frequent interaction with others forms a state of interdependence. College students depend on their instructors, but just as importantly, they depend on other students in many ways.

As important as our interactions with others are, we don't automatically have the skills that help us form good relationships and make the most of our experiences. Consider how these two college students are different:

> John often arrives just as class is beginning and leaves immediately afterward. He makes little effort to talk with other students in the class, and after class he goes off to study alone or to his part-time job, where he spends most of his time at a computer screen. He is diligent in his studies and generally does well. After two months, he has not gotten to know his roommate very well, and he generally eats alone with a book in hand. On weekends and holidays he often hangs out at his parents' house or sees old friends.

> Kim likes to get to class early and sits near others so they can talk about the reading for class or compare notes. She enjoys running into other students she knows from her classes and usually stops to chat. Although she is an older working student who lives alone off campus, she often dines in a campus café and asks students she meets in her classes to join her. After two months, with the approach of midterms, she formed a study group with other students. A few weeks into the term, she spent a weekend with a student from another country and learned much about a culture about which she had previously known little.

These students are very different. Which do you think is more fully enjoying the college experience? Which do you think is more likely to do well academically? Most of us fall somewhere between these two extremes, but we can learn to be more like Kim and more actively engage with others.

2.2   Recognize the Value of Social Interaction

Building good relationships is important for happiness and a successful college experience. College offers the opportunity to meet many people you would likely not meet otherwise in life. Make the most of this opportunity to gain a number of benefits:

- A growing understanding of diverse other people, how they think, and what they feel that will serve you well throughout your life and in your future career
- A heightened sense of your own identity, especially as you interact with others with different personalities and from different backgrounds
- Emotional comfort from friendship with someone who understands you and with whom you can talk about your problems, joys, hopes, and fears
- An opportunity to grow with wider intellectual and emotional horizons

College often offers an opportunity to be stimulated and excited by new relationships and interactions with people. Still, it can be difficult to get started with new relationships in college.

2.3   Making New Friends in College

Some people just make friends naturally, but many first-year college students are more shy or quiet and may need to actively seek new friends. Here are some starting points:

1. **Keep doors open for meeting new people.** If you live in a dorm, literally keep the door open. Try to sit with different people at meals so you can get to know them better. Study in a common area or lounge where you'll be among others.
2. **Be open in your interests.** Don't limit yourself to people who share only certain interests. Meeting people by studying together is an excellent way to get to know people with different interests.
3. **Don't try to get involved in everything going on around you.** Committing to too many activities or joining too many social groups will spread your time too thin, and you may not spend enough time with anyone to get to know them.
4. **Let others see who you really are.** Let people find out what you're interested in, your real passions. People who really know you are more likely to become good friends.
5. **Make an effort to get to know others, too.** Show some interest. Don't talk just about *your* interests—ask them about theirs. Show others that you're interested, that you think they're worth spending time with, and that you really do want to get to know them.
6. **Once a friendship has started, be a good friend.** Respect your friends for what they are and don't criticize them or talk about them behind their back. Give emotional support when they need it and accept their support when you need it.

Are You Shy?

If you're shy, try meeting and talking to people in situations where you can interact one-to-one, such as talking with another student after class. Start with what you have in common—"How'd you do on the test?"—and let the conversation grow from there. Start conversations with others who look interesting to you. You'll soon find other "shy" or quiet people eager to interact with you as well and get to know you.

Shy people may be more likely to feel lonely at times, especially while still feeling new at college. Loneliness is usually a temporary emotional state, however. For tips for how to overcome feelings of loneliness, see the section on loneliness in Chapter 10.

2.4   Communication Skills

Communication is at the heart of social interaction. Communication with others has a huge effect on our lives, what we think and feel, and what and how we learn. Communication is, many would say, what makes us human.

Oral communication involves not only speech and listening but also **nonverbal communication**: facial expressions, tone of voice, and many other **body language** signals that affect the messages sent and received. People generally pay more attention, often unconsciously, to *how* people say something than to *what* they are saying. When the nonverbal message is inconsistent with the verbal (spoken) message, just as when the verbal message itself is unclear because of poorly chosen words or vague explanations, then miscommunication may occur.

Miscommunication is at the root of many misunderstandings among people and makes it difficult to build relationships.

Chapter 7 discusses oral communication skills in general and guidelines for communicating well with your instructors. The same communication skills are important for building and maintaining social relationships.

Remember that communication is a two-way process. Listening skills are critical for most college students simply because many of us have not learned how to really listen to another person. Here are some guidelines for how to listen effectively:

- **Talk less to listen more.** Most people naturally like to share their thoughts and feelings, and some people almost seem unable to stop talking long enough to ever listen to another person. Try this: next time you're in a conversation with another student, deliberately try not to speak very much but give the other person a chance to speak fully. You may notice a big difference in how much you gain from the conversation.

- **Ask questions.** To keep the conversation going, show your interest in the other person by asking them about things they are saying. This helps the other person feel that you are interested in them.

- **Watch and respond to the other person's body language.** You'll learn much more about their feelings for what they're saying.

- **Show the other person that you're really listening and that you care.** Make eye contact and respond appropriately with nods and brief comments like "That's interesting!" or "I know what you mean" or "Really?" Be friendly, smile, and encourage the person to keep speaking.

- **Give the other person feedback.** Show you understand by saying things like "So you're saying that…" or asking a question that demonstrates you've been following what they're saying and want to know more.

As you improve your listening skills, think also about what you are saying and how. Here are guidelines for effective speaking:

- **Be honest, but don't be critical**. Strongly disagreeing may only put the other person on the defensive—an emotion sure to disrupt the communication. You can disagree, but keep the conversation from becoming emotional. Say "I don't know, I think that maybe it's…" instead of "That's crazy! What's *really* going on is…."

- **Look for common ground.** Make sure that your side of a conversation relates to what the other person is saying and that it focuses on what you have in common. There's almost no better way to stop a conversation dead in its tracks than to ignore everything the other person has just said and launch into an unrelated story or idea of your own.

- **Avoid sarcasm and irony unless you know the person well.** Sarcasm is easily misunderstood and may be interpreted as an attack on the other person's ideas or statements.

- **Don't try to talk like the other person,** especially if the person is from a different ethnic or cultural background or speaks with an accent or heavy slang. The other person will feel that you are imitating them and maybe even making fun of them. Be yourself and speak naturally.

- **Understand that assertive communication is better than passive or aggressive communication.** "Assertive" in this context means you are honest and direct in stating your ideas and thoughts; you are confident and clear and willing to discuss your ideas while still respecting the thoughts and ideas of others. A passive communicator is reluctant to speak up, seems to agree with everything others say, hesitates to say anything that others might disagree with, and therefore seldom communicates much at all. **Passive communication** simply is not a real exchange in communication. **Aggressive communication**, at the other extreme, is often highly critical of the thoughts and ideas of others. This communication style may be sarcastic, emotional, and even insulting. The other is not prompted to respond honestly and openly, preventing real communication.

- **Choose your conversations wisely.** You don't have to engage in all conversations. Try to form relationships and engage in interactions that help you learn and grow as a person.

nonverbal communication

Communication that occurs outside of the written and spoken word, including meanings inferred from facial expressions and body positions.

body language

Another term for forms of nonverbal communication, including gestures, postures, and facial expressions.

FIGURE 9.2

Miscommunication is at the root of many misunderstandings.

© *Thinkstock*

feedback

Evaluative information derived from a person's reaction or response to a particular activity, such as from a listener's response to a speaker.

assertive communication

Communication that is self-assured, positive, and honest but still tactful and nonaggressive.

Passive communication

Communication characterized by acceptance of things expressed by others, without taking an active or confident role in sharing one's own ideas or thoughts.

Aggressive communication

One-sided communication in which a speaker attacks what others say or uses a pushy, domineering style to express ideas or thoughts.

Some students may have difficulty in the opposite direction: their social lives may become so rich or so time consuming that they neglect their studies. Online social media, for example, may eat up a lot of time.

2.5   Online Social Networking

social networking

The use of a Web site to connect with people who share personal or professional interests.

Most college students know all about Facebook, Twitter, blogging, chat rooms, and other **social networking** sites. Over 90% of college students use Facebook regularly, although older students may do so less. The media often emphasize negative stories involving safety concerns, obsessive behavior, the superficiality of much online social interaction, and so on. But online social networking also has several benefits. Many professionals regularly network via LinkedIn and other sites.

Following are some of the benefits of social media:

- Facebook and other social media make it easy to stay in touch with friends and family at a distance. College students who have moved away from former friends seem to make the transition more easily when they stay in touch. Maintaining past relationships does not prevent most people from making new friends at college.

- Facebook provides users with increased "social capital," which is a sum of resources gained through one's relationships with people. Facebook users gain information and learn about activities and groups.

- Facebook makes it easier for people who are shy or otherwise slow to initiate or respond to interactions with others to participate socially in a group. Online network sites also offer an outlet for self-expression and sharing.

- For many college students, interactions on Facebook strengthen personal relationships rather than detracting from them.

- Acknowledging that online social networking is a reality for most college students, many college administrators and instructors also use it to stay in better touch with students, to provide information and encouragement, and to help students experience the full richness of the college experience. Your college may have a Facebook page where you can learn much about things happening around campus, and you may receive tweets about important announcements.

FIGURE 9.3

Still, online social networking is not 100% beneficial for all college students. Someone who becomes obsessed with constantly updating their profile or attracting a huge number of friends can spend so much time at this that they miss out on other important aspects of college life. Students have shown that some students may also compare themselves with all the positive posts made by others and become depressed that their own lives are less glamorous. Finally, by now most students know why you should never post inappropriate photos or information about yourself anywhere online, even as a joke: employers, college admissions offices, and others may find this compromising material in the future and deny you the job, internship, graduate program, or other position that you want, even if you think you've protected your identity and privacy on online sites.

Overall, online networking in moderation can help enrich one's life. When used to build relationships, gain information, and stay in touch with a larger community, it can contribute to success in college. But if you're on Facebook more than ten to thirty minutes a day, ask yourself if you're maybe missing out on something else.

2.6   Balancing Schoolwork and Social Life

Virtually all college students say they don't have enough time to do everything they want. Once you've developed friendships within the college community and have an active social life, you may feel you don't have enough time for your studies, work, and other activities. The numerous social opportunities of college can become a distraction, and with less attention to one's studies, academic performance can drop. Here are some tips for balancing your social life with your studies:

- **Keep working on your time management skills,** as discussed in Chapter 2. You can't just go with the flow and hope that, after spending time with friends, you'll have enough time and energy left over for studying. Make a study schedule that with enough time for what you need to do. Study first; socialize after.

- **Keep working on your study skills,** as you learned in Chapter 4, Chapter 5, and Chapter 6. When you have only limited time for studying, be sure you're using that time as effectively as possible as you read assignments and prepare for class, organize your notes after class, and prepare for tests.

- **If you can't resist temptations, reduce them.** If you are easily distracted by talking with your roommate, spouse, or family members because you study where you live, then go to the library to study.

- **Make studying a social experience.** If your studying keeps you so busy that you feel like you don't have much of a social life, form a study group. You will learn more than you would alone, and you can enjoy interacting with others without falling behind.

- **Keep your social life from affecting your studying.** Simply scheduling study time doesn't mean you'll use it well. If you stayed up late last night, you may not be able to concentrate well now as you study for that big test. This is another reason for good time management and scheduling your time well, looking ahead.

- **Get help if you need it.** If you're still having difficulty balancing your study time with other activities, talk with your academic advisor or a counselor. Maybe you need some additional study skills or you need to get some extra help from a tutor or campus study center. Remember, your college wants you to succeed and will try to help those who seek help.

A Note on Greek Life

Fraternities and sororities appeal to many students on many campuses. You meet a lot of people quickly and automatically gain a social life along with many events and parties. Many people have formed lasting, even lifelong relationships with their fraternity and sorority friends. On the other hand, this living and social experience may limit the kinds of people you meet and present fewer opportunities to interact with others outside the Greek system. You may have to learn to say no at times when studying is the priority. If you are interested in but not yet committed to this life, it's worthwhile to find out what the houses at your school are really like, consider what your life would likely be like in a fraternity or sorority, and think about how it may impact your college goals.

2.7   Overcoming Difficulties and Resolving Conflicts

Conflicts among people are natural. People have many differences in opinions, ideas, emotions, and behaviors, and differences sometimes cause conflicts. Here are just a few examples of conflicts that may occur among college students:

- Your roommate is playing loud music in your room, and you need some quiet to study for a test.
- You want to have a nice dinner out, but your spouse wants to save the money to buy new furniture.

- Your instructor gave you a C on a paper because it lacks some required elements, but you feel it deserves a better grade because you think it accomplished more important goals.
- Others at your Greek house want to invite only members of other fraternities and sororities to an upcoming party, but you want the party to be more inclusive and to invite more diverse students.

So how can such conflicts be resolved? Two things are necessary for **conflict resolution** that does not leave one or more of the people involved feeling negative about the outcome: attitude and communication.

A conflict cannot be resolved satisfactorily unless everyone involved has the right attitude:

- **Respect the options and behaviors of others.** Accept that people are not all alike and learn to celebrate your differences. Most situations do not involve a single right or wrong answer.
- **Be open minded.** Even if you think you're right, do not close the door to other possibilities. Look at the other's point of view. Be open to change—even when that means accepting constructive criticism.
- **Calm down.** You can't work together to resolve a conflict while you're still feeling strong emotions. Agree with the other to wait until you're both able to discuss it without strong emotions.
- **Recognize the value of compromise.** Even if you disagree after calmly talking over an issue, agree to disagree and understand that a compromise may be necessary in order to get along with others.

With the right attitude, you can then work together to resolve the issue. This process depends on good communication:

- **Listen.** Don't simply argue for your position, but listen carefully to what the other says. Pay attention to their body language as you try to understand their point of view, and ask questions to ensure that you do. Paraphrase what you think you hear to give the other a chance to correct any misunderstanding.
- **Use "I statements" rather than "you statements."** Explain your perspective in a way that does not put the other person on the defensive and evoke emotions that make resolution more difficult. Don't say, "You're always playing loud music when I'm trying to study." Instead, say, "I have difficulty studying when you play loud music, and that makes me frustrated and irritable." Don't blame the other for the problem—that would just get emotions flowing again.
- **Brainstorm together to find a solution that satisfies both of you.** Some compromise is usually needed, but that is usually not difficult to reach when you're calm and have a good attitude about working together on a solution. Sometimes you may have to accept a result that you still do not agree with, simply in order to move on.

The process of conflict resolution is discussed more fully in Chapter 10. In most cases, when the people involved have a good attitude and are open to compromise, conflicts can be resolved successfully. Yet sometimes it seems impossible, and you may have to decide not to see that person anymore or find other ways to avoid the conflict in the future. But it's seldom a good solution to run away from a problem that will continue to surface and keep you from being happy with your life.

Roommate Issues

Many students live in campus residence halls or in a shared apartment with roommates. This is the first time many students have had to share a room, suite, or apartment with others who were not family members, and this situation may lead to conflicts and strong feelings that can even affect your academic success.

As in all interactions, the keys to forming a good relationship with a roommate are communication and attitude. From the beginning, talk about everyone's expectations of the other(s) and what matters most to you about where you live. Don't wait until problems happen before talking. It's often good to begin with the key practical issues: agreeing on quiet hours for study (limiting not only loud music but also visits from others), time for lights out, neatness and cleaning up, things shared and private things not to touch.

Show respect for the other's possessions, respect their privacy, and try to listen more than you talk. Even if your roommate does not become a close friend, you can have a harmonious, successful relationship that makes your residence a good home for both of you. Follow these guidelines to help ensure you get along well:

- **Anticipate problems before they happen.** Think about things that you consider essential in your living environment and talk with a new roommate about them now.
- **Deal with any problem promptly.** Don't wait until a behavior is well established before speaking up, as if the other person will somehow catch on that it aggravates you. It may be as simple as a

roommate using your toothpaste without asking, but if you say nothing, trying to be polite, the habit may expand to other things.

- **Be patient, flexible, and willing to compromise.** It may take a while for you to get used to each other and to establish an open communication pattern so that you can be honest with each other about what really matters.

- **Be warm, use humor, and be sensitive.** Telling someone that they're doing something bothersome can be very difficult for many people. Think before speaking, looking for the best way to communicate what you feel. Remember, you'll be spending a lot of time around this person, so do you really want them to think of you as bossy or obsessive-compulsive?

- **Get out more.** Sometimes it helps to spend more time elsewhere, studying in the library or another quiet place. You just might need a certain amount of time a day alone. That's fine, but don't expect your roommate to have to leave just to give you that time alone!

But What If You *Really* Have a Roommate Problem?

With some people who will not compromise and do not respect you and your needs, a roommate can be a serious problem. Room changes usually are usually not granted simply because you don't get along, but certain circumstances may justify a change, as in these examples:

- Your roommate uses illegal drugs, drinks alcohol underage, or conducts other illegal activities in the room.

- Your roommate repeatedly refuses to limit activities at any hour to allow you to sleep.

- Your roommate does anything that threatens your physical well-being or safety.

- Your roommate denies you your rights to practice your religion or other basic rights.

If you have a problem like this, first talk with your resident advisor (RA) or other residence hall authority. They will explain the process for a room change, if warranted, or other ways for managing the problem,

2.8   Dealing with Harassment

Although college campuses are generally safe, secure, and friendly places, harassment can occur in any setting. **Harassment** refers to behavior that is intended to disturb or threaten another person in some way, often psychologically. Typically a person doing the harassment targets the victim because of a difference in race, ethnicity, religion, nationality, sex, age, sexual orientation, or disability.

Acts of harassment may be verbal, physical, psychological, or any other behavior intended to disturb another person. Bullying behavior, name-calling, belittling, gesturing obscenely, stalking, mobbing—any action intended to torment or deliberately make another person uncomfortable or feel humiliated is harassment. Harassment may also be intended to manipulate a targeted person to act in some specific way.

Sexual harassment is a special term referring to persistent, unwanted sexual behaviors or advances. Sexual harassment may begin with words but progress to unwanted touching and potentially even rape. Sexual harassment is discussed in more detail in Chapter 10

Many types of harassment are illegal. In the workplace, a supervisor who tells sexual jokes around an employee may be guilty of sexual harassment. Students who deliberately malign members of another race may be guilty of committing a hate crime. Physically tormenting another student in a hazing may be judged assault and battery. Any discrimination in the workplace based on race, religion, age, sex, and so on is illegal. On a college campus, any harassment of a student by a faculty member or college employee is expressly forbidden, unethical, and also possibly illegal.

Harassment of any type, at any time, of any person, is wrong and unacceptable. You will know it if you are harassed, and you should know also that it is your basic right to be free of harassment and that your college has strict policies against all forms of harassment. Here's what you should do if you are being harassed:

1. Tell the person to stop the behavior—and if you feel at any risk of harm, get out of the situation immediately.

2. Document the incident, particularly with ongoing harassment. Keep notes of the details. Tell someone you trust about the situation.

3. Report the harassment to the appropriate college authority. If you are unsure whom to talk to, go to the dean of students first.

Harassment

Actions or words meant to disturb, belittle, or torment another person.

2.9 Changing Family Relationships

The college years are a time of many changes, including relationships with parents, siblings, and one's own children and partner. Any time there is change, issues may arise.

FIGURE 9.4

A video communication program like Skype makes it easy to stay in touch with friends and family.

© *Thinkstock*

As in other relationships, try to understand the other's perspective. Honesty is important, along with tact and understanding. Here are some tips for getting along:

- Understand that your parents may not change their attitudes toward you as quickly as you are changing. They may still think of you as a younger person in need of their guidance. They will worry about you and fear that you might fall in with the wrong crowd or engage in risky behavior. Be patient. Take the time to communicate, and don't close yourself off. Let them gradually accept you as a more mature person who can make your own decisions wisely.

- Stay in touch. You may be busier than ever and feel you haven't time for a phone call or e-mail, but communication is very important for parents—especially if they are now empty-nesters without other children at home. Even if they seem to want to be too involved in your life and make decisions for you, realize this is partly just a desire to stay in touch with you—and to feel they still matter in your life.

- Use your best listening skills. Understanding what they're feeling, which is often simply a concern for you born of their love for you, usually helps you know how to respond.

- Over time your parents and other family members will get used to your being on your own and will accept that you can make your own decisions. Time itself often solves issues.

- With your own family, now that you are busier than ever with classes and work, pay special attention to family relationships. Schedule times for family outings and make room in your days for casual interactions. But remember, it's not how much time you spend together but the quality of that time, so give your family your full attention when you are together.

KEY TAKEAWAYS

- A rich, diverse social life is an important dimension of the college experience that contributes to academic success.
- Getting along with others requires communication skills and a willingness to interact with different people in different ways.
- Effective listening skills are as important as expressing yourself well verbally and nonverbally.
- Online social networking used in moderation can be beneficial.
- Balancing your social life with studies requires time management skills and good study habits.
- Since conflicting values, behaviors, or ideas are common, it's important to respect others, stay open minded, be open to compromise, and understand how to resolve conflicts.
- Acknowledge that family relationships will likely change after you enter college, and work to ease the transition for everyone.

CHECKPOINT EXERCISES

1. List three or four guidelines for interacting successfully with others.

   _____

   _____

   _____

   _____

2. You are talking after class with another student with whom you'd like to be friends, but you're worried about a test you have to study for. If you're not careful, what nonverbal communication signals might you accidentally send that could make the other person feel you are *not* friendly? Describe two or three nonverbal signals that could give the wrong impression.

   _____

   _____

   _____

3. What are the best things *to say* when you're actively engaged in *listening* to another?

   _____

   _____

   _____

4. For each of the following statements about effective communication, circle T for true or F for false:

T	F	Avoid eye contact until you've gotten to know the person well enough to be sure they will not misinterpret your interest.
T	F	Using the same slang or accent as other people will show them that you respect them as they are.
T	F	Communicating your ideas with honesty and confidence is usually more effective than just agreeing with what others are saying.
T	F	Communicating with people online is seldom as effective as calling them on the telephone or seeing them in person.
T	F	Always accept a spontaneous invitation from someone else because you'll always have time later for your studies.

5. You are upset because your roommate (or a family member) always seems to have friends over just when you need to study most. Write in the space below what you might say to this person to explain the problem, using "I statements" rather than "you statements."

   _____

   _____

   _____

6. If another person is acting very emotionally and is harassing you, what should you *not* do at that moment?

   _____

   _____

3. LIVING WITH DIVERSITY

L E A R N I N G   O B J E C T I V E S

1. Define diversity and explain the benefits of a diverse college campus for all students.
2. List ten or more ways in which different groups of people can have significant differences, experiences, and perspectives.
3. Explain why all college students are more successful academically in a diverse environment and list several additional benefits of diversity for all students.
4. Describe the valuable characteristics of "nontraditional" older college students.
5. Explain what students can do to foster multiculturalism and celebrate diversity on campus. For students who have few experiences with diversity in the past, outline steps that can be taken to gain cultural sensitivity and a multicultural outlook.
6. Describe how instructors help create a positive, inclusive learning environment in the classroom.

diversity

A condition of having differences, generally referring to meaningful differences among various groups of people.

Ours is a very diverse society—and increasingly so. Already in many parts of the country, non-Hispanic whites comprise less than 50% of the population, and by 2020 an estimated one in three Americans will be a person of color, as will be about half of all college students. But "diversity" means much more than a variety of racial and ethnic differences. As we use the term here, **diversity** refers to the great variety of human characteristics—ways that we are different even as we are all human and share more similarities than differences. These differences are an essential part of what enriches humanity.

We'll look first at some of the ways that people differ and explore the benefits of diversity for our society generally and for the college experience. While we should all celebrate diversity, at the same time we need to acknowledge past issues that grew from misunderstandings of such differences and work together to bring change where needed.

3.1 What Diversity Really Means

Differences among people may involve where a person was born and raised, the person's family and cultural group, factual differences in personal identity, and chosen differences in significant beliefs. Some diversity is primarily cultural (involving shared beliefs and behaviors), other diversity may be biological (race, age, gender), and some diversity is defined in personal terms (sexual orientation, religion). Diversity generally involves things that may significantly affect some people's perceptions of others.

stereotype

A simplified and standardized image of what a certain type or group of people is like, often held in common by members of a different group.

When discussing diversity, it is often difficult to avoid seeming to generalize about different types of people—and such generalizations can seem similar to dangerous **stereotypes**. The following descriptions are meant only to suggest that individuals are different from other individuals in many possible ways and that we can all learn things from people whose ideas, beliefs, attitudes, values, backgrounds, experiences, and behaviors are different from our own. This is a primary reason college admissions departments frequently seek diversity in the student body. Following are various aspects of diversity:

- **Diversity of race. Race** refers to what we generally think of as biological differences and is often defined by what some think of as skin color. Such perceptions are often at least as much social as they are biological.

- **Diversity of ethnicity. Ethnicity** is a cultural distinction that is different from race. An ethnic group is a group of people who share a common identity and a perceived cultural heritage that often involves shared ways of speaking and behaving, religion, traditions, and other traits. The term "ethnic" also refers to such a group that is a minority within the larger society. Race and ethnicity are sometimes interrelated but not automatically so.

- **Diversity of cultural background. Culture**, like ethnicity, refers to shared characteristics, language, beliefs, behaviors, and identity. We are all influenced by our culture to some extent. While ethnic groups are typically groups within a larger society, the larger society itself is often called the "dominant culture." The term is often used rather loosely to refer to any group with identifiable shared characteristics.

- **Diversity of educational background.** Colleges do not use a cookie-cutter approach to admit only students with identical academic skills. Diversity of educational background helps ensure a free flow of ideas and challenges those who might become set in their ways.

- **Diversity of geography.** People from different places within the United States or the world often have a range of differences in ideas, attitudes, and behaviors.

- **Diversity of socioeconomic background.** People's identities are often influenced by how they grow up, and part of that background may involve socioeconomic factors. Socioeconomic diversity can contribute a wide variety of ideas and attitudes.

- **Diversity of gender roles.** Women fill virtually all professional and social roles, including those once dominated by men, and men have taken on many roles, such as raising a child, that were formerly held mostly by women. These changing roles have brought diverse new ideas and attitudes to college campuses.

- **Diversity of age.** While younger students attending college immediately after high school are generally within the same age range, older students returning to school bring a diversity of age. Because they often have broader life experiences, many older students bring different ideas and attitudes to the campus.

- **Diversity of sexual orientation.** Lesbian, gay, bisexual, and transgender (LGBT) people make up a significant percentage of people in American society and students on college campuses. Exposure to this diversity helps others overcome stereotypes and become more accepting of human differences.

- **Diversity of religion.** For many people, religion is a spiritual force that infuses their lives. Religion helps shape different ways of thinking and behaving, and thus diversity of religion brings a wider benefit of diversity to college.

- **Diversity of political views.** A diversity of political views helps broaden the level of discourse on campuses concerning current events and the roles of government and leadership at all levels. College students are frequently concerned about issues such as environmentalism and civil rights and can help bring about change.

- **Diversity of physical ability.** Some students have athletic talents. Some students have physical disabilities. Physical differences among students brings yet another kind of diversity to colleges—a diversity that both widens opportunities for a college education and also helps all students better understand how people relate to the world in physical as well as intellectual ways.

- **Diversity of extracurricular abilities.** As you remember from your college applications, colleges ask about what you do outside of class—clubs, activities, abilities in music and the arts, and so on. A student body with diverse interests and skills benefits all students by helping make the college experience full and enriching at all levels.

These are just some of the types of diversity you are likely to encounter on college campuses and in our society generally.

Race

A human group with biological differences, typically referring to skin color and appearance.

Ethnicity

A set of cultural and sometimes physical characteristics of a group of people with a shared cultural background and identity.

Culture

In anthropology, culture is the total of characteristic ways in which a group of people live and interact, transmitted from one generation to another; more generally, culture is the behaviors and beliefs characteristic of a particular social, ethnic, or age group.

gender roles

The roles that society or a cultural group traditionally assigns to males and females based on their gender.

3.2 The Benefits of Diversity

FIGURE 9.5

Diversity in the classroom is a goal of college admissions offices.

© *Thinkstock*

Discrimination

Treatment of a person based on some group, class, or category to which that person belongs rather than on individual merit.

The goal of many college admissions departments is to attract diverse students. But why is diversity so important? There are many reasons:

- **Experiencing diversity in college prepares students for the diversity they will encounter the rest of their lives.** Learning to understand and accept people different from ourselves is very important in our world. While many high school students may not have met or gotten to know many people with different backgrounds, this often changes in college. Success in one's career and future social life also requires understanding people in new ways and interacting with new skills. Experiencing diversity in college assists in this process.

- **Students learn better in a diverse educational setting.** Encountering new concepts, values, and behaviors leads to thinking in deeper, more complex, and more creative ways, rather than furthering past ideas and attitudes. Students who experience diversity in their classes are more engaged in active thinking processes and develop more intellectual and academic skills (and have higher grade point averages) than others with limited experience of diversity.

- **Attention to diversity leads to a broader range of teaching methods, which benefits the learning process for all students.** Just as people are different in diverse ways, people from different backgrounds and experiences often learn in different ways. College teaching has expanded to include many new teaching techniques. All students gain when instructors make the effort to address the diverse learning needs of all students.

- **Experiencing diversity on campus is beneficial for both minority and majority students.** Students have more fulfilling social relationships and report more satisfaction and involvement with their college experience. Studies show *all* students on campus gain from diversity programs. All the social and intellectual benefits of diversity cited in this list hold true for all students.

- **Diversity experiences help break the patterns of segregation and prejudice that have characterized American history. Discrimination** against others—whether by race, gender, age, sexual orientation, or anything else—is rooted in ignorance and sometimes fear of people who are different. Getting to know people who are different from you is a step in accepting those differences, furthering the goal of a society free of all forms of prejudice and the unfair treatment of people.

- **Students of a traditional college age are in an ideal stage of development for forming healthy attitudes about diversity.** The college years are a time of growth and maturation intellectually, socially, and emotionally, and a sustained experience of diversity is an opportunity to heighten this process.

- **Experiencing diversity makes us all better citizens in our democracy.** When people can better understand and consider the ideas and perspectives of others, they are better equipped to participate meaningfully in our society. Democratic government depends on shared values of equality and the public good. An attitude of "us versus them," in contrast, does not further the public good or advance democratic government. Studies have shown that college graduates with a good experience of diversity generally maintain patterns of openness and inclusivity in their future lives.

- **Diversity enhances self-awareness.** We gain insights into our own thought processes, life experiences, and values as we learn from people whose backgrounds and experiences are different from our own.

While all the benefits described above have been demonstrated repeatedly on campuses all across the country in study after study, and while admissions and retention programs on virtually all campuses promote and celebrate diversity, some problems still remain. Society generally changes slowly, and sadly, many students in some areas still feel marginalized in the dominant culture of their campuses. Even in a country that elected an African American president, racism exists in many places. Gays and lesbians are still fighting for full equal rights under the law and acceptance everywhere. Women still earn less than men in the same jobs. Thus society as a whole, and colleges in particular, need to continue to work to destroy old stereotypes and achieve a full acceptance of our human differences.

multiculturalism

Accepting, respecting, and preserving different cultures or cultural identities within a unified society.

Multiculturalism is *not* political correctness. We've all heard jokes about "political correctness," which suggests that we do or say certain things not because they are right but because we're expected to pay lip service to them. Unfortunately, some people think of colleges' diversity programs as just the politically correct thing to do. Use your critical thinking skills if you hear such statements. In the world of higher education, truth is discovered through investigation and research—and research has shown repeatedly the value of diversity as well as programs designed to promote diversity.

Older "Nontraditional" Students and Diversity

nontraditional students

A general term for college students who do not attend college within a year or so after graduating high school and who therefore are usually older than seventeen to nineteen years of age and have significant work or other noneducational experiences.

Sometimes overlooked among the types of diversity on most college campuses are older students, often called **nontraditional students**, who return to education usually after working a number of years. While many college students are younger and enroll in college immediately after high school, older students help bring a wider range of diversity to campuses and deserve special attention for the benefits they bring for all students. As a group, older students often share certain characteristics that bring unique value to the college experience overall. Older students often:

- Have well-established identities and broader roles and responsibilities on which to base their thinking
- More fully represent the local community and its values
- Have greater emotional independence and self-reliance
- Have well-developed skills for problem solving and decision making
- Can share important life lessons and insights not found in textbooks
- Have relationships and experience with a greater variety of people
- Can be positive role models for younger students with less experience and maturity

In many ways, nontraditional students benefit the campus as a whole and contribute in meaningful ways to the educational process. Both instructors and traditional students gain when older students share their ideas and feelings in class discussions, study groups, and all forms of social interaction.

3.3   Accepting and Celebrating Diversity and Working for Change

More than anything, multiculturalism is an attitude. Multiculturalism involves accepting and respecting the ideas, feelings, behaviors, and experiences of people different from oneself—all the forms of diversity described earlier. America is not actually a "melting pot" in the sense that people from diverse backgrounds somehow all become the same. America has always included a great diversity of ideas, attitudes, and behaviors. For example, the constitutional separation of church and state, a fundamental principle present since early days in the United States, ensures that people of all religions have the same freedoms and rights for worship and religious behavior. People of diverse religious backgrounds are not expected to "melt" together into one religion. Other laws guarantee the equal rights of all people regardless of skin color, gender, age, and other differences. The United States does not even have an official national language—and many government and other publications in various geographical areas are offered in a variety of languages as well. In short, America as a nation has always recognized the realities and benefits of diversity.

Colleges similarly make commitments to respect and value differences among people and promote a wide understanding of such differences. Most colleges have formal diversity programs to help all students not only accept and understand differences among students but also celebrate the benefits for all.

What Students Can Do

While diversity exists in most places, not everyone automatically understands differences among people and celebrates the value of those differences. Students who have never thought about diversity and who make no conscious effort to experience and understand people different from themselves gain less than others who do. In many ways you can experience the benefits of diversity on your college campus, beginning with your own attitudes and by taking steps to increase your experiences with diverse individuals.

Acknowledge your own uniqueness, for you are diverse, too. Diversity doesn't involve just other people: you may be just as different to other people as they are to you. Don't mistakenly think of the other person as the one who is different, that you are somehow the "norm." Your religion may seem just as odd to them as theirs does to you, and your clothing may seem just as strange looking to them as theirs is to you—until you accept there is no one "normal" or right way to be. Look at yourself in a mirror and consider why you look as you do. Why do you use the slang you do with your friends? Why did you just have that type of food for breakfast? How is it that you prefer certain types of music? Read certain books? Talk about certain things? Much of this has to do with your cultural background—so it makes sense that someone from another cultural or ethnic background is different in some ways. But both of you are also individuals with your own tastes, preferences, ideas, and attitudes—making you unique. It's only when you realize your own uniqueness that you can begin to understand and respect the uniqueness of others, too.

Consider your own (possibly unconscious) stereotypes. A stereotype is a fixed, simplistic view of what people in a certain group are like. It is often the basis for prejudice and discrimination: behaving differently toward someone because you stereotype them in some way. Stereotypes are generally learned and may emerge in the dominant culture's attitudes toward those from outside that dominant group. A stereotype may be explicitly racist and destructive. It may also be a simplistic generalization applied to any group of people, even if intended to be flattering rather than negative. As you have read this chapter so far, did you find yourself thinking about any group of people, based on any kind of difference, and perhaps thinking in terms of stereotypes? If you walked into a party and saw many different kinds of people standing about, would you naturally avoid some and move toward others? Remember, we learn stereotypes from our family or cultural background—so it's not a terrible thing to admit you have inherited some stereotypes. Thinking about them is a first step in breaking out of these irrational thought patterns.

Examples of Cultural Differences in Body Language

While we should be careful not to stereotype individuals or whole cultures, it is important to be aware of potential differences among cultures when interacting with other people. For example, body language often has different meanings in different cultures. Understanding such differences can help you in your interaction with others. Here are a few examples:

- Some Americans clap their hands together to emphasize a point, while some French clap to end a conversation.
- Many Americans cross their legs when seated and thus may point the bottom of their shoe toward another person; many Japanese find this gesture offensive.
- Many Americans may wave their index fingers at someone else to make a point, but this gesture is often offensive to Mexicans and Somali, who may use that gesture only for dogs.
- In America, men and women shake hands with each other, but in some other cultures, handshakes across genders are not acceptable.
- In America, eye contact is generally considered polite and a sign of interest, whereas in many Asian cultures, people show their respect for others by bowing their head slightly and consider steady eye contact aggressive.

ACTIVITY: CHALLENGE YOUR THINKING

Read each of the following scenarios quickly and respond immediately without stopping to think. There are no right or wrong answers.

Scenario 1. You are walking home down a dark sidewalk when ahead you see three people standing on the street corner. Something about the way they are hanging out makes you a little frightened to walk past them.

Be honest with yourself: what did you just imagine these people looked like?

_____

Why do think you might have associated this particular mental image with the emotion of feeling frightened?

_____

Scenario 2. In a café on campus, you see a student from another country sitting alone—someone you know casually from a class—and you walk over and are just about to ask if you can join him, when two other students also from his country appear and sit down with him. You hesitate.

Would you have hesitated if this person had the same cultural background as you? What makes this situation different?

_____

As you hesitate, you overhear them conversing in a language other than English.

Be honest with yourself: how does that make you feel now?

_____

Scenario 3. A couple you know invites you to join them and one of their friends, whom you have not met, for a movie and dinner. When you meet them outside the theater, you see that their friend, your date, is of a race different from your own.

Are you surprised? What is your first reaction?

_____

Do you anticipate more difficulty making conversation with your date than with anyone else whom you have just met?

_____

Should your friends have told you in advance? Why or why not?

_____

If they had told you, would that have made any difference? Explain.

_____

Now think for a minute about how you responded in these scenarios. Did your mental image in the first scenario involve a negative stereotype? What images in the media or society might have contributed to that response? The second and third scenarios involve situations in which you couldn't help but note some difference between you and another person. What might you feel in such situations in real life? Again, there is no "right" answer, and an awareness of differences is normal and natural even if it may cause some discomfort at first. On the other hand, if you have had significant experiences with diverse others, you might have read these scenarios and simply wondered, "So what? What's the big deal?" _It's worthwhile thinking about what that means._

Do not try to ignore differences among people. Some people try so hard to avoid stereotyping that they go to the other extreme and try to deny any differences at all among people. But as we have seen throughout this chapter, people *are* different in many ways, and we should accept that if we are to experience the benefits of diversity.

Don't apply group generalizations to individuals. People are individuals first, members of a group second, and any given generalization simply may not apply to an individual. Be open minded and treat everyone with respect as an individual with his or her own ideas, attitudes, and preferences.

Develop cultural sensitivity for communication. Realize that your words may not mean quite the same thing in different cultural contexts or to individuals from different backgrounds. This is particularly true of slang words, which you should generally avoid until you are sure the other person will know what you mean. Never try to use slang or expressions you think are common in the cultural group of the person you are speaking with. Similarly, since body language often varies among different cultures, avoid strong gestures and expressions until the responses of the other person signify he or she will not misinterpret the messages sent by your body language.

Take advantage of campus opportunities to increase your cultural awareness. Your college likely has multiculturalism courses or workshops you can sign up for. Special events, cultural fairs and celebrations, concerts, and other programs are held frequently on campuses. There may also be opportunities to participate in group travel to other countries or regions of cultural diversity.

Take the initiative in social interactions. Many students just naturally seem to hang out with other students they are most like. Even when we're open minded and want to learn about others different from ourselves, it often feels easier and more comfortable to interact with others of the same age, cultural group, and so on. If we don't make a small effort to meet others, however, we miss a great opportunity to learn and broaden our horizons. Next time you're looking around the classroom or dorm for someone to ask about a class you missed or to study together for a test or group project, choose someone different from you in some way. Making friends with others who are different is often one of the most fulfilling experiences of college students.

Work through conflicts as in any other interaction. Conflicts simply occur among people, whether of the same or different background. If you are too afraid of making a mistake when interacting with someone from a different background, you might avoid interaction altogether—and thus miss the benefits of diversity. Nothing risked, nothing gained. If you are sincere and respect the other, there is less risk of a misunderstanding occurring. If conflict does occur, work to resolve it as you would any other tension with another person, as described earlier.

Take a Stand against Prejudice and Hate

Unfortunately, prejudice and hate still exist in America, even on college campuses. In addition to racial prejudice, some people are also prejudiced against women, people with disabilities, older adults, LGBT individuals—virtually anyone that anyone else may characterize as "different." All campuses have policies against prejudice and discriminatory behaviors. But it is not enough for college administrators to fight prejudice and hate—this is a responsibility for all good citizens who take seriously the shared American value of equality for all people. So what can you as a college student do?

- **Decide that it does matter.** Prejudice threatens us all, not just the particular group being discriminated against in a specific incident. Don't stand on the sidelines or think it's up to the people who may be victimized by prejudice or hate to do something about it. We can all do something.

- **Talk with others.** Communication has great value on campuses. Let others know how you feel about any acts of prejudice or hatred that you witness. The more everyone openly condemns such behavior, the less likely it is to reappear in the future. This applies even if you hear another student telling a racist joke or putting down the opposite sex—speak up and tell the person you find such statements offensive. You don't want that person to think you agree with them. Speaking up can be difficult to do, but it can be done tactfully. People can and do learn what is acceptable in a diverse environment.

- **Report incidents you observe.** If you happen to see someone spray-painting a hateful slogan, for example, be a good citizen and report it to the appropriate campus office or the police.

- **Support student groups working for change.** America has a great tradition of college students banding together to help solve social problems. Show your support for groups and activities that celebrate diversity and condemn prejudice. Even if you are a shy, quiet person, your attendance at a parade or gathering lends support. Or you can write a letter to the editor in a student newspaper, help hand out leaflets for a rally, or put up posters on campus. Once you become aware of such student activities on campus, you'll find many ways you can help take a stand.

- **Celebrate diversity.** In many ways, you can learn more about diversity through campus programs and activities. The more all students participate, the closer the campus will come to being free of prejudice and hate. Be a role model in how you act and what you say in relation to diversity, and you may have more effect on others than you realize.

3.4 Dealing with Prejudice

If you yourself experience prejudice or discrimination related to your race or ethnicity, gender, age, disability, sexual orientation, religion, or any other aspect of diversity, don't just try to ignore it or accept it as something that cannot be changed. College students can do much to fight intolerance on campus. Many overt forms of discrimination are frankly illegal and against college policies. You owe it to yourself, first and foremost, to report it to the appropriate college authority.

You can also attack prejudice in other ways. Join a campus organization that works to reduce prejudice, or start a new group and discuss ways you can confront the problem and work for a solution. Seek solidarity with other groups. Organize positive celebrations and events to promote understanding.

Write an article for a campus publication explaining the values of diversity and condemning intolerance.

What if you are directly confronted by an individual or group making racist or other discriminatory remarks? In an emotionally charged situation, rational dialogue may be difficult or impossible, and a shouting match or name-calling seldom is productive. If the person may have made an offensive remark inadvertently or because of a misunderstanding, then you may be able to calmly explain the problem with what they said or did. Hopefully the person will apologize and learn from the experience. But if the person made the remark or acted that way intentionally, confronting this negative person directly may be difficult and may not have a positive outcome. Most important, take care that the situation does not escalate toward violence. Reporting the incident instead to college authorities may better serve the larger purpose of working toward harmony and tolerance.

JOURNAL ENTRY

If you are in the dominant cultural group on your campus, write a paragraph describing values you share with your cultural group. Then list things that students with a different background may have difficulty understanding about your group. If your racial, ethnic, or cultural background is different from the dominant cultural group on your campus, write a paragraph describing how students in the dominant culture seem to differ from your own culture.

Look back at what you just wrote. Did you focus on characteristics that seem either positive or negative? Might there be any stereotypes creeping into your thinking?

Write a second paragraph focusing on yourself as a unique individual, not a part of a group. How would others benefit from getting to know you better?

KEY TAKEAWAYS

- Diversity refers to a great variety of human characteristics and ways in which people differ.
- Diversity in the college environment has many benefits for all students and faculty. Students learn more in a diverse setting, are better prepared for the future, and contribute more fully in positive ways to society.
- Nontraditional students bring many unique characteristics to the college environment that help enrich all students' social and educational experiences.
- Multiculturalism involves respecting the ideas, feelings, behaviors, and experiences different from one's own in any way. Colleges promote both diversity in the student body and multiculturalism among all students.
- As an individual, each of us can gain the benefits of diversity as we challenge our own stereotypes, understand and celebrate differences in others, and learn to interact well with others different from ourselves. Take advantage of campus opportunities to increase your cultural awareness and to form social relationships with diverse others.
- Although we would hope that all college campuses would be free of hate and discrimination, it can become necessary to take a stand against prejudice.

CHECKPOINT EXERCISES

1. List as many types of diversity as you can think of.

   _____
   _____
   _____

2. Write a description of someone who is of a different race from yourself but who may not be different ethnically.

   _____
   _____

3. List several characteristics of *your own* cultural background that may be different from the cultural background of some others on your campus.

   _____
   _____
   _____

4. For each of the following statements about diversity, circle T for true or F for false:

T	F	A diverse educational environment is primarily good for students from minority groups.
T	F	Students of traditional college age are usually already too old to be open to new ideas and attitudes learned from others with diverse backgrounds.
T	F	We gain insights into ourselves when we learn from others who are different from ourselves.
T	F	You can better understand an individual from a cultural group other than your own if you apply generalizations about that other culture to the person.
T	F	The best way to avoid a conflict that may arise from cultural differences is to interact only politely and in superficial ways with people who seem different from yourself.

5. Is it a cultural observation or a stereotype to say, for example, that Mexicans are more relaxed about time commitments than Americans? (Think a minute before answering. How would you justify and explain your answer if challenged? Could both answers be right in some way?)

   _____
   _____
   _____
   _____

6. List at least three ways you may be able to increase your cultural awareness and understanding of diversity on your campus.

   _____
   _____
   _____
   _____

4. CAMPUS GROUPS

LEARNING OBJECTIVES

1. **Describe several benefits of participating in campus life by joining organized groups and campus activities.**
2. **Identify how participation in organized activities can promote multiculturalism and a better understanding of diversity.**
3. **List ways you can learn about groups and activities on your own campus.**

The college social experience also includes organized campus groups and activities. Participating in organized activities requires taking some initiative—you can't be passive and expect these opportunities to come knocking on your door—but is worthwhile for enriched college interactions. The active pursuit of a stimulating life on campus offers many benefits:

- **Organized groups and activities speed your transition into your new life.** New students can be overwhelmed by their studies and every aspect of a new life, and they may be slow to build a new life. Rather than waiting for it to come along on its own, you can immediately begin broadening your social contacts and experiences by joining groups that share your interests.

- **Organized groups and activities help you experience a greater variety of social life than you might otherwise.** New students often tend to interact more with other students their own age and with similar backgrounds. But if you don't actively reach out, you are much less likely to meet and interact with others from the broader campus diversity: students who are older and may have a perspective you may otherwise miss, upper-level students who have much to share from their years on campus, and students of diverse heritage or culture with whom you might otherwise be slow to interact.

- **Organized groups and activities help you gain new skills—technical, physical, intellectual, and social.** Such skills may find their way into your résumé when you seek a job or apply for a scholarship or another educational opportunity. Employers and others like to see well-rounded students with a range of proficiencies and experiences.

- **Organized groups and activities are fun and a great way to stay healthy and relieve stress.** As Chapter 10 discusses, exercise and physical activity are essential for health and well-being, and many organized activities offer a good way to keep moving.

4.1   Participating in Groups and Activities

College campuses offer a wide range of clubs, organizations, and other activities open to all students. When you decided to attend your college, you likely received printed materials or studied the college's website and saw many opportunities. But you may have been so busy studying that you haven't thought of these groups since. It's a good time now to check out the possibilities:

- Browse the college website, where you're likely to find links for student clubs and organizations.

- Watch for club fairs, open houses, and similar activities on campus. Especially near the beginning of the year, an activity fair may represent many groups providing information. Talk with the representatives from any group in which you are interested.

- Look for notices on bulletin boards around campus. Student groups want new students to join, so they usually try to post information where you can find it.

- Stop by the college's office of student affairs or student activities or cultural center.

- If you are looking for a very specialized group, check with the academic departments where students with that interest may be majoring.

- Consider a variety of organizations. Some are primarily social; some are political or activist; some are based on hobbies (photography, chess, equestrianism, bird watching, videogames, computer programming); some involve the arts (instrumental music, choral singing, painting, poetry writing, drama club); some are forms of physical recreation (rock-climbing, ballroom dancing, archery, yoga, table tennis, tai chi, team sports); some focus on volunteerism (tutoring other students, community service projects, food drives); and others are related to academic or intellectual pursuits (nursing club, math club, chess club, engineering club, debate club, student literary magazine).

- Consider other activities beyond clubs. Gain leadership experience by running for office in student government or applying for a residence hall position. If you are looking for a job, consider what kinds of people you'll have the opportunity to interact with. Chapter 11 will give you more tips for finding a job.

- If your campus doesn't have a group for a particular activity you enjoy, think about starting a new club. Your college will help you get started; talk with the student activities or affairs office.

FIGURE 9.6

Check bulletin boards on campus to learn about cultural events.

© *Thinkstock*

Whatever your interests, don't be shy about checking out a club or organization. Take chances and explore. Attending a meeting or gathering is not a commitment—you're just going the first time to see what it's like, and you have no obligation to join. Keep an open mind as you meet and observe other students in the group, especially if you don't feel at first like you fit in: remember that a benefit of the experience is to meet others who are not necessarily just like everyone you already know.

EXERCISE: EXPLORE YOUR INTERESTS FOR COLLEGE CLUBS AND ORGANIZATIONS

Write things in which you may be interested in each of these categories.

Clubs Related to Hobbies and Personal Interests	Sports, Exercise, Physical Fitness	Interests Related to Your Major Area of Study	Purely for Fun

Bridging the Generation Gap

Is there still a "generation gap" in our society? Maybe not in the same sense as when that phrase came into being in the 1960s, but it remains generally true that most people gravitate toward others of similar age. Even in the accepting environment of most colleges, many students interact primarily with others of similar age—which, sadly, misses a great opportunity for both older and younger students to learn from each other.

This opportunity is one of the great benefits of organized campus groups and activities, however. Regardless of your age or background, you can attend a meeting of those with similar interests and meet people you simply would not have crossed paths with otherwise. Age barriers rapidly break down when people share the same interests.

4.2   When and How to Say No

For all the benefits of an active social and campus life, too much of a good thing can also cause trouble. If you join too many groups, or if you have limited time because of work and family commitments, you may spend less time with your studies—with negative results. Here are some guidelines for finding a good balance between social life and everything else you need to do:

- Don't join too many organizations or clubs. Most students can handle no more than two or three regular activities.
- Work on your time management skills, as described in Chapter 2. Plan ahead for study time when you don't have schedule conflicts. If you have a rich social life, study in the library or places where you won't be tempted by additional social interaction with a roommate, family member, or others passing by.
- Don't be afraid to say no. You may be active in a club and have plenty of time for routine activities, but someone may ask you to spend extra time organizing an upcoming event just when you have a major paper deadline coming up. Sometimes you have to remember the main reason you're in college and just say you can't do it because you have to get your work done.
- If you really can't resolve your time conflicts, seek help. Talk with your advisor or a college counselor. They'll help you get back on track.

KEY TAKEAWAYS

- College students with an active social life and who interact with the campus community are generally more successful academically as well.
- Organized groups and activities promote a more varied and diverse social experience.
- Students participating in organized groups and activities gain skills that may become important for job and other professional applications.
- Most campuses offer a large variety of opportunities for involvement in clubs, associations, and other activities.
- Take the initiative to find organizations and activities you will most enjoy.
- To balance your social life and academic studies, avoid joining too many organizations, and use your time management skills.

CHECKPOINT EXERCISES

1. List two specific skills (technical, intellectual, or social) that you may gain or improve by participating in a campus club or organization.

   _____

   _____

2. What events or campus groups have you noticed on a campus bulletin board or poster recently that caught your eye?

   _____

   _____

3. What academic subject might you major in? Imagine yourself joining a club formed by students in that major. What kinds of things might you do or talk about in such a club? (Use your imagination as you consider how you can have fun with others in such a club.)

   _____

   _____

   _____

5. CHAPTER ACTIVITIES

Chapter Takeaways

- Social interaction with a variety of people on campus contributes to college students' well-being and overall academic success.
- Successfully interacting with diverse others requires effective communication skills, including both listening skills and assertive communication rather than passive or aggressive communication.
- Social interaction can be heightened by moderate online networking.
- Time management and study skills help one balance social life and academic studies.
- To prevent or resolve conflicts that may occur in any social interaction, maintain an attitude of respect for others, be open minded and willing to compromise, and know how to work together calmly to resolve conflicts.
- Diversity on campus is beneficial for all students, not just those from ethnic or minority groups. The wider perspectives of students from different backgrounds and the greater variety of teaching methods help everyone learn better, develop a more mature worldview, and prepare for interacting with a diverse world in the future.
- Multiculturalism involves an attitude of respect for the ideas, feelings, behaviors, and experiences of others who differ from oneself in any way. Colleges promote both diversity in the student body and multiculturalism among all students.
- To gain a multicultural perspective, challenge your own learned stereotypes while you learn more about other cultural groups. Understanding what can be learned from others leads to celebrating the diversity found on most campuses.
- Take a personal responsibility for speaking out against prejudice and discrimination wherever encountered.

- Take advantage of campus opportunities to increase your cultural awareness and to form social relationships with diverse others. Organized campus groups and events can help you broaden your horizons.
- Participation in campus clubs and other organizations is not only fun and a good way to reduce stress but also helps develop social, intellectual, and technical skills.

CHAPTER REVIEW

1. List at least three benefits of social interaction with a variety of different people on your college campus.

   _____

   _____

   _____

2. Describe what is involved in being a "good friend" to someone you have just recently met.

   _____

   _____

3. What can you do to demonstrate that you are really listening to another person in a conversation?

   _____

   _____

4. Mark each of the following communication strategies as passive, assertive, or aggressive:

   - Showing your very critical reaction to another's ideas: _____
   - Agreeing with everything another person says: _____
   - Hesitating to say something another may disagree with: _____
   - Being honest and confident when expressing your ideas: _____
   - Joking sarcastically about something the other says: _____
   - Offering your opinion while respecting other opinions: _____

5. True or false: Interactions with online social media can strengthen one's personal relationships with others and make it easier to participate socially in a group.

6. Give two examples of how you can use time management skills to get your studies done while still maintaining an active social life.

   _____

   _____

7. Write an "I statement" sentence you might say to prevent a heated argument with another student who has just told a sexist joke.

   _____

   _____

8. Imagine this scenario: Eight white college students between the ages of eighteen and twenty from a large U.S. city are spending a summer in a poverty-stricken rural Indonesian village in a volunteer project. Describe several behavioral characteristics of these American students who are now the ethnic minority group that may not be understood by the villagers.

   _____

   _____

9. Imagine yourself working in your chosen career five years from now. Describe two experiences you might have in that career for which your current experience with diverse people on campus may help prepare you.

   _____

   _____

10. What insights into your own attitudes, behaviors, or values have you gained through interactions with others different from yourself? Think of specific aspects of yourself that you have come to view in a new light.

    _____

    _____

11. What's wrong with the following statement? "People are what they are and you can't change them. The best thing you can do when someone shows their prejudice is just walk away and don't let it bother you."

    _____

    _____

12. Read this case study and answer the following questions:

    The International Student Office is sponsoring Asian Night, a celebration in which different student goups will showcase their cultures and ethnic foods. Two groups of students have had disagreements during the planning and rehearsals. They have argued about how much time each group is allotted for their performances and how high on the evening's agenda their performances are scheduled. The conflict escalates and threatens cancellation of the whole celebration.

    a. If you were the director of the International Student Office, how would you handle this situation?

       _____

       _____

    b. What would you say to these two groups of students? What process would you use?

_____

_____

OUTSIDE THE BOOK

1. Visit your college's website and look for a page on student activities and organizations. Try to identify two or three groups you might be interested to learn more about.

2. Next time you walk across campus or through the student center, stop to look at bulletin boards and posters. Look for upcoming events that celebrate cultural diversity in some way. Read the information and imagine how much fun the event might be while you also learn something new. Then ask a friend to go with you.

3. Go to http://www.understandingrace.org/lived/sports/index.html—a website of the American Anthropological Association—and take the short online sports quiz. Many things have been said about why certain races or people from certain geographic areas excel at certain sports. People often talk about differences in biology and other differences among ethnic groups related to sports. How much is true, partly true, or blatantly false? How much do you know about what are real or not real differences?

MAKE AN ACTION LIST

Friendships

Sometimes I'm not as good a friend as I could be because I

_____

_____

I will work on the following things to be a better friend:

_____

_____

Social Interaction

Sometimes I have difficulty interacting well with these people:

_____

_____

I will use these communication techniques for more successful interactions in the future:

_____

_____

Communication Style

Sometimes I am too passive when talking with these people:

_____

_____

I can do these things to be more assertive in my communication:

_____

_____

Balance of Studies and Social Life

I sometimes don't get enough studying done because I am busy doing these things:

_____

_____

I will ensure I have enough time for studying by taking these steps:

_____

_____

Family Life

Since I am so busy with college now, I may have ignored my relationship(s) with

_____

_____

I will do better to stay in touch by

_____

_____

Diversity on Campus

I admit to knowing very little about these groups of people I often see on campus:

_____

_____

By this time next year, I hope to be more culturally aware as a result of doing these things more often:

_____

_____

Campus Activities

I would really enjoy doing the following one thing more often with other people:

_____

_____

To participate in this activity with a variety of people, I will look on campus for a club or group such as the following:

_____

_____

I can do these things to learn more about this club:

_____

_____

CLASS DISCUSSION QUESTIONS

1. A student in your college starts harassing you online after asking you on a date and you turned them down. You're not worried about the situation escalating to violence, but the harassment is really bothering you. You think maybe you should report it to someone, but you don't want to be known as a snitch if the word got out. What are your options?

2. You are having a conversation with a student of a different race from you, and without thinking, you mention you really admire a certain person who is of the same race. The person then says you've made a racist comment. What should you do or say? Can you "prove" you're not racist?

3. Visualize your dorm room, apartment, or house. What object there might provoke the most curiosity in someone just arrived here from halfway around the world? Is there anything you'd be embarrassed about if that person asked you to explain it? (Is any stereotyping occurring in your thinking?)

Taking Control of Your Health

FIGURE 10.1

© Thinkstock

Where Are You Now?

Assess your present knowledge and attitudes.

	Yes	Unsure	No
1. I usually eat well and maintain my weight at an appropriate level.			
2. I get enough regular exercise to consider myself healthy.			
3. I get enough restful sleep and feel alert throughout the day.			
4. My attitudes and habits involving smoking, alcohol, and drugs are beneficial to my health.			
5. I am coping in a healthy way with the everyday stresses of being a student.			
6. I am generally a happy person.			
7. I am comfortable with my sexual values and my knowledge of safe sex practices.			
8. I understand how all of these different health factors interrelate and affect my academic success as a student.			

Where Do You Want to Go?

Think about how you answered the questions above. Be honest with yourself. On a scale of 1 to 10, how would you rate your level of personal health at this time?

Not very healthy   **Very healthy**

1   2   3   4   5   6   7   8   9   10

In the following list, circle the three most important areas of health in which you think you can improve:

- Nutrition
- Weight control
- Exercise
- Sleep
- Smoking
- Alcohol use
- Drug use
- Stress reduction
- Emotional health
- Romantic relationships
- Sexual health

Are there other areas in which you can improve your physical, emotional, and mental health and become happier? Write down other things you feel you need to work on.

_____

_____

_____

How to Get There

Here's what we'll work on in this chapter:

- Eating well to stay healthy and at a weight you feel good about
- Finding regular physical activities you enjoy that will make you healthier and cope better with the stresses of being a student
- Determining how much sleep your body and mind really need—and how to get it

- Developing a healthy attitude toward smoking, alcohol, and drugs and learning how to change your habits if needed
- Understanding why everyone feels stressed at times and what you can do about it
- Knowing what to do if you're feeling lonely or anxious about school or your personal life and how to stay balanced emotionally
- Feeling good about your sexuality, having safe sex, and protecting against unwanted pregnancy and sexual assault

1. INTRODUCTION

Health and wellness are important for everyone—including students. Not only will you do better in school when you're healthy, but you'll be happier as a person. And the habits you develop now will likely persist for years to come. What you're doing now will have a huge influence on your health throughout life and can help you avoid many serious diseases.

Considerable research has demonstrated that the basic elements of good health—nutrition, exercise, not abusing substances, stress reduction—are important for preventing disease. You'll live much longer and happier than someone without good habits. Healthy habits can lower the risks of diseases like these:

- Cardiovascular issues such as heart attacks and strokes (most common causes of death)
- Some cancers
- Diabetes (currently reaching epidemic proportions)
- Lung diseases related to smoking
- Injuries related to substance abuse

Wellness is more than just avoiding disease. Wellness involves mind and spirit as well as the body. Good health habits also offer these benefits for your college career:

- More energy
- Better ability to focus on your studies
- Less stress, feeling more resilient and able to handle day-to-day stress
- Less time lost to colds, flu, infections, and other illnesses
- More restful sleep

This chapter examines a wide range of topics from nutrition, exercise, and sleep to substance abuse and risks related to sexual activity. All of these involve personal attitudes and behaviors. And they are all linked to one of the biggest problems students face: stress.

Everyone knows about stress, but not everyone knows how to control it. Stress is the great enemy of college success. Learning how to reduce and cope with it puts you on the road to becoming the best student you can be.

2. NUTRITION AND WEIGHT CONTROL

LEARNING OBJECTIVES

1. Explain why good nutrition is important.
2. List health problems related to being overweight and obesity.
3. Explain the general principles of good nutrition.
4. Make good choices about foods for meals and snacks.

Most Americans have a real problem with food. Overeating causes health problems, but what and how you eat can also affect how well you do as a student.

2.1   Why Are So Many Americans Overweight?

Americans are eating too much—much more so than in the past. A third of all Americans twenty years or older are obese. Another third of all adults are overweight. That means that two-thirds of us are not eating well or getting enough exercise for how we eat. There are many intertwined causes of this problem in American culture.

Why are being **overweight** and **obesity** a problem? Obesity is associated with many medical conditions, including diabetes, cardiovascular disease, and some cancers. Although some health problems may not appear until later in life, diabetes is increasing rapidly in children and teenagers. Worse, the habits young adults may already have or may form during their college years often continue into later years.

But it's not just about body weight. Good nutrition is still important even if you don't have a health problem. What you eat affects how you feel and how well you function mentally and physically. Food affects how well you study and how you do on tests. Doughnuts for breakfast can lower your grades!

overweight

Having more body fat than is optimally healthy, often defined as a body mass index between 25 and 29.9.

obesity

Condition in which body fat has accumulated to the point of having adverse health effects, often defined as a body mass index of 30 or greater.

2.2   Why Do Students Find It So Hard to Eat Healthily?

If Americans have trouble eating well in an environment that encourages overeating and low-nutrition fast food, college students often have it even worse. It seems like food is everywhere, and students are always snacking between classes. Fast food restaurants abound. If there's not enough time to get back to your dorm or apartment for lunch, it's just so easy to grab a quick pastry at a nearby coffee shop.

It's the eating by habit, or mindlessly, that usually gets us in trouble. If we're mindful instead, however, it's easy to develop better habits. Take the Nutrition Self-Assessment to evaluate your present eating habits.

NUTRITION SELF-ASSESSMENT

Check the appropriate boxes.

	Usually	Sometimes	Seldom
1. I take the time to eat breakfast before starting my day.			
2. I eat lunch rather than snack throughout the day.			
3. When I'm hungry between meals, I eat fruit rather than chips or cookies.			
4. I consciously try to include fruit and vegetables with lunch and dinner.			
5. There is food left on my plate at the end of a meal.			
6. I try to avoid overeating snacks at night and while studying.			
7. Over the last year, my eating habits have kept me at an appropriate weight.			
8. Overall, my eating habits are healthy.			

2.3   Eating Well: It's Not So Difficult

The key to a good diet is to eat a varied diet with lots of vegetables, fruits, and whole grains and to minimize fats, sugar, and salt. The exact amounts depend on your calorie requirements and activity levels, but you don't have to count **calories** or measure and weigh your food to eat well. Following are the U.S. Department of Agriculture's (USDA) current general dietary guidelines:

calories

The basic unit of food energy; consuming more calories in one's diet than are used leads to weight gain.

Balancing Calories to Manage Weight

- Prevent and/or reduce overweight and obesity through improved eating and physical activity behaviors.
- Control total calorie intake to manage body weight. For people who are overweight or obese, this will mean consuming fewer calories from foods and beverages.

- Increase physical activity and reduce time spent in sedentary behaviors.
- Maintain appropriate calorie balance during each stage of life—childhood, adolescence, adulthood, pregnancy and breastfeeding, and older age.

Foods and Food Components to Reduce

- Reduce daily sodium intake to less than 2,300 milligrams (mg) and further reduce intake to 1,500 mg among persons who are 51 and older and those of any age who are African American or have hypertension, diabetes, or chronic kidney disease. The 1,500 mg recommendation applies to about half of the U.S. population, including children, and the majority of adults.
- Consume less than 10% of calories from saturated fatty acids by replacing them with monounsaturated and polyunsaturated fatty acids.
- Consume less than 300 mg per day of dietary cholesterol.
- Keep trans fatty acid consumption as low as possible by limiting foods that contain synthetic sources of trans fats, such as partially hydrogenated oils, and by limiting other solid fats.
- Reduce the intake of calories from solid fats and added sugars.
- Limit the consumption of foods that contain refined grains, especially refined grain foods that contain solid fats, added sugars, and sodium.
- If alcohol is consumed, it should be consumed in moderation—up to one drink per day for women and two drinks per day for men—and only by adults of legal drinking age.

Foods and Nutrients to Increase

- Increase vegetable and fruit intake.
- Eat a variety of vegetables, especially dark-green and red and orange vegetables and beans and peas.
- Consume at least half of all grains as whole grains. Increase whole-grain intake by replacing refined grains with whole grains.
- Increase intake of fat-free or low-fat milk and milk products, such as milk, yogurt, cheese, or fortified soy beverages.
- Choose a variety of protein foods, which include seafood, lean meat and poultry, eggs, beans and peas, soy products, and unsalted nuts and seeds.
- Increase the amount and variety of seafood consumed by choosing seafood in place of some meat and poultry.
- Replace protein foods that are higher in solid fats with choices that are lower in solid fats and calories and/or are sources of oils.
- Use oils to replace solid fats where possible.
- Choose foods that provide more potassium, dietary fiber, calcium, and vitamin D, which are nutrients of concern in American diets. These foods include vegetables, fruits, whole grains, and milk and milk products.

For more detailed information, visit the Dietary Guidelines website to download the full Guidelines pdf booklet, available at http://www.health.gov/dietaryguidelines/dga2010/ DietaryGuidelines2010.pdf.

2.4 If You Need to Lose Weight

If you need to lose weight, don't try to starve yourself. Gradual steady weight loss is healthier and easier. Try these guidelines:

1. Check your **body mass index (BMI)** to see the normal weight range for your height (see "Additional Resources" below for more information).
2. Go to http://www.choosemyplate.gov for help determining your ideal caloric intake for gradual weight loss.
3. Set your goals and make a plan you can live with. Start by avoiding snacks and fast foods. Try to choose foods that meet the guidelines listed earlier.
4. Stay active and try to exercise frequently.

body mass index (BMI)

A measure of a person's weight in relation to height, used medically to determine whether a person is underweight, of normal weight, overweight, or obese.

5. Keep a daily food journal and write down what you eat. Simply writing it down helps people be more aware of their habits and motivated to eat better.

6. Visit your college's student health center and ask for more information about weight loss programs.

7. Remember, no one plan works for everyone. Visit the online resources listed later for a variety of approaches for weight loss.

2.5 Avoiding the "Freshman Fifteen"

The "freshman fifteen" refers to the weight gain many students experience in their first year of college. Even those whose weight was at an appropriate level when they entered college often gain unwanted pounds because of changes in eating habits.

Look back at the boxes you checked in the earlier Nutrition Self-Assessment. Be honest with yourself. If your first choice for a snack is cookies, ice cream, or chips, think about that. If your first choice for lunch is a burger and fries, have you considered other choices?

Tips for Success: Nutrition

- Eat a variety of foods every day.
- Take a multivitamin every day.
- Take an apple or banana with you for a snack in case you get hungry between meals.
- Avoid fried foods.
- Avoid high-sugar foods. After the rush comes a crash that can make you drowsy, and you'll have trouble paying attention in class. Watch out for sugary cereals—try other types with less sugar and more fiber.
- If you have a soft drink habit, experiment with flavored seltzer and other zero- or low-calorie drinks.
- Eat when you're hungry, not when you're bored or just because others are eating.
- If you find yourself in a fast food restaurant, try a salad.
- Watch portion sizes and never "supersize it"!

2.6 Eating Disorders

The most common eating disorders are anorexia, bulimia, and binge eating.

Anorexia is characterized by excessive weight loss and self-starvation. The individual usually feels "fat" regardless of how thin she or he becomes and may continue to eat less and less. If your BMI is lower than the bottom of the normal range, you may be developing anorexia.

Bulimia is characterized by frequent binge eating followed by an attempt to compensate for or "undo" the overeating with self-induced vomiting or laxative abuse.

Binge eating disorder is characterized by frequent binge eating without compensatory behavior to "undo" the overeating. Binge eating usually leads to weight gain and eventual obesity.

More than ten million Americans suffer from an eating disorder. The causes are complex, and the individual usually needs help to overcome the problem. Eating disorders hurt one's health in a variety of ways and can become life threatening. The signs of a possible eating disorder include the following:

- Eating secretly when others can't see you
- Having a strong fear of being overweight or gaining weight
- Only eating a limited number of foods
- Exercising obsessively
- Lacking a monthly menstrual period

Get Help for Eating Disorders

Don't feel ashamed if you obsess over food or your weight. If your eating habits are affecting your life, it's time to seek help. As with any health problem, professionals can provide help and treatment. Talk to your doctor or visit your campus student health center.

anorexia

An eating disorder involving a loss of the desire to eat, often as a result of psychological problems related to how a person perceives her or his appearance.

Bulimia

An eating disorder involving frequent binge eating followed by compensatory behaviors such as vomiting.

binge eating

An eating disorder involving frequent binge eating not followed by compensatory behaviors.

Additional Resources

BMI calculator. Find out how your weight compares with normal ranges at http://www.cdc.gov/healthyweight/assessing/bmi.

Diet planning. How much should you eat to maintain the same weight? What if you want to lose weight? Find out at http://www.choosemyplate.gov.

Calorie counter, nutritional database, and personal diet log. If you're really serious about losing weight and want to keep a daily log of your progress, try this online tool: http://www.caloriecount.about.com. Many smartphone apps are also available for tracking calorie consumption.

Eating disorders. For information about causes and treatment of eating disorders, go to http://www.nationaleatingdisorders.org.

KEY TAKEAWAYS

- Good nutrition and an appropriate body weight are important for health and wellness as well as academic success.
- Eating well does not require counting calories or obsessing over everything you eat. Focus on whole grains, lots of fruits and vegetables, and low-fat meats and dairy products. Minimize processed snacks and foods high in saturated fats, trans fats, sodium, and sugar.
- If you need to control your weight, a variety of healthful plans are available to help you eat foods you like and still lose weight.

CHECKPOINT EXERCISES

1. What health problems may result from obesity?

   _____

2. List three or more snacks that are healthier than cookies, chips, ice cream, and doughnuts.

   _____

3. How many cups of fruit and vegetables should you eat every day?

   _____

3.   ACTIVITY AND EXERCISE

LEARNING OBJECTIVES

1. **List the physical and mental health benefits of regular exercise.**
2. **Plan a program of regular exercise that you enjoy and can maintain.**

3.1 Does Exercise Really Matter?

Exercise is good for both body and mind. Indeed, physical activity is almost essential for good health and student success. The physical benefits of regular exercise include:

cardiovascular fitness

Having a healthy heart and blood vessels.

immune system

The body system, involving many different organs and body tissues, responsible for defending the body against infection and disease.

cholesterol

A fat-like substance, made by the body and found naturally in animal foods, that when in excess levels in the body contributes to cardiovascular disease.

diabetes

A disease in which the body has high levels of sugar in the blood because of an inability to manage blood glucose; diabetes is associated with a range of serious health problems.

wellness

A state of physical, emotional, mental, and social well-being, not merely the absence of disease.

- Improved fitness of the whole body, not just the muscles
- Greater **cardiovascular fitness** and reduced disease risk
- Increased physical endurance
- Stronger **immune system**, providing more resistance to disease (fewer colds!)
- Lower **cholesterol** levels, reducing the risks of cardiovascular disease
- Lowered risk of developing **diabetes**
- Weight maintenance or loss

Perhaps more important for college students are the mental and psychological benefits of exercise:

- Stress reduction
- Improved mood, less anxiety and depression
- Improved mental focus
- Better sleep
- Feeling better about oneself

For all of these reasons, it's important to regularly exercise or engage in physical activity. Like good nutrition and getting enough sleep, exercise is a key habit for overall **wellness** and promotes college success. First, use the following Exercise and Activity Self-Assessment to consider your current habits and attitudes.

EXERCISE AND ACTIVITY SELF-ASSESSMENT

Check the appropriate boxes.

	Usually	Sometimes	Seldom
1. I enjoy physical activity.			
2. Exercise is a regular part of my life.			
3. I get my heart rate up for 20-30 minutes several times a week.			
4. I enjoy exercising or engaging in physical activities or sports with others.			

Write your answers.

1. What physical activities do you enjoy?

_____

_____

2. How often each week do you engage in a physical activity?

_____

_____

3. If you feel you're not getting much exercise, what stands in your way?

_____

_____

4. Overall, do you think you get enough exercise to be healthy?

_____

_____

5. Do you feel a lot of stress in your life?

_____

_____

6. Do you frequently have trouble getting to sleep?

_____

_____

3.2 How Much Exercise and What Kind?

With **aerobic exercise**, your heart and lungs are working hard enough to improve your cardiovascular fitness. This generally means moving fast enough to increase your heart rate and breathing. Try to exercise at least three days a week for at least 20-30 minutes at a time. If you really enjoy exercise and are motivated, you can exercise as often as six days a week, but take at least one day of rest. When you're first starting out, or if you've been inactive for a while, take it gradually, and let your body adjust between sessions. Note that the old expression "No pain, no gain" is *not* true—if you feel pain in any activity, stop or cut back. The way to build up strength and endurance is through a plan that is consistent and gradual.

For exercise to have aerobic benefits, try to keep your heart rate in the **target heart rate** zone for at least 20-30 minutes. The target heart rate is 60% to 85% of your maximum heart rate, which can be calculated as 220 minus your age. For example, if you are 24 years old, your maximum heart rate is 196, and your target heart rate is 118 to 166 beats per minute. If you are just starting an exercise program, stay at the lower end of this range and gradually work up over a few weeks. The "Additional Resources" below includes online information for estimating your target heart rate depending on your present level of fitness.

Enjoy It!

Most important, find a type of exercise or activity that you enjoy, or else you won't stick with it. This can be as simple and easy as a brisk walk or slow jog through a park or across campus. Swimming is excellent exercise, and so is dancing. Think about what you like to do and explore activities that provide exercise while you're having fun.

Do whatever you need to make your chosen activity enjoyable. Many people listen to music or even read when using workout equipment. Try different activities to prevent boredom. Be more active in your daily life by taking the stairs instead of elevators, walking farther across campus instead of parking as close to your destination as you can get, and so on.

Exercise with a friend is more enjoyable, including jogging or biking together. Some campuses have even installed equipment for students to play "Dance Dance Revolution." Many Wii and Kinect games can get your heart rate up.

You may stay more motivated using exercise equipment. An inexpensive pedometer can track your progress walking or jogging, or a bike computer can monitor your speed and time. A heart rate monitor makes it easy to stay in your target zone; many models also calculate calories burned. Devices such as Fitbit and the Apple Watch have sensors that track your activities, such as number of steps in a day, and with the associated apps can help motivate you to stay active. Many devices input your activity and exercise into an app or software to track your progress and chart your improvements. These apps and devices help make it fun to increase your activity level.

The biggest obstacle to getting enough exercise, many students say, is a lack of time. Actually, we all have the time, if we manage it well. Build exercise into your weekly schedule on selected days. You'll find that regular exercise actually saves you time because you'll sleep better and concentrate better. Time you used to fritter away is now used for activity that provides many benefits.

3.3 Campus Activities Can Help

Most campuses have resources to make exercise easier and more enjoyable for their students. Take a look around and think about what you might enjoy. A fitness center may offer exercise equipment. There may be regularly scheduled aerobic or spin classes. You don't have to be an athlete to enjoy casual sports such as playing tennis or shooting hoops with a friend. If you like more organized team sports, see if your college has intramural sports.

Additional Resources

Exercise guidelines and more information. See http://www.cdc.gov/physicalactivity/everyone/guidelines/index.html.

How to measure exercise intensity. How to judge your heart rate to experience the benefits of aerobic exercise at http://www.mayoclinic.org/healthy-lifestyle/fitness/in-depth/exercise-intensity/art-20046887.

Target heart rate calculator based on age and current fitness level. See http://exercise.about.com/cs/fitnesstools/l/bl_THR.htm.

aerobic exercise

Brisk physical activity that requires the heart and lungs to work harder to meet the body's increased oxygen needs.

target heart rate

The level of heartbeat that gives you the best workout: about 60 to 85 percent of your maximum heart rate, which is typically calculated as 220 minus your age.

KEY TAKEAWAYS

- Regular exercise has many benefits for your body and mind. You'll also be a better student.
- It is easier to make exercise a regular part of your life if you explore your interests and join activities with others. The time you spend exercising will be made up for with better concentration when it's time to study.

CHECKPOINT EXERCISES

1. College students should get _____ minutes of aerobic exercise at least _____ times a week.
2. List at least two ways to make exercise more fun.

    _____

4. SLEEP

LEARNING OBJECTIVES

1. **Explain why students need adequate sleep to succeed in college.**
2. **Determine how much sleep you need.**
3. **Change your habits and routines in ways to ensure you get the sleep you need.**

Like good nutrition and exercise, adequate sleep is crucial for wellness. Sleep is particularly important for students because there seem to be so many time pressures—to attend class, study, maintain a social life, work—that most college students have difficulty getting enough. Yet sleep is critical for concentrating well. First, use the Sleep Self-Assessment to consider your current habits and attitudes.

SLEEP SELF-ASSESSMENT

Check the appropriate boxes.

	Usually	Sometimes	Seldom
1. I usually get enough sleep.			
2. I feel drowsy or unfocused during the day.			
3. I take a nap when I need more sleep.			
4. I have fallen asleep in class or had trouble staying awake.			
5. I have fallen asleep while studying.			
6. I have pulled an "all-nighter" when studying for a test or writing a class paper.			

Write your answers.

1. How many hours of sleep do you usually get on weeknights?

   _____

   _____

2. How many hours of sleep do you usually get on weekends?

   _____

   _____

3. How would you rank the importance of sleep in relation to studying, working, spending time with friends, and other activities?

   _____

   _____

4. How many hours of sleep do you think you ideally need?

   _____

   _____

5. Generally, do you believe you are getting as much sleep as you think you need?

   _____

   _____

4.1   The Importance of a Good Night's Sleep

You may not realize the benefits of sleep, or the problems associated with being sleep deprived, because most likely you've had the same sleep habits for a long time. Or maybe you know you're getting less sleep now that you're in college, but how can you tell if some of your stress or problems studying are related to not enough sleep?

On the positive side, a healthy amount of sleep has these benefits:

- Improves your mood during the day
- Improves your memory and learning abilities
- Gives you more energy
- Strengthens your immune system
- Promotes wellness of body, mind, and spirit

In contrast, not getting enough sleep over time can lead to a wide range of health issues and student problems. **Sleep deprivation** can have these results:

- Affects mental health and contributes to **stress** and feelings of anxiety, depression, and general unhappiness
- Causes sleepiness, difficulty paying attention in class, and ineffective studying
- Weakens the immune system, making it more likely to catch colds and other infections
- Increases the risk of accidents (such as while driving)
- Contributes to weight gain

Sleep deprivation

A chronic lack of sufficient restorative sleep.

stress

A natural response of the body and mind to a demand or challenge, often associated with feelings of tension and negative emotions.

4.2 How Much Sleep Is Enough?

College students are the most sleep-deprived group in the country. With so much to do, who has time for sleep?

Most people need seven to nine hours of sleep a night, and the average is around eight. Some say they need much less than that, but often their behavior during the day shows they are actually sleep deprived. Some do need only about six hours a night. New research indicates there may be a "sleep gene" that determines how much sleep a person needs. So how much sleep do *you* actually need?

There is no simple answer, in part because the quality of sleep is just as important as the number of hours a person sleeps. Sleeping fitfully for nine hours and waking during the night is usually worse than seven or eight hours of good sleep, so you can't simply count the hours. Do you usually feel rested and alert all day long? Do you rise from bed easily without struggling with the alarm clock? Do you have no trouble paying attention to your instructors and never feel sleepy in a lecture class? Do you not need to drink coffee or caffeine-heavy "power drinks" during the day to stay attentive? Are you able to get through work without feeling exhausted? If you answered yes to all of these, you likely are in that 10% to 15% of college students who consistently get enough sleep.

4.3 How to Get More and Better Sleep

You have to allow yourself enough time for a good night's sleep. Using the time management strategies discussed in Chapter 2, schedule at least eight hours for sleeping every night. If you still don't feel alert and energetic during the day, try increasing this to nine hours. Keep a sleep journal, and within a couple weeks you'll know how much sleep you need and will be on the road to making new habits to ensure you get it.

Myths about Sleep

- **Having a drink or two helps me get to sleep better.** *False:* Although you may seem to fall asleep more quickly, alcohol makes sleep less restful, and you're more likely to awake in the night.
- **Exercise before bedtime is good for sleeping.** *False:* Exercise wakes up your body, and it may be some time before you unwind and relax. Exercise earlier in the day, however, is beneficial for sleep.
- **It helps to fall asleep after watching television or surfing the web in bed.** *False:* Rather than helping you unwind, these activities can engage your mind and make it more difficult to get to sleep.

nicotine

A habit-forming stimulant found in tobacco, which raises blood pressure, increases heart rate, and has toxic effects throughout the body.

caffeine

A stimulant found in coffee, tea, many soft drinks, and other foods and drinks that increases alertness and wakefulness but also may have adverse effects in large quantities.

Tips for Success: Sleep

- Avoid **nicotine**, which can keep you awake—yet another reason to stop smoking.
- Avoid **caffeine** for six to eight hours before bed. Caffeine remains in the body for three to five hours on the average, and much longer for some people. Remember that many soft drinks contain caffeine.
- Don't eat two to three hours before bed. Avoid alcohol before bedtime.
- Stay away from your computer and devices for at least an hour before going to bed.
- Don't nap during the day. Napping is the least productive form of rest and often makes you less alert. It may also prevent you from getting a good night's sleep.
- Exercise earlier in the day (at least several hours before bedtime).
- Try to get to bed and wake about the same time every day—your body likes a routine.
- Make sure the environment is conducive to sleep: dark, quiet, comfortable, and cool.
- Use your bed only for sleeping, not for studying, watching television, or other activities. Going to bed will become associated with going to sleep.
- Establish a presleep winding-down routine, such as taking a hot bath, listening to soothing music, or reading (not a textbook). Try one of the relaxation techniques described in Chapter 10and Section 6

If you can't fall asleep after ten to fifteen minutes in bed, it's better to get up and do something else rather than lie there fitfully for hours. Do something you find restful (or boring). Read, or listen to a recorded book. Go back to bed when you're sleepy. If you frequently wake during the night, keep a sleep journal and write down what you were doing during the day before a poor night's sleep. Your goal is to first identify and then try to reduce factors that later cause wakefulness. You may also find it helpful to use a sleep-monitoring device such as a Fitbit, Basis watch, smartphone app like SleepCycle, or Apple

Watch to learn more about your sleep patterns and identify factors that keep you awake or that promote a good night's sleep.

If you frequently cannot get to sleep or are often awake for a long time during the night, you may be suffering from **insomnia**, a medical condition. Resist the temptation to try over-the-counter sleep aids. If you have tried the tips listed here and still cannot sleep, talk with your health-care provider or visit the student health clinic. Many remedies are available for those with a true sleep problem.

insomnia

An inability to sleep; chronic sleeplessness.

KEY TAKEAWAYS

- Getting enough sleep is very important for wellness and success in college. It's easy to determine if you're getting enough sleep.
- Don't fall for popular myths about sleep. Getting enough sleep gives you an improved ability to focus and apply yourself more efficiently in your studies and work.

CHECKPOINT EXERCISES

1. List at least three things you should *not* do before going to bed in order to get a good night's sleep.

   _____

2. Identify one or two things you can do as a regular presleep routine to help you relax and wind down.

   _____

5. SUBSTANCE USE AND ABUSE

LEARNING OBJECTIVES

1. **Define the terms "substance," "abuse," and "addictive."**
2. **Describe physical and mental effects associated with smoking and frequent or heavy drinking.**
3. **List the risks of using drugs.**
4. **Know how to get help if you have a substance use habit to break.**

Substance is the word health professionals use for most things you might take into your body besides food. When people talk about substances, they often mean **drugs**—but alcohol and nicotine are also drugs and are substances that can be abused.

Substance

A drug or other chemical typically used in an overindulgent manner for its effects on the body or mind.

drugs

A substance used for treating, curing, or preventing disease (prescription and over-the-counter drugs) or used without medical reason to alter the body or mind (illegal drugs or prescription drugs used without prescription).

addictive

Having the characteristic of becoming physically or psychologically habit forming, causing cravings; the person becomes dependent on the substance and suffers adverse effects on withdrawal.

abuse

The use of illegal drugs or the use of prescription or over-the-counter drugs or alcohol for other than their intended purposes or in excessive amounts.

People use substances for their effects. But many substances have negative effects, including being physically or psychologically **addictive**. It's important to be aware of any substance's effects on your health and on your life as a student, and to make smart choices. Use of any substance to the extent that it has negative effects is considered **abuse**.

First, consider your own habits and attitudes with the Substance Use Self-Assessment.

SUBSTANCE USE SELF-ASSESSMENT

Check the appropriate boxes.

	Daily	Sometimes	Never
1. I smoke cigarettes or use smokeless tobacco or e-cigarettes.			
2. I drink beer or other alcohol.			
3. I have missed a class because I was hung over from drinking the night before.			
4. I have taken a medication that was not prescribed for me.			
5. I have used an illegal drug.			

Write your answers.

1. If you smoke cigarettes, how many a day do you usually smoke?

   _____

   _____

2. If you drink alcohol (including beer), on how many days in a typical week do you drink?

   _____

   _____

3. If you drink at parties or when out with friends, how many drinks (or beers) do you typically have at one time?

   _____

   _____

4. If you use a pharmaceutical or illegal drug, how often do you take it?

   _____

   _____

5. Are your habits of smoking, drinking, or using other drugs affecting your studies or grades?

   _____

   _____

5.1   Smoking and Tobacco: Why Start, and Why Is It So Hard to Stop?

Everyone knows smoking is harmful to one's health. Smoking causes cancer and lung and heart disease. Most adult smokers continue smoking not because they really think it won't harm them but because it's very difficult to stop.

If you have never smoked or used smokeless tobacco, feel good about your choices. But read this section anyway because you may have friends now or in the future who smoke, and it's important to understand it. If you do smoke, even only rarely as a "social smoker," be honest with yourself—wouldn't you like to stop if you thought you could without suffering? Simply by going to college you've shown that you care about your future and your life. You likely care about your health, too.

Many young smokers think there is plenty of time to quit later. Social smokers, who may have a cigarette only occasionally with a friend, usually think they won't develop a habit. But smokers are fooling themselves. **Nicotine** is one of the most addictive drugs in our society today. Admitting this to yourself is the first step toward becoming smoke free.

nicotine

A habit-forming stimulant found in tobacco, which raises blood pressure, increases heart rate, and has toxic effects throughout the body.

First, the good news. Stopping smoking brings immediate health benefits, and the benefits get better over time. Just twenty minutes after quitting, your heart rate drops. After two weeks to three months, your heart attack risk begins to drop and your lung function begins to improve. After one year, your added risk of **coronary heart disease** is half that of a smoker's. And every year your health continues to improve.

coronary heart disease

A heart disease caused by damage to the arteries that supply blood and oxygen to the heart.

Tips for Stopping Smoking

Stopping isn't easy. Many ex-smokers say it was the hardest thing they ever did. Still, over 45 million adults in the United States once smoked and then successfully stopped.

You know it's worth the effort. And it's easier if you think it through and make a good plan. There's lots of help available. Before you quit, the National Cancer Institute suggests you START with these five important steps:

1. **S** = Set a quit date.
2. **T** = Tell family and friends you plan to quit.
3. **A** = Anticipate and plan for challenges while quitting.
4. **R** = Remove cigarettes and other tobacco from your home, car, and work.
5. **T** = Talk to your doctor or pharmacist about quit options.

To get ready, download the booklet "Clearing the Air: Quit Smoking Today" at http://smokefree.gov/sites/default/files/pdf/clearing-the-air-accessible.pdf. The table of contents of that booklet (Figure 10.2) outlines the basic steps that will help you be successful. You can also explore a variety of different quitting methods to see what may work best for you.

FIGURE 10.2

"Clearing the Air," a downloadable booklet available at http://www.smokefree.gov, presents a plan for stopping smoking that works for many smokers.

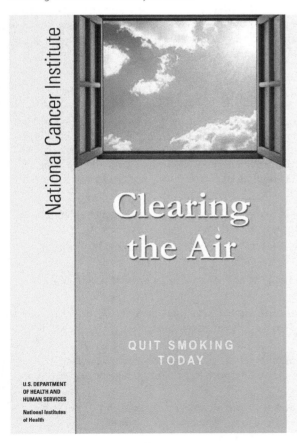

When You Really Crave a Cigarette

Remember that the urge to smoke will come and go. Try to wait it out. Use these tips:

- Keep other things around instead of cigarettes. Try carrots, pickles, sunflower seeds, apples, celery, raisins, or sugar-free gum.
- Wash your hands or the dishes when you want a cigarette very badly. Or take a shower.
- Learn to relax quickly by taking deep breaths.
    - Take ten slow, deep breaths and hold the last one.
    - Then breathe out slowly.
    - Relax all of your muscles.
    - Picture a soothing, pleasant scene.
    - Just get away from it all for a moment.
    - Think only about that peaceful image and nothing else.
- Light incense or a candle instead of a cigarette.
- Where you are and what is going on can make you crave a cigarette. A change of scene can really help. Go outside or go to a different room. You can also try changing what you are doing.
- No matter what, don't think, "Just one won't hurt." It will hurt. It will undo your work so far.
- Don't believe it if you've heard that e-cigarettes are safer or an easier way to stop smoking. There are still negative health consequences, and the nicotine is just as addictive.
- Remember that trying something to beat the urge is always better than trying nothing.[1]

Get Help to Stop Smoking

nicotine-replacement therapy

The use of a nicotine product (in gum, patches, etc.) intended to replace nicotine obtained from smoking, thereby making it easier for the person to stop smoking.

smoking cessation

The general term for any of many different programs developed to help people stop smoking, including use of medications, counseling, group therapy and support, hypnosis, and other programs.

dependence

Being abnormally tolerant to and dependent on something that is psychologically or physically habit forming (especially alcohol or narcotic drugs); addiction.

A lot of people are not able to stop smoking by themselves, so don't feel bad if you aren't successful the first try. Ask your doctor about other ways to stop. Maybe **nicotine-replacement therapy** is what you need. Maybe you need prescription medication. Stop by your college's student health center and learn about **smoking cessation** programs. Your doctor and other health professionals at your school have a lot of experience helping people—they can help you find what works for *you.*

5.2 What's the Big Deal about Alcohol?

Of all the issues that can affect a student's health and success in college, drinking causes more problems than anything else. Everyone knows what happens when you drink too much. Your judgment is impaired and you may behave in risky ways. Your health may be affected. Your studies are likely affected.

Most college students report drinking at least sometimes—and even those who do not drink are often affected by others who do. Here are a few facts about alcohol use among college students from the National Institute on Alcohol Abuse and Alcoholism:

- **Death.** Each year, over 1,800 college students between the ages of 18 and 24 die from alcohol-related unintentional injuries, and 599,000 students are injured.
- **Assault.** More than 696,000 students between the ages of 18 and 24 are assaulted by another student who has been drinking.
- **Sexual abuse.** More than 97,000 students between the ages of 18 and 24 are victims of alcohol-related sexual assault or date rape.
- **Unsafe sex.** 400,000 students between the ages of 18 and 24 have unprotected sex and more than 100,000 students between the ages of 18 and 24 report having been too intoxicated to know if they consented to having sex
- **Academic problems.** About 25% of college students report academic consequences of their drinking, including missing class, falling behind, doing poorly on exams or papers, and receiving lower grades overall.
- **Health problems.** More than 150,000 students develop an alcohol-related health problem.
- **Alcohol abuse and dependence.** In a recent year 31% of college students met criteria for a diagnosis of alcohol abuse and 6% for a diagnosis of alcohol **dependence**.[2]

So why is drinking so popular if it causes so many problems? You probably already know the answer: lots of college students say they have more fun when drinking. They're not going to stop drinking just because someone lectures them about it.

Like everything else that affects your health and happiness—eating, exercise, use of other substances—drinking is mostly a matter of personal choice. Like most decisions we all face, there are trade-offs. The most we can reasonably ask is to be smart in your decisions. That means understanding the effects of alcohol and deciding to take control.

Myths about Alcohol

Myth: I can drink and still be in control.

Fact: Drinking impairs your judgment, which increases the likelihood that you will do something you'll later regret such as having unprotected sex, being involved in date rape, damaging property, or being victimized by others.

Myth: Drinking isn't all that dangerous.

Fact: One in three 18- to 24-year-olds admitted to emergency rooms for serious injuries is intoxicated. And alcohol is also associated with homicides, suicides, and drownings.

Myth: I can sober up quickly if I have to.

Fact: It takes about three hours to eliminate the alcohol content of two drinks, depending on your weight. Nothing can speed up this process—not coffee or a cold shower.

Myth: I can manage to drive well enough after a few drinks.

Fact: About half of all fatal traffic crashes among 18- to 24-year-olds involve alcohol. If you are under 21, driving after drinking is illegal and you could lose your license.

Myth: Beer doesn't have as much alcohol as hard liquor.

Fact: A 12-ounce bottle of beer has the same amount of alcohol as a standard shot of 80-proof liquor (either straight or in a mixed drink) or 5 ounces of wine.[3]

College Alcohol Awareness Programs

Colleges have recognized the problems related to alcohol use and have designed programs to help students become more aware of these problems. If you are a new student, you may be in such a program now. Two popular online programs, AlcoholEdu and My Student Body, are used at many schools.

The goal of these courses is not to preach against drinking. You'll learn more about the effects of alcohol on the body and mind. You'll learn about responsible drinking versus high-risk drinking. You'll think about your own attitudes and learn coping strategies to help prevent or manage a problem. These courses are designed for you—to help you succeed in college and life. They're worth taking seriously.

How Much Alcohol Is Too Much?

There's no magic number for how many drinks a person can have and how often. If you're of legal drinking age, you may not experience any problems if you have one or two drinks from time to time. "Moderate drinking" is not more than two drinks per day for men or one per day for women. More than that is heavy drinking.

As with most things that can affect your well-being, most important is being honest with yourself. You're likely drinking too much or too often if:

- You have missed classes or work because you were hung over or overslept after drinking
- Your friends or family members have hinted that you drink too much, or you've hidden your drinking from others
- Your drinking is causing trouble in a relationship
- You can't remember what you did or said while drinking
- You need to drink to have a good time at a party or with friends
- You've driven a car when you know you shouldn't have after drinking
- You binge drink (consume five or more drinks at a time)

Did you know that one night of heavy drinking can affect how well you think for days afterward? This can really affect how well you perform as a student.

Pressures to Party

Most of us can remember times when we were influenced by our friends and others around us to behave in some way we might not have otherwise. I have a big test tomorrow, and I've been studying for hours, and just when I knock off to relax for a while, a friend stops by with a six-pack of beer. I'd planned to get to bed early, but my friend pops open a beer and sticks it in my hand, saying it will help me relax. So I tell myself just one, or maybe two—after all, that's not really *drinking*. And let's say I stop after two (or three) and get to bed. Maybe I don't sleep quite as well, but I still pass the test in the morning, even if my grade wasn't as good as I'd have liked. So—was it peer pressure or my decision?

There are no easy answers. What matters is that you think about your own habits and choices and how to take control of your own life.

Read this case study about a student who joins a college fraternity and feels pressured to drink. You may be very different from him—maybe you're older and work full time and are taking night courses—but you can still relate to his issues. As you answer the questions about his situation, think about how similar questions might also apply to someone in your own situation.

CASE STUDY

Pressured to Drink

When John decided to pledge a fraternity in college, he knew there would likely be drinking in the house. He had had a few beers at parties through high school but had never binged and felt there was nothing wrong with drinking as long as he kept it under control. But he was surprised how much alcohol flowed through the fraternity house, and not just at parties—and the house adviser just seemed to look the other way. He wanted to fit in, so he usually had a few whenever his roommate or others called him away from studying. One night he definitely drank too much. He slept late, missed his first two classes, and felt rotten most of the day. So he told himself he'd drink only on weekends and only a few at a time. Being underage didn't bother him. His grades hadn't been all that great in high school, and he didn't want to screw up his first year in college. But only a day later some of the older fraternity brothers interrupted his studying again and stuck a beer in his hand. He didn't know what to do.

1. Is John at risk for developing problems if he tries to fit in with the drinkers while promising himself he would drink only moderately? Why or why not?

   _____

   _____

2. If John decides to hold firm and drink only on weekends when he didn't have to study, is he still at any risk for developing a problem? Why or why not, depending on what circumstances?

   _____

   _____

3. If John decides to tell his fraternity brothers he does not want to drink, what should he say or do if they continue to pressure him?

   _____

   _____

What to Do

If you think you may be drinking too much, then you probably are. Can you stop—or drink moderately if you are of age—and still have fun with your friends? Of course. Here are some tips for enjoying yourself in social situations when others are drinking:

- Drink only moderately (if above legal age) and slowly. Your body processes alcohol at a rate of about one drink an hour—drinking faster than that leads to problems. Sip slowly. Set yourself a limit and stick to it.
- Try a mixer without the alcohol. It tastes just as good or better. Alternate alcoholic drinks with nonalcoholic ones to slow down the pace.
- Rather than just standing around with others who are drinking, stay active: move about and mingle with different people, dance, and so on.
- If someone tries to make you uncomfortable for not drinking, go talk to someone else.

Because drinking is a serious issue in many places, it's a good idea to know what to do if you find yourself with a friend who has had too much to drink:

- Stay with the person if there is any risk of him hurting himself (driving, biking) or passing out. Take away his keys if necessary.

- If he passes out after drinking a great deal of alcohol fast and cannot be awakened, get medical help.

- An intoxicated person who falls asleep or passes out on his back is at risk of choking on vomit—roll him on his side or face down.

- Do not try to give him food or other substances in an effort to sober him up.

- Don't put him in a cold shower, which could cause unconsciousness.

If You Feel You Need Help

Visit the student health center or talk with your college counselor. They understand how you feel and have a lot of experience with students feeling the same way. They can help.

5.3   Prescription and Illegal Drugs

People use drugs for the same reasons people use alcohol. They say they enjoy getting high. They may say a drug helps them relax or unwind, have fun, enjoy the company of others, or escape the pressures of college. While alcohol is a legal drug for those above the drinking age, most other drugs—including the use of many **prescription drugs** not prescribed for the person taking them—are illegal. They usually involve more serious legal consequences if the user is caught. Some people may feel there's safety in numbers: if a lot of people are using a drug, or drinking, then how can it be too bad? But most other drugs carry risks for health problems, a risk of death or injury, and a serious impact on your ability to do well as a student.

As with alcohol, the choice is yours. What's important is to understand what you're doing and make smart choices. What's the gain, and what are the risks and costs?

While society may seem to condone drinking, and the laws regarding underage drinking or being drunk in public may not seem too harsh, the legal reality of being caught with an illegal drug can impact the rest of your life. Arrest and conviction may result in being expelled from college—even with a first offense. A conviction is a permanent legal record that can keep you from getting the job you may be going to college for.

Although the effects of different drugs vary widely, even a single use of a drug can have serious effects and consequences. Even if you're told that a pill is a prescription medication whose effects are mild or safe, can you really be sure of the exact ingredients and strength of that pill? Do you fully understand how it can affect you with repeated use? Can it be addictive? Could it show up on an unexpected random drug test at work?

Table 10.1 lists some of the possible effects of drugs used by college students. Good decisions also involve being honest with yourself. Why do I use (or am thinking about using) this drug? Am I trying to escape some aspect of my life (stress, a bad job, a boring class)? Could the effects of using this drug be worse than what I'm trying to escape?

prescription drugs

A drug prescribed to a specific person for a specific medical condition by a health-care provider; many prescription drugs are illegal when used by someone other than the person for whom it was prescribed.

TABLE 10.1 Common Prescription and Illegal Drugs on Campuses

Drug and Common Names	Intended Effects	Adverse Effects	Common Overdose Effects
Anabolic Steroids	Muscle development	Liver cancer, sterility, masculine traits in women and feminine traits in men, aggression, depression, mood swings	—
Barbiturates	Reduced anxiety, feelings of well-being, lowered inhibitions	Addiction; slowed pulse and breathing; lowered blood pressure; poor concentration; fatigue; confusion; impaired coordination, memory, and judgment	Coma, respiratory arrest, death
Prescription Opioids: OxyContin, Vicodin, Demerol	Pain relief, euphoria	Addiction, nausea, constipation, confusion, sedation, respiratory depression	Respiratory arrest, unconsciousness, coma, death
Heroin	Pain relief, anxiety reduction	Addiction, slurred speech, impaired vision, respiratory depression	Respiratory failure, coma, death
Morphine	Pain relief, euphoria	Addiction, drowsiness, nausea, constipation, confusion, sedation, respiratory depression	Respiratory arrest, unconsciousness, coma, death
Ritalin	Stimulant: mood elevation, increased feelings of energy	Fever, severe headaches, paranoia, excessive repetition of movements and meaningless tasks, tremors, muscle twitching	Confusion, seizures, aggressiveness, hallucinations
Amphetamines: Dexedrine, Benzedrine, methamphetamine	Stimulant: mood elevation, increased feelings of energy	Addiction, irritability, anxiety, increased blood pressure, paranoia, psychosis, depression, aggression, convulsions, dizziness, sleeplessness	Convulsions, death
Cocaine, Crack	Stimulant: mood elevation, increased feelings of energy	Addiction, paranoia, hallucinations, aggression, insomnia, and depression, elevated blood pressure and heart rate, increased respiratory rate, insomnia, anxiety, restlessness, irritability	Seizures, heart attack, death
Ecstasy	Stimulant: mood elevation	Panic, anxiety, depression, paranoia, nausea, blurred vision, increased heart rate, hallucinations, fainting, chills, sleep problems	Seizures, vomiting, heart attack, death
Marijuana, Hash	Euphoria	Impaired or reduced comprehension, altered sense of time; reduced ability to perform tasks requiring concentration and coordination; paranoia; intense anxiety attacks; impairments in learning, memory, perception, and judgment; difficulty speaking, listening effectively, thinking, retaining knowledge, problem solving	—
LSD	Hallucinogen: altered states of perception and feeling	Elevated blood pressure, sleeplessness, tremors, chronic recurring hallucinations (flashbacks)	—

Resources for Help

If you have questions or concerns related to drug use, your doctor or student health center can help. Check these websites for additional information:

- Drug Information Online: http://www.drugs.com/drug_information.html
- Substance Abuse and Mental Health Services Administration: Alcohol, Tobacco, and Other Drugs: http://www.samhsa.gov/atod
- Drug and alcohol National Helpline: 1-800-662-HELP

KEY TAKEAWAYS

- Excessive drinking or substance abuse is a common—but unhealthy—response to college stresses. While the decisions are yours, you should understand the effects of tobacco, alcohol, and drugs and how they impact your life.

- Quitting smoking is hard, but it's clearly worth it—and lots of help is available. If you're a smoker, make this the year you become proud of yourself for quitting.

- If you like to drink, be honest with yourself. How much does drinking enrich your life, and how much do the effects of drinking interfere with your life? Make smart decisions so that you live your life to its fullest without regrets about losing control.

- Avoiding drugs can be a complicated issue, certainly not as simple as simply deciding to say no. But you've already made the decision to attend college, and that's a smart decision. Make smart choices in other areas of your life as well.

CHECKPOINT EXERCISES

1. "Social smoking"—having a cigarette just every now and then with a friend—may not have significant health effects, but why is this still a problem?

   _____

2. For each of the following statements about drinking, circle T for true or F for false:

T	F	After a few drinks, you can sober up more quickly by eating or drinking coffee.
T	F	A fourth of college students experience academic consequences from their drinking.
T	F	A 12-ounce beer has about half the alcohol of a standard shot of 80-proof liquor.
T	F	Moderate drinking is defined as no more than four drinks a day for men or two drinks a day for women.
T	F	A night of heavy drinking affects your thinking ability for several days afterward.

3. If smoking marijuana relaxes you, can it minimize the stress you may feel over time in your life? Why or why not?

   _____

6. STRESS

LEARNING OBJECTIVES

1. **List common causes of stress for college students.**
2. **Describe the physical, mental, and emotional effects of persistent stress.**
3. **List healthy ways college students can manage or cope with stress.**
4. **Develop your personal plan for managing stress in your life.**

We all live with occasional stress. Since college students often feel even more stress than most people, you need to understand it and learn ways to deal with it so that it doesn't disrupt your life.

Stress is a natural response of the body and mind to a demand or challenge. The thing that causes stress, called a **stressor**, captures our attention and causes a physical and emotional reaction. Stressors include physical threats, such as a car we suddenly see coming at us too fast, and the stress reaction likely includes jumping out of the way—with our heart beating fast and other physical changes. Most of our stressors are not physical threats but situations or events like an upcoming test or an emotional break-up. Stressors also include long-lasting emotional and mental concerns such as worries about money or finding a job. Take the Stress Self-Assessment.

stress

A natural response of the body and mind to a demand or challenge, often associated with feelings of tension and negative emotions.

stressor

Anything, such as an event or situation, that causes a person stress.

STRESS SELF-ASSESSMENT

Check the appropriate boxes.

	Daily	Sometimes	Never
1. I feel mild stress that does not disrupt my everyday life.			
2. I am sometimes so stressed out that I have trouble with my routine activities.			
3. I find myself eating or drinking just because I'm feeling stressed.			
4. I have slept poorly because I was feeling stressed.			
5. Stress has affected my relationships with other people.			

Write your answers.

1. What is the number one cause of stress in your life?

   _____

   _____

2. What else causes you stress?

   _____

   _____

3. What effect does stress have on your studies and academic performance?

   _____

   _____

4. Regardless of the sources of your own stress, what do you think you can do to better cope with the stress you can't avoid?

   _____

   _____

6.1 What Causes Stress?

eustress

A positive and stimulating kind or level of stress.

Not all stressors are bad things. Exciting, positive things also cause a type of stress, called **eustress**. Falling in love, receiving an unexpected sum of money, acing an exam you'd worried about—all of these positive things also affect the body and mind in ways similar to negative stress: you can't help thinking about it, you may lose your appetite and lie awake at night, and your routine life may be momentarily disrupted.

But the kind of stress that causes most trouble results from negative stressors. Life events that usually cause significant stress include the following:

- Serious illness or injury
- Serious illness, injury, or death of a family member or loved one
- Losing a job or sudden financial catastrophe
- Unwanted pregnancy
- Divorce or ending a long-term relationship (including parents' divorce)
- Being arrested or convicted of a crime
- Being put on academic probation or suspended
- Fearing failing a course

Life events like these usually cause a lot of stress that may begin suddenly and disrupt one's life in many ways. Fortunately, these stressors do not occur every day and eventually end—though they can be very severe and disruptive when experienced. Some major life stresses, such as having a parent or family member with a serious illness, can last a long time and may require professional help to cope with them.

Everyday kinds of stressors are far more common but can add up and produce as much stress as a major life event:

- Anxiety about not having enough time for classes, job, studies, and social life
- Worries about grades, an upcoming test, or an assignment
- Money concerns
- Conflict with a roommate, someone at work, or family member

- Anxiety or doubts about one's future or difficulty choosing a major or career
- Frequent colds, allergy attacks, other continuing health issues
- Concerns about one's appearance, weight, eating habits, or abilities
- Relationship tensions, poor social life, loneliness
- Time-consuming hassles such as a broken-down car or the need to find a new apartment

- _____
- _____
- _____

Take a moment and reflect on the list above. How many of these stressors have you experienced in the last month? The last year? Circle all the ones that you have experienced. Now go back to your Stress Self-Assessment and look at what you wrote there for causes of your stress. Write any additional things that cause you stress on the blank lines above.

How many stressors have you circled and written in? There is no magic number of stressors that an "average" or "normal" college student experiences—because everyone is unique. In addition, stressors come and go; the stress caused by a midterm exam tomorrow morning may be gone by noon, replaced by feeling good about how you did. Still, most college students are likely to circle about half the items on this list.

But it's not the *number* of stressors that counts. You might have circled only one item on that list—but it could produce so much stress for you that you're just as stressed out as someone who circled all of them. The point of this exercise is to start by understanding what causes your own stress as a base for learning what to do about it.

6.2   What's Wrong with Stress?

Physically, stress prepares us for action: the classic "fight-or-flight" reaction when confronted with a danger. Our heart is pumping fast, and we're breathing faster to supply the muscles with energy to fight or flee. Many physical effects in the body prepare us for actions we may need to take to survive a threat.

But what about nonphysical stressors, like worrying about grades? Are there any positive effects there? Imagine what life would feel like if you never had worries, never felt any stress at all. If you never worried about grades or doing well on a test, how much studying would you do? If you never thought at all about money, would you make any effort to save it or make it? Obviously, stress can be a good thing when it motivates us to do something, whether it's study, work, resolving a conflict with another, and so on. So it's not stress itself that's negative—it's *unresolved or persistent stress* that starts to have unhealthy effects. Chronic (long-term) stress is associated with many physical changes and illnesses, including the following:

immune system

The body system, involving many different organs and body tissues, responsible for defending the body against infection and disease.

blood pressure

The pressure blood exerts on the walls of blood vessels, resulting from complex processes in the body; high blood pressure is associated with several diseases and health problems.

diabetes

A disease in which the body has high levels of sugar in the blood because of an inability to manage blood glucose; diabetes is associated with a range of serious health problems.

insomnia

An inability to sleep; chronic sleeplessness.

- Weakened **immune system**, making you more likely to catch a cold and to suffer from any illness longer
- More frequent digestive system problems, including constipation or diarrhea, ulcers, and indigestion
- Elevated **blood pressure**
- Increased risk of **diabetes**
- Muscle and back pain
- More frequent headaches, fatigue, and **insomnia**
- Greater risk of heart attack and other cardiovascular problems over the long term

Chronic or acute (intense short-term) stress also affects our minds and emotions in many ways:

- Difficulty thinking clearly or concentrating
- Poor memory
- More frequent negative emotions such as anxiety, depression, frustration, powerlessness, resentment, or nervousness—and a general negative outlook on life
- Difficulty dealing with others because of irritability, anger, or avoidance

No wonder we view stress as such a negative thing! As much as we'd like to eliminate all stressors, however, it just can't happen. Too many things in the real world cause stress and always will.

6.3   Unhealthy Responses to Stress

Since many stressors are unavoidable, the question is what to do about the resulting stress. A person can try to ignore or deny stress for a while, but it keeps building and starts causing all those problems. So we have to do *something*.

Consider first what you have typically done in the past when you felt most stressed; complete this Past Stress-Reduction Habits Self-Assessment:

PAST STRESS-REDUCTION HABITS SELF-ASSESSMENT

On a scale of 1 to 5, rate each of the following behaviors for how often you have experienced it because of high stress levels.

Stress Response	Never	Seldom	Sometimes	Often	Usually	Always
1. Drinking alcohol	0	1	2	3	4	5
2. Drinking lots of coffee	0	1	2	3	4	5
3. Sleeping a lot	0	1	2	3	4	5
4. Eating too much	0	1	2	3	4	5
5. Eating too little	0	1	2	3	4	5
6. Smoking or drugs	0	1	2	3	4	5
7. Having arguments	0	1	2	3	4	5
8. Sitting around depressed	0	1	2	3	4	5
9. Watching television or surfing the web	0	1	2	3	4	5
10. Complaining to friends	0	1	2	3	4	5
11. Exercising, jogging, biking	0	1	2	3	4	5
12. Practicing yoga or tai chi	0	1	2	3	4	5
13. Meditating	0	1	2	3	4	5
14. Using relaxation techniques	0	1	2	3	4	5
15. Talking with an instructor or counselor	0	1	2	3	4	5

Total your scores for questions 1–10: _____

Total your scores for questions 11–15: _____

Subtract the second number from the first: _____

Interpretation: If your final, subtracted score is a positive number, then your past coping methods for dealing with stress have not been as healthy and productive as they could be. Items 1 to 10 are generally not effective ways of dealing with stress, while items 11 to 15 usually are. If you final score is over 20, you're probably like most beginning college students—feeling a lot of stress and not yet sure how best to deal with it.

What's wrong with those stress-reduction behaviors listed first? Why not watch television or get a lot of sleep when you're feeling stressed, if that makes you feel better? While it may feel better temporarily to escape feelings of stress in those ways, ultimately they may cause *more* stress themselves. If you're worried about grades and being too busy to study as much as you need to, then letting an hour or two slip by watching television will make you even more worried later because now you have even less time. Eating too much may make you sluggish and less able to focus, and if you're trying to lose weight, you'll now feel just that much more stressed by what you've done. Alcohol, caffeine, smoking, and drugs all generally increase one's stress over time. Complaining to friends? Over time, your friends will tire of hearing it or tire of arguing with you because it isn't much fun to be around a complaining person. So eventually you may find yourself even more alone and stressed.

Yet there is a bright side: there are lots of very positive ways to cope with stress that will also improve your health, make it easier to concentrate on your studies, and make you a happier person overall.

6.4 Coping with Stress

Look back at the list of stressors that you circled earlier. For each, consider whether it is an external factor (like bad job hours or not having enough money) or an internal factor originating in your attitudes and thoughts. Mark each item with an E (external) or an I (internal).

You may be able to eliminate many external stressors. Talk to your boss about changing your work hours. If you have money problems, work on a budget you can live with (see Chapter 11), look for a new job, or reduce your expenses by finding a cheaper apartment, selling your car, and using public transportation.

What about other external stressors? Taking so many classes that you don't have the time to study for all of them? Keep working on your time management skills (Chapter 2). Schedule your days carefully and stick to the schedule. Take fewer classes next term if necessary. What else can you do to eliminate external stressors? Change apartments, get a new roommate, find better child care—consider all your options. And don't hesitate to talk things over with a college counselor, who may offer other solutions.

Internal stressors, however, are often less easily resolved. We can't make all stressors go away, but we can learn how to cope so that we don't feel so stressed out most of the time. We can take control of our lives. We can find healthy coping strategies.

All the topics in this chapter involve stress one way or another. Many of the healthy habits that contribute to our wellness and happiness also reduce stress and minimize its effects.

Get Some Exercise

aerobic exercise

Brisk physical activity that requires the heart and lungs to work harder to meet the body's increased oxygen needs.

hormones

A substance produced in the body that has physical, mental, or emotional effects.

Exercise, especially **aerobic exercise**, is a great way to help reduce stress. Exercise increases the production of certain **hormones**, leading to a better mood and helping counter depression and anxiety. Exercise helps you feel more energetic and focused so that you are more productive in your work and studies and thus less likely to feel stressed. Regular exercise also helps you sleep better, further reducing stress.

Get More Sleep

When sleep deprived, you feel more stress and are less able to concentrate on your work or studies. Many people drink more coffee or other caffeinated beverages when feeling sleepy, and caffeine contributes further to stress-related emotions such as anxiety and nervousness.

Manage Your Money

Worrying about money is one of the leading causes of stress. Try the financial management skills in Chapter 11 to reduce this stress.

Adjust Your Attitude

You know the saying about the optimist who sees the glass as half full and the pessimist who sees the same glass as half empty. Guess which one feels more stress?

Much of the stress you feel may be rooted in your attitudes toward school, your work—your whole life. If you don't feel good about these things, how do you change? To begin with, you really need to think about yourself. What makes you happy? Do you expect college to be perfect and always exciting, with never a dull class or reading assignment? Or can you be happy that you are in fact succeeding in college and foresee a great life and career ahead?

Maybe you just need to take a fun elective course to balance that "serious" course that you're not enjoying so much. Maybe you just need to play an intramural sport to feel as good as you did in high school sports. Maybe you just need to take a brisk walk every morning to feel more alert and stimulated. Maybe listening to some great music on the way to work will brighten your day. Maybe calling up a friend to study together for that big test will make studying more fun.

No one answer works for everyone—you have to look at your life, be honest with yourself about what affects your daily attitude, and look for ways to make changes. The good news is that although negative habits can be hard to break, once you've turned positive changes into new habits, they will last into a brighter future.

Learn a Relaxation Technique

Relaxation techniques

Any specific physical or mental practice developed to help a person calm the mind, relax the body, or both to lower stress and promote rest or concentration.

Relaxation techniques can be used to help minimize stress. Following are a few tried-and-tested ways to relax when stress seems overwhelming. You can learn most of these through books, online exercises, CDs or MP3s, and DVDs available at your library or student health center. Practicing one of them can have dramatic effects.

- **Deep breathing.** Sit in a comfortable position with your back straight. Breathe in slowly and deeply through your nose, filling your lungs completely. Exhale slowly and smoothly through your mouth. Concentrate on your breathing and feel your chest expanding and relaxing. After five to ten minutes, you will feel more relaxed and focused.

- **Progressive muscle relaxation.** With this technique, you slowly tense and then relax the body's major muscle groups. The sensations and mental concentration produce a calming state.

- **Meditation.** Different forms of meditation may involve focusing on your breathing, a specific visual image, or a certain thought, while clearing the mind of negative energy. Many apps, podcasts, and online resources are available to help you find a form of meditation that works best for you.

- **Yoga or tai chi.** Yoga, tai chi, and other exercises that focus on body position and slow, gradual movements are popular techniques for relaxation and stress reduction. You can learn these techniques through a class or from a DVD.

- **Music and relaxation CDs and MP3s.** Many different relaxation techniques have been developed for audio training. Simply play the recording and relax as you are guided through the techniques.

- **Massage.** Regular massages are a way to relax both body and mind. If you can't afford a weekly massage but enjoy its effects, a local massage therapy school may offer affordable massage from students and beginning practitioners.

Get Counseling

If stress is seriously disrupting your studies or your life regardless of what you do to try to reduce it, you may need help. There's no shame in admitting that you need help, and college counselors and health professionals are there to help.

Tips for Success: Stress

- Pay attention to, rather than ignore, things that cause you stress, and change what you can.
- Accept what you can't change and resolve to make new habits that will help you cope.
- Get regular exercise and enough sleep.
- Evaluate your priorities, work on managing your time, and schedule restful activities in your daily life. Students who feel in control of their lives report feeling much less stress than those who feel that circumstances control them.
- Slow down and focus on one thing at a time—don't check for e-mail or text messages every few minutes! Know when to say no to distractions.
- Break old habits involving caffeine, alcohol, and other substances.
- Remember your long-range goals and don't obsess over short-term difficulties.
- Make time to enjoy being with friends.
- Explore new activities and hobbies that you enjoy.
- Find a relaxation technique that works for you and practice regularly.
- Get help if you're having a hard time coping with emotional stress.

JOURNAL ENTRY

All college students feel some stress. The amount of stress you feel depends on many factors, as discussed in this chapter. As you look at your present life and how much stress you may be feeling, what short-term changes can you start making in the next week or two to feel less stressed and more in control? By the end of the semester or term, how would you ideally like your life to be different—and how can you best accomplish that? Write your thoughts here.

_____

_____

_____

_____

_____

_____

KEY TAKEAWAYS

- Everyone feels stress, and many of the things that cause stress won't go away regardless of what we do. But we can examine our lives, figure out what causes most of our stress, and learn to do something about it.
- Stress leads to a lot of different unhealthy responses that actually increase our stress over the long term. But once we understand how stress affects us, we can begin to take steps to cope in healthier ways.

CHECKPOINT EXERCISES

1. Why should it *not* be your goal to try to eliminate stress from your life completely?
   _____

2. List three or more unhealthful effects of stress.
   _____

3. Name at least two common *external* stressors you may be able to reduce or eliminate from your life.
   _____

4. Name at least two common *internal* stressors you may feel that you need to learn to cope with because you can't eliminate them.
   _____

5. List at least three ways you can minimize the stress you feel.
   _____

---

7. EMOTIONAL HEALTH AND HAPPINESS

LEARNING OBJECTIVES

1. **Explain common causes of anxiety, depression, and other negative emotions in college-age people.**
2. **Describe changes you can make in your life to achieve or maintain emotional balance.**
3. **List characteristics of healthy relationships.**
4. **Describe the steps of conflict resolution.**

Your emotional health is just as important as your physical health—and maybe more so. If you're unhappy much of the time, you will not do as well as in college—or life—as you can if you're happy. You will feel more stress, and your health will suffer.

Most of us are not happy nor unhappy *all the time.* Life is constantly changing, and our emotions change with it. But sometimes we experience more negative emotions than normally, and our emotional health may suffer. Use the Emotional Self-Assessment to evaluate your emotional health.

EMOTIONAL SELF-ASSESSMENT

Check the appropriate boxes.

	Daily	Sometimes	Never
1. I sometimes feel anxious or depressed—without disruption of my everyday life.			
2. I sometimes feel so anxious or depressed that I have trouble with routine activities.			
3. I sometimes feel lonely.			
4. I sometimes feel that I have little control over my life.			
5. Sometimes I have just wanted to give up.			
6. Negative emotions have sometimes kept me from studying or getting my work done.			
7. Negative emotions have affected my relationships with others.			

Write your answers.

1. Describe your emotional mood on most days.

   _____

   _____

2. Describe what you'd ideally like to feel like all the time.

   _____

   _____

3. What specific things are keeping you from feeling what you'd ideally like to feel like most of the time?

   _____

   _____

4. Are you happy with your relationships with others?

   _____

   _____

5. What do you think you can do to be a happier person?

   _____

   _____

7.1   Problematic Emotions

When is an emotion a problem? Is it bad to feel anxious about a big test coming up or to feel sad after a romantic relationship breakup?

Many negative emotions are normal from time to time. College students face so many demands and stressful situations that many naturally feel anxious, depressed, or lonely. These emotions become problematic only when they persist and begin to affect your life in negative ways. That's when it's time to work on your emotional health—just as you'd work on your physical health.

Anxiety

Anxiety is one of the most common emotions of college students, often as a result of the demands of college, work, and family and friends. It's difficult to juggle everything, and you may end up feeling not in control, stressed, and anxious.

Anxiety

Feelings of worry, tension, and nervousness with or without a specific focus of concern; severe or persistent anxiety can be a mental disorder.

stress

A natural response of the body and mind to a demand or challenge, often associated with feelings of tension and negative emotions.

Anxiety typically results from **stress**. Anxiety can be a good thing if it leads to studying for a test, focusing on a problem that needs to be resolved, managing your time and money better, and so on. But if anxiety disrupts your focus and makes you freeze up rather than take action, then it's problematic. Using stress-reduction techniques often helps reduce anxiety to a manageable level.

Anxiety is easier to deal with when you know its cause. Then you can take steps to control the part of your life causing the anxiety. But anxiety can become excessive and lead to a dread of everyday situations. There are five types of more serious anxiety:

1. **Generalized anxiety disorder** is characterized by chronic anxiety, exaggerated worry and tension, even when there is little or nothing to provoke it. The person may have physical symptoms, especially fatigue, headaches, muscle tension, muscle aches, difficulty swallowing, trembling, twitching, irritability, sweating, and hot flashes.

2. **Obsessive-compulsive disorder (OCD)** is characterized by recurrent, unwanted thoughts (obsessions), repetitive behaviors (compulsions), or both. Repetitive behaviors such as hand washing, counting, checking, or cleaning are often performed with the hope of preventing obsessive thoughts or making them go away.

3. **Panic disorder** is characterized by unexpected and repeated episodes of intense fear accompanied by physical symptoms that may include chest pain, heart palpitations, shortness of breath, dizziness, or abdominal distress.

4. **Posttraumatic stress disorder (PTSD)** can develop after exposure to a terrifying event or ordeal involving grave physical harm or its threat. Traumatic events that may trigger PTSD include violent personal assaults, natural or human-caused disasters, accidents, or military combat.

5. **Social phobia (or social anxiety disorder)** is a persistent, intense, and chronic fear of being watched and judged by others and being embarrassed or humiliated by one's own actions. The fear may be so severe that it interferes with work or school and other ordinary activities. Physical symptoms often accompany the intense anxiety of social phobia and include blushing, profuse sweating, trembling, nausea, and difficulty talking.

These five types of anxiety go beyond the normal anxiety everyone feels at some times. If you feel your anxiety is like any of these, see your health-care provider. Effective treatments are available to help you regain control.

Loneliness

loneliness

An emotional state of sadness and feeling isolated from or not connected to others.

Loneliness is a normal feeling that most people experience at some time. College students away from home for the first time are likely to feel lonely at first. Older students may also feel lonely if they no longer see their old friends. Loneliness involves not feeling connected with others. One person may need only one friend to not feel lonely; others need to feel more connected with a group. There's no set pattern for feeling lonely.

If you are feeling lonely, there are many things you can do to meet others and feel connected. Don't sit alone in your room bemoaning the absence of friends—that would only cause more stress and emotional distress. You will likely start making new friends through going to classes, working, studying, and living in the community. But you can jump-start that process by taking some active steps:

- Realize you don't have to be physically with friends in order to stay connected. Many students use social Web sites to stay connected with friends at other colleges or in other locations. Telephone calls, instant messaging, and e-mail work for many.

- Understand that you're not alone in feeling lonely. Many others like you are just waiting for the opportunity to connect, and you will meet them and form new friendships fast once you start reaching out.

- Become involved in campus opportunities to meet others. Every college has a wide range of clubs for students with different interests (see Chapter 9). If you're not the "joiner" type, look for individuals in your classes with whom you think you may have something in common and ask them if they'd like to study for a test together or work together on a class project.

- Remember that loneliness is a temporary thing—it's only a matter of time until you make new friends.

If your loneliness persists and you seem unable to make friends, then it's a good idea to talk with your counselor or someone at the student health center. They can help.

Depression

Depression, like anxiety and loneliness, is commonly experienced by college students. It may be a mild sadness resulting from specific circumstances or be intense feelings of hopelessness and helplessness. Many people feel depressed from time to time because of common situations:

- Feeling overwhelmed by pressures to study, work, and meet other obligations
- Not having enough time (or money) to do the things you want to do
- Experiencing problems in a relationship, friendship, or work situation
- Feeling overweight, unhealthy, or not in control of oneself
- Feeling that your new life as a student lacks some of the positive dimensions of your former life
- Not having enough excitement in your life

Depression, like stress, can lead to unhealthy consequences such as poor sleep, overeating or loss of appetite, substance abuse, relationship problems, or withdrawal from activities that formerly brought joy. For most people, depression is a temporary state. But lasting or severe depression can have crippling effects. Not everyone experiences the same symptoms, but these are most common:

- Persistent sad, anxious, or "empty" feelings
- Feelings of hopelessness or pessimism
- Feelings of guilt, worthlessness, or helplessness
- Irritability or restlessness
- Loss of interest in activities or hobbies once pleasurable, including sex
- Fatigue and decreased energy
- Difficulty concentrating, remembering details, and making decisions
- Insomnia, early morning wakefulness, or excessive sleeping
- Overeating or appetite loss
- Thoughts of suicide or suicide attempts
- Persistent aches or pains, headaches, cramps, or digestive problems

If you have feelings like this that last for weeks at a time and affect your life, your depression is more severe than "normal," temporary depression. It's time to see your health-care provider and get treatment as you would for any other illness.

Suicidal Feelings

Severe depression often makes a person feel there is no hope—and therefore many people with depression do not seek help. In reality, depression can be successfully treated, but only if the person seeks help.

Suicidal feelings, which can result from severe depression, are more common in college students than in the past. Suicide is the second leading cause of death for American college students (after accidents). In most cases, the person had severe depression and was not receiving treatment. Recognizing severe depression and seeking treatment are crucial.

Depression can strike almost anyone, at any age, at any kind of college. It is a myth that high-pressure colleges have higher suicide rates or that students who feel compelled to excel because of college pressures are more likely to commit suicide. In reality, anyone can be ill with severe depression and, if not treated, become suicidal.

Following are risk factors for suicide:

- Depression and other mental disorders or a substance-abuse disorder (more than 90% of people who die by suicide have these risk factors)
- Prior suicide attempt
- Family history of mental disorder, substance abuse, or suicide
- Family violence, including physical or sexual abuse
- Exposure to the suicidal behavior of others, such as family members, peers, or media figures

Warning Signs for Suicide

- Being depressed or sad most of the time
- Having feelings of worthlessness, shame, or hopelessness about the future

depression

A despondent emotional state with feelings of pessimism and sometimes feelings of inadequacy; severe or persistent depression affecting one's daily life can be a mental disorder.

- Withdrawing from friends and family members
- Talking about suicide or death
- Being unable to get over a recent loss (broken relationship, loss of job, etc.)
- Experiencing changes in behavior, sleep patterns, or eating habits

If you or a friend is in a crisis and needs help at any time, call the National Suicide Prevention Lifeline: 1-800-273-TALK (8255). Call for yourself or for someone you care about. All calls are confidential.

If you think someone is suicidal, do not leave him or her alone. Try to get the person to seek immediate help by calling the hotline number. Many campuses also have twenty-four-hour resources. In an emergency, call 911. Try to ensure that the person does not have access to a firearm or other potential tool for suicide, including medications.

7.2 Achieving Emotional Balance

wellness

A state of physical, emotional, mental, and social well-being, not merely the absence of disease.

Emotional balance is an essential element of **wellness**—and for succeeding in college. Emotional balance doesn't mean that you never experience a negative emotion, because these emotions are usually natural and normal. Emotional balance means we balance the negative with the positive, that we can be generally happy even if we're saddened by some things.

Emotional balance starts with being aware of our emotions and understanding them. If you're feeling angry, stop and think about the real cause of your anger. Are you really angry because your friend said something about one of your bad habits, or are you angry because you haven't been able to break that habit? Are you feeling anxiety because you're worried you might not be cut out for college, or are you just anxious about that test tomorrow?

See the "Tips for Success" for ways you can achieve and maintain a healthy emotional balance.

Tips for Success: Emotional Health

- Accept that most emotions can't be directly controlled. But the things you do—like getting exercise, using a relaxation technique, trying a stress-reduction method discussed earlier—do improve your emotional state.
- Connect with others. Your emotional state is less likely to change when you keep to yourself and "stew over" the feeling.
- Develop your empathy for others. Empathy involves recognizing the emotions that others are feeling. You'll find yourself in better emotional balance as a result, and your relationships will improve.
- Be honest in your relationships. If you try to hide your feelings, the other person will know something is wrong and may react the wrong way.
- Understand that negative emotions are temporary. You may be feeling bad now, but this will pass in time. But if a negative feeling does last a long time, recognize that you likely need help resolving it—and that help is available.
- If you've just become a college student, know that the first term is usually the hardest. Hang in there. Once you've developed effective study habits and time management skills, each term will be easier and happier than the one before.

7.3 Relationships

Romantic relationships are often as much a part of a rich emotional life for college students as for anyone else. But the added challenges of college, especially while also working and maintaining a family life, often stress these relationships. You may have to give extra attention to a relationship to keep it healthy.

Building Relationships

Ideally, a healthy relationship should have these characteristics:

- Both partners should respect each other as individuals. Don't expect your partner to be just like you. Both partners should be supportive of each other.

- Both partners should trust each other and be honest with each other. You must feel that you can open up emotionally to the other without fear of rejection.

- Both partners should be understanding and have **empathy** for each other. Good communication is essential. Many relationship problems are rooted in misunderstandings.

These positive characteristics of a good relationship don't happen overnight. The relationship may begin with romantic attraction and only slowly develop into a trusting, mutually supportive friendship as well. These signs may indicate that a dating relationship is not developing well:

- Your partner is pressuring you for sex when you're not ready
- Your partner seems angry or abusive when you disagree about something
- Your partner seems possessive when others want to spend time with you
- Your partner treats you unequally in any way
- Your partner is emotionally or physically abusive (whether it happens once or many times)

If you recognize any of these things happening with someone you're dating, it may be time to reconsider, even if you still feel attracted. Any relationship that begins this way is not likely to end well.

Resolving Conflicts

Conflict will eventually happen in any friendship or relationship. This is just natural because people are different. If a conflict is ignored or not resolved, it may simmer and continue to cause tension, weakening the relationship. It's better to take steps to resolve it.

Conflict resolution is a process for understanding what's really going on and finding a solution. The same general steps of conflict resolution can work to solve a relationship conflict or a conflict between any people or groups because of a disagreement about anything. Following are the general principles of conflict resolution:

1. **Allow things to cool off.** It's difficult to resolve a conflict while either party is still emotional. Wait a few minutes or agree to talk about it later.

2. **Using "I statements" rather than "you statements," each party explains what bothers him or her about the cause of the conflict.** For example, don't say, "You're always playing loud music when I'm trying to study." Instead, say, "I have difficulty studying when you play loud music, and that makes me frustrated and irritable." "You statements" put the other person on the defensive and evoke emotions that make resolution more difficult.

3. **Listen carefully to what the other person says.** Then restate the message in your own words to give the other a chance to clarify their thoughts and feelings. Each party should listen to the other and restate the other's message to ensure the real issue is out on the table for discussion.

4. **Accept responsibility for your role in the conflict, instead of blaming the other.** A good example of accepting responsibility is to say, "I know I'm always studying and need the quiet. I guess that makes it hard for you to listen to your music."

5. **Brainstorm together to find a solution that satisfies both of you.** Some compromise is usually needed, but that is usually not difficult to reach when you're calm and are working together on a solution. In this example, you might compromise by going elsewhere to study at selected times when the other has friends over and wants to listen to music, and the other may compromise by agreeing to use headphones at other times and never to play music aloud after 10 p.m.

6. **Apologize, thank, and forgive.** After reaching a resolution, emotional closure is needed to restore your relationship and end on a positive, affirming note. When appropriate, apologize for your past anger or arguing. Thank the other for being willing to compromise to resolve the conflict. In your mind, forgive the person for past misunderstandings and actions so that you do not carry a grudge into the future.

empathy

The ability to understand and share the feelings of another person.

Conflict resolution

A step-by-step process designed to resolve a dispute or disagreement.

KEY TAKEAWAYS

- Emotional health is just as important as physical health. We can take steps to reduce the negative emotions that plague us from time to time and gain control over our emotional health.

- Emotional balance results from a variety of things in our lives. We need to connect with others, to be honest and empathetic in our relationships, and to resolve conflicts that can cause bad feelings and threaten our daily happiness. We can learn skills in these areas just as in other areas of our lives.

CHECKPOINT EXERCISES

1. For each of the following statements about emotional health, circle T for true or F for false:

T	F	Anxiety is always a mental health disorder.
T	F	It's normal to feel depressed sometimes about the pressures of studying, working, and other obligations in your life.
T	F	When you're feeling depressed or anxious, it's best to keep to yourself and not try to connect with others until after these feelings pass.
T	F	If someone says he is feeling suicidal, he is only seeking attention and is unlikely to actually try to kill himself.

2. List at least two things you can do to make new friends at college.

   _____

3. Describe three characteristics of a good relationship.

   _____
   _____
   _____
   _____

4. List the six steps for effective conflict resolution.

   a. _____
   b. _____
   c. _____
   d. _____
   e. _____
   f. _____

8. SEXUAL HEALTH

LEARNING OBJECTIVES

1. **Explain the importance of understanding your sexual values and making wise decisions regarding your sexuality.**
2. **Describe guidelines for sexually active college students to protect themselves against sexually transmitted infections and unwanted pregnancy.**
3. **List actions to protect against sexual assault.**

Sexuality is normal, natural human drive. As an adult, your sexuality is your own business. Like other dimensions of health, however, your sexual health depends on understanding many factors involving sexuality and your own values. Your choices and behavior may have consequences. Learning about sexuality and thinking through your values will help you make responsible decisions. Begin with the Sexual Health Self-Assessment.

SEXUAL HEALTH SELF-ASSESSMENT

Check the appropriate boxes.

	Often	Sometimes	Never
1. I think about issues related to sexuality.			
2. I have experienced unwanted sexual advances from another.			
3. If I am sexually active, I protect myself from the risk of sexually transmitted infections.			
4. If I am sexually active, I protect myself from the risk of unwanted pregnancy.			
5. I am proud of the choices I have made regarding sexual activity.			
6. I am concerned about the possibility of sexual assault including date rape.			
7. I have been in situations involving some risk of date rape.			

Write your answers.

8. How comfortable are you with your past and present decisions related to sexual behavior?
_____
_____

9. If you are not presently sexually active, do you feel prepared to make responsible decisions about sexual activity if you become active in the near future?
_____
_____

10. If you are sexually active, how well protected are you against the risks of sexually transmitted infection? If you are not active now, how well do you understand protections needed if you become active?
_____
_____

11. If you are sexually active, how well protected are you against the risk of unwanted pregnancy? If you are not active now, how well do you understand the different types of protection available if you become active?
_____
_____

12. If you suddenly found yourself in a situation with a potential for sexual assault, including date rape, would you know what to do?
_____
_____

8.1   Sexual Values and Decisions

It's often difficult to talk about sexuality and sex. Not only is it a very private matter for most people, but the words themselves are often used loosely, resulting in misunderstandings. Surveys have shown, for example, that about three-fourths of college students say they are "sexually active"—but survey questions rarely specify exactly what that phrase means. To some, sexual activity includes passionate kissing and fondling, while to others the phrase means sexual intercourse. Manual and oral sexual stimulation may or may not be included in an individual's own definition of being sexually active.

We should therefore begin by defining these terms. First, sexuality is not the same as sex. **Human sexuality** is a general term for how people experience and express themselves as sexual beings. Since all people are sexual beings, everyone has a dimension of human sexuality regardless of their behavior. Someone who practices complete abstinence from sexual behavior still has the human dimension of sexuality.

human sexuality

A general term for how people experience and express themselves as sexual beings, including feelings, thoughts, and actions.

gender identity

A person's sense of self in terms of being male or female.

sexual orientation

A sexual preference or choice that determines whether one chooses a member of the same or the opposite sex, or both, for sexual satisfaction.

sexual activity

Any behavior involving genital stimulation, including vaginal, oral, and anal intercourse, that carries the risk of acquiring a sexually transmitted disease.

intercourse

An act of physical sexual contact between individuals that involves the genitalia of at least one person, typically with penetration of the vagina, mouth, or anus.

sexual intercourse

As used here, referring to heterosexual intercourse in which the penis penetrates the vagina.

FIGURE 10.3

Drinking alcohol increases the likelihood of having unprotected sexual activity.

© Thinkstock

safer sex

The use of protective actions or devices during sexual activity to minimize the risk of sexually transmitted infections and unwanted pregnancy.

Sexuality involves **gender identity**, or how we see ourselves in terms of maleness and femaleness, as well as **sexual orientation**, which refers to the gender qualities of those to whom we are attracted. The phrase **sexual activity** is usually used to refer to behaviors between two (or more) people involving the genitals—but the term may also refer to solo practices such as masturbation or to partner activities that are sexually stimulating but may not involve the genitals. For the purposes of this chapter, with its focus on personal health, the term sexual activity refers to any behavior that carries a risk of acquiring a sexually transmitted disease. This includes vaginal, oral, and anal **intercourse**. The term **sexual intercourse** will be used to refer to vaginal intercourse, which also carries the risk of unwanted pregnancy. We'll avoid the most confusing term, sex, which in strict biological terms refers to reproduction but is used loosely to refer to many different behaviors.

College students are often stereotyped as having frequent sexual activity. One survey found that most college students think that *other* students have an average of three sexual partners a year, yet 80% of those answering said that they *themselves* had zero or one sexual partner. In other words, college students as a whole are not engaging in sexual activity nearly as much as they think they are. Another study revealed that about 20% of eighteen- to twenty-four-year-old college students had never been sexually active and about half had not been during the preceding month.

In sum, some college students are sexually active and some are not. Misperceptions of what others are doing may lead to unrealistic expectations or feelings. Most important, however, is to be aware of your own values and to make responsible decisions that protect your sexual health.

Information and preparation are the focus of this section of the chapter. People who engage in sexual activity in the heat of the moment—often under the influence of alcohol—without having protection and information for making good decisions are at risk for disease, unwanted pregnancy, or abuse.

Alcohol and Sexual Activity

Almost all college students know the importance of protection against sexually transmitted infections and unwanted pregnancy. So why then do these problems still occur so often? Part of the answer is that we don't always do the right thing even when we know it—especially in the heat of the moment, particularly when drinking or using drugs. Some 400,000 eighteen- to twenty-four-year-old college students a year engage in unprotected sexual activity after drinking, and 100,000 report having been too intoxicated to know if they had consented to the sexual activity.

8.2 What's "Safe Sex"?

It has been said that *no* sexual activity is safe because there is always some risk, even if very small, of protections failing. The phrase "**safer sex**" better describes actions one can take to reduce the risk of sexually transmitted infections and unwanted pregnancy.

Sexually Transmitted Infections (STIs)

About two dozen different diseases can be transmitted through sexual activity. **Sexually transmitted infections (STIs)** range from infections that can be easily treated with medications to diseases that may have permanent health effects to **HIV (human immunodeficiency virus)** infections, the cause of AIDS, a fatal disease. Despite decades of public education campaigns and easy access to protection, STIs still affect many millions of people every year. Often a person feels no symptoms at first and does not realize he or she has the infection and thus passes it on unknowingly. Or a person may not use protection because of simple denial: "It can't happen to me."

Table 10.2 lists facts about common STIs for which college students are at risk. Although there are some differences, in most cases sexual transmission involves an exchange of **body fluids** between two people: semen, vaginal fluids, or blood (or other body fluids containing blood). The same precautions to prevent the transmission of HIV will prevent the transmission of other STIs as well.

Although many of these diseases may not cause dramatic symptoms, or not at first, always see a health-care provider if you have the slightest suspicion of having acquired an STI. Not only should you receive treatment as soon as possible to prevent the risk of serious health problems, but you are also obligated to help not pass it on to others.

Sexually transmitted infections (STIs)

Any infection predominantly transmitted through sexual activity between two individuals, usually through direct contact with the genitals or an exchange of body fluids.

HIV (human immunodeficiency virus)

Virus transmitted via body fluids during sexual activity and by other means such as drug needle sharing; the cause of AIDS, a fatal disease.

body fluids

In general, any fluid within the body, but more specifically used for those fluids that may carry a sexually transmitted disease: blood, semen, and vaginal secretions.

TABLE 10.2   Common Sexually Transmitted Infections

Infection	U.S. Incidence	Transmission	Symptoms	Risks
HIV (Human Immunodeficiency Virus) Causing AIDS	About 56,000 new HIV infections per year	Contact with infected person's blood, semen, or vaginal secretions during any sexual act (and needle sharing)	Usually no symptoms for years or decades. Later symptoms include swollen glands, weight loss, and susceptibility to infections.	Because medical treatment can only slow but not cure AIDS, the disease is currently eventually fatal.
Chlamydia Bacteria	Over 1 million new cases reported annually, with many more not reported	Vaginal, anal, or oral sex with infected person	Often no symptoms. Symptoms may occur 1–3 weeks after exposure, including burning sensation when urinating and abnormal discharge from vagina or penis.	In women, pelvic inflammatory disease may result, with permanent damage to reproductive tissues, possibly sterility. In men, infection may spread and cause pain, fever, and rarely sterility.
Genital HPV (Human Papilloma Virus) Causing Genital Warts	6.2 million new cases a year (before vaccine)	Genital contact, most often during vaginal and anal sex	Most infected people have no symptoms at all and unknowingly pass on the virus. Warts may appear in weeks or months.	Of the 40 types of HPV, many cause no health problems. Some types cause genital warts; others can lead to cancer. Vaccine is now recommended for girls and young women and protects against cancer-causing HPV.
Genital Herpes Virus	An estimated 45 million Americans have had the infection	Genital-genital or oral-genital contact	Often no symptoms. First outbreak within 2 weeks of contact may cause sores and flu-like symptoms. Outbreaks occur less frequently over time.	Many adults experience recurrent painful genital sores and emotional distress. Genital herpes in a pregnant woman puts the infant at risk during childbirth.
Gonorrhea Bacteria	700,000 new cases each year	Direct contact with the penis, vagina, mouth, or anus; ejaculation does not have to occur	Often no recognized symptoms. Burning sensation when urinating. Abnormal discharge from vagina or penis. Rectal infection symptoms include itching, soreness, or bleeding.	If untreated, it may cause serious, permanent health problems, including pelvic inflammatory disease in women with permanent damage to reproductive tissues and possibly sterility in both men and women.
Trichomoniasis Protozoa	7.4 million new cases each year	Genital contact, most often during vaginal sex	Most men have no symptoms or may have slight burning after urination or mild discharge. Some women have vaginal discharge with strong odor and irritation or itching of genital area.	Trichomoniasis makes an infected woman more susceptible to HIV infection if exposed to the virus. Trichomoniasis is easily treated with medication.
Syphilis Bacteria	36,000 cases reported a year	Direct contact with a syphilis sore, which occurs mainly on the external genitals, vagina, anus, or in the rectum but can also occur on the lips and in the mouth; during vaginal, anal, or oral sex	Often no recognized symptoms for years. Primary stage symptom (a small painless sore) appears in 10–90 days but heals without treatment. Secondary stage symptoms (skin rashes, fever, headache, muscle aches) may also resolve without treatment. Late-stage symptoms occur after 10–20 years, including severe internal organ damage and nervous system effects.	Because the infected person may feel no symptoms, the risk of transmission is great. Syphilis is easy to treat in the early stages, but treatment in late stages cannot repair damage that has already occurred. Untreated, syphilis is often fatal.

Follow these guidelines to protect yourself against STIs if you are sexually active:

- Know that only **abstinence** is 100% safe. Protective devices can fail even when used correctly, although the risk is small. Understand the risks of not always using protection.

- Talk with your partner in advance about your sexual histories and health. Agree that regardless of how sure you both are about not having an STI, you will use protection because you cannot be certain even if you have no symptoms.

- Avoid sexual activity with casual acquaintances whose sexual history you do not know and with whom you have not talked about health issues. Sexual activity is safest with a single partner in a long-term relationship.

- Use a latex condom for all sexual activity (except when intending pregnancy). A male condom is about 98% effective when used correctly, and a female condom about 95% effective when used correctly. With both, incorrect use increases the risk. If you are unsure how to use a condom correctly and safely, do some private online reading. Good information can be found at http://www.emedicinehealth.com/how_to_use_a_condom/article_em.htm. You can watch a video demonstration of how to use condoms correctly at http://www.plannedparenthood.org/teen-talk/watch/how-use-condom-26797.htm.

- If you are sexually active with multiple partners, see your health-care provider twice a year for an STI screening even if you are not experiencing symptoms.

Preventing Unwanted Pregnancy

Heterosexual couples who engage in vaginal intercourse are also at risk for an unwanted pregnancy. There are lots of myths about how a woman can't get pregnant at a certain time in her menstrual cycle or under other conditions, but in fact, there's a risk of pregnancy after vaginal intercourse at any time. All couples should talk about protection before reaching the stage of having intercourse, and take appropriate steps.

While a male condom is about 98% effective, that 2% failure rate could lead to tens of thousands of unintended pregnancies among college students. When not used correctly, condoms are only 85% effective. In addition, a couple who have been healthy and **monogamous** in their relationship for a long time may be less faithful in their use of condoms if the threat of STIs seems diminished. Other methods of birth control should also therefore be considered. With the exception of male **vasectomy**, at present most other methods are used by the woman. They include intrauterine devices (IUDs), implants, injected or oral **contraceptives** (the "pill"), hormone patches, vaginal rings, diaphragms, cervical caps, and sponges. Each has certain advantages and disadvantages.

Birth control methods vary widely in effectiveness as well as potential side effects. This is therefore a very personal decision. In addition, two methods can sometimes be used together, such as a condom along with a diaphragm or spermicide, which increases the effectiveness. (Note that a male and female condom should not be used together, however, because of the risk of either or both tearing because of friction between them.) Because this is such an important issue, you should talk it over with your health-care provider or a professional at your student health center or an agency such as Planned Parenthood.

In cases of unprotected vaginal intercourse, or if a condom tears, **emergency contraception** is an option generally for up to five days after intercourse. Sometimes called the "morning after pill" or "plan B," emergency contraception is an oral hormone that prevents pregnancy from occurring. It is *not* an "abortion pill." Planned Parenthood offices around the country can provide more information and confidential contraceptive services including emergency contraception.

8.3   Sexual Assault and Date Rape

Sexual assault is a serious problem in America generally and among college students especially:

- About a third of all dating relationships involve some physical violence.
- One in six women and one in ten men will be sexually assaulted in their lifetimes.
- About a fourth of sexual assault victims are in the typical college age range of eighteen to twenty-four years old.
- As many as one in four women experience unwanted sexual intercourse while attending college.
- In more than three fourths of rape cases, the victim knows the perpetrator.

abstinence

Not engaging in sexual activity.

monogamous

A relationship involving a single mate for a significant period of time.

vasectomy

A surgical procedure that causes a man to be sterile and permanently incapable of reproducing unless the procedure is later reversed.

contraceptives

A drug, device, or procedure used for the deliberate prevention of pregnancy.

emergency contraception

Contraceptive measures, such as a drug, used to prevent pregnancy after sexual intercourse has already occurred.

Sexual assault

Any form of coerced sexual contact or sexual activity without the other person's voluntary consent.

Rape

Unlawful sexual intercourse with or sexual penetration of another person without that person's consent, typically with force or threat of force.

Sexual assault is any form of sexual contact without voluntary consent. **Rape** is usually more narrowly legally defined as forced sexual intercourse, a specific type of sexual assault. Both are significant problems among college students. Although men can also be victims of sexual assault and rape, the problem more often involves women, so this section focuses primarily on the issue for women in college. Men must also understand what is involved in sexual assault and help build greater awareness of the problem and how to prevent it.

Sexual assault is so common in our society in part because many people believe myths about certain kinds of male-female interaction. Common myths include "It's not really rape if the woman was flirting first" and "It's not rape unless the woman is seriously injured." Both statements are not legally correct. Another myth is the idea that "Saying no is just playing hard to get, not really no." Men who really believe these myths may not think that they are committing assault, especially if their judgment is impaired by alcohol. Other perpetrators of sexual assault and rape, however, know exactly what they're doing and may deliberately plan to overcome their victim by using alcohol or a date rape drug.

College administrators and educators have worked very hard to promote better awareness of sexual assault and to help students learn how to protect themselves. Yet colleges cannot prevent things that happen at parties and behind closed doors. Students must understand how to protect themselves.

Perpetrators of sexual assault fall into three categories:

1. Strangers
2. Acquaintances
3. Dating partners

Among college students, assault by a stranger is the least common on campus because campus police departments take many measures to help keep students safe. Nonetheless, use common sense to avoid situations where you might be alone in a vulnerable place. Walk with a friend if you must pass through a quiet place after dark. Don't open your door to a stranger. Don't take chances. For more information and ways to reduce your risk of sexual assault, see http://www.rainn.org/get-information/sexual-assault-prevention.

Most sexual assaults are perpetrated by acquaintances or date partners. Typically, an acquaintance assault begins at a party. Typically, both the man and the woman are drinking—although assault can happen to sober victims as well. The interaction may begin innocently, perhaps with dancing or flirting. The perpetrator may misinterpret the victim's behavior as a willingness to share sexual activity, or a perpetrator intent on sexual activity may simply pick out a likely target. Either way, the situation may gradually or suddenly change and lead to sexual assault.

Prevention of acquaintance rape begins with the awareness of its likelihood and then taking deliberate steps to ensure you stay safe at and after the party:

- Go with a friend and don't let someone separate you from your friend. Agree to stick together and help each other if it looks like things are getting out of hand. If your friend has too much to drink, don't leave her or him alone. Plan to leave together and stick to the plan.
- Be especially alert if you become separated from your friend, even if you are only going off alone to look for the bathroom. You may be followed.
- Be cautious if someone is pressuring you to drink heavily.
- Trust your instincts if someone seems to be coming on too aggressively. Get back to your friends.
- Know where you are and have a plan to get home if you have to leave abruptly.

date rape

The rape of a person by someone whom the person is dating.

These preventions can work well at a party or in other social situations, but they don't apply in many dating situations when you are alone with another person. About half of sexual assaults on college students are **date rape**. An assault may occur after the first date, when you feel you know the person better and perhaps are not feeling concerned about the risk. This may actually make you more vulnerable. Until you really get to know the person well and have a trusting relationship, follow these guidelines to lower the risk of sexual assault:

- Make it clear that you have limits on sexual activity. Take care that your body language or appearance does not send a message that you might be "easy." If there is any question that your date may not understand your limits, talk about your values and limits.
- If your date initiates unwanted sexual activity of any sort, do not resist passively. The other may misinterpret passive behavior as consent. Make your "no" explicit and obvious.
- Be careful if your date is drinking heavily or using drugs. Avoid drinking yourself, or drink very moderately.
- Stay in public places where there are other people. Do not invite your date to your home before your relationship is well established.

- Trust your instincts if your date seems to be coming on too strong. End the date if necessary.
- Pay attention for signs of an unhealthy relationship (described in Section 7).

If you are sexually assaulted, always talk to someone. Call a rape crisis center, your student health center, or the **National Sexual Assault Hotline at 1-800-656-HOPE (4673)** for a confidential conversation. Even if you do not report the assault to law enforcement, it's important to talk through your feelings and seek help if needed to prevent an emotional crisis.

Date Rape Drugs

In addition to alcohol, sexual predators use certain commonly available drugs to sedate women for sexual assault. They are odorless and tasteless and may be added to a punch bowl or slipped into your drink when you're not looking. These drugs include the sedatives GHB, sometimes called "liquid ecstasy," and Rohypnol, also called "roofies." Both cause sedation in small doses but can have serious medical effects in larger doses. Date rape drugs are typically used at parties. Use the following tips to protect yourself against date rape drugs:

- Don't put your drink down where someone else may get to it. If your drink has been out of your sight for even a moment, don't finish it.
- Never accept an open drink. Don't accept a mixed drink that you did not see mixed from pure ingredients.
- Never drink anything from a punch bowl, even if it's nonalcoholic. You can't know what may have been added into the punch.
- If you experience unexpected physical symptoms that may be the result of something you drank or ate, get to an emergency room and ask to be tested.

KEY TAKEAWAYS

- Sexual health is an important dimension of wellness and something we should all think about to affirm our values and make responsible decisions.
- Your time in college and your overall health and well-being would be seriously impacted if you were to acquire a sexually transmitted infection or experience an unwanted pregnancy. You owe it to yourself—and anyone with whom you are in a relationship—to have the facts and know how to protect yourself.
- Sexual assaults are rampant on college campuses and in society in general. You need to know what's involved—and what to do to protect yourself from the pain of becoming a victim.

CHECKPOINT EXERCISES

1. For each of the following statements about sexual health, circle T for true or F for false:

T	F	As long as you always use a condom, you don't have to worry about an STI from sexual activity.
T	F	You may have a very serious STI without feeling any symptoms at all.
T	F	Abstinence is the only 100% effective method of birth control.
T	F	It's not rape if a man has sexual intercourse with a woman after she says no as long as he does not use force.

2. List at least three things a woman can do at a party to ensure she does not become a victim of sexual assault.
_____

3. Describe a first date scenario in which a woman is well protected from the risk of sexual assault. List at least three things she should make sure of.
_____
_____

9. CHAPTER ACTIVITIES

Chapter Takeaways

- Good health helps you be more successful in college.
- For good nutrition, eat a varied diet with lots of vegetables, fruits, and whole grains, and minimize fats, sugar, and salt.
- Regular exercise is not only important for good health but is a great way to reduce stress in your life.
- Sleep is one of the first areas where college students cut back when they find themselves too busy with classes, work, and other activities. Taking the time to get enough sleep, however, makes you so much more efficient when studying that it can actually save you time.
- Substance use and abuse not only take a toll on the body but also contributes to problems in college, at work, and in the future. You may need to make a smart decision between short-term pleasures and long-term success.
- Since many stressors are unavoidable in life, we all need to find good ways to minimize their effects. The best stress-reducers over time become good habits that increase our wellness and help us succeed in college and careers.
- If you are having an emotional or relationship problem that persists and affects your life, don't hesitate to seek help. Most colleges have counselors and health professionals trained to help you get through any crisis.
- Sexual health is your own business—except that sexuality usually affects and is affected by others. Smart choices focus on protecting yourself from potential problems, regardless of your choices about sexual activity.

CHAPTER REVIEW

1. Whose fault is it if I'm overweight now? _____

2. Whose fault is it if I'm overweight two years from now? _____

3. Whom can I talk to if I want to find a weight loss program that will work best for me? _____

4. Complete these sentences:

   a. What I think most needs change in my diet is

   _____

   b. The main reason I don't get enough exercise is

   _____

   c. When I feel stressed, I often _____ (How healthy is that? Should you choose healthier activities instead?)

   d. The first step in resolving a conflict you are having with someone else is to

   _____

5. How do you know if you're drinking too much or too often?

   _____

   _____

6. As a college student, why should you care about how much stress you feel and what you do about it?

   _____

   _____

7. If you have a friend who has seemed very depressed lately, what signs should you look for that might indicate he or she is becoming suicidal?

   _____

   _____

8. If you do see signs of suicide in your friend, what should you do?

   _____

   _____

9. If you are sexually active, can you be certain you are at zero risk for acquiring HIV? If so, when? If not, what can you do?

   _____

   _____

OUTSIDE THE BOOK

1. Choose a friend you enjoy spending time with and see if he or she will help you with an "experiment." Together, make a list of fun things to do together in the next week that will help minimize your stress. Choose activities that are different from your usual habits. Below are some ideas, but be creative and try to include your own healthy ideas. At the end of the week, talk about the experiment and how you felt during and afterward. Did you have fun? Did you get some ideas for other or better things to do? Plan to keep doing some of these activities.

   - Cook a healthy meal together (if you have a kitchen) or shop together for snacks you can carry with you for when you're hungry between classes.
   - Go for a jog, bike ride, or long walk at least three times during the week.
   - Study together early in the evening, with snacks and drinks that won't slow you down or keep you up, and then get to bed on time.

2. Spend 20-30 minutes online getting more ideas about healthy ways to minimize the stress you feel as a student. Start by typing the phrase "stress reduction" into your search engine. Look for specific ideas and activities not already covered in this chapter. Write them down here to share with other students and your instructor.

   a. _____
   b. _____
   c. _____
   d. _____
   e. _____

3. Go to http://www.englishclub.com/health/stress-quiz.htm and take the ten-question stress quiz to see how much you understand about stress-related topics. (The EnglishClub.com website also has a lot of good information for students who speak English as a second language.)

MAKE AN ACTION LIST

Nutrition

My worst eating habits are

_____

_____

My action plan to eat better includes the following:

_____

_____

Exercise

I don't get enough exercise because

_____

_____

I'll try to do these things to become more active:

_____

_____

Sleep

I sometimes/often don't get enough sleep because

_____

_____

I can better manage my time to get enough sleep in these ways:

_____

_____

Substances

I tend to overuse or abuse these substances:

_____

_____

My action plan to avoid substance problems includes:

_____

_____

Stress

These things cause me the most stress:

_____

_____

I will take these steps to better cope with these stresses:

_____

_____

Emotional Health

I am happiest when I

_____

_____

I'll be happier if I make these changes:

_____

_____

Sexual Health

I am/might be putting myself at risk when/if I do these things:

_____

_____

What I should always do to reduce these risks is to

_____

_____

CLASS DISCUSSION QUESTIONS

1. It seems that medical research studies are continually issuing new guidelines about what is or is not healthy, often contradicting previous studies. How can we trust any guidelines about what to eat, how much exercise or sleep is needed, and so on? Why not just do what feels right?

2. Can a person be experiencing persistent stress and not feel "stressed out"? If so, how would you know if you're having effects from too much stress?

3. Many colleges now have guidelines that state that for sexual consent to occur, it is not enough just that a woman does not say "no": she must actually say "yes" for a man to proceed with sexual advances. Do you feel this will make a difference in preventing sexual assaults? Explain.

ENDNOTES

1. Smokefree.gov, "Quit Guide: Quitting," http://www.smokefree.gov (accessed July 13, 2010).

2. National Institute on Alcohol Abuse and Alcoholism, "A Snapshot of Annual High-Risk College Drinking Consequences," College Drinking—Changing the Culture, http://www.collegedrinkingprevention.gov/StatsSummaries/snapshot.aspx (accessed April 27, 2015).

3. National Institute on Alcohol Abuse and Alcoholism, "Alcohol Myths," College Drinking—Changing the Culture, http://www.collegedrinkingprevention.gov/CollegeStudents/alcoholMyths.aspx (accessed July 13, 2010).

Taking Control of Your Finances

FIGURE 11.1

© Thinkstock

Where Are You Now?

Assess your present knowledge and attitudes.

	Yes	Unsure	No
1. I am confident I will make it through college without any financial hardships.			
2. I realize that while in college I won't have as much money to spend on things as in the past.			
3. I plan to avoid debt as much as possible while in college so I don't have unnecessarily large loans to pay back after college.			
4. I am willing to make sacrifices and spend less on some things while in college.			
5. I keep track of all my expenditures and maintain a budget so that I know when I am spending too much.			
6. I believe I can have a happy and fulfilling life while a student without having a lot of money.			
7. I know the best kinds of jobs to seek while in college.			
8. I always pay off the full balance on my credit cards when the statement arrives.			
9. I have applied for every possible form of financial aid to help pay for college.			

Where Do You Want to Go?

Think about how you answered the questions above. Be honest with yourself. On a scale of 1 to 10, how would you rate your financial health at this time?

In financial trouble   **Very financially secure**

1   2   3   4   5   6   7   8   9   10

In the following list, circle the three most important financial areas in which you think you may need to improve:

- Making more money
- Finding the best job
- Spending less money
- Living more cheaply
- Paying bills on time
- Avoiding overdraft and late-payment fees
- Making a budget
- Sticking to a budget
- Controlling credit card spending
- Getting help with personal finances
- Saving money
- Keeping good financial records
- Building a good credit history
- Applying for financial aid

Are there other areas in which you can improve your financial well-being and avoid potential money problems while in college? Write down other things you feel you need to work on.

_____

_____

_____

How to Get There

Here's what we'll work on in this chapter:

- Setting realistic financial goals for your college years
- Accepting college loans no greater than needed
- Choosing between making more money and spending less money
- Accepting the financial realities of college and being happy with your financial choices
- Discovering what kinds of jobs are more fulfilling while in college and how to find them
- Tracking spending using a budget and managing your budget to stay on track
- Spending less while still having fun, eating well, and having a social life
- Using a credit card without getting into debt
- Avoiding future financial problems while building a good credit history now
- Getting all the financial aid you can

1. INTRODUCTION

What is a chapter on personal finances doing in a book on student success? If you're a new college student you may not yet have money problems or issues—but most college students soon do. It doesn't matter whether you're a "traditional" college student enrolled in college just after high school or a "nontraditional" student returning to school.

Younger students are likely to confront money issues for several reasons:

- If you are living away from home for the first time, you may have less experience setting and sticking to a budget and handling money in general.
- Because you need more time for studying and other aspects of college life, you may have less time to work and make money.
- Even if you receive financial support from your family, your funds are not unlimited, and you'll need to learn to live within a budget.
- You will have many new expenses including tuition and fees, room and board or housing and food bills, books and supplies, and so on.

Nontraditional students who have worked or started a family before attending college may have already learned to manage their money well but usually still confront some financial issues:

- Because you need more time for studying and courses, you likely have less time to work and make money.
- You will have many new expenses including tuition and fees, books and supplies, and so on.
- You are more likely to have to juggle a budget that may include a family, mortgage, and other established expenses.

The money issues almost everyone eventually has in college can impact your academic success. Money problems are stressful and can keep you from concentrating on your studies. Spending too much may lead you to work more hours than you might otherwise, giving you less time to study. Or you might take fewer classes and thus spend more years in college than needed. Worse yet, money problems cause many students to drop out of college entirely.

But it doesn't have to be this hard. Like other skills, financial skills can be learned, and they have lifelong value. This chapter will help you:

- Set financial goals
- Consider jobs and making money
- Learn how to spend less and manage a budget
- Avoid credit card debt
- Determine how best to finance your college expenses

2.   FINANCIAL GOALS AND REALITIES

LEARNING OBJECTIVES

1. Set financial goals to match your realities.
2. Establish financial priorities appropriate for your college years.
3. Make choices between spending less and making more.

It's expensive to go to college. College tuition has risen for decades at virtually all schools, and very few students are fortunate enough to not have to be concerned with this reality. Still, there are things you can do to help control costs and manage your finances while in college. Begin by thinking about your financial goals.

2.1   What Are Your Financial Goals?

Whatever it is you plan to do in your future, your financial goals in the present should be realistic to enable you to fulfill your plan. Consider these two different students:

Keri entered college planning to major in business. Her family could not give her much financial support, but she chose to attend an expensive private college because she thought it would help her get into a good business school after graduation. She had to take large loans to pay her tuition, but she wasn't concerned about a budget because she assumed she'd make a lot later on and be able to easily pay off the loans. Yet when she graduated and had to begin paying off her private bank loans, she discovered she couldn't afford to go straight to business school after all. She put her dream on hold for a few years and took a job she didn't much like.

Jorge worked a few years after high school but finally decided that he needed a college degree to get the kind of job he wanted. He kept his nice apartment and car and enrolled in a couple night classes while continuing to work full time during the day. He was surprised how much he had to study, however, and after a couple months he felt he was struggling. He just didn't have enough time to do it all—so he dropped first one class and then, a couple weeks later, the other. He told himself that he'd try it again in a year or two, but part of him wondered how anyone could ever get through college while working.

What Keri and Jorge have in common is a conflict between their financial goals and realities. Both were motivated to succeed in college, and both had a vision for their future. But both were unsuccessful in finding ways to make their dreams come true—because of money issues.

Could they have done things differently? Maybe Keri could have gone to a less expensive college and still reached her goal, or maybe she could have avoided such heavy student loans by working summers and part time during the school year. Maybe Jorge could have reduced his living expenses and cut back his work hours to ensure he could balance school and work better. Maybe both were spending thousands of dollars a year on things they could have done without if only they'd thought through their goals and learned to live within a budget.

Taking control of your personal finances begins with thinking about your goals and deciding what really matters to you. Here are some things to think about:

internships

A paid or unpaid position in a formal program designed for a student to gain practical experience in a career field.

- Is it important for you to graduate from college without debt? Is it acceptable to you, or necessary, to take some student loans?

- What are your priorities for summers and other "free time"? Working to earn money? Taking nonpaying **internships** or volunteering to gain experience in your field? Enjoying social activities and time with friends?

- How important is it to take a full load of classes so that your college education does not take longer than necessary?

- How important is it to you to live in a nice place, or drive a nice car, or wear nice clothes, or eat in nice restaurants? How important are these compared to your educational goals?

There are no easy answers to such questions. Most people would like enough money to have and do what they want, low enough expenses that they don't have to work too much to stay on budget, and enough financial freedom to choose activities without being swayed by financial concerns. Few college students live in that world, however. Since you will have to make choices, it's important first to think about what really matters to you—and what you're willing to sacrifice for a while in order to reach your goals.

2.2 Is College Debt Worth It?

In recent years there has been much media attention to the size of student loans many students graduate with. We hear numbers about loans in the tens of thousands of dollars and the many years it will take to pay them off. It's scary to think of having so much debt in the future that you might have to wait a long time to buy a house or start a family. Such stories in the media can make one wonder if it really makes sense to go to college only to be saddled with such debt afterwards.

Unfortunately, there's no one easy answer that applies to everyone. What everyone should do is confront some basic questions with eyes open and then make smart decisions. Let's start with a fact. Current research indicates that for the great majority of college graduates, their student loan debt is manageable and that their higher earnings in better jobs as a result of having a college degree more than compensate for having loans that must be paid off. In short, for most students, college is still well worth the cost.

But that does not automatically apply to *everyone*. If a student goes to an expensive college, indulges in an unnecessarily expensive lifestyle, chooses not to work summers or part-time during school, and then fails to find a job that pays reasonably well, that student's student loan debt can in fact be a crushing experience for years to come. Note that this student has made several choices that led to that reality, however. Did he or she *have* to go to a college with such high tuition and other costs? Did he or she *have* to spend so much during the college years? *Could* he or she have worked and avoided some of that final debt? *Could* he or she have done more while in college to increase the odds for finding a successful job after graduation?

Those are questions you can only answer for yourself. Again, what matters most at this point, as you begin college, is being honest with yourself when you think about money and your future. There's nothing wrong with taking student loans, which are simply necessary for many students. There's also nothing wrong with a student choosing to begin college at a less expensive community college and planning later to attend a state university to complete a four-year program. There's nothing wrong with a student transferring from an expensive private college to a state college after a year or two in order to reduce the overall costs of a degree. We are not arguing for options like these—we're simply suggesting that every student has unique circumstances and goals, and it always helps to gather realistic information about the costs of college and the prospects of future earnings.

Chapter 12 discusses the process of choosing a college major and a potential future career. If you are unsure of your interests or future job earnings, you might want to look ahead at some of the resources for information on career prospects and expected salary levels in different careers. While you might change your major or intended career in the next few years, or may not land that dream job immediately upon graduation, it is helpful to project your financial future when it comes to decisions you'll make almost every day as a student.

Finally, although it's good to stay upbeat about the values and benefits of being in college, there is a dark side of the financial picture to be aware of. As mentioned above, for the great majority of college students, the future financial benefits of a better job do clearly outweigh the costs of taking on debt to obtain a degree. But those dire news stories about crippling debt can be true for one group of students: those who take large loans but then drop out of college before finishing. That can be the worst of both worlds, having to make large loan payments but having a lower-paying job and not earning enough to pay off the loans while living a good life. How to avoid this situation? Make your personal commitment to succeed in college and then work to do it. Those who end up dropping out almost always have not made the commitment. You can succeed in college and avoid this unfortunate financial situation, and everything in this book will help you reach that success.

2.3   Make More or Spend Less?

That's often an issue for college students, who want to live well on limited means. What is your budget? Have you worked out a detailed budget to avoid money problems through your college years? A **budget** is the best way to balance the money that comes in with the money that goes out.

For most college students, the only way to increase the "money coming in" side of the budget is to work. Even with financial support from your family, **financial aid** from the college, your savings from past jobs, and the like, you may need to work if all your resources do not equal the "money going out" side of the budget. **The major theme of this chapter is avoiding debt except when absolutely necessary to finance your education.** Why is that so important? Simply because money problems and debt cause more people to drop out of college than almost any other single factor—and as we saw earlier, being in debt and not having a degree can be the worst of both worlds.

The next section of this chapter discusses how students can earn money while in college, along with the benefits of working. But working too much can have a negative impact by taking away time from studying. It's crucial, therefore, when you think about your own financial situation and need to work, to also think about *how much* you need to work—and consider whether you would be happier spending less if that meant you could work less and enjoy your college life and studies more. As we'll see later, students often spend more than they actually need to and are often happier once they learn to spend less.

budget

An organized plan for coordinating income and expenditures.

financial aid

Funds or a tuition waiver in a formal program designed to help students pay for college; forms of financial aid include scholarships, grants, student loans, and work study programs.

KEY TAKEAWAYS

- Almost every college student faces money issues, but you can learn to take control of your finances.
- Being able to complete your college career should be a key priority when setting financial goals.
- Since college students need time for classes and studying, it is generally more important to spend less money rather than work more hours.

1. What is the leading reason some students have to drop out of college?

   _____

2. List three or more things you would be willing to give up or cut back on in order to be able to finance your college education.

   _____

3. MAKING MONEY

LEARNING OBJECTIVES

1. **Understand the value of different kinds of jobs while you're in college.**
2. **List questions to consider when considering a particular job.**
3. **Be able to perform an effective job search.**

Most college students work while in school. Whether you work summers only or part time or full time all year, work can have both benefits and drawbacks. The difference depends on both the type of job and the number of hours you work.

3.1 A Job Can Help or Hurt

In addition to helping pay the bills, a job or internship while in school has other benefits:

- Experience for your **résumé**
- Contacts for your later job search network
- Employment references for your résumé

résumé

A document used to summarize the experience of a person.

Work or internship experience related to your future career has significant value. Although students often can't find such opportunities in their community, even a job or volunteering outside your field of study can have value and say something about you to future employers. The job may demonstrate that you have initiative, are responsible, are a team player or can work independently, and can take on financial responsibility. Potential future employers will check your work references. Having an employer from your college years say you did a good job, were always on time to work, and were honest and responsible in doing your job definitely gives you an advantage over students who graduate without having worked at all.

Some types of jobs, however, contribute more to your overall college experience. Remember, you're in college for an education and to gain a wide range of skills—not just for the degree. The best student jobs engage you more deeply in the college experience, while the wrong kind of job gets in the way of that experience. Here are some factors to consider as you look for a job:

- **What kinds of people will you be interacting with?** Other students, instructors, researchers? Interacting with others in the world of college can broaden your college experience, help motivate you to study, and help you feel part of a shared experience. You may work with or meet people who in the future can refer you to employers in your field. On the other hand, working in a business far from campus, for example, may offer a steady paycheck but can separate you from the academic community and detract from a positive college experience.

- **Is the job flexible enough to meet your needs in college?** Will you be able to change your work hours during final exam week or when a special project is due? A rigid work schedule may cause difficulty at times when you really need to focus on your classes.

- **What will you be able to say about your work in your future résumé?** Does it involve any skills—including people skills or financial or managerial responsibilities—that your employer can someday praise you for? Will working this job help you get a different, better job next year?

Factors like that can make a job ideal for college students, but in the real world many students have to work less-than-ideal jobs. Working at a fast food restaurant or overnight shipping company may not seem very glamorous or offer other benefits, but it may be the only job available at present. Don't despair—things can always change. Make the money you need to get by but don't become complacent and stop looking for more meaningful work. Keep your eyes and ears open for other possibilities. Check in with the campus student employment office frequently for new postings. Talk to other students.

But even if you have a dull job, do your best and keep a good attitude. Remember that your boss or supervisor may someday be a work reference who can help (or hurt) your chances of getting a job you really want.

3.2 Student Jobs

The number of hours college students work per week varies considerably, from five to ten hours a week to full time and everywhere in between. Before deciding how much you need to work, make a detailed budget (described later). Your goal should be to make as much as you need, and hopefully a little more to save—but first you need to know your real need. Remember your goals for college and stay focused on your education. Cut back on your optional spending so that you don't have to work so many hours that your studies are impacted.

Where to Find a Job

Start at your campus financial aid office or student employment office. If they don't have anything right for you at first, check back frequently for new job postings.

For off-campus jobs, check local newspaper classified ads and **Craigslist**. Many jobs are never advertised, however, so ask friends, family members, and other students. Visit companies in your area and ask if they have openings.

If you applied for financial aid when you applied to your college, you already know whether you qualify for a work study program. Often these jobs are ideal because they are designed for students. If your financial circumstances change, be sure to check in with the financial aid office because your eligibility may have changed.

Many government agencies also have summer jobs or internships for college students. This work may be an ideal way to gain experience related to your chosen field. (See "Additional Resources" below for more information.)

> **Craigslist**
>
> A free online listing of classified ads, organized by city, useful for job searches; access through Craigslist.org.

Go to Work for Yourself

If you have energy and initiative, you can create your own work. While it may take some time to get started, flexibility and being your own boss can make up for this drawback. Students often make money in ways like these:

- Tutor classmates in a subject you are good in.
- Sell your technical skills: help others set up new computer hardware, teach software skills such as PowerPoint or Excel, or design websites.
- Sell things you no longer need (video games, DVDs, textbooks) on eBay or Craigslist. Earn a commission by helping others sell their stuff online.
- Provide services to faculty members and residents in the nearby community: lawn mowing, snow shoveling, housecleaning, babysitting, pet sitting, dog walking, and so on.

Additional Resources

Campus jobs and work study. Check with your campus student employment or financial aid office.

Broad listing of links for federal government jobs and internships for students. See https://www.usajobs.gov/StudentsAndGrads.

Student Opportunities at the Environmental Protection Agency (EPA). See http://www.epa.gov/careers/stuopp.html.

Student Opportunities at the U.S. Department of Defense. See http://godefense.cpms.osd.mil/internships.aspx.

Student Opportunities at the U.S. Department of Health and Human Services. See http://www.hhs.gov/careers/pathways/index.html.

Student Opportunities at the National Science Foundation. See http://www.nsf.gov/careers/careertypes/pathways.jsp.

Student Internships at the State Department. See http://careers.state.gov/intern/which-program-is-right-for-you.

3.3 Balancing the Job You Have with Your Ideal Job

More students these days are working full time when they return to school, and many continue in the same jobs. If you're in this situation, you know how difficult it is to balance work and college. You're used to working—but not used to finding time for class and studying at the same time. You likely feel harried and frustrated at times, and you may start to wonder if you're cut out for college. You may even start thinking about dropping classes or leaving college altogether. It may be hard to stay motivated.

If you start feeling this way, focus on your big goals and don't let the day-to-day time stresses get you down. As difficult as it may be, try to keep your priorities, and remember that while you face temporary difficulties now, a college degree is forever.

- Acknowledge that sacrifice and compromise may be needed.
- Reduce your expenses, if you can, so you can cut back on how many hours you work. This may mean temporarily giving up some things you enjoy in order to reach your goals.
- If you cannot cut your expenses and work hours and simply do not have the time to do well in your classes, you may have to cut back on how many classes you take per term. Try everything else first, but know that it's better to succeed a little at a time than to push too hard and risk not succeeding. If you do have to cut back, keep a positive attitude: you're still working toward your future ideal.

If you ever feel the temptation to quit, see your college counselor to explore all your options. Resources may be available that you don't know about.

KEY TAKEAWAYS

- The best student jobs have value for your college experience and future résumé and network, while the wrong kinds of jobs may detract from your college experience.
- How much you work should be based on a realistic budget and your financial goals and needs.
- To find the best job for you, use all the resources available.

CHECKPOINT EXERCISES

1. What are the primary benefits of a student job on campus? (List as many as you can.)

   _____
   _____
   _____

2. Considering your abilities and interests, what would be your ideal job while a college student?

   _____

4. SPENDING LESS

LEARNING OBJECTIVES

1. Identify how you are spending your money and what optional expenditures you can cut back on.
2. Develop a positive attitude for spending less while still enjoying a full college experience.
3. Create and manage a workable budget by tracking expenditures to reach your financial goals.
4. Recognize if you are getting in financial trouble and know what to do about it.
5. List the benefits of saving money even while in college.

Where Does the Money Go?

Most people aren't really sure where a lot of their money goes. Take this survey to see how much you remember about how you have spent money recently. (Print out the attachment below and write it in.)
Do your best to remember how much you have spent in the last thirty days in each of the following categories:

Category	Amount in Dollars (Per Month)
Coffee, soft drinks, bottled water	
Newspapers, magazines	
Movies, music concerts, sports events, night life	
Fast food lunches, snacks, gum, candy, cookies, and so on	
Social dining out with friends (lunch, dinner)	
Music, DVDs, other personal entertainment	
Ringtones, mobile phone apps	
Bank account fees, ATM withdrawal fees	
Credit card finance charges	
Lottery tickets	
Cigarettes, smokeless tobacco	
Beer, wine, liquor purchased in stores	
Beer, wine, liquor purchased in restaurants and bars	
Gadgets, video or computer games, and so on	
Gifts	
Hobbies	
Travel, day trips	
Total:	

Now be honest with yourself: is this *really* all you spent on these items? Most of us forget small, daily kinds of purchases or underestimate how much we spend on them—especially when we pay with cash.

You'll notice also that this list does not include essential spending for things like room and board or rent, groceries, utilities, college tuition and books, and so on. The greatest potential for cutting back on spending is in the area of optional things.

4.1 Spending on Essentials, Spending on Optionals

More people get into financial trouble because they're spending too much than because they're making (or receiving) too little. While spending may seem a simple matter—"I need to buy this, I'd like to buy that"—it's actually very complex. America is a consumer society, and we're deluged by advertisements promising that we'll be happier, more successful, better liked by more people, sexier, and everything else if only we buy *this*. Companies have spent billions of dollars researching how to manipulate our buying behavior. No wonder it's so tough to resist those pressures!

Why does a person feel compelled to buy fast food for lunch, or a new song they just heard on the radio, or a new video game a friend says is good, or a new article of clothing? We owe it to ourselves to try to understand our own attitudes about money and spending. Here's a good place to start:

- **Having money or not having money doesn't define who you are.** Your real friends will think no less of you if you make your own lunch and eat it between classes or take the bus to campus rather than drive a new car. You are valued more by others for who you are as a person, not for what things you have.

- **You don't have to spend as much as your friends to be one of the group.** Some people always have more money than others and spend more. Resist any feeling that your friends who are big spenders are the norm. Don't feel you have to go along with whatever expensive activities they propose just so you fit in.

- **A positive attitude leads to success.** Learn to relax and not get stressed out about money. If you need to make changes in how you spend money, view this as an exciting accomplishment, not a depressing fact. Feel good about staying on a budget and being smart about how you spend your money.

- **Be realistic about what you can accomplish.** Most students have financial problems, and they don't just go away by waving a magic wand of good intentions. If your budget reveals you don't have enough money even while working and carefully controlling your spending, you may still need a student loan or larger changes in your lifestyle to get by. That's OK—there are ways to deal with that. But if you unrealistically set your sights so high about spending less and saving a lot, you may become depressed or discouraged if you don't meet your goals.

Before you can make an effective budget, you need to look at what you're actually spending money on now and consider what's essential and what's optional. Essential costs are the big things:

- Room and board or rent/mortgage, utilities, and groceries
- College tuition, fees, textbooks, supplies
- Transportation
- Insurance (health insurance, car insurance, etc.)
- Dependent care if needed
- Essential personal items (*some* clothing, hygiene items, etc.)

These things are sometimes called fixed costs, but that term can be misleading. If you have the option to move to a less expensive apartment that is smaller or a few blocks farther away, you can partly control that cost, so it's not really "fixed." Still, for most people, the real savings come from spending less on optional things.

Look back at the amounts you wrote in the earlier exercise "Where Does the Money Go?" These things are "optional" expenses—you can spend more or less on them as you choose. Most people spend by habit, not really thinking about where their money goes or how quickly their spending adds up. If you knew you were spending more than a thousand dollars a year on the coffee you buy every day between classes, would that make you think twice? Or another thousand on fast food lunches rather than taking a few minutes in the morning to make your lunch? When people actually start paying attention to where their money goes, most are shocked to see how it all adds up. If you can save a few thousand dollars a year by cutting back on little things, how far would that go to making you feel much better about your finances?

Below are some general principles for learning to spend less. The following "Tips for Success" then list specific ways you can try to apply these principles in your daily life. **Remember, spending money doesn't define who you are!**

- **Be aware of what you're spending.** Carry a small notebook and write down everything—*everything*—you spend for a month. You'll see your habits and be able to make a better budget to take control.

- **Look for alternatives.** If you buy a lot of bottled water, for example, you may feel healthier than people who drink soft drinks or coffee, but you're probably spending hundreds of dollars a year on something that is virtually free! Carry your own refillable water bottle and save the money.

- **Plan ahead to avoid impulse spending.** If you have a healthy snack in your backpack, it's easier to not put a dollar in a vending machine when you're hungry on the way to class. Make a list before going grocery shopping and stick to it. Shopping without a list usually results in buying all sorts of unneeded (and expensive) things that catch your eye in the store.

- **Be smart.** Shop around, compare prices, and buy in bulk. Stopping to think a minute before spending is often all it takes.

Tips for Success: Spending Less

- Make your own lunches and snacks.
- Read newspapers and magazines online or in the library.
- Cancel cable television and watch programs online for free.
- Use free campus and local wifi spots and cancel your home high-speed Internet connection.
- Buy **generic** products instead of name brands.
- Shop at thrift stores and yard sales.
- Pay with cash instead of a credit card.
- Cancel your health club membership and use a free facility on campus.
- Compare prices online.
- Avoid ATM fees by finding a machine on your card's network (or change banks); avoid checking account monthly fees by finding a bank with free checking.
- Get cash from an ATM in small amounts so you never feel "rich."
- With larger purchases, postpone buying for a couple days (you may find you don't "need" it after all).
- Look for free fun instead of movies and concerts—most colleges have frequent free events.
- If you pay your own utility bills, make it a habit to conserve: don't leave lights burning or your computer on all night.
- Use good study skills to avoid failing a class—paying to retake a course is one of the quickest ways to get in financial trouble!

FIGURE 11.2

Paying with cash rather than a credit card helps you stay aware of your spending habits.

© *Thinkstock*

> **generic**
>
> Any product commonly marketed under a brand name that is sold in a package without a brand.

4.2   Managing a Budget

Budgeting involves analyzing your income and expenses so you can see where your money is going and then making adjustments to stay in control. At first budgeting can seem complex or time consuming, but once you've gone through the basics, you'll find it easy and a valuable tool for managing your personal finances.

Why create and manage a budget? Without a budget, it's just human nature to spend more than you have coming in, as evidenced by the fact that most Americans today are in debt. Debt is a major reason why students drop out of college. So it's worth it to go to the trouble to create and manage a budget.

Budgeting involves three steps:

1. Listing all your sources of income on a monthly basis.
2. Calculating all your expenditures on a monthly basis.
3. Making adjustments to ensure the money isn't going out faster than it's coming in.

Tracking Income

Many college students receive money or financial assistance from a number of sources. To track income in a monthly budget, consider all your sources of funds and convert them to a monthly number. For example, you may receive a student loan once during the year or you may work only in the summer and earn money then. To calculate your monthly projected income, add up your income sources and divide that number by the number of months you will be using the income. For example, if you have saved $4,800 that you can spend over a year of college, divide the $4,800 by twelve months to arrive at a monthly income of $400 from those savings. Do the same with scholarship grants, student loans, monetary gifts, and so on.

If some of your college costs are being paid directly by parents or others, do not include that money in your budget as either income or an expense. Base your monthly budget on just those funds and expenses that involve you directly.

Use Table 11.1 to record and total all your income on a monthly basis. (Print out the attachment below and write it in.) If you must estimate some sources, estimate low rather than high; it's a bad trap to assume you'll have more money coming in than you actually do—that's a real budget buster.

TABLE 11.1 Monthly Income and Funds

Source of Income/Funds	Amount in Dollars
Job income/salary (take-home amount)	
Funds from parents/family/others	
Monthly draw from savings	
Monthly draw from financial aid	
Monthly draw from student/other loans	
Other income source: _____	
Other income source: _____	
Other income source: _____	
Total Monthly Incoming:	

Tracking Expenses

Tracking expenditures is more difficult than tracking income. Some fixed expenses (tuition, rent, etc.) you should already know, but until you've actually written down everything you spend in a typical month, it's hard to estimate how much you're really spending on coffee or smoothies between class, groceries, entertainment, and the like. The best way to itemize this side of your budget is to write down everything you spend—*everything*, every bottle of water and cookie, coins into parking meters, and so forth—for a full month. Then you can total up the different categories of expenses. We urge you to immediately start writing everything down in a small notebook you carry with you. You may be astonished how small purchases add up.

While you're writing this down for a month, go ahead and work through the expenditure half of your budget, using Table 11.2. (Print out the attachment below and write it in.) Set aside an hour or two to look through your past financial records, checkbook register and **debit card** transactions, past utility bills, credit card statements, and so on to get the numbers to put in your expenses budget. Make estimates when you have to, but be honest with yourself and don't underestimate your usual spending. There will be plenty of time down the road to adjust your budget—but don't start out with an unrealistic plan. Write "est" (for estimated) next to numbers in your budget that you're guessing at.

Once you have listed your routine expenditures using Table 11.2, write out your own budget categories that fit how *you* actually spend money. Everyone is unique, and you want your budget to be easy to use for your own life and habits.

debit card

A card like a credit card that functions like a check and through which a purchase or cash withdrawal from an automated teller machine (ATM) is made directly from the holder's bank account.

As noted previously with income, if some of your expenses are paid directly by others, do not include them here. Base your monthly budget on just those funds and expenses that involve you directly.

TABLE 11.2 Monthly Expenditures

Expenditures	Amount in Dollars
Tuition and fees (1/12 of annual)	
Textbooks and supplies (1/12 of annual)	
Housing: monthly mortgage, rent, or room and board	
Home repairs	
Renter's insurance	
Property tax	
Average monthly utilities (electricity, water, gas, oil)	
Optional utilities (cell phone, Internet service, cable television)	
Dependent care, babysitting	
Child support, alimony	
Groceries	
Meals and snacks out (including coffee, water, etc.)	
Personal expenses (toiletries, cosmetics, haircuts, etc.)	
Auto expenses (payments, gas, tolls) plus 1/12 of annual insurance premium—or public transportation costs	
Loan repayments, credit card pay-off payments	
Health insurance (1/12 of annual)	
Prescriptions, medical expenses	
Entertainment (movies, concerts, nightlife, sporting events, purchases of CDs, DVDs, video games, etc.)	
Bank account fees, ATM withdrawal fees, credit card finance charges	
Newspapers, magazines, subscriptions	
Travel, day trips	
Cigarettes, smokeless tobacco	
Beer, wine, liquor	
Gifts	
Hobbies	
Major purchases (computer, home furnishings) (1/12 of annual)	
Clothing, dry cleaning	
Memberships (health clubs, etc.)	
Pet food, veterinary bills, and so on	
Other expenditure:	
Other expenditure:	
Other expenditure:	
Other expenditure:	
Other expenditure:	
Total Monthly Outgoing:	

Balancing Your Budget

Now comes the moment of truth: compare your total monthly incoming with your total monthly outgoing. How balanced are they at this point? Remember that you estimated some of your expenditures. You can't know for sure until you actually track your expenses for at least a month and have real numbers to work with.

What if your spending total is higher than your income total? The first step is to make your budget work on paper. Go back through your expenditure list and see where you can cut. Don't try to live like a working professional. Maybe you are used to a nice haircut every month or two—but maybe you can go to a cheaper place or cut it yourself. There are dozens of ways to spend less, as suggested earlier. **The essential first step is to make your budget balance on paper**.

Then your job is to live within the budget. It's normal to have to make adjustments at first. Just be sure to keep the overall budget balanced as you make adjustments. For example, if you must spend more for textbooks, you can decide to spend less eating out—and subtract the amount from that category that you add to the textbook category. Get in the habit of thinking this way instead of reaching for a credit card when you don't have enough money left for something you want or need.

Don't be surprised if it takes several months to make the budget process work. Be flexible, but stay committed to the process and don't give up if it feels like too much work to keep track of your money. Without a budget, you may have difficulty reaching your larger goal: taking control of your life while in college.

Budgeting on Your Computer

If you are good at Excel or another spreadsheet program, you can create your own budget in a spreadsheet that allows you to monitor your income and expenditures month to month, with the calculations done for you. Other budget calculators can be found online. Apps are also available, but it's easier to work with a budget on a computer than a phone. Figure 11.3 shows a simple online budget calculator available at http://www.ed.gov/offices/OSFAP/DirectLoan/BudgetCalc/budget.html. The categories in this one are general, but you can add up your numbers from Table 11.2 in these categories and enter them in the online budget form, which then does the calculations for you.

FIGURE 11.3   Simple Online Budget Calculator[1]

Budget Calculator	
Expenses	**Resources/Incomes**
Education: $ 0.00	Family Contribution: $ 0.00
Housing: $ 0.00	Financial Assistance: $ 0.00
Food: $ 0.00	Non-Taxable Income: $ 0.00
Transportation: $ 0.00	Financial Aid Grants: $ 0.00
Health: $ 0.00	Federal Direct Loans: $ 0.00
Personal/Misc.: $ 0.00	Loans: $ 0.00
Entertainment: $ 0.00	Scholarships: $ 0.00
In-School Interest: $ 0.00	Employment: $ 0.00
Dependent Care: $ 0.00	Other Inc./Resources: $ 0.00
Emergencies: $ 0.00	
Other Expenses: $ 0.00	
Total Expenses: $	**Total Income: $**

Calculate   Reset

Your balance (income - expense) is: $

Most college students can do well with a simple budget that helps you track monthly income and expenditures so that you can make adjustments as needed. If your financial life is more complicated or you would enjoy full financial tracking and control using your computer, a software program like Quicken has all the power you need and can download your banking and credit card records to easily track categories of expenses over time. A free online budget and tracking system is available at Mint.com.

What If Your Budget Doesn't Work?

Your budget may be unbalanced by a small amount that you can correct by reducing spending, or you may have a serious imbalance. If your best efforts fail to cut your expenditures to match your income, you may have a more serious problem, unless you plan in advance to manage this with student loans or other funds.

First, think about how this situation occurred. When you decided to go to college, how did you plan to finance it? Were you off in your calculations of what it would cost, or did you just hope for the best? Are you still committed to finding a way to continue in college?

If you are motivated to reach your college goal, good! Now look closely at your budget to determine what's needed. If you can't solve the budget shortfall by cutting back on optional expenses, you may need more dramatic changes. Are you paying a high rent because your apartment is spacious or near campus? Can you move a little farther away and get by temporarily in a smaller place, if the difference in rent makes a big difference for your overall finances? If you're spending a lot on your car, can you sell it and get by with public transportation for a year or two? Play with the numbers for such items in your budget and see how you can cut expenses to stay in college without getting deeply in debt. If you worry you won't be as happy if you change your lifestyle, remember that money problems are a key source of stress for many college students and that stress affects your happiness as well as how well you do in college. It's worth the effort to work on your budget and prevent this stress.

If all else fails, see a financial aid counselor at your college. Don't wait until you're in real financial trouble before talking to someone who can help.

Why People Spend Too Much, Even on a Budget

- **Old habits die hard.** Keep monitoring your spending habits and watch for things you're spending money on without really thinking about it.
- **Credit cards.** Never use them if at all possible. They make it easy to spend too much or not see how much you're spending. Save them for emergencies only or online purchases when needed.
- **Easy access to cash.** Just put your card in an ATM and get some cash! It's so easy to do, and an automatic habit for so many, that it's easy to bust your budget with small amounts daily.
- **Temptations are everywhere.** Even when we're careful, we're often easily influenced by friends to go out or spend in other ways. Remember why you made your budget in the first place and keep your priorities in mind. The guilt you'll feel tomorrow about spending a whole week's food budget on one expensive dinner out probably isn't worth that brief pleasure!
- **We buy things to feel good.** If that's been a longtime habit for you, it will be hard to break. Often it's better to find small things that make you feel good rather than trying to go without everything. Rewarding yourself with an ice cream treat for a week's budgeting success won't break your budget.

What If You Get in Financial Trouble?

People often don't admit to themselves that they have a problem until it becomes unmanageable. We humans are very good at rationalizing and making excuses to ourselves! Here are some warning signs of sliding into financial trouble:

- For two or three months in a row, your budget is unbalanced because you're spending more than you are bringing in.
- You've begun using your savings for routine expenses you should be able to handle with your regular budget.
- You've missed a deadline for a bill or are taking credit card cash advances or overdrawing your checking account.
- You have a big balance on your credit card and have paid only the required minimum payment for the last two months.
- You have nothing in the bank in case of an emergency need.
- You don't even know how much total debt you have.
- You're trying to cut expenses by eliminating something important, such as dropping health insurance or not buying required textbooks.

If you are experiencing any of these warning signs, first acknowledge the problem. It's not going to solve itself—you need to take active steps before it gets worse and affects your college life.

Second, if you just cannot budget your balance, admit that you need help. There's no shame in that. Start with your college counselor or the financial aid office; if they can't help you directly, they can refer you to someone who can. Take your budget and other financial records with you so that they can see what's really involved. Remember that they're there to help—their goal is to ensure you succeed in college.

Balance Your Checkbook!

Lots of people don't balance their checkbook every month, thinking it's just too much trouble. But it's important to keep your checkbook balanced for several reasons:

- Banks sometimes make errors, and you can't catch one without checking your record against your monthly bank statement.
- If you make a math error or forget to record a check or ATM withdrawal, you may have to pay overdraft fees.
- If you balance your checkbook only every few months, it can take many hours to examine records to find a problem.

If you're not sure how exactly to balance your checkbook, ask a teller at your bank or get instructions online. It takes only a few minutes each month and is well worth it to avoid the stress and lost hours caused by a problem.

4.3 Saving for the Future

If you're having problems just getting by on your budget, it may seem pointless to even think about saving for the future. Still, if you can possibly put aside some money every month into a savings plan, it's worth the effort:

- An emergency or unexpected situation may occur suddenly. Having the savings to cope with it is much less stressful than suddenly having to take out a loan or run up your credit cards.
- Saving is a good habit to develop. Saving for the future prepares you for the increasing financial complexities of life after graduation.
- You may need your savings to help launch your career after graduation. If you're broke when you graduate, you may feel you have to take the first job that comes along, but some savings may give you time to find the job that's perfect for you.
- You may change your mind about future plans. Maybe you now think that you'll go to work at a good job right after graduation, so you're not concerned about saving—but maybe in a couple years you'll decide to go to graduate school, law school, or business school—or to start your own business, or to join a volunteer program. Your savings will make it easier to pursue your new goal.

credit union

A cooperative association that offers banking services to employees and often students at a particular college, possibly at rates more competitive than a private bank.

money market

A specific type of investment and spending account offered at many banks that may pay a higher interest rate.

certificates of deposit (CDs)

A bank deposit, usually made for a fixed term, at a specified interest rate that is typically higher than the rate of a regular savings account, involving a penalty for early withdrawal.

Start by saving in a savings account at your bank or campus **credit union**. You can have a certain amount transferred from your checking account every month into a savings account—that makes it easier and more routine. A savings account allows a withdrawal anytime but pays lower interest than certain other types of accounts. Ask at your bank about **money market** accounts and **certificates of deposit (CDs)**, which generally pay higher interest but have restrictions on minimum balances and withdrawals. Savings bonds are another option. All of these options are federally insured, so your money stays safe. Risky investments like the stock market are generally not appropriate for college students on a budget.

KEY TAKEAWAYS

- Financial success while in college depends on understanding and controlling your expenditures.
- There are many ways you can spend less on optional expenses, and even essentials, and still have a full life and enjoy your college experience.
- A detailed monthly budget listing income and expenditures makes it easier to track expenses and avoid sliding into financial trouble.
- Spending too much can quickly lead to financial problems. If you see the signs that you're starting to have money problems, take steps quickly to prevent trouble before the situation snowballs out of control.
- While it may seem difficult just to make ends meet, make it a goal to try to save something for future needs.

CHECKPOINT EXERCISES

1. List the top three optional expenditures you usually make every week.

   _____

   _____

   _____

2. List three tips for spending less that you feel you can use routinely to avoid running out of money while in college.

   _____

   _____

   _____

3. For each of the following statements, circle T for true or F for false:

T	F	It's OK to miss the payment deadline for your phone as long as you pay on time at least half of the time.
T	F	There's really nothing wrong with not having any money in the bank as long as you have a credit card for emergencies and major purchases.
T	F	You should balance your checkbook every month when you receive your bank statement.
T	F	A good way to save money is to get by without buying expensive textbooks.
T	F	You only need to write up a budget if you've gotten deeply into debt and need to see a financial advisor to get out of debt.

5.   CREDIT CARDS

LEARNING OBJECTIVES

1. **Identify the benefits of having a credit card and choosing one wisely.**
2. **Set personal limits for credit card use to minimize your debt.**
3. **Describe steps to take to avoid overusing a credit card.**
4. **Understand the importance of a good credit history and how to obtain and review your credit report.**

Credit cards are such a big issue because they're easy to get, easy to use—and for many people, addictive. Until new regulations in 2009 and 2010, many college students got deeply in debt and experienced financial disaster. The new regulations set limits to prevent such serious problems for students under age twenty-one, but many older students still experience problems from overuse.

Credit cards have legitimate purposes:

credit rating

The classification of credit risk based on a person's financial resources, past payment pattern, and personal history of debts.

- In an emergency, you may need funds you cannot obtain otherwise.
- You generally need a credit card for travel, for hotels, and other needs.
- Often it's less expensive to make significant purchases online, and to do that you usually need a credit card. (Debit cards are less safe for online purchases.)
- If you are young, responsible use of a credit card is a good way to start building a **credit rating**.

Even though federal regulations require banks to disclose all credit card fees and make it more difficult to increase fees or rates without warning credit card holders in advance, many people overuse credit cards and pay high interest rates and fees for making late payments. The average American household has credit card debt of $5,000 to $8,000 (reports vary). College students reportedly are more likely to be late with payments and incur additional fees.

The first goal is to understand what you're getting into and how you are charged. Read the fine print on your monthly statements. Watch for rate increases and know what happens if you miss a payment, pay less than the minimum, or pay late. It also pays to shop around. Two good websites—http://www.cardtrak.com and http://www.bankrate.com—compare rates of many credit cards and provide more information about how credit cards work.

5.1 Setting Limits

All credit cards have a maximum total for what you can charge, but this is not the same as the limit *you* should set for how you use the card based on your budget. If you buy something that costs $400, for example, will your monthly budget let you pay it off when the bill comes? If it will take you two or three months to have that much available in your budget, are you also including the interest you'll be paying? What if an unexpected need then arises and you need to charge more?

Set your personal use limit by calculating how much your budget allows you to charge. If you are using the card just for convenience, such as to pay for meals or regular purchases, be sure you have enough in those budget categories left at the end of the month to make the payment. When tempted to buy a significant item with your credit card, do those calculations in advance.

5.2 Avoiding Credit Card Debt

If your credit card debt is not limited by your age, that balance can rapidly rise. Following are tips that will help you avoid slipping into credit card debt:

overdraft

The act of withdrawing (or purchasing with a debit card) more funds from an account than are in the account at the time.

- **Pay with cash when you can.** Use your budget as a guide for how much cash to carry with you. A good way is to plan how much you'll need for a week (lunches, parking meters, snacks or drinks between classes) and start the week with that amount from an ATM. Carrying that exact amount helps you stay informed of how you're doing on your budget and keeps you from "accidentally" spending too much on a whim.
- **When possible, use a debit card instead of a credit card.** A debit card can be used just like a credit card in most places, but remember that purchases are subtracted immediately from your account. Don't risk **overdraft** fees by using a debit card when you don't have the balance to back it up. Record a debit card purchase in your checkbook register as soon as possible.
- **Make it a priority to pay your balance in full every month.** If you can't pay it all, pay as much as you can—and then remember that balance will still be there, so try not to use the card at all during the next month.
- **Don't get cash advances on your credit card.** With most cards, you begin paying interest from that moment forward—so you'll pay an interest charge even if you pay the bill in full at the end of the month. Cash advance interest rates are often considerably higher than purchase rates.
- **Don't use more than one credit card.** Multiple cards make it too easy to misuse them and lose track of your total debt.
- **Get and keep receipts for all credit card purchases.** Don't throw them away because you'll see the charges on your monthly statement. Write the amounts down in your spending budget. You also need the receipts in case your monthly statement has an error.
- **Stop carrying your credit card.** If you don't have enough willpower to avoid spontaneous purchases, be honest with yourself about that. Don't carry the card at all—after all, the chances of having an emergency need for it are likely to be very small. Having to go home to get the card also gives you a chance to consider whether you really need whatever it is that you were about to buy.

5.3 Credit History and Reports

Many younger college students are just beginning to develop a **credit history**. Older students likely have had credit cards for years, as well as a car loan and other financial transactions that add up to a credit history. It is important to understand what a credit history is and how your monetary habits now can affect your future financial well-being and options. For example, frequent overdrafts on a debit card can prevent you from being approved for a credit card, or late credit card payments can prevent you in the future from obtaining a car loan or cause you to have to pay a higher interest rate.

Credit bureaus collect financial data on everyone and then make it available to companies when you apply for a loan. Your **credit report** has a detailed history of many years of your financial habits (Figure 11.4). It includes:

- Current and past credit accounts (credit cards and store charge cards)
- History of balances and credit payments
- History of late or missed payments
- Inquiries into your credit status (e.g., if you've applied for a number of credit cards, this is recorded even if you did not receive the cards)
- Bankruptcy or mortgage foreclosure proceedings

All this information remains in your credit report for seven to ten years. What you do today can really come back to haunt you!

credit history

A general term referring to a person's past use of credit and payment patterns.

credit report

A written report, compiled by a credit bureau, listing the details of a person's credit history, possibly including a credit rating, FICO score, or both.

FIGURE 11.4 First Page of a Typical Credit Report[2]

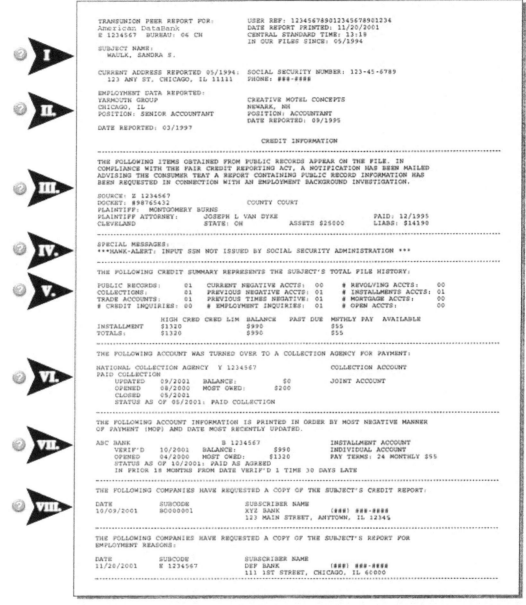

HAWK messages play a critical role in warning you of suspected fraudulent activity, such as misuse of a SSN, address, or telephone number.

LOOK identifies subscriber's name, complete address, and telephone, if available, for quicker, easier reference.

Phone Append verifies applicant's phone number provided on the application.

Reviewing Your Credit History

If you have ever had a loan or credit card, you already have a credit history, and you should know what is in your report. Errors are common in credit histories and, if not corrected, can hurt you in the future.

You are entitled to a free copy of your credit report every year, and ideally you should check it every year for possible errors. To obtain a copy online, go to http://www.annualcreditreport.com. This is website is authorized by the federal government, and the report is free.

You may also visit the website of any of the three main credit bureaus, but be aware that each has for-fee services they may attempt to sell you while obtaining your report.

- Experian: http://www.experian.com
- TransUnion: http://www.transunion.com
- Equifax: http://www.equifax.com

Once you have your credit report, go over it carefully to make sure its information is accurate. If you have paid off and closed an account, for example, it should not be listed as still open. Make sure all accounts listed actually belong to you and that the balances listed are correct. If you find an error, report it promptly, following the procedure on the credit bureau's website.

It's also important to keep good financial records. Don't immediately throw away your credit card statements or loan papers. You may need these to prove an error in your credit history.

Your FICO Credit Score

To sum up your creditworthiness, credit bureaus analyze all your data to come up with a single number, called your credit score or **FICO score**. The calculations of the credit bureaus differ somewhat. The score may be anywhere between 250 to 336 (poor credit risk) and 843 to 900 (excellent credit risk). The score is based on the following:

- The length of your credit history
- The total amount you owe
- Your payment history
- The types of credit you have

Credit bureaus are not required to tell you the FICO score that they report to a lender who inquires about your credit history. Check with any of the individual credit bureaus if you need to know your score, or you may be able to get it from a lender with whom you have a loan. Most students have no need to know their credit score, except to understand how banks and other lenders make their decisions if you are applying for any type of loan.

Protecting Your Financial Identity

Identity theft is a serious, growing problem. **Identity theft** is someone else's use of your personal information—usually financial information—to make an illegal gain. A criminal who has your credit card number or bank account information may be able to make purchases or transfer funds from your accounts. Someone with the right information about you, such as your social security number along with birth date and other data, can even pretend to be you and open new credit accounts that you don't know about until the bank or collection agency tries to recover amounts from you. Even though you are innocent, you'll have to spend a lot of time and effort dealing with the problem.

Follow these guidelines to prevent identity theft:

- Never put in the trash any document with personal or financial information (e.g., your social security number, credit card number). Shred it first.
- Carefully review bank statements, credit card bills, etc. when you receive them. If the balance seems incorrect or you do not recognize charges, contact the bank or credit card company immediately.
- Never give your social security number, credit card number, or other sensitive data when requested by telephone or e-mail. Many schemes are used to try to trick people to reveal this information, but legitimate companies do not make such requests.
- Do not use online banking or make online purchases with a credit card using a public computer or an unsecured wifi connection. Your data can be picked up by others lurking within the wifi signal range.

FICO score

A standard credit score often included in a credit report generated by a credit bureau, used to measure a person's credit risk; an acronym for the Fair Isaac Credit Organization, which devised the basic formula for calculating this score.

Identity theft

A fraudulent use of someone's identifying or personal data or documents, such as a credit card.

CASE STUDY

Maria's Financial Dilemma

When Maria enrolled in community college after working full time a few years, she was sure she could afford it. She had saved enough money to pay tuition for two years, and she cut back to part-time work that paid enough, she calculated, to live on. With great enthusiasm she registered for the fall term.

Her money problems began in November when her car broke down on her way to work. The mechanic said her transmission had to be rebuilt and her car also really needed new rear shocks The bill was over a thousand dollars. She paid with her Visa card. At the end of the month, she didn't have enough to pay the credit card bill in full. She almost decided just to pay the minimum, but then she checked her statement and saw the 15% interest rate and decided to pay the full balance from her savings. She wouldn't need that money for tuition until next year anyway, and that gave her a long time to save it up.

The first week in December, she slipped on an icy sidewalk and sprained her ankle. She had student health insurance, but she had to make a copayment. Unfortunately, she couldn't do her job on crutches, so she lost two weeks' pay.

Still, "that's life," she thought. But now she was so worried about money that she decided to increase her work hours for a couple months to help her get caught up financially. As midterm exams grew closer, she felt unprepared because she hadn't had enough time for studying. Because of the stress she wasn't sleeping well, and one day she fell asleep in class. Always rushing around, she was eating more junk food than ever and feeling too guilty to even get on the scale to see if she was gaining weight. She found herself daydreaming about the coming summer and being free of classes. To feel better, she started taking long drives in her car on the weekends, even though the gas was expensive.

She passed her midterms but did not do as well as she'd hoped. She still hadn't been able to save enough for next year's tuition but felt that she had the summer to work full time and make up for it.

In April, her boss told her that business was too slow and he couldn't increase her hours to full time for the summer. He was very sorry, but she could keep working part time if she wanted.

Now Maria really doubted if she'd be able to make it. Her family could spare no money to help her out. She had enough for rent, food, and her car, but that was about it. If she didn't figure something out, she couldn't afford tuition in the fall. Even with an installment plan to break up tuition payments, she just wasn't making enough to cover it. She didn't know what to do.

1. What is the first step Maria should take to start sorting out her financial situation and learn about her options?

   _____

2. Maria's original financial planning had been based on making enough to cover what she spends and using her savings for tuition. If she now made a monthly budget and analyze every expenditure, might she be able to cut back and save more for unexpected expenses that come up? List areas in which she would likely be able to spend less if she used a budget.

   _____
   _____
   _____

3. Maria's attitude toward her credit card is a healthy indicator that she wants to avoid debt. If a student loan to cover tuition proved to be the only solution, should she consider it for her second year? Why or why not?

   _____
   _____

4. If Maria was considering dropping out of college and looking for a new full-time job to start saving up tuition money again, what advice might you give her?

   _____
   _____

KEY TAKEAWAYS

- Credit cards have important benefits when used carefully, including building a credit history and having emergency funds available.
- Don't charge purchases up to the credit card's limit but set your own personal limit that allows you to pay the balance in full every month.
- Avoid high credit card balances by using the card minimally, paying cash when you can, and not taking cash advances.
- How you manage your credit and finances now affects your credit history and creditworthiness in the future.

CHECKPOINT EXERCISES

1. What is the best number of credit cards to have and carry with you?
   _____

2. For each of the following statements, circle T for true or F for false:

T	F	The more credit cards you have, and the larger the balances you keep, the better is your credit rating as long as you make the minimum payments every month on time.
T	F	Most credit cards charge the same interest rate.
T	F	An overdraft on an ATM cash advance won't cost you anything as long as you pay it off at the end of the month.
T	F	Your credit history begins only after graduation from college, so it doesn't matter how well you manage money while still in school.
T	F	Identity theft happens only to senior citizens.

3. How often can one obtain a free credit report?
   _____

6. FINANCING COLLEGE AND LOOKING AHEAD

LEARNING OBJECTIVES

1. **Understand the importance of researching and applying for financial aid every year even if you don't think you qualify for assistance.**
2. **Identify key differences among scholarships and grants, student loans, and work study programs.**
3. **Avoid excessive student loans.**

You may already be receiving financial aid or understand what types of financial aid are available. Even if you are not receiving financial aid, however, you should understand the basics because your financial situation may change and you may need help paying for college. You owe it to yourself to learn about potential types of aid .

Every college has a financial aid office that can give you information about standard financial aid programs. Certain kinds of financial aid, however, such as private **scholarships**, are not administered by the college, so you may need to do some research. There are three main categories of financial aid:

scholarship

A sum of money or other financial aid granted to a student based on academic merit or other ability, intended to help meet the expenses of attending college.

1. Scholarships and **grants** (money or tuition waivers that do not need to be repaid)
2. **Student loans** (money that does need to be repaid, usually starting after graduation)
3. **Work study** programs (money that is earned for tuition or other expenses)

These are described in general in the following sections, but you should be sure to get more information from your college's financial aid office and the online sources listed here.

6.1 Applying for Financial Aid

For financial aid administered by your college, often only one general application form is required, the **FAFSA (Free Application for Federal Student Aid)**, along with detailed information on your financial situation (and that of your parents or guardians, if you are receiving their support). If you have not already done this application, learn more at http://www.fafsa.ed.gov. Virtually all colleges require the FAFSA.

Outside loans and scholarships are generally applied for separately. Follow these general rules to ensure you receive any aid for which you are qualified:

1. Apply to your college for financial aid every year, even if you do not receive financial aid in your first year or term. Your situation may change, and you want to remain eligible at all times in the future by filing the application.
2. Talk to the financial office immediately if you (or your family) have any change in your circumstances.
3. Complete your application accurately, fully, and honestly. Financial records are required to verify your data. Pay attention to the deadlines for all applications.
4. Research possible outside financial aid based on other criteria. Many private scholarships and grants are available, for example, for the dependents of employees of certain companies, students pursuing a degree in a certain field, or students of a certain ethnic status or from a certain religious or geographical background, and the like.
5. Do not pay for financial aid resource information. Some online companies try to profit from the anxieties of students about financial aid by promising to find financial aid for you for a fee. Legitimate sources of financial aid information are free.

6.2 Scholarships and Grants

Scholarships and grants are "free" money—you do not have to pay them back, unlike student loans. A scholarship is generally based on merit rather than demonstrated financial need—based on past grades, test scores, achievements, and experiences, including personal qualifications such as athletic ability, skills in the arts, community or volunteer experiences, and so on. Don't make the mistake of thinking scholarships go only to students with high grades. Many scholarships, for example, honor those with past leadership or community experience or the promise of future activities. Even the grades and test scores needed for academic scholarships are relative: a grade point average (GPA) that does not qualify for a scholarship at one college may earn a scholarship at another. Never assume that you're not qualified for any kind of scholarship or grant.

A grant also does not need to be paid back. Most grants are based on demonstrated financial need. A grant may be offered by the college, a federal or state program, or a private organization or civic group. The largest grant program for college students is the federal government's Pell Grants program (Figure 11.5). Learn more about Pell Grants and other scholarship and grant programs from your college's financial aid office or the online resources listed later.

FIGURE 11.5

FEDERAL STUDENT GRANT PROGRAMS

StudentAid.gov

The federal government provides grant funds for students attending colleges, career schools, and universities. Grants, unlike loans, do not have to be repaid. The major federal student grant programs are briefly described below.

Federal Grant Program	Program Details	Annual Award (subject to change)
Federal Pell Grant	• Awarded to undergraduate students who have exceptional financial need and who have not earned a bachelor's or graduate degree; in some cases, however, students enrolled in a postbaccalaureate teacher certification program might receive a Federal Pell Grant • Federal Pell Grant lifetime eligibility is limited to 12 semesters or the equivalent	Up to $5,730
Federal Supplemental Educational Opportunity Grant (FSEOG)	• Awarded to undergraduate students who have exceptional financial need and who have not earned a bachelor's or graduate degree • Federal Pell Grant recipients receive priority • Not all colleges participate in the FSEOG program • Funds depend on availability at the college; apply by your college's deadline	Up to $4,000
Teacher Education Assistance for College and Higher Education (TEACH) Grant	• For undergraduate, postbaccalaureate, or graduate students who are or will be taking coursework necessary to become elementary or secondary teachers • Must agree to serve, for a minimum of four years (within eight years of completing academic program), as a full-time teacher in a high-need field in a school or educational service agency that serves low-income students • Must attend a participating college and meet certain academic achievement requirements • Failure to complete the teaching service commitment will result in the grant being converted to a Direct Unsubsidized Loan that must be repaid	Up to $4,000
Iraq and Afghanistan Service Grant	• For students whose parent or guardian was a member of the U.S. armed forces and died as a result of performing military service in Iraq or Afghanistan after the events of 9/11 • Must be ineligible for a Federal Pell Grant due only to having less financial need than is required to receive Pell funds • Must have been less than 24 years old or enrolled at least part-time at an institution of higher education at the time of the parent's or guardian's death	Up to $5,311.71 For grants first disbursed on or after Oct. 1, 2014, and before Oct. 1, 2015

Looking for more sources of free money? Try **StudentAid.gov/scholarships** for tips on where to look and for a link to a free online scholarship search.

https://studentaid.ed.gov/sites/default/files/federal-grant-programs.pdf

6.3 Student Loans

Many different student loan programs are available for college students. Because many colleges cannot offer full grants to students with financial need, financial aid packages often include a combination of grant and loan money. While ideally one would like to graduate without a loan to repay, almost two-thirds of full-time college students do need student loans to pay for college. The amount of money students borrow has risen in recent years because tuition and fees have risen faster than inflation. The average amounts are over $20,000 for students at four-year colleges and over $10,000 at two-year colleges.

Unfortunately this is a necessary reality for many students. With smart choices about the type of loan and a structured repayment program for your working years after graduation, there's no reason to fear a loan. Just remember that the money eventually has to be repaid—it's not "free" money even though it may feel that way while you're in school.

All student loans are not the same. Interest terms vary widely, and with most private loans the interest starts building up immediately. The best loan generally is a **subsidized federal Stafford loan**. "Subsidized" in this case means the interest does not begin on the loan until after graduation. Otherwise, if you borrowed $20,000 over four years and interest accrued during this time, you could owe as much as $25,000 upon graduation. Be sure to talk with your college financial office first about getting a federal subsidized Stafford loan. With the current maximum of this type of loan, you ideally should not have to consider other types of loans—if you qualify for the Stafford with demonstrated financial need.

subsidized federal Stafford loan

A type of federal college student loan that does not begin accruing interest until after graduation.

How Much Should You Borrow?

Many financial analysts urge college students not to borrow more than about $5,000 per year, or about $10,000 for two years of college, or $20,000 for four years. Even if you qualify for more, that doesn't mean you should take it, and if you can, you may want to borrow much less. Think about this seriously before jumping to any conclusions about your future earning potential and how much you may have to struggle then to pay off your student loans. During an economic downturn, for example, many students have difficulty finding a job that pays well enough to cover their loan payments without hardship.

First learn the repayment rate for a loan amount. Then research the starting salary you can realistically expect after graduation. You can find this information online at many sites (such as this salary finder: http://www.salary.com/category/salary). Assume the starting salary will be at the low end of the salary range for any given career; the linked salary finder allows you to limit your search by location and experience. Finally, make sure that your loan payments do not total more than 10% of your starting salary. If the payment amount is more than 10%, you are setting yourself up for future financial problems. Try to find ways to cut back on expenses instead. Many experts advise attending a less expensive college, if necessary, rather than risking your future well-being.

6.4 Work Study Programs

Work study programs are the third type of financial aid. They are administered by colleges and are a common part of the financial aid package for students with financial need. You work for what you earn, but work study programs often have advantages over outside jobs. The college runs the program, so you don't have to spend valuable time looking for a job. Work study students usually work on or near campus, and work hours are controlled to avoid interfering with classes and study time. Work study students are more engaged with the academic community than students working off campus.

Some students who have special skills or job experience can make a higher hourly rate than in a work study program. If so, you might make the same income working fewer hours, leaving more for studying and other college activities. If this is your situation, carefully weigh the pros and cons before deciding about a work study program.

Tips for Success: Applying for Financial Aid

- Talk to your college's financial aid office early and get the appropriate forms.
- Start your application early to ensure you make the deadline.
- Do online research to learn about additional private scholarships you may be qualified for.
- Evaluate student loans carefully and do not borrow more than you need or can repay without hardship after graduation.

6.5 Resources

Start with your local college offices to gather information about financial aid. Do additional research to make sure you're considering all your options. Even though this takes some effort, it will prove worthwhile if you find other sources of funds for your college years. Start with the online resources listed here.

Additional Resources

Federal government information about federal grants and student loans. See http://studentaid.ed.gov.

U.S. Department of Labor's Free Scholarship Search Tool. See http://www.careerinfonet.org/scholarshipsearch/ScholarshipCategory.asp?searchtype=category&nodeid=22.

FinAid.org. See this private information website on scholarships, grants, and student loans at http://www.finaid.org.

CollegeScholarships.org. See this private information website on scholarships, grants, and student loans at http://www.collegescholarships.org.

Salary Finder. To estimate future earning potential, use this tool available at http://www.salary.com/category/salary.

<table>
<tr><td colspan="1">

KEY TAKEAWAYS

- Many forms of financial aid are available for college students. Apply every year, and notify the college financial aid office if you have a significant change in circumstances.
- Consider all forms of financial aid—not just the aid managed by your college. Look into private scholarships and grants.
- Carefully consider how much to borrow with student loans.

</td></tr>
</table>

CHECKPOINT EXERCISES

1. What is the best kind of college financial aid to seek?

   _____

2. For each of the following statements, circle T for true or F for false:

T	F	You don't need to complete the FAFSA if you are applying only for a federal student loan.
T	F	If you apply to your college's financial aid office, they will tell you about all possible scholarships for which you may be qualified.
T	F	After graduation, you have to begin repaying the money you received in a grant.
T	F	A work study program job often has advantages over a job you find on your own.

3. As a general rule, your future payments on a student loan should not be more than _____ percent of what you expect to make with your starting salary.

7. CHAPTER ACTIVITIES

Chapter Takeaways

- Controlling your finances while in college is important both for your future well-being and for eliminating stress that can impede your academic success.
- Meeting your financial goals while in college may require some financial sacrifice but need not result in hardship.
- The best student jobs offer benefits beyond just the money.
- There are many ways to reduce expenditures while in college. Tracking your spending with an effective budget is the first step in taking control of your finances.
- Understanding your own spending habits and practicing a few simple principles for spending less help prevent unnecessary debt. Make and use a budget to manage your financial life.
- Credit card spending is the leading cause of out-of-control debt in America today. Use credit cards minimally and wisely.
- Protect your financial identity by maintaining good records and preventing criminals from obtaining your personal or financial information.
- Look into all forms of financial aid and apply for all aid for which you may be qualified. But do not take more in student loans than you really need.

CHAPTER REVIEW

1. Why is it necessary to track all your expenditures if your goal is to spend less to avoid financial problems while in college?

    _____
    _____

2. Imagine several situations in which a friend asks you to join some activity that would break your budget. Write down positive, upbeat things you can say in these situations instead of glumly saying "I can't afford it."

    _____
    _____

3. List as many ways as you can think of to locate job openings for which you might apply.

    _____
    _____

4. Who should you talk to if you are having difficulty paying for college or meeting your expenses?

    _____
    _____

OUTSIDE THE BOOK

1. Although you may not need a résumé until you seek full-time employment after graduation, go online to learn what kinds of experience are typically listed in a résumé. Make a list of your experiences, qualifications, and references so far that you might put on your future résumé. What areas seem weak to you? What kind of job, internship, or other experience could you potentially have in your college years that will strengthen your résumé?

2. Choose a friend you enjoy spending time with and see if he or she will help you with an "experiment." Together, make a list of fun free things to do over the next two weeks. For example, look for free concerts and other campus activities. Make it your goal to spend as little as possible for two weeks, cooking meals together if practical, taking lunches and snacks to classes, and finding new ways to enjoy your free time inexpensively. At the end of this experiment, compare what you spent with your past habits. How successful were you? Think about how you can continue saving in the future.

3. Make a budget as described in this chapter, based on realistic estimates of your daily and monthly expenditures. Choose two or three categories of expenses and pay special attention to these for a month. For every $10 less that you spend in these categories during the month, put $3 in a new category to reward yourself. Then at the end of the month, use this new fund to celebrate your success with something special.

4. It's never too early to think about summer jobs. Go online to check out summer jobs and internships you might find interesting. Check out the application process and deadlines and write these on your calendar for the winter or spring to remind yourself to apply early. Start with this site: https://www.usajobs.gov/StudentsAndGrads

5. Go to the following Web site and take the "Finance Quiz To Test Knowledge Of College Students"—then check other resources on this site for more financial information you may need:

    http://www.familyresource.com/parenting/money-management/
    finance-quiz-to-test-knowledge-of-college-students

M A K E   A N   A C T I O N   L I S T

Spending

I usually spend too much money every week on:

_____

_____

My action plan to spend less includes the following:

_____

_____

Lifestyle

The area of my lifestyle where I know I spend more than most other college students is:

_____

_____

I can make these adjustments in my lifestyle to reduce spending in this area:

_____

_____

Job in College

Ideally, I'd like to work no more than _____ hours a week.

What I'd most enjoy doing is:

_____

_____

I can learn more about possible jobs close to my ideal by:

_____

_____

Saving Money

I believe I can realistically save this amount of money a month if I watch my spending:

_____

_____

This is where I will put my savings:

_____

_____

I will allow myself to spend this money only for something major like:

_____

_____

Budgeting and Tracking Spending

Here's how I have kept track of what I spent in the past:

_____

_____

So that I can maintain a budget now and in the future, I know I need to record every expenditure. I will do this by:

_____

_____

Credit Card Use

In the past, I usually used my credit card to buy things like:

_____

_____

If you have not always been able to pay off your balance every month: I will try to avoid using my credit card as much by taking these steps:

_____

_____

CLASS DISCUSSION QUESTIONS

1. At the end of your first year of college, you've landed a good summer job and you're feeling pretty good about your finances. Better yet, a friend is selling his 8-year-old car with only 75,000 miles on it, and you're thinking how much fun it will be to have a car and it looks like you can afford it. Before you decide to buy it, what things should you think about?

2. After lunch with a friend in a campus cafe, you take out your pocket notebook and jot down what you just spent on lunch as part of your budget tracking. Your friend makes fun of you for being "compulsive." What can you say that will make you feel better and maybe help educate your friend as well?

3. You've heard a lot about how terrible it is to have big student loans, but after a year you've burned through your savings faster than you thought you would, and it would sure make things easier to just take out a loan and not stress about money. What calculations should you do before deciding to apply for a loan?

ENDNOTES

1. Federal Student Aid, "Budget Calculator," Federal Student Aid Direct Loans, http://www.ed.gov/offices/OSFAP/DirectLoan/BudgetCalc/budget.html (accessed April 28, 2015).

2. American DataBank, "Trans Union Sample Credit Report," http://www.americandatabank.com/trans_report.htm (accessed July 15, 2010).

CHAPTER 12

Taking Control of Your Future

FIGURE 12.1

© Thinkstock

Where Are You Now?

Assess your present knowledge and attitudes.

	Yes	Unsure	No
1. I have a good understanding of my career options.			
2. I have a good understanding of the work-related skills I will need in the future and a plan to get them.			
3. I know where I can get useful information about careers.			
4. I have created a transferable skills inventory.			
5. I have an up-to-date résumé.			
6. I know how to prepare an effective cover letter.			
7. I have both professional and social networks.			
8. I have discussed my career objectives with my academic advisor.			
9. I am comfortable in interviews.			
10. I have chosen my major based on the job market.			
11. I have chosen my major based on my personal interests.			

Where Do You Want to Go?

Think about how you answered the questions above. Be honest with yourself. On a scale of 1 to 10, how would you rate your preparation for your future at this time?

I'm adrift (no idea)					I have a clear direction and plan to get there				
1	2	3	4	5	6	7	8	9	10

In the following list, circle the three most important areas in which you think you can improve:

- Following my dreams to successful employment
- Networking for employment
- Completing informational interviews
- Completing employment interviews
- Writing a résumé
- Researching potential employers
- Writing effective cover letters
- Researching and choosing a college major
- Researching potential careers
- Understanding the financial implications of career choices
- Defining short-, medium-, and long-term plans for career development
- Discovering my transferable skills
- Addressing required work-based skills

Are there other areas in which you can improve your career planning? Write down other things you feel you need to work on.

_____

_____

_____

How to Get There

Here's what we'll work on in this chapter:

- Learning how the employment market has changed over the past ten years and what that means to you

- Discovering your dream for the future
- Choosing a major
- Working with your faculty advisor
- Learning the difference between jobs and careers
- Exploring career options
- Learning what work-based skills and transferable skills you really need
- Transferring to a four-year college
- Building your experience base
- Writing résumés
- Writing cover letters
- Completing informational interviews
- Interviewing for a job
- Networking for employment
- Preparing your life-work plan

1. A JOURNEY BEGINS…

If you don't know where you are going, you might wind up someplace else.
  - *Yogi Berra*

This popular saying attributed to Yogi Berra suggests a good reason to have a pretty clear picture of where we are headed. And college, for many of us, is a key step toward a fulfilling and exciting career. But the fact is that the employment market and job-seeking techniques have changed significantly over recent years and will continue to change; it is not as easy as it once was to map out a clear career path. However, a clear direction can still provide enough flexibility to respond to the changing needs of today's job market. In fact, having flexibility in your career plans is a requirement for achieving a successful career.

Consider these ways in which the job market has changed—and what they may mean for your planning:

- You will likely be employed by many organizations in your lifetime. The U.S. Department of Labor found that on average, people hold to eleven jobs between the ages of eighteen and forty-two.[1] This means graduates need to be very flexible in their career plans and that they should make an effort to identify and develop transferable skills to navigate the changing employment market.

- Five years from now, you may be working in a job that doesn't even exist right now. As technology accelerates and national and global priorities (such as going green or national security) take on a new sense of urgency, new needs are identified, and new jobs will be created to fill those needs. For example, not long ago, a search engine optimization (SEO) specialist was a job in only a handful of web-centric companies. With the meteoric growth of Google, SEO is now a common role in just about any marketing department—and a job in relatively high demand. In the same way, the aging population has created new opportunities in elder care, the threat of terrorism has led to a whole new category of jobs in homeland security, and new discoveries and approaches in science have created fields like biotechnology and nanotechnology. Today's students and job hunters must become lifetime learners to keep up with new trends.

- The physical location of a job is no longer as important as it once was. Many companies have off-site employees who stay connected via the Internet. This means that job hunters should be able to demonstrate the ability to work independently and produce results without consistent, direct personal supervision.

- The growth of online job applications has led to a glut of applicants for most posted positions. You have online access to millions of job opportunities, but so do millions of other job seekers. Each employer must cull through hundreds of résumés received for each job posted online. Strategies for standing out in this crowded field become very important.

These factors have combined to create a job environment very different from the past. How you prepare for a career needs to be more flexible and more personalized. Technology will play an important role in your career development. Linking your demonstrable skills to the needs of a job will be a key to your success. This chapter will help you get ready for this challenging environment.

2. THE DREAM OF A LIFETIME

LEARNING OBJECTIVES

1. **Use your life mission to inform career decisions.**
2. **Understand how you are already on your way to fulfilling your dream.**
3. **Work with changing life objectives and goals.**

This book has covered many techniques for *how* to get things done effectively: how to study, how to read, how to take notes, how to manage your personal finances and your social life. This last chapter challenges you to really think about the *why*. Why did you decide to attend college? Why is it important to you?

We all have life goals or objectives—some are clearer than others, but even the less defined one are still there. You may think of your objectives in terms of finances (to get a job that makes you be financially independent, for example) or your personal life (for example, to be married and have a family). Your goals might be specific (to pay off my student loans within three years of leaving college) or very general (to do good). Regardless of what they are, your goals are all important because they influence the decisions you are making today about your future.

Understanding your goals and aspirations is essential because then you can better prioritize your thoughts about the future and identify new options you may not have thought of before. Beware of goals set by others ("I want to finish college to make my parents proud" or "I want to complete my degree because my boyfriend says I can get a better job"). These are not necessarily bad dreams, but they will lead to genuine fulfillment only if they are *your* dreams.

EXERCISE 1: WHAT ARE MY DREAMS?

In the table that follows, list the four most important dreams you have for your future. Include your personal, professional, and economic goals. Now take some time to think about *why* these dreams are important to *you*. Revisit your answers frequently over the next week or two and fine-tune them. What do they tell you about what is important to you? How are they linked to each other?

My dreams for the future	Why they are important to me

Since you were a child and first definitively stated, "When I grow up I want to be a _____," you have been making decisions in order to fulfill your dreams. Most likely you are in college today as a step toward fulfilling a lifetime goal. But very few of us are still passionate about our childhood dream. As we grew up, we discovered new options; were influenced by people we met; or perhaps even learned that being a fireman, nurse, circus clown, pro baseball player, or princess is not all we thought it might be. Your evolving life dreams may continue even today and should be embraced. But for most people, the motivators behind the dreams—the answers to "Why they are important to me" in Exercise 1—change very little over time. If as a child you wanted to be a princess so your kingdom would have a kind ruler, today you may want to be a teacher to help children learn—and both of these dreams, at their core, are motivated by the desire to help others.

Take a close look at your "importance" statements in Exercise 1. What do they tell you about the direction you want to take in your life? What are your priorities? Will some dreams need to be put on the back burner while you pursue others? Using your dream statements as a guide, write a two- or three-sentence mission for yourself. You don't need to share it with anyone, but you should refer to it a few times a year and ask yourself, "Am I living up to my mission?" and "Am I taking the right steps toward this mission?" You may also want to fine-tune it as you progress.

KEY TAKEAWAYS

- The world is changing quickly around you, but your dreams and aspirations may provide a sense of direction in unknown territory.
- The reasons dreams or aspirations are important to you are as important as the dreams themselves and are likely to be more consistent than your literal dreams.
- A mission statement can be very useful in helping you to make important personal decisions, but you should consider it often and fine-tune it as needed.

3. CAREER EXPLORATION

LEARNING OBJECTIVES

1. **Define the difference between a job and a career.**
2. **Identify the primary types of work and which you are best suited for.**
3. **Learn how to explore work options.**

A **job**: yes, it's something you would like to have, especially if you want to pay your bills. A job lets you enjoy a minimal level of financial security. A job requires you to show up and do what is required of you; in exchange, you get paid. In contrast, a **career** involves holding a job, but it is more a means of achieving personal fulfillment. In a career, your jobs follow a sequence that leads to increasing mastery, professional development, and personal and financial satisfaction. A career requires planning, knowledge, and skills. If it is to be a fulfilling career, it requires that you bring into play your full set of analytical, critical, and creative thinking skills to make informed decisions that will affect your life in both the short term and the long term.

Why is planning so important? Isn't it enough, as college commencement speakers so often say, to use college to "find yourself" and "follow your dream"? Well, yes and no. If you're not thinking about your future at all, just taking courses for fun without much of a goal in mind, you could end up as in the common joke about the graduate in his first job who learns to ask "Do you want fries with that?" This is *not* to say you need to map out your whole life and single-mindedly stay on a specific educational career track. But we all have heard of graduates who played around in college for four years and never "found" themselves or their dream—and then it could be disillusioning to enter the job market only to find employers aren't looking for just *anyone* with a degree. This could be especially devastating if you're starting out with large student loans. In other words, just as you should think about your dreams, you should think about how best to reach them. That's what this section is all about.

job

Routine work done for an agreed price.

career

An occupation or profession requiring special skills or training; a progression of jobs followed as one's life pursuit.

3.1 What Do You Want to Do When You "Grow Up"?

The Department of Labor defines 840 occupations in its Standard Occupation Classification system[2] —and new occupations are being created at an ever-faster rate. A decade ago, who would have imagined the job of a social media marketing specialist? As new careers develop and old careers morph in new directions, it's OK if you aren't able to pinpoint exactly what occupation or career will capture your passion for a lifetime. However, it is important to define as best you can what field you will want to develop your career in, because that will help dictate your major and your course selections.

The process of career exploration can be a lot of fun, as it allows you to discover a world of possibilities. Even those students who have a pretty clear idea of what they want to do should go through this process because they will discover new options as backups and maybe a new direction even more attractive than their original choice. The career exploration process involves four phases.

Phase A: Who Am I?

Getting to know who you are—who you *really* are—is the first step. As in Exercise 1, be careful to base your self-discovery on what you think, not what Auntie Ethel always said about you or the hopes that Dad had for you to join in the family business. This is all about *you*.

You are a unique individual with a distinct combination of likes, dislikes, personality traits, and skills. But you are not so different that you can't be identified with certain personality types, and those types may help you narrow your career choices. Visit your campus career guidance or placement office. They will likely be able to offer you a variety of tests to define your personality type; you can also find tests online at websites such as http://www.careertest.net or http://www.theguardian.com/lifeandstyle/2014/nov/11/-sp-questionnaire-what-job-would-make-you-happiest.

Many personality tests are based on the career theory developed by Dr. John Holland. Holland defined six categories of people based on personality, interests, and skills:

1. **Realistic.** These people describe themselves as honest, loyal, and practical. They are doers more than thinkers. They have strong mechanical, motor, and athletic abilities; like the outdoors; and prefer working with machines, tools, plants, and animals.

2. **Investigative.** These people love problem solving and analytical skills. They are intellectually stimulated and often mathematically or scientifically inclined; like to observe, learn, and evaluate; prefer working alone; and are reserved.

3. **Artistic.** These people are the "free spirits." They are creative, emotional, intuitive, and idealistic; have a flair for communicating ideas; dislike structure and prefer working independently; and like to sing, write, act, paint, and think creatively. They are similar to the investigative type but are interested in the artistic and aesthetic aspects of things more than the scientific.

4. **Social.** These are "people" people. They are friendly and outgoing; love to help others, make a difference, or both; have strong verbal and personal skills and teaching abilities; and are less likely to engage in intellectual or physical activity.

5. **Enterprising.** These people are confident, assertive risk takers. They are sociable; enjoy speaking and leadership; like to persuade rather than guide; like to use their influence; have strong interpersonal skills; and are status conscious.

6. **Conventional.** These people are dependable, detail oriented, disciplined, precise, persistent, and practical; value order; and are good at clerical and numerical tasks. They work well with people and data, so they are good organizers, schedulers, and project managers.

EXERCISE 2: WHAT'S MY TYPE?

Using the descriptions above, choose the three types that most closely describe you and list them in order in the following table. Most people are combinations of two or sometimes three types. Then list the specific words or attributes that made you think you fit in that type description.

	Occupational type	Words and attributes that closely describe me
Primary type (the one I identify with *most closely*)		
Secondary type		
Tertiary type		

Note: Your Holland occupational code is made up of the initials of the three personality types you selected, in order.

Phase B: What's Out There?

Once you have determined your occupational type, you can begin to explore what types of careers might be best suited to you. Exercise 2 is just a rough beginning to find your occupational type, but you should still seek out more detailed results through your career guidance or placement office or by taking the Self-Directed Search (SDS) online through sites such as http://www.lamission.edu/careercenter/SDS Exercise.pdf, which will provide you with a profile of careers you might want to consider. In addition, you can explore information from your college's career guidance or placement office.

The SDS and other career guidance tests are based on Holland's work. Holland studied people who were successful and happy in many occupations and matched their occupations to their occupational type, creating a description of the types of occupations that are best suited to each personality type. Just as many individuals are more than one personality type, many jobs show a strong correlation to more than one occupational type.

TABLE 12.1   Examples of Occupational Options by Type

Type	Ideal Environments	Sample Occupations
Realistic	■ Structured ■ Clear lines of authority ■ Work with **things** and **tools** ■ Casual dress ■ Focus on tangible results or well-thought-out goals	■ Contractor ■ Emergency medical technician (EMT) ■ Mechanic ■ Military career ■ Packaging engineer
Investigative	■ Nonstructured ■ Research oriented ■ Intellectual ■ Work with **ideas** and **data**	■ Pharmacist ■ Lab technician ■ Nanotechnologist ■ Geologist ■ College professor
Artistic	■ Nonstructured ■ Creative ■ Rewards unconventional and aesthetic approaches ■ Creation of products and **ideas**	■ Advertising career ■ Architect ■ Animator ■ Musician ■ Journalist
Social	■ Collaborative ■ Collegial ■ Work with **people** and on people-related problems/issues ■ Work as a team or community	■ Teacher ■ Geriatric counselor ■ Correctional officer ■ Coach ■ Nurse
Enterprising	■ Typical business environment ■ Results oriented ■ Driven ■ Work with **people** and **data** ■ Entrepreneurial ■ Power focused	■ Sales manager ■ Banker ■ Lawyer ■ Business owner ■ Restaurant manager
Conventional	■ Orderly ■ Clear rules and policies ■ Consistent **processes** ■ Work with systems to manipulate and organize **data** ■ Control and handling of money	■ Auditor ■ Insurance underwriter ■ Bank teller ■ Office manager ■ Database manager

Use the occupational code you defined in Exercise 2 to identify careers you might want to consider. Your career guidance or placement office should be a good resource for this activity, or you can look at Gottfredson and Holland's *Dictionary of Holland Occupational Codes* in the reference section of your library.

Use the Department of Labor's O*Net (http://www.onetonline.org/find) to get a deeper understanding of your occupation. For each occupation, O*Net lists the type of work, the work environment, the skills and education required, and the job outlook for that occupation. This is a truly rich resource that you should get to know.

Phase C: What Factors Might Affect My Choice?

You may now have a list of careers you want to explore. But there are other factors you should consider as well. Use your creative thinking skills to come up with alternative "right" answers to factors that may present an obstacle to pursuing the right career.

- **Timing.** How much time must I invest before I actually start making money in this career? Will I need to spend additional time in school? Is there a certification process that requires a specific amount of experience? If so, can I afford to wait?
- **Finances.** Will this career provide the kind of income I need in the short term and the security I'll want in the longer term? What investment must I make to be successful in this field (education, tools, franchise fees, etc.)?
- **Location.** Does this career require me to relocate? Is the ideal location for this career somewhere I would like to live? Is it somewhere my family would like to live?
- **Family/personal.** How will this career affect my personal and family life? Do friends and family members who know me well feel strongly (for or against) about this career choice? How important is their input?

Phase D: Where Do I Go from Here?

It may seem odd to be thinking about life after school if you are just getting started. But you will soon be making decisions about your future, and regardless of the direction you choose, there is a lot you can do while still in college. You will need to focus your studies by choosing a major. Look for opportunities to explore the careers that interest you. Try to ensure that you are building the right kind of experience on which to base a successful career. These steps help bring your dreams to life and make them achievable.

Start by developing a relationship with a counselor in your college's career guidance or placement office. All too often students speak with these counselors only near the end of their college days, when the pressure is just on getting a job—any job—after having completed a degree. But these counselors can be of great help in matching your interests to a career and ensuring you are gathering the right kind of experience to put you at the top of the recruiting heap.

Keep in mind that deciding on and pursuing a career is an ongoing process. The more you learn about yourself and the career options that best suit you, the more you may need to fine-tune your career plan. Don't be afraid to consider new ideas, but don't make changes without careful consideration. Career planning is exciting: learning about yourself and about career opportunities, and considering the factors that can affect your decision, should be a core part of your thoughts while in college.

KEY TAKEAWAYS

- The right career for you depends on your interests, your personality, and your skills.
- Defining your occupational type may confirm career choices you have already made or open entirely new options for you.
- Career planning is an ongoing process involving knowing yourself, knowing about career options, and understanding the context in which your decisions will be made.

CHECKPOINT EXERCISES

1. Using your occupational type, identify a career opportunity you might be suited for that you have not yet considered. Now write a paragraph on what life might be like if you were to pursue that career.

2. Name the six Holland occupational types, and then circle what each type likes to work with:

1.	data	ideas	people	process	tools
2.	data	ideas	people	process	tools
3.	data	ideas	people	process	tools
4.	data	ideas	people	process	tools
5.	data	ideas	people	process	tools
6.	data	ideas	people	process	tools

3. Visit O*Net (http://www.onetonline.org/find) and look up one of the careers you may be considering. What kinds of things does O*Net tell you about a career?

4. CHOOSING YOUR MAJOR

LEARNING OBJECTIVES

1. **Understand how a chosen major relates to your career.**
2. **Practice skills for selecting a good major.**

Choosing a college major can have a big impact on your career choices, especially if you are following a technical or vocational program of study. After all, you can't become a pharmacist by studying computer programming. But students often get too anxious about choosing a major or program of studies. Certainly many two-year students have a very clear idea of what they are studying and the job they expect to land after completing their degree, and you probably feel confident enough in your choice of program of study to make the investment for tuition in that program. But there is no need to panic over your choice of major or program of studies:

- Your choice of major or program will be important mostly for your first job after college; most people change careers (not just jobs, but careers) five times or more in their lifetime, and no possible major has that much flexibility.

- Many majors and programs share foundation courses with other majors, so you can usually change your major without having wasted your time in courses unrelated to your new major. Chances are that if you change your major, it will be to something similar, especially if you do an occupational interest survey as recommended earlier in this chapter.

- Most students change their major at least once, and many will change majors two or three times before they graduate.

- If a change in major does delay your degree, it may still be a good investment of time to follow a career path you are truly happy with. Before making a decision, consider the factors outlined in phase C of the previous section. Use your creative thinking skills to find a second right answer to any dilemmas a delay like this may cause.

While these thoughts might remove some of the stress, it is still not always easy to make the choice. The following tips may make it a little easier… and perhaps fun!

- **Follow your dreams.** Your first instinct in choosing a field of study is probably based on your dreams and life experience. Make sure you base your choice on your own dreams and interests and not those of a parent, spouse, or friend.

- **Make it fun.** What do you like to do for fun? What kinds of magazines do you read? What websites do you visit often? What kinds of volunteer work have you done? What do the answers to these questions tell you about the kind of career you would enjoy?

- **Build on your skills.** Choose a program of study not just based on your likes—also consider your skills. What were your best courses in high school? Consider also courses that you found challenging in which you learned a lot (it's hard to keep a level of determination to tackle a tough subject if you don't enjoy it). What do these courses tell you about what you are skilled at studying?

- **Ask around.** Find people who are in the majors you are considering, and ask them what they like and dislike. If you can find recent graduates with that major, ask them about the value of their major.
- **Two is better than one.** Talk to your faculty advisor about a double major or a combined program, which can be an effective preparation for the uncertainties and options of future employment. Think about declaring a minor if your college allows it.
- **What makes you unique?** If you have a major that you'd like to pursue that is not offered at your college, find out if you can plan your own major. This option is especially attractive if you want to combine two seemingly different disciplines into a major (Dance and athletics? Sociology and film? Women's studies and economics?).
- **Be open to change.** Once you have selected a major, don't panic if it later turns out to be the wrong choice; consider it a step toward finding the right program for *you*. Repeat the major selection process, but carefully consider what you learned from your first choice. Why was it not the right major? (Did it not match your interests? Was the workload too heavy? Were the courses too tough?) What do you know now that you should consider in making a new choice?

KEY TAKEAWAYS

- There is no need to panic over the choice of a major or program of studies.
- Most students will change their major during their college years.
- Many people work and have successful careers in disciplines they did not major in.

CHECKPOINT EXERCISES

1. How is your choice of major important? Why do you want to be sure you do a good job selecting one?

   _____

2. What are some of the reasons you should not panic over the choice of major?

   _____

---

5. GETTING THE RIGHT STUFF

LEARNING OBJECTIVES

1. **Explore the benefits of a four-year college education.**
2. **Understand differences between work-based skills and transferable skills.**
3. **Learn how to use jobs, internships, and volunteering to pursue your goals.**

What do you need to launch a good career? Employers will look at your education, skills, and experience. Making sure you have the "right stuff" in these three areas in your college experience.

5.1 The Transfer Ticket

Are you in a two-year program or community college? Perhaps to save some money or to be able to explore a career before committing to a four-year program? Now you may find that a bachelor's degree is worth pursuing if it is a requirement for the career you want or because it can boost your income opportunities. If you are thinking about transferring to a four-year program, be sure to follow these steps:

1. Find out about the transfer program at your college. Most two-year colleges have a program to make sure you have the right general education courses, electives, and courses related to your major to help you transfer seamlessly into a junior year at a four-year college.

2. Make sure your credits are transferable. Each four-year college or university has its own policies about what kind of credits it accepts. If you are planning for a particular four-year college, find out about its transfer policies as you plan your studies now. These policies are typically described in the college's website or catalog. Read them carefully to ensure you can transfer most if not all of your credits.

3. Talk to your advisor. Now. If you haven't met with your advisor to discuss your ideas about transferring, do so soon. Your advisor can help you formulate a plan of studies that meets your requirements for your associate's degree and maximizes your transferable credits.

4. Does your college have **articulation agreements**? These agreements between your college and four-year institutions define specific requirements for transferring and make it easier for you to transfer from your college to the bachelor's program in a four-year school.

If you are in a four-year college already but think your career objectives might be better met by a program at another college, you should also go through steps two and three as soon as possible. It can save you a great deal of time, money, and heartbreak.

5.2   Developing Skills

The second requirement for employment is skills. Many of the skills you will need are career specific: we call those **work-based skills**. They include knowing how to use equipment that is specific to the career and mastering processes used in the field. While some of these skills are learned and perfected on the job, you may be in a vocational track program (such as for homeland security officers, nurses aides, or paralegals) where you are learning your work-based skills.

These are not the only skills you will need for a career. A second set of skills are called **transferable skills** because they can be used in almost all occupations. These include thinking skills, communication skills, listening skills—in fact, most of the skills for college success we have been stressing throughout this book are transferable skills because they are also key to success in life. This skill set is very broad, and your mastery will vary from skill to skill; therefore, you should identify the skills that are most important to your career objective and plan to develop them. Review your occupation profile on O*Net (http://www.onetonline.org/find) to determine which skills you need to demonstrate to potential employers.

articulation agreements
An agreement between a community college and four-year institution that allows for seamless transfer into a four-year bachelor's program.

work-based skills
Skills that are specific to a single occupation but are not likely to be used for others.

transferable skills
Skills that contribute to success in any number of occupations.

EXERCISE 3: TRANSFERABLE SKILLS INVENTORY

In the following list of forty transferable skills, *underline* five skills you believe you have mastered and then describe specific ways in which you have used each skill successfully. Then *circle* five skills that you think are important to your career but that you have not mastered yet. Describe specific steps you plan to take to master those skills.

Active listening	Decision making	Negotiating	Researching
Active learning	Editing	Observing	Selling
Analyzing	Evaluating	Organizing	Speaking a second language
Budgeting	Forecasting	Perceiving Feelings	Supervising
Coaching	Goal setting	Persuading	Teaching
Communicating	Handling a crisis	Planning	Teamwork
Consulting	Handling details	Problem solving	Time management
Creative thinking	Manipulating numbers	Public speaking	Training
Critical thinking	Mentoring	Reading	Visualizing
Customer service	Motivating	Reporting	Writing

Skills I have mastered	Examples of how I used them

Skills I still need to master	How I will master them

As you examine the list of skills in Exercise 3, you likely find that you have at least some experience in many of them, but you probably haven't thought all that much about them because you take them for granted. But it is important to think about all your activities and consider the skills you have applied successfully. Your transferable skills inventory may be larger than you think. For example, if you volunteer as a big brother or big sister, you have skills in active listening, mentoring, time management, and probably coaching. If you have written a college paper, you have skills in visualizing, researching, communicating, and writing.

Think of the ways you have developed and mastered transferable skills. Build a list of your skills for a future resume, and update it every year. It will be a valuable tool for you as you work with your career development and ultimately with job applications.

5.3 Gaining Relevant Experience

Are you frustrated by the fact that even entry-level jobs often require some experience? Experience is the third set of qualifications employers look for, and it's the one that often stumps students. Relevant experience gained while in college is not only important as a job qualification; it can also be a way to explore occupational options and build contacts of value for the future.

But how to gain relevant experience without experience to begin with? Consider three options: volunteering, internships, and part-time employment.

Volunteering is especially good for students looking to work in social and artistic occupations, but other too should consider the options. You can master many transferable skills through volunteering. Volunteering at a museum or performance center provides relevant experience to students in the arts. But what if you want to work in engineering? Volunteering for an organization promoting green energy would be helpful. Looking for a career in homeland security? Do volunteer work with the Red Cross or the Coast Guard Auxiliary. With a little brainstorming and an understanding of your field, you can find relevant volunteer experiences for just about any career.

Internships focus on gaining practical experience related to a program of study. Interns work for an organization or company for a stipend or volunteer in exchange for practical experience. A successful internship program is a win-win situation: the intern adds value to the company's efforts, and the student learns or practices work-related skills. Most internships are typically held during summers or school vacation periods, though on occasion they can be scheduled for a set block of time each week during the course of a regular school term.

Once you secure an internship (usually through a normal job application process aided by a faculty member or the career guidance or placement office), it is important to have a written agreement with the employer stating:

1. The learning objective for the internship

2. The time commitment

3. The work the company expects you to do

4. What your supervisor will do for you and your college (internship progress reports, evaluations, etc.)

This written agreement may seem like overkill, but it is critical to ensure that the internship experience doesn't degrade into unsatisfying tasks such as photocopying and filing.

Remember that a key objective of your internship is to develop relationships you can use for mentoring and networking during your career. Befriend people, ask questions, go the extra mile in terms of what is expected of you, and generally participate in the enterprise. Your extra effort will pay dividends in the future.

Part-time employment may be an option if your study schedule allows. First investigate opportunities in your field of study. Ask instructors and the career guidance or placement office about job leads, even if not specifically in the area where you want to work.

If you are lucky enough to have a job in your field of study already, be sure to relate what you are learning to what you do on the job—and what you do on the job to what you are learning. Ask your job supervisor about ideas you have learned in classes, and ask your instructors about the practices you apply at work. This cross-linking will make you a much stronger candidate for future opportunities and a much better student in the short term.

KEY TAKEAWAYS

- Employers look for candidates who have the right education, the right skills, and the right experience.
- Be sure you can identify and demonstrate transferable skills as well as work-related skills.
- Experience gained through volunteering, internships, and part-time jobs will show potential employers that you can work in your chosen field, and it helps you create a network of colleagues to enhance your career development.

CHECKPOINT EXERCISES

1. Read the famous "fence whitewashing" story in Mark Twain's *The Adventures of Tom Sawyer* (http://www.inspirational-short-stories.com/tom-sawyer-fence.html). What transferable skills does Tom demonstrate? What work-related skills does he demonstrate?

_____
_____
_____

2. Why is having a written internship agreement important?

_____
_____
_____

6. CAREER DEVELOPMENT STARTS NOW

LEARNING OBJECTIVES

1. **Understand that career development starts now, not when you are searching for a job.**
2. **Know how to get organized for career development.**
3. **Use resources for career development.**

Think of developing your career as if you were working in a start-up venture, because in a sense, you are. What you are developing is yourself as a professional. Start by getting organized. Create a file for all your career-related documents on your computer. Use a folder in your browser's bookmarks exclusively for keeping track of websites of good resources, interesting companies, and leading ideas from your targeted occupation. In your contact management system or personal directory, flag individuals who may help you in your exploration and search. Create group folders for them in your social networking sites. There may not be many people in those groups now, but as you go through the processes described in this chapter, their numbers will multiply, and it pays to have a system in place to identify key professional contacts.

Start identifying resources that you can use to explore your planned career and those to help land that first (or next) job in your career. Consider the various resources and websites already described in this chapter. You may want to add an alumnus who has been helpful or a relative who already practices in your target occupation. Record such resources in your notes.

To avoid putting off career development until it is too late (at graduation), set goals now to guide the process. Include simple, everyday steps that keep you moving in the right direction, such as "investigate metallic arts sculpture as a business" or "make an appointment to see a counselor at the guidance office." Keep adjusting and building on your goals as you continue to develop career plans for the future.

KEY TAKEAWAYS

- Career exploration and job hunting are not short-term projects but processes that continue over time.
- Being organized helps set you up for success.
- Setting goals will keep your actions organized and keep you moving forward in a long-term process.

CHECKPOINT EXERCISES

1. What are two things you should do to get organized with your career development?

_____

_____

_____

2. Why is setting goals important in this process?

_____

_____

7. THE POWER OF NETWORKING

LEARNING OBJECTIVES

1. **Learn how to develop a network.**
2. **Keep track of your contacts.**
3. **Attend conferences and trade shows.**

There is some wisdom in the saying that it's who you know that brings success in getting a job. Consider the following:

- It is estimated that only 20% of new jobs and vacancies are advertised or posted.
- A web posting for a job typically yields over 150 applicants for a position.
- Some 60% to 80% of jobs are found through personal contact and networking.

What exactly is **networking**? In its simplest terms, it is the process of engaging others to help you reach an objective. Three words in this definition deserve a closer look:

1. **Process.** Networking doesn't happen casually but requires thought, planning, and deliberate activity.
2. **Engaging.** You are looking to have others do something for you—give you information, guidance, other contacts, or perhaps a recommendation.
3. **Objective.** You need to be clear about your purpose for networking—it is not merely to collect people's contact information but to further your career development.

networking

The process of engaging others in helping reach an objective.

The process of networking involves three basic phases: prospect identification, making contact, and follow-up.

Student FAQs

- **I won't graduate and be in the job market for a couple years. Do I need to work on my résumé and networking now?** Yes, absolutely! There are many benefits to starting now. As a student, you are likely applying for part-time jobs, internships, and volunteer positions. Networking is a process of building relationships, and the strongest relationships are built over time. Having a good network will help you find interesting and relevant opportunities. Having a résumé that summarizes your strengths and skills will give you an advantage over other candidates who apply without a résumé, because job application forms rarely give the opportunity to highlight your strengths. It makes sense to capture your accomplishments in a résumé as they happen, saving you a lot of time in the future.

- **I don't have any work experience. How can I write a résumé?** You may not have any work experience yet, but you do have experience and skills. Focus on your transferable skills, and list examples of how you have used them. Think of organizations you have been involved in and volunteer work you have done. It is OK to include high school accomplishments; you can replace them with college accomplishments as you gain them. It is also OK to include your GPA, particularly if it is over 3.0, because that helps show you are disciplined and organized.

7.1 All Contacts Matter, but Some More So Than Others

The first phase of networking involves identifying whom you should be speaking to and finding people who can introduce you to them. This is like the game "Six Degrees of Kevin Bacon" applied to your own life. Whom do you need to speak to? That really depends on your objectives. If you are trying to learn about an occupation, it can be just about anyone involved with that field. If you are in the process of trying to land an internship or a job, you want to reach the person who will make the hiring decision.

Your objective also suggests how to get started with your networking. To learn about a career, you might want to start with people you meet at an industry conference; to land a job or internship, think about whom you know in that company or who might know someone in that company. If you don't have any contacts who fit that description, whom do you know who lives in the town in which the company is based or in a nearby town?

As important as having contacts is your ability to access them when you need to. Think of this as contact management. Don't be caught wishing you could call someone you met three weeks ago... if you could only remember what you did with their business card! There are countless ways to keep track of contacts, from writing names in a notebook to maintaining digital contacts on your computer or smartphone. Use a system you are comfortable with and use regularly.

Building a network requires consistent work, and a strong network will take time to achieve. That is why we recommend starting to build your professional network now—even early in your college career. Your network should include anyone who might have a connection that will help: family, friends, neighbors, past and present coworkers, bosses, people you met through associations and clubs (especially business associations), instructors and alumni from your college, and acquaintances you have met via online networking.

When you capture your contact data, use relevant keywords to help you search your database and shape your contact activity. Be sure to record the source of the contact. For example, if a friend introduced you, be sure to note that friend's name; if you met at a party, note the name of the host and the occasion; if you met at a conference, note the conference and date. You'll use this information later on when you renew the contact. Also use other keywords so that you can quickly find contacts who are best for each of your objectives. Keywords might describe the person's area of specialization, organization membership, or type of contact (family, friend, colleague, etc.).

Personal Contact

Being in the right place at the right time has less to do with luck than with the art of personal contact. Contacts are everywhere, and you never know when you might turn one to your advantage. You may feel a little awkward following these tips at first, but with practice you will become quite adept at meeting new people and adding them to your network.

- **Be prepared.** If you are going to a conference, a party, or even a class, know ahead of time which people or kinds of people you want to meet. Be prepared with topics to steer the contact into real conversation so you don't waste time awkwardly talking about the weather and then slink away.
- **Be confident.** Prepare a short introduction for yourself. Be factual, don't brag, and give enough information about yourself to prompt your contact to ask questions.
- **Be curious.** The best way to get contacts to want to know you is to show you want to know them. Observe them before starting a conversation. Is there something unique about them, or perhaps something you overheard that you can ask about? "You have such an interesting accent; do you mind if I ask where you're from?" or "I hear you're doing some interesting work in Asia...?" After asking question, listen actively to keep the conversation going.
- **Be prepared (part 2).** Have personal cards to give out to contacts; that will prompt them to give you their contact information, too. You don't have to be in business to have a business card.
- **Be courteous.** If someone you know comes up to you while you are speaking with a contact, introduce them; if you see that the contact is getting antsy, tell them you enjoyed meeting them and then move on. Don't trap them!
- **Be prepared (part 3).** Set yourself up for networking success by discreetly writing a word or two on the back of their card to jog your memory in the future. "World-class rodeo clown" would certainly help you remember Jack Smith at Triangle Financial.

7.2   Make the Call

What you say in a networking call or e-mail depends on the objective of your networking effort. (Is it to learn about an career or industry? Seek a job-shadowing opportunity? Ask for a job?) Some networking basics and elements of etiquette apply to all contacts:

- **Be mindful of your contact's time.** Keep your calls and e-mails courteous but brief. If you are calling, ask if it is a good time to talk.
- **In the first contact, tell the contact where you got his or her name or remind them where you met.** "I was referred to you by our friend Janet Smith" or "My colleague Richard Stewart suggested I call you" or "I met you after you spoke at the International Genius Conference" (remember the contact source information in your contact database?). This turns an interrupting cold call into a warm call with an interested individual.
- **Be specific about how the contact can help you.** Know what you are asking for and do so directly. Don't be shy.
- **Use your network for more than just asking for jobs.** Networking is great for learning about new trends in the industry, for launching "trial balloons" for ideas or concepts you are developing, and for seeking advice on practical aspects of your occupation.
- **Help others in your network.** Networking works both ways. Be willing to offer your assistance to others whenever you can; the fact that you are still in college doesn't mean you can't be of value. You may be able to get an introduction to an instructor for a person in the industry or help that person's daughter learn about your college.

7.3   Care and Feeding of Your Network

Much of the success of your networking efforts depends on what you do after having a phone call or receiving an e-mail reply. The first step is to **thank your contact** for his or her help. Do this right away; any thank-you after twenty-four hours may seem late. Find a reason (not just an excuse) to **keep in touch** with people in your network. If you read an article that you think people in your network would be interested in, send them the link. If you run across a problem one of your contacts might help you with, don't be shy—give him or her a call to **ask for help**. If you meet someone you think a contact would like, make introductions. **Send a follow-up note of thanks** to a person who gave you a particularly productive lead. Let him or her know what you were able to accomplish. People like to know they are on a successful team. Finally, if a person in your network asks you for help, **do what you say you will do**.

KEY TAKEAWAYS

- Networking is an ongoing process that involves identifying and managing prospects, making contact, and following up.
- All contacts are good contacts.
- Common courtesy and follow-through are the catalysts of good networking.

CHECKPOINT EXERCISES

1. Take twenty minutes to list fifty or more people you know. (You may want to think of groups first and then see how quickly you can list people within them.) Now take another twenty minutes to write one or two words next to each name to describe how he or she could help you network.

2. List three things you should do whenever you contact someone the first time.

   _____

   _____

   _____

3. Describe two things you can do to overcome shyness and network effectively in a person-to-person setting.

   _____

   _____

8. RÉSUMÉS AND COVER LETTERS

LEARNING OBJECTIVES

1. **Understand the purpose of a résumé.**
2. **Describe the elements of successful résumés.**
3. **Know how to prepare a good cover letter.**

résumé

A document used to summarize the experience of a person.

A **résumé** is basically a summary of your experience. Just as an advertiser condenses the essence of his or her product into a thirty-second ad for the Super Bowl, condensing the essence of your experience onto one or two pages can be a challenging task. Fine-tuning, updating, and rewriting your résumé will become an ongoing process as you move through your career, and it is not too early to get started now. The purpose of a résumé is to get you invited for an interview. Unfortunately, however, too often a résumé becomes a reason to exclude a candidate. Poor grammar, misspelled words, lengthy listings of irrelevant experience, and messy formatting motivate hiring managers to move quickly to the next candidate.

There is no such thing as a perfect format for a résumé, though hiring managers and recruiters generally agree on the following principles:

- A short résumé is generally better than a long one. One page should usually be enough—two pages only if you have a lot of experience.
- Focus on your accomplishments, not just the positions you held. Your résumé should point out your strengths. Use dynamic verbs (see "101 Action Verbs" below).
- Include numbers. Be sure to include dollar amounts and percentages that support achievements. For example, you might write "Reduced costs by 20%." Keep track of your accomplishments in your recorded notes so that you don't have to go back and recreate history later on when you are revising your résumé.
- Use keywords. Most recruiters and hiring managers look for résumés online and review submitted résumés with software that looks for keywords.
- Keep information easy to find. Use the standard convention of a reverse chronological listing of experience, starting with your current or most recent job and moving backward in time, unless there is a valid reason for following a different format (a function-based résumé might be appropriate if you need to cover two or more long periods of unemployment).

Deciding what to include in your résumé is much of the work, because it is in the careful wording of the body of your résumé that you can really sell yourself for a position. Ideally, revise your résumé for each position you are applying for, particularly to include any accomplishments that you would not include in your "general résumé" but that are relevant to a particular job. Your résumé should include these elements:

- **Header.** Include your full name and complete contact information. Use your personal phone number and e-mail address, not your work contact information.
- **Objective.** Include a short one- or two-sentence summary of the kind of position you are looking for. Some experts now recommend replacing or following the objective with a listing of skills, particularly when posting the résumé online, because that provides a great opportunity to include keywords. Look to your list of transferable skills for this kind of list.
- **Résumé body.** Starting with your current or most recent job, internship, or volunteer position, list your experience in reverse chronological order. Each entry should include the title, the name and location of the company, and the dates you held the position. This should be followed by your major achievements in that position. Use strong action verbs and a quantitative measure for achievements. Look for things that will show that you are a better candidate than others. Consider accomplishments such as the following:
  - Being promoted
  - Gaining expanded responsibilities
  - Being recruited by a former employer or boss, or being asked to follow him or her to another company
  - Having your accomplishment copied by other departments or, even better, by other companies

- Recruiting and training others
- Receiving awards and recognitions, including speaking at conferences, writing, or being written about. If these are online and you are short on space, just include links or even omit these types of accomplishments, because you will be Googled.

101 Action Verbs

Here are the kinds of verbs that help sell you to potential employers. Expand on this list with other good verbs specific to your accomplishments found in an online search for "action verbs for résumés."

acted	delegated	implemented	persuaded
adapted	demonstrated	improved	planned
advised	designed	increased	prepared
analyzed	developed	influenced	prioritized
arranged	devised	informed	produced
assembled	diagnosed	initiated	promoted
assessed	directed	inspected	publicized
assigned	edited	instituted	recruited
attained	educated	instructed	rehabilitated
authored	enabled	integrated	represented
balanced	encouraged	introduced	researched
budgeted	engineered	invented	reviewed
built	enlisted	investigated	revitalized
calculated	established	lectured	scheduled
chaired	evaluated	managed	set goals
coached	executed	marketed	shaped
collected	fabricated	mediated	solved
communicated	facilitated	moderated	spoke
compiled	forecasted	motivated	stimulated
computed	formulated	negotiated	strengthened
conceptualized	founded	organized	supervised
consolidated	generated	originated	trained
contracted	guided	overhauled	translated
coordinated	identified	oversaw	upgraded
counseled	illustrated	performed	wrote
created			

8.1   The Finishing Touches

Once you have written the body of your résumé, review and discuss it with people you respect. Ask them what stands out, what puts them to sleep or turns them off, and whether anything is missing. Make sure your résumé is short and sweet and that it demonstrates your strengths. Be sure you can support every point you make on your résumé during an interview (an interviewer will quickly uncover any exaggeration).

Great résumés are a combination of a business document, marketing piece, and personal preferences. Expect conflicting opinions from others and don't get hung up on them; the final decision is yours.

Finally, here are some tips on format. Name your résumé file clearly. Don't give the file the name "résumé" or "My Résumé." Include your name, abbreviated job title, and the company name to which you are applying in the file name. For example, if Victor Smith applies for a marketing project manager job at XYZ Company, his résumé file might be named "VictorSmith-MktPM-XYZ.doc."

Format your document wisely. Use a readable font! You have approximately thirty seconds to make an impact on the person reading your résumé, and nothing turns off a reader faster than a résumé that is difficult to read.

- Serif fonts, such as Times New Roman, should be no smaller than eleven points, and sans-serif fonts, like Arial, should be no smaller than ten points.
- Keep margins at one inch all the way around.
- Print your résumé on a high-grade, bright white paper. Do not use cream-colored paper or paper with visible fibers, as these papers can confuse scanners and optical character recognition software that employers may use to digitally store and search résumés.

8.2 Cover Letters

cover letter

A letter to potential employers to entice them to read a résumé.

The purpose of a **cover letter** is to entice the recipient to read your résumé. There is no better way to entice someone to read further than to demonstrate that you fit his or her needs. A successful cover letter should emphasize how your knowledge, skills, or experiences make you an ideal candidate for the specific job.

When writing a cover letter, look over the job posting carefully. What are the keywords in the posting? Underline or highlight them. Think about how your experience and skills are related to those keywords. What examples can you give in short sentences? Now you can begin to write.

Be sure to state what job you are applying for and why in your opening paragraph. If you don't hook the reader here, you will not be considered for the job. Here you begin to show that you are a unique and qualified candidate. This, in marketing terms, is your selling proposition. Write this paragraph two or three different ways and then choose the best. When you are happy with your opening paragraph, add one or two paragraphs that illustrate your proposition from the opening paragraph.

Remember that your cover letter also demonstrates your communication skills. Be clear, be concise, and be careful. You won't have another opportunity to make a first impression. Be sure your spelling and grammar are correct. Did you double-check the spelling of the company name? Read the document; look for mistakes your spellchecker won't catch (like the word "you" instead of "your"). Put it down for a while and then reread it again.

Keep your formatting simple. Often you have to copy and paste your letter and résumé into a predetermined form on a company's website. In this process you will likely lose formatting such as tabbing, tables, and bulleted lists.

KEY TAKEAWAYS

- The purpose of a résumé is to secure an interview.
- A good résumé is action based and focused on accomplishments.
- The purpose of a cover letter is to entice the recipient to read your résumé.

CHECKPOINT EXERCISES

1. Explain some ways a résumé could block consideration of a candidate. What are some strategies for ensuring this doesn't happen?

   _____

   _____

   _____

2. List your top three accomplishments to date. What were the key transferable skills you used to achieve them? Do both the accomplishments and the skills play a prominent role in your résumé?

Accomplishments	Transferable skills

3. Write your résumé. Everyone should have one. They are useful not only to apply for jobs but also to secure internships and to explain who you are to your network. If you are a student who has no work experience, what kinds of accomplishments can you use to illustrate your skills?

9. INTERVIEWING FOR SUCCESS

LEARNING OBJECTIVES

1. **Understand the types of interviews.**
2. **Know how to prepare for an interview.**
3. **Be successful in an interview.**

In a job search, nothing is more exciting or more intimidating than an interview. Reaching the interview stage means that you are in serious consideration for the position, and the pressure feels cranked up. This section explores how to prepare yourself to excel in this process.

9.1   Types of Interviews

In the process of exploring occupations and landing a job, you will likely participate in a variety of interviews. They are defined by their objective:

- **Informational or networking interviews**. Informational interviewing is particularly useful for exploring career options. This is an interview that *you* have requested to learn about a particular job, company, or industry and how best to present yourself to potential hiring managers. An informational interview also gives you an opportunity to create a positive impression. Be sure to get referrals, leads, and recommendations for other networking contacts.

- **Screening interviews**. Generally conducted by a representative of the company or a recruiter, a screening interview is used to determine whether you are qualified or overqualified to do the job. This initial type of interview is often done over the phone. As the name implies, the objective of this interview is to find reasons to remove, not include, people from a candidate pool. Do not consider it lightly just because someone other than the hiring manager is conducting it.

- **One-on-one interviews**. In a one-on-one interview, the interviewer asks a set of questions to learn if you have the knowledge and skills to handle the job for which you have applied. The hiring manager conducting the one-on-one interview also wants to see what it would be like working with you and how you would fit in the organization. The interview will explore how you behaved in past situations as a predictor of how you are likely to behave in the future. Expect to be asked "Tell me about a time when…" or "Give me an example…" questions. This interview is the one a hiring decision is based on.

Informational or networking interviews

An interview *you* request to learn more about a job, company, or industry.

Screening interviews

An interview used to confirm qualification and narrow the pool of candidates down to a small group of "finalists."

One-on-one interviews

An interview or series of interviews with hiring managers to get to know candidates and determine their fit with the organization. Hiring decisions are largely based on these interviews.

9.2 Preparing for Interviews

Just as preparation is important for an exam, preparation is key to success in interviews. Many of the principles for preparation are actually the same, but in an employment interview, the subject is *you*. Just as for an exam, the first step in preparation is to know your material.

Learn about the organization. In almost every interview you'll be asked something like "What can you do for this company?" Practice your answer. Research press releases, stories in the *Wall Street Journal*, annual reports, blogs, websites, the news, and so on. Know the company's philosophies, goals, plans, new products, targeted customers, new executives, and major directional changes.

Use your network. Do you know anyone who works for or has worked for this company or organization? Call or have lunch with them before your interview to learn more. If you do your homework better than your competition, the employer will notice.

Review the job description. Be prepared to explain how your background qualifies you for the job. Did you find the job posting online? Make a printout now because later it may have been removed from the website before the company starts calling people in for interviews. Bring it with you to the interview. Be prepared to focus on your qualifications related to the specifics of the job description.

Review your résumé. Think of examples in your past experiences that describe or illustrate your accomplishments. You will be asked about items on your résumé, and you need to be able to support them and go into more detail.

Use your study guide. Employment interviews, especially screening interviews, seldom stray far from a standard list of questions. Find a quiet one to two hours to review the interview study guide below, prepare your answers, and actually practice them. Your answers should be short but complete.

Interview Study Guide

The following types of questions[3] are typical in many employment interviews. If you prepare answers ahead of time, you will not be caught off guard during an interview.

- **Tell me about yourself.** Remember that one-minute elevator introduction you worked on for networking? Here's your starting place.

- **What can you offer us? Why should we hire you?** Make a list of your qualifications for the job. Include years of experience, education, special training, technical skills, inside knowledge of a product or market, and so on. Are you a customer of this product or service?

  Use your list of transferable skills like communication, leadership, organization, attention to detail, and work ethic. Review your list objectively. Which items are most valuable to the employer? Use this information to write a brief "sales pitch" that describes your qualifications for the job. Structure the information in a logical fashion and then practice saying it aloud until your delivery is smooth, natural, and confident.

- **What are your strengths?** Provide context and scope when answering this question. Elaborating on your strengths should make it easier for the employer to see where and how you excel.

  Think about your noteworthy and unusual achievements or experiences. What did you do to accomplish them? What kind of preparation did they require? How are they unique?

  Think about performance reviews you have received in a job. Have you won awards or received positive feedback from others in the organization or from a happy customer? What were the reasons for the positive attention?

  If you are a student or recent graduate with limited professional experience, think about your papers, reports, projects, or group assignments. Think about the assignment and what you did to complete it. The same strengths that helped you academically will also help you succeed professionally.

- **What are your weaknesses?** Remember that employers are human and appreciate honesty. It's OK to acknowledge your weaknesses and explain steps you've taken to address them. It's also fair to point out how you've turned a weakness into a strength.

- **Where do you see yourself three to five years from now?** Think about your personal goals and answer as genuinely as possible. This is a good opportunity to ask the interviewer about the opportunities available to a person who succeeds in this job.

- **What attracted you to our company?** Draw from your research and personal knowledge of the company to answer this question. Keep in mind that this interview is about what you can do for them, so answering that you're attracted to the free snacks in the break room won't score any points.

- **Tell me about a time you were under pressure to meet a deadline and what you did.** When did you find pressure at school or work because something was due? Describe the problem, the actions you took, and the outcome. Choose examples in which you received positive feedback.

- **What will former employers say about you?** Be honest. Think about the positive things they will
- say about you.

What salary are you expecting? This is a landmine question and one you'll almost certainly face. Typically a company has a certain salary range for a position and will stay within it. A general rule for salary discussions is that he or she who says the first number loses. Ask what the salary range is and where the interviewer sees you fitting into that range.

You owe it to yourself to find out before the interview what the salary range is for a comparable position in the geographical region. You can learn this through your network or an online salary search.

■ **What questions do you have for me?** Before the interview, think of things you would like to know about the company, the job, or the industry. Having good questions will demonstrate your interest in the position and your degree of preparation. If you can, relate your questions to something the interviewer said earlier. Remember, an interview is not just the company checking you out—it's also you checking out the company.

Trick Questions in Interviews

Be prepared also for a question intentionally designed to put you on the spot, such as a sudden "What would you do if...?" The only wrong answer is "I don't know." Hiring managers are looking for employees who think through tough challenges. They want to know if you keep your cool under pressure, if you can think on your feet, whether you fake it or maintain your credibility, and how you respond to the unfamiliar. So show them: think aloud.

Talk about what you know about the problem; work out the process in front of them. You are being judged not only on your ability to solve problems but also on your intelligence, creativity, initiative, and potential. There is no potential in "I don't know."

Prepare yourself physically. Like a final exam, an interview can cause anxiety, and too much anxiety can result in a poor interview. Make sure you eat well and get a good night's sleep before the interview. Hunger, using energy drinks, and lack of sleep all contribute to interview anxiety.

Take extra copies of your résumé. Although you can expect the main interviewer to have it already, you may meet others—often extemporaneously—and it is appropriate to offer them a copy of your résumé if they join in the interview.

Dress to impress. Research shows many job applicants have unsuccessful interviews because they didn't dress professionally. If you're not sure, ask the person who schedules you for the interview what the dress code is. A suit or jacket, dress slacks, dress shirt, and a tie are usually fine for men—although many companies now have moved to less formal "business casual" attire. A suit or blouse and a skirt or slacks are fine for women. The rule of thumb is to dress one notch above that group's normal attire. Just remember, you're going to a job interview, not a casual event.

Punctuality counts. Confirm the date and time of the interview a day or two before. Make sure you know how to get there and how long it takes. Arrive at least ten to fifteen minutes before your interview. You may be asked to complete an application or other form when you arrive. If not, it's a good time to do some relaxation exercises.

9.3 Tips for Success during the Interview

Now is the time to demonstrate your listening, thinking, and communication skills. Avoid unexpected distractions, and turn off your cell phone before you even enter the building. Be sure to know in advance the name of the interviewer and his or her role in the company; if possible, get something in writing from the interview coordinator with names spelled out (for follow-up purposes). Once you are face-to-face with the interviewer, do the following:

■ Relax, take a deep breath, and smile. You should be genuinely pleased to be there, as you were selected from a pool of many other candidates.

■ Be yourself. That's whom you want them to hire, not someone you're trying to act like.

■ Keep your tone conversational but not too informal. Avoid slang and expletives.

■ Make eye contact but don't stare.

■ When answering questions, keep your answers focused on your skills and knowledge.

■ Avoid one-word answers, but be succinct and direct; don't ramble.

■ Be truthful. Any statements discovered to be untrue are grounds for not hiring you.

■ If you don't understand a question, ask for clarification.

- If you don't have the exact fact an interviewer is asking for, offer to find out and get back to them.
- At the end of the interview, thank the interviewer and tell him or her you enjoyed your conversation. If the interviewer hasn't already told you, it is appropriate to ask about the next steps.

9.4 After the Interview

Be sure to send a thank you note to each person with whom you interviewed. It is also courteous to send a short note of thanks to the person who coordinated your schedule with the company, even if he or she didn't interview you. This person may be asked for his or her impressions of you. Keep your notes short but personal; refer to a comment or question from the interview that you found significant. An e-mail is usually acceptable, especially if you applied online. Be sure to send it within twenty-four hours.

KEY TAKEAWAYS

- Successful interviewing depends on careful preparation.
- Most interview questions can be anticipated and prepared for.
- An interview is as important for you to evaluate the company and its working environment as it is for the company to evaluate your skills and fit.

CHECKPOINT EXERCISES

1. Practice, even with phone interviews, helps you be more comfortable in any interview situation. Set up and complete three informational interviews about a field or industry you are interested in. Write about what you learned about yourself and your approach to interviews.
2. Practice, even with mock interviews, will make you more comfortable in interview situations. Invite a friend to do a mock employment interview with you for a job you select from an online posting. Then switch roles. Write about what you learned about yourself and your approach to interviews.

10. CHAPTER ACTIVITIES

CHAPTER REVIEW

1. Explain the difference between a job and a career.

   _____

2. List three ways in which the employment environment is changing. What does this mean to you?

   _____

   _____

   _____

3. What is your life's mission?

   _____

4. What is your Holland occupational type? What kinds of occupations should you explore based on your results?

   _____

5. List two work-related skills and five transferable skills you have.

   _____

   _____

   _____

   _____

6. What are some ways you can gain more experience and explore career options before you get your degree?

   _____

   _____

   _____

7. What are some of the factors you should consider when choosing a major or field of study?

   _____

   _____

   _____

8. Why is networking so important?

   _____

9. List four or five qualities of successful networking.

   _____

   _____

   _____

   _____

10. Many people are shy about networking. How would you recommend they overcome this?

    _____

11. What is the primary purpose of a résumé?

    _____

12. What should the body of a résumé focus on?

    _____

13. What is the purpose of a cover letter?

    _____

14. List the three types of interviews and their objectives.

    _____

    _____

    _____

15. List three things you should do to prepare for an interview.

    _____

    _____

    _____

MAKE AN ACTION LIST

Two things I will do to further my career exploration in...	Actions	How I will know I accomplished each action
The next two weeks	1.	
	2.	
The next two months	1.	
	2.	
The next two years	1.	
	2.	

CLASS DISCUSSION QUESTIONS

1. Suppose that as you are thinking about your choice of a college major, you decide on a field of study based purely on your enjoyment of classes—but then when you begin exploring possible careers related to that field, you discover only limited possibilities and they don't excite you. What should you do now?

2. Suppose that the only jobs you've had were part-time working in fast food restaurants. You are majoring in history and applying for an intern position with a team doing a research project. Should you include your work experience on your résumé? Why or why not? If you do, is there anything to say about that experience, or simply list the places and dates?

3. Suppose that you have one more year of college before you actively begin your job search. You have not done much networking, but now you realize the importance of making new contacts in your field. Think of as many ways as possible to make new contacts within your college environment. Be creative in your thinking.

ENDNOTES

1. U.S. Census Bureau, "Table 597. Average Number of Jobs Held From Ages 18 to 42: 1978 to 2006," *U.S. Department of Labor: National Longitudinal Survey of Youth 2007*, https://www.census.gov/compendia/statab/2010/tables/10s0597.xls (accessed July 13, 2010).

2. U.S. Bureau of Labor Statistics, *U.S. Department of Labor: Standard Occupational Classification User Guide 2010*, http://www.bls.gov/soc/soc_2010_user_guide.pdf (accessed July 13, 2010).

3. SuccessHawk, "Interview Questions to Anticipate," http://www.successhawk.com/Interviewing/Interview-Questions-to-Anticipate (accessed July 13, 2010).

Index

CPSIA information can be obtained
at www.ICGtesting.com
Printed in the USA
LVHW02s0123310818
588707LV00005B/57/P